World Wisdom
The Library of Perennial Philosophy

The Library of Perennial Philosophy is dedicated to the exposition of the timeless Truth underlying the diverse religions. This Truth, often referred to as the *Sophia Perennis*—or Perennial Wisdom—finds its expression in the revealed Scriptures as well as the writings of the great sages and the artistic creations of the traditional worlds.

The Perennial Philosophy provides the intellectual principles capable of explaining both the formal contradictions and the transcendent unity of the great religions.

Ranging from the writings of the great sages of the past, to the perennialist authors of our time, each series of our Library has a different focus. As a whole, they express the inner unanimity, transforming radiance, and irreplaceable values of the great spiritual traditions.

Ye Shall Know the Truth: Christianity and the Perennial Philosophy appears as one of our selections in the Perennial Philosophy series.

The Perennial Philosophy Series

In the beginning of the Twentieth Century, a school of thought arose which has focused on the enunciation and explanation of the Perennial Philosophy. Deeply rooted in the sense of the sacred, the writings of its leading exponents establish an indispensable foundation for understanding the timeless Truth and spiritual practices which live in the heart of all religions. Some of these titles are companion volumes to the Treasures of the World's Religions series, which allows a comparison of the writings of the great sages of the past with the perennialist authors of our time.

Ye Shall Know the Truth

Christianity and the Perennial Philosophy

Edited by
Mateus Soares de Azevedo

Foreword by
William Stoddart

World Wisdom

Ye Shall Know the Truth: Christianity and the Perennial Philosophy
© 2005 World Wisdom, Inc.

Library of Congress Cataloging-in-Publication Data

Ye shall know the truth : Christianity and the perennial philosophy / edited by
Mateus Soares de Azevedo ; foreword by William Stoddart.
    p. cm. – (Perennial philosophy series)
 Includes bibliographical references and index.
 ISBN 0-941532-69-0 (pbk. : alk. paper)
 1. Christianity. 2. Philosophy. 3. Spirituality. 4. Philosophy and religion. I.
Azevedo, Mateus Soares de, 1959- II. Series.
 BR50.Y4 2005
 230'.01–dc22

2005001069

Printed on acid-free paper in Canada

For information address World Wisdom, Inc.
P.O. Box 2682, Bloomington, Indiana 47402-2682
www.worldwisdom.com

Cognoscetis Veritatem et Veritas liberabit vos.
Ye shall know the Truth
and the Truth shall make you free.

—John 8:32

Vincit omnia Veritas.
Truth conquers all.

—I Esdras 3:12

CONTENTS

V. The Universality of the Christian Mystics

VI. The Modern Deviation

FOREWORD

Let me start with the subtitle of this book. The term "perennial philosophy" has existed since the Renaissance, but in modern times it became familiar to the English-speaking world thanks to the book of the same name by Aldous Huxley. The central idea of the perennial philosophy is that Divine Truth is one, timeless, and universal, and that the different religions are but different languages expressing that one Truth. The symbol most often used to convey this idea is that of the uncolored light and the many colors of the spectrum which are made visible only when the uncolored light is refracted. In the Renaissance, the term betokened the recognition of the fact that the philosophies of Pythagoras, Plato, Aristotle, and Plotinus incontrovertibly expounded the same truth as lay at the heart of Christianity. Subsequently the meaning of the term was enlarged to cover the metaphysics and mysticisms of all of the great world religions, notably, Hinduism, Buddhism, and Islam.

In point of fact, Huxley was not the first exponent of this idea in modern times. It had already been propounded by the Bengali saint Ramakrishna (1836-1886), who was intimately familiar—and at a much deeper level than Huxley—, not only with Hinduism, but also with Christianity and Islam. Given the "exotism" and unfamiliarity of the great Ramakrishna, however, and also the dubious religious credentials of the eclectic Huxley, the term and the idea "perennial philosophy" did not get off to a good start with conservative religious seekers, Christian and other.

But a development that no one could have foreseen occurred. In the 1920s, the books of the French philosopher René Guénon began to appear. These expounded, in irrefutably Platonic fashion, the oneness of supra-formal Truth, and the multiplicity of the formal expressions thereof. From this one could perceive that the reason for being of the different religions is not that they are "all the same", but, precisely, that they are all *different*! The essence (concerning God, man, and salvation) is of course the same, but the *forms* are significantly different. The principle of religious unity lies in God alone, and it is a rash man who declares that God has expressed Himself in only one language!

Guénon's books were followed, in the 1930s, by the long series of writings of the German philosopher Frithjof Schuon, who carried to incredible heights the exposition of timeless truth, *and its saving quality*. Schuon's message was indeed one of truth, beauty, and salvation. It is difficult to dispute the profundity and expertise of these two authors. The current of intellectuality and spirituality of which they were the pioneers became known in time as the "traditionalist" or "perennialist" school. Two other writers who have contributed to making this school known are Ananda Coomaraswamy and Titus Burckhardt. The editor of this anthology has judiciously included seminal examples of the writings of all four of these authors.

Nothing can take away from the originality of vision of Guénon and Schuon, but it is useful to mention some of the great precursors to whom they most frequently refer. These include Shankara (Hinduism), Plato (Ancient Greece), Eckhart (Western Christianity), and Ibn 'Arabî (Islam). Yet the perennialist vision does not require lengthy expression: it is summed up in the title of this book, which is taken from the words of Christ: "*Ye shall know the Truth*, and the Truth shall make you free". For the perennial philosophy, this is indeed the whole story: timeless truth, and its liberating quality. Some of the more detailed aspects are taken up by the editor of the present anthology in his informative Introduction.

Perhaps because of the superficiality of early 20th century Huxley, and late 20th century "new-age" notions, the perennialist school, with its universalist ideas and "extra-Christian" references, is still in some quarters regarded with suspicion. Some people indeed seem to confuse two opposites: "new-age" phantasies and the perennial philosophy. Others, again, think that the perennial philosophy has to do only with something which is pejoratively referred to as "Eastern mysticism", forgetting that the term itself is of Christian origin, and that it was brought into service in the first place by the Christian recognition of the eternal truths of Platonism. These eternal truths are precisely what the perennial philosophy is all about, and the central virtue of the present anthology is to make this abundantly clear and so dispel many distressing illusions.

The perennial philosophy is not for fools—and neither is Christianity!—and it is precisely this that the modern sophisticated man needs to know. The perennial philosophy—which is true universalism and true ecumenism—is, at least extrinsically, a recognition of the divine origin of each religion. The essence of each religion is pure truth, and the various religious forms clothe that truth in garments of different designs and colors. "In my Father's house are many mansions". This saying of Christ's applies not only to Heaven, but also to earth. The function of the various religions is to express the truth, and to offer a way of salvation, in a manner suited to the needs of the different segments and ethnicities of mankind. Each religion comes from God, and each religion leads back to God. Each religion, moreover, comprises a doctrine and a method, that is to say, it is an enlightening truth coupled with a saving means. Were this not so, it would not be a question of religion, but of an empty man-made ideology (humanism, marxism, freudianism, "new-age"-ism, and many others) that can save no one.

As Frithjof Schuon has repeatedly pointed out, intelligence comprises not only acuity of mental discernment and correctness of logical operation, but also virtue and beauty. If logic, which in itself is sacred, is not accompanied by a love of virtue and an intuition of beauty, it runs the risk of being untrue to itself and ending up as something sterile. This necessary harmony of the various components of integral intelligence is expressed by the Platonic teaching that beauty is the splendor of the truth; that beauty is outward virtue; and that virtue is inward beauty. Nicholas of Cusa expressed the same doctrine thus: *Mens sine desiderio non intelligit; mens sine intellectu non desiderat.* ("The mind without love cannot understand; the mind without intelligence cannot love.") St. Thomas Aquinas said that, while the virtues do not form part of contemplation, they are nevertheless an indispensable condition for it, and Meister Eckhart said that the sufficient reason of the virtues is not primarily their extrinsic usefulness, but their intrinsic beauty.

The problem with modern intellectuals is that they are not intellectual; they are, in fact, much less intellectual (in the true sense of this word) than people of simple faith. It is forgotten that man is not "mind" alone, but also "Spirit" or "Intellect". Man's composition is summed up by the classical ternary: *Spiritus [Intellectus], anima, corpus* ("Spirit [Intellect], soul, body"). This is not the place to expound traditional metaphysics, but let us say in summary that "Spirit" or "Intellect" is universal or supra-formal, whereas "soul" (one of whose contents is "mind") is individual or formal. The "Intellect", understood in this Medieval sense, is man's only guarantee of objectivity, for soul and body belong to the realm of subjectivity. The central fault of Jung and other modern psychologists is their confusion of Intellect and soul (or indeed their complete exclusion of Intellect). As C. S. Lewis would say, this is the "abolition of man" with a vengeance!

As already emphasized, the relationship of Christianity—or for that matter, of any religion—to the perennial philosophy is that of one particular color to the uncolored light. The essays included in this book, therefore, envisage Christianity on the background of a perennial and universal truth. In the *Rig-Veda* (1.164.46), it is said that "sages call the one Reality by many names", and a man is not debarred from understanding this truth simply because he is a Christian. St. Augustine alluded to this perennial and universal truth when he said: "That which today is called the Christian religion existed among the Ancients, and has never ceased to exist from the origin of the human race, until the time when Christ himself came, and men began to call Christian the true religion which already existed beforehand." The perennial philosophy could be said to be perennial Platonism. Others might call it perennial Vedanta. Others again, like C. S. Lewis, might call it the *Tao*.

The editor's selection of contributors is very wide-ranging. From a large number of authors, of a variety of denominations, he has chosen many surprising and unique items of great relevance which one would be very unlikely to come across elsewhere. One matter of contemporary importance on which the book offers some encouraging perspectives is the question of relations between Christianity and Islam. Here too the editor has unearthed contributions which, often in unexpected ways, shed considerable light.

—William Stoddart

INTRODUCTION

To expound in a new key the spiritual, philosophical, and artistic patrimony of the Christian tradition in its intellectually challenging dimension—as well as to consider its future possibilities—this, in a nutshell, is what *Ye Shall Know the Truth: Christianity and the Perennial Philosophy* intends. Behind it lies the belief that one of the main factors responsible for the contemporary decadence, lack of vigor, and indeed tragic crisis, in traditional religion is the indifference, and even suspicion, that is shown towards its sapiential or "knowledge" dimension.

Religion in general aims at addressing all men without distinction, with a view to providing them with the means of salvation, but not necessarily with a view to providing explanations regarding pure Truth and the fundamental nature of things—and this despite the fact that these explanations are also provided, at least symbolically, for those with "eyes to see" and "ears to hear." In the case of Christianity, especially in its Western form, this loss has been particularly apparent since the time of the so-called "Renaissance" of the 15th and 16th centuries, a veritable revolution which signified not a "rebirth," but the death of many crucial things, notably Medieval art, as represented, for example, by Romanesque abbeys, Gothic cathedrals, Byzantine icons, and also by such a masterpiece as the *Divine Comedy*—and, above all, by the intangible spiritual kernel of these manifestations.

This spiritual, or rather, intellectual, dimension is not to be identified with mere quantitative information, cerebral ability, or bookish study, since it is much more profound, and comprises, on the contrary, qualitative dimensions that involve the whole being of man, and not merely his mental capacity. Wisdom makes man think clearly, and live well, in accordance with the nature of things. Since the time when the influence and insights of sages such as Meister Eckhart (1260-1327) and Dante Alighieri (1265-1321) in the West, and Gregory Palamas (1296-1359) in the Christian East, began to wane, a more and more emotional and conventional kind of faith has predominated, leading to a sentimental view of things which is situated at a level well below the capacity and the needs of the human mind. Despite its importance in the total scheme of things, this "sentimental faith"—or "fideism"—unaccompanied by an intellectual component, constitutes only a part of the integral religious message of Christianity. Too often, intelligence has been envisaged as a manifestation of spiritual—or intellectual—pride, without its being realized that this is a contradiction in terms, pride being at the antithesis of spirituality or intellectuality. True intelligence is characterized by the capacity to see things as they really are, and therefore by an implacable objectivity, which excludes pride, precisely.

Nowadays, most of the usual arguments advanced in favor of religion have, as Frithjof Schuon (1907-1998) has shrewdly pointed out, become "psychologically outworn"; considerations of a superior order have been relegated to a sort of limbo. In this connection, Ananda K. Coomaraswamy (1887-1947) has observed: "Today religion is presented in such a sentimental manner that it is not surprising that the best of the new generations rebel. The solution is once again to present religion in its intellectually challenging form."

There is no doubt that in our times an indifference and even a calculated disdain of religion is "in the air," especially among the "shouting classes" (journalists, academics, scientists, "celebrities"). This is not only because the typical modern man is ignorant of and uninterested in religion—he has no religious sensibility and no intuition for the sacred—but also because religion has for long presented itself in a banal and superficial manner that is far from anything that could be called "intellectually challenging." If this were not so, what could explain the interest shown by some of our contemporaries in the Oriental religions and, regrettably, in the so-called "new age" movement? Part of this turning away from their own religion comes from misinformation regarding the more profound and beautiful dimensions of Christianity, that is to say, its intellectual content, its spiritual practices, and its arts.

If on the one hand it seems correct to address the average man with sentimental and moral arguments—that is to say, with a non-intellectual approach—the fact remains that there are still men and women—and more perhaps than we might think—who are moved by considerations of a higher order, and these people too need to be given "solid food." In addition, when distanced from, or totally lacking in, the true spiritual element, the intelligentsia ends up by exerting a deleterious influence upon the whole of society, as is all-too-clearly demonstrated by most of the so-called Western "intellectuality" of the 20th century. One might mention, for instance, the unquestioning support it showed towards Marxism and Freudianism.

Introduction

If the pair "sentimentalism-fideism" seems to be most appropriate to influence the will of the average man, one must nevertheless keep in mind the somewhat different pair "knowledge-faith," for without faith, intelligence is incomplete and prone to error. If left completely to itself, purely cerebral intelligence ends up by being consumed in a sterile mental agitation, without utility or finality—as is abundantly proved by modern philosophy and art. Faith acts within us as a stabilizing element; it enriches and fortifies discernment.

The two elements in the pair "knowledge-faith" have not always been regarded as contradictory. A realization that the two are necessarily partners was the norm during the Middle Ages, and has appeared intermittently since then. This is to be seen above all in the concept of the "Perennial Philosophy"—a view which, as we shall indicate below, has been present in the West for several centuries. The essays in the present anthology point precisely in this direction; religion is here envisaged primarily as knowledge of a sacred character —not as "social service" or as a merely ethical system. The authors presented here support the vision that the intellective dimension is central to the human being; knowledge, profoundly understood, is the very heart of man. "To know is to be."

The specific characteristic of this anthology is therefore that it deals primarily with the sapiential aspect of religion. The reader will not find in it anything that smacks of "religious nationalism," formalism without spirit, or expedients intended to appeal to anything less than the central intellectual faculty of man. The essays contained in *Ye Shall Know the Truth: Christianity and the Perennial Philosophy* do not espouse the idea that Christian spirituality as a whole can be equated with the voluntaristic mysticism associated with the great Spanish Carmelite Saint John of the Cross (1542-1591). While we gladly recognize his undisputed sanctity, we must take care not to assume that his "non-intellectual" approach is the only possible form of Christian spirituality. For example, the perspectives of Saint Francis of Assisi (1182-1226) and of Saint Bernard of Clairvaux (1090-1153) constitute a spirituality of a deeper and more contemplative order. This spirituality may be compared with what in Hinduism is called *bhakti-marga*, that is to say, a "way of devotion" which is nevertheless accompanied by an "intellectual" element which distinguishes it sharply from the "non-intellectual" mysticism of Saint John of the Cross. It should be noted in passing that this "intellectual" element was not entirely lacking from the mysticism of another Spanish saint of approximately the same period, namely, Saint Ignatius Loyola (1491-1556).

Christianity possesses a deep, if somewhat unknown, dimension and this is sapiential or "gnostic" spirituality. Though the term "gnostic" may frighten some people, the reality it signifies must not be confused with the heresy of Gnosticism which appeared during the first centuries of the Christian era. The early mystical theologian Clement of Alexandria (c.150-c.215), in his *Stromata* ("Miscellanies"), was emphatic in distinguishing between authentic and spurious gnosis. St. Paul himself, in the Epistle to the Romans (11:33) refers to gnosis as "the knowledge of God" (*gnôsis tou Theou*). Meister Eckhart, the German Dominican esoterist of the Middle Ages, together with the sapiential poet Angelus Silesius (1624-1677), and the early mystical theologian Dionysius the Areopagite (500?-555?), are amongst the best known representatives of this mode of spirituality. In the Christian East, one could say that in a certain sense the Hesychasts of Greece, Russia, Romania, etc., follow a similar pattern. The chapter, "Characteristics of Voluntaristic Mysticism" deals with this important subject in a detailed and masterly manner.

"God made Himself what we are, in order to make us what He is." This audacious saying of Saint Irenaeus (c.120-c.202) epitomizes the specific message of Christianity. It shows the intrinsically "gnostic" character of the religion, together with its characteristic emphasis on the practical or "operative" consequences. To know completely and totally means to realize what one knows. The saint's words also show that Christianity cannot be reduced to a mere social activity, to a system of ethics, or to a sequence of events, and that its very heart is pure Spirit. Christianity in its kernel is a spiritual path that starts from God and, through man, ends in God; a path that leads to what Saint Irenaeus' words indicate, that is to say, *deificatio*.

In all of the great world religions, this dimension has had important spokesmen throughout the centuries; in the case of Christianity, some of its luminaries have just been mentioned. If a large "historical jump" may now be permitted, we will introduce the names of the principal contemporary spokesmen of this perennial wisdom. For it was at the beginning of the 20th century that the French philosopher René Guénon (1886-1951), followed later by the Anglo-Indian art critic Ananda Kentish Coomaraswamy, began to expound the treasures of the Perennial Philosophy in the contemporary West. It was indeed in the West that the term *Philosophia Perennis* was first used, namely by

Augustin Steuco, in the 16th century. Steuco was the Vatican's chief librarian and, influenced by Plato, Aristotle, and Nicholas of Cusa, he perceived the essential convergence of Jewish and Christian theologies and Greek philosophy. We can thus see that the notion of the Perennial Philosophy, from its beginning, was linked to Christianity and the Occident.

It was in the second half of the 20th century that the greatest exponent of this "school of thought" arose, namely, the German-Swiss metaphysician Frithjof Schuon. In this endeavor Schuon's closest collaborator and friend was the distinguished Swiss art historian Titus Burckhardt (1908-1984). In truth, one should not speak of a "school of thought," since in this case thought is no more than the medium in which concepts which go beyond discursive thinking are expressed, and which in reality are "seen" and contemplated by the Intellect. Such philosophers, in the lineage of Plato, are best described as "visionaries" rather than as "thinkers." Unlike post-Cartesian and post-Kantian philosophers, they do not seek to invent and propagate a "system" of their own, but rather to convey, in new forms, ideas and ideals that have existed everywhere and always. These authors have not "invented" anything; rather, they have brought a renovated and reinvigorating approach to the diverse aspects and dimensions of religion in general and of Christianity in particular.

René Guénon explained with amazing clarity the meaning of symbols in ritual, art, and culture, while at the same time making a devastating critique of materialism, relativism, and pseudo-spirituality, emphasizing on the contrary the truth and greatness of what he called the Primordial Tradition. Ananda Kentish Coomaraswamy, with his encyclopedic knowledge of Vedanta, Platonism, and Scholasticism, pointed out the profound convergence of the Greek, Christian, and Oriental traditions, especially in the fields of philosophy and art. Titus Burckhardt, for his part, made a fresh evaluation of sacred art, whose patrimony he demonstrated in all its splendor, especially in the Gospel manuscripts and the great cathedrals of early Medieval Europe, clarifying also their correspondences with the sacred arts of other civilizations, such as the Hindu and the Islamic. The pivotal role of figures such as Dante, Saint Bernardino of Siena, and Saint Catherine of Siena in the understanding of Christian mysticism was also expounded by him.

Above all, it was Frithjof Schuon who, with his "eagle eye," re-evaluated the Christian legacy in its essential aspects. Taking full account of its specificities and particularities, he situated it clearly among the world religions, and especially its relationships with the two other monotheistic traditions, Judaism and Islam. The idea of a "transcendent unity of religions" is one of his main contributions in the field of religious studies. The profound significance of the different branches of Christianity, notably Catholicism, Orthodoxy, and Protestantism, as well as some smaller branches such as the Coptic church, was brilliantly explained by him. The organic role played by the "way of sacred knowledge" (gnosis) in all these considerations was clearly displayed. Schuon also corrected a certain limitation in Guénon's view concerning the esoteric vis-à-vis the exoteric in Christianity, demonstrating the essentially "esoteric" or "initiatic" character of its dogmas and sacraments. The centrality of prayer, as the main channel of communication between the Divine and the human, was emphasized by Schuon in all his writings; he described prayer under its three main modes: personal (individual), canonical (collective), and jaculatory ("prayer of the heart"). Finally, the place of virtue in the economy of spiritual practice was not forgotten: Schuon constantly emphasized the practice of humility (*vacare Deo*), charity, and fidelity to truth as the conditions *sine qua non* of the spiritual life.

The Perennial Philosophy is not the "invention" of either René Guénon or Frithjof Schuon, but they are its main contemporary expositors. Guénon was a metaphysician and a professor of mathematics; he expounded universal principles with the rigor and schematization of an arithmetician. His main works were written during the first half of the 20th century, and he manifested in them a discernment that exposed the errors of positivism, occultism, and spiritism (or spiritualism). Schuon was a philosopher, poet, and painter. He surpassed Guénon's pioneering contribution in that he expounded and applied the universal principles to moral and social life, to art, culture, and the diverse religious patrimonies of the world. His principal works were written in the second half of the 20th century, during the full deployment of the Marxist blitzkrieg and the Freudian, nihilist, and new-age relativisms. Both authors showed that the seeds of the Perennial Philosophy are to be found in the contemplative dimensions of the traditional religions: in the Advaita Vedanta (non-dualism) of Hinduism, in Zen Buddhism, in the Kabbalah of Judaism, in the Hesychasm of the Orthodox Church, and in Islamic

Sufism. Traces of it are to be found "behind the veils" of the great sacred Scriptures, in the metaphysical insights of the Old and New Testaments, for example, in the Ecclesiastes of Solomon and in the Gospel according to St. John; and also in the insights of the great spiritual masters throughout the centuries.

As the reader will see, *Ye Shall Know the Truth: Christianity and the Perennial Philosophy* envisages the Christian phenomenon in both the singular and the plural: in the plural, because it is considered in its diverse dimensions—metaphysical, theological, ritual, moral, artistic, historical—and also in the context of its relationship with the other great world traditions such as Hinduism, Buddhism, Islam, and the Native American religion of the Sun Dance and the Sacred Pipe. Each of these religions manifests in its own way the two fundamental dimensions, namely, the exoteric (the outward law, morality, conventions) and the esoteric (the mystical, the inward, the sapiential). Essentially coinciding with the inward dimension of religion, esoterism points the way to that mysterious "Kingdom of God" that "is within you" (Luke 17:21) of which Christ speaks. Christianity is also envisaged in the singular, in its intrinsic universality and in the specificity of its doctrines, rites, art, and culture.

The essays included here indicate the analogies that exist between the Christian way and the paths of the other religions, and also the elements in Christianity which betoken the Perennial Philosophy. They deal with topics such as the metaphysical basis of the Christian faith, the meaning of its sacraments, its forms of prayer, and its cultural and artistic achievements—and how these artistic forms contribute to man's enlightenment and salvation. Also included are references to the lives and works of its principal figures in our own day, not forgetting incisive and detailed criticism of the tendencies prevalent in our postmodern and desacralized world.

After all, for the thousand years following the collapse of the Greco-Roman civilization, Christianity and Western civilization were practically synonymous. But ever since the revolution that was the Renaissance, and through a long series of subsequent revolutions, the last of which was Vatican II in the second half of the 20th century (the very period in which the "perennialist" works of Frithjof Schuon began to appear), the Occident has been separating itself ever more radically from its Christian origin and its Christian mold. The divorce is now almost complete and irreversible; the chaos and instability engendered by the materialism and secularism of the modern world has finally penetrated the citadel of religion, with tragic results for society as a whole. In order not to become submerged in this chaos, the authors in the present anthology are unanimous in saying that religion must turn towards its kernel of wisdom, to that "Truth that shall make you free" (John 8:32). And it is precisely this that they do, discussing religion profoundly and objectively, and putting at our disposal the keys that will enable us to love it sincerely, and to live it "with all our heart, and with all our soul, and with all our mind, and with all our strength" as the Gospel says (Mark 12:30).

*
*   *

Ye Shall Know the Truth: Christianity and the Perennial Philosophy is organized into six sections which comprise the main aspects of the subject matter. The first section, "Foundations," presents a penetrating and original synthesis of Christianity—including its three main branches, Catholicism, Orthodoxy, and Protestantism—according to the perennialist perspective, and discusses the roles which esoterism, exoterism, and mysticism play within it. The second section, "Spirituality," focuses on the contemplative discipline of "quintessential prayer" or "prayer of the heart" especially in the form of the Jesus Prayer and the Rosary. The third section, "Sacred Art," presents the artistic forms and the crafts in their most profound dimensions, as a powerful means of furthering the spiritual life. The fourth section, "Comparative Religion," deals with the historical and cultural relationships between Christianity and the other traditional religions, such as Hinduism, Buddhism, Judaism, and especially Islam—the least known and most misunderstood of the world's major religions. The fifth section, "The Universality of the Christian Mystics," deals with the "universal" character and appeal of some of the most influential figures of Christian mysticism, from the Middle Ages through to the modern period. The sixth and final section, "The Modern Deviation," offers strong, perspicacious, and soundly based criticism of the modern mentality in its various forms; clear indication is given that, of all the pollutions that beset contemporary man, the worst by far is intellectual pollution. The last item in the book, by one of the "founding fathers" of the perennialist school, Titus Burckhardt, constitutes as it were a synthesis of the whole volume and summons us, even amid the chaos and perplexities of present circumstances, to focus on the essential. It offers a positive message, for *vincit omnia Veritas* ("Truth conquers all"), the same Truth that will "make us free"; for only Truth is all-liberating and all-conquering.

At the beginning of sections I-VI the reader will also find an extensive selection of quotations. These have primarily been garnered from the Christian scriptures as well as the long legacy of its saints and sages. They are intended both to introduce the reader to the major themes of the various sections, as well as expose them to the Christian tradition at its most rich and profound.

For the discerning reader who perceives the universal and sapiential nature of Christianity, the essays collected together here offer a substantial and precious viaticum. They bring to life what we believe to be the only authentic and solid alternative to the shallow, tedious, and in fact erroneous, forms that pass for "religion" today. For the authors in this volume, Christianity remains alive; it has the power to convey light and warmth to all who truly seek. As the very source of understanding and compassion; and as the way to truth, beauty, and salvation—this, in a nutshell, is how religion in general, and Christianity in particular, are presented in this book.

—MATEUS SOARES DE AZEVEDO

1

Foundations

"Blessed is the man who has found wisdom. . . . Her ways are good ways, and all her paths are peaceful. She is a tree of life to all that lay hold upon her."—Proverbs 3:13; 17-18

"The ultimate goal of the universe is truth, and the contemplation of truth is the essential activity of wisdom."—St. Thomas Aquinas (1224-1274)

Magna est veritas et praevalebit.
"Great is truth and it shall prevail."—I Esdras 4:41

Quod ubique, quod semper, quod ab omnibus creditum est.
"That which has been believed everywhere, always, and by everybody."— Definition of orthodoxy by St. Vincent de Lérin (d.c.450)

"If I had to choose between God and Truth, I would choose Truth; but God is Truth."—Meister Eckhart (1260-1327)

Aliquid est in anima quod est increatum et increabile; si tota anima esset talis, esset increata et increabilis; et hoc est Intellectus.
"There is something in the soul which is uncreated and uncreatable; if the whole soul were such, it would be uncreated and uncreatable; and this is the Intellect."—Meister Eckhart (1260-1327)

"I do perceive that never can our Intellect be sated, unless the Truth do shine upon it."—Dante Alighieri (1265-1321)

"The eye with which I see God is the same eye with which God sees me."— Meister Eckhart (1260-1327)

"The purpose of temporal tranquility, which well-ordered policies establish and maintain, is to give opportunities for contemplating truth."—St. Thomas Aquinas (1224-1274)

"We define 'God' as the greatest possible object of thought. Now, if any object of thought does not exist, another exactly like it which does exist, is greater. Therefore the greatest of all objects of thought must exist, since, otherwise, another, still greater, would be possible. Therefore, God exists."—St. Anselm (1033-1109)

Mens sine desiderio non intelligit; mens sine intellectu non desiderat.
"The mind without love cannot understand; the mind without intelligence cannot love."—Nicholas of Cusa (1401-1464)

"Unto you, O men, I [Wisdom] call; and my voice is to the sons of man. O ye simple, understand wisdom: and, ye fools, be ye of an understanding heart. Hear; for I will speak of excellent things; and the opening of my lips shall be right things. For my mouth shall speak truth; and wickedness is an abomination to my lips. All the words of my mouth are in righteousness; there is nothing froward or perverse in them. They are all plain to him that understandeth, and right to them that find knowledge. Receive my instruction, and not silver; and knowledge rather than choice gold. For wisdom is better than rubies; and all the things that may be desired are not to be compared to it. I, Wisdom, dwell with prudence, and show the way to knowledge. The fear of the Lord is to hate evil: pride, and arrogancy, and the evil way, and the froward mouth, do I hate. Counsel is mine, and sound wisdom; I am understanding; I have strength. By me kings reign, and princes decree justice. By me princes rule, and nobles, even all the judges of the earth. I love them that love me; and those that seek me early shall find me. Riches and honor are with me; yea, durable riches and righteousness. My fruit is better than gold, yea, than fine gold; and my revenue than choice silver. I lead in the way of righteousness, in the midst of the paths of judgment: that I may cause those that love me to inherit substance; and I will fill their treasures. The Lord possessed me in the beginning of his way, before his works of old. I was set up from everlasting, from the beginning, or ever the earth was. When there were no depths, I was brought forth; when there were no fountains abounding with water. Before the mountains were settled, before the hills was I brought forth: while as yet he had not made the earth, nor the fields, nor the highest part of the dust of the world. When he prepared the heavens, I was there: when he set a compass upon the face of the depth: when he established the clouds above: when he strengthened the fountains of the deep: when he gave to the see his decree, that the waters should not pass his commandment: when he appointed the foundations of the earth: then I was by him, as one brought up with him: and I was daily his delight, rejoicing always before him; rejoicing in the habitable part of his earth; and my delights were with the sons of men. Now therefore hearken unto me, O ye children: for blessed are they that keep my ways. Hear instruction, and be wise, and refuse it not. Blessed is the man that heareth me, watching daily at my gates, waiting at the posts of my doors. For whoso findeth me findeth life, and shall obtain favor of the Lord."—Proverbs 8:4-35

THE QUESTION OF EVANGELICALISM

Frithjof Schuon

Christianity is divided into three great denominations: Catholicism, Orthodoxy, Evangelicalism, not to mention the Copts and other ancient groups close to Orthodoxy. This classification may astonish some of our regular readers since it seems to place Protestantism on the same level as the ancient Churches; now we have in view here, not liberal Protestantism or just any sect, but Lutheran Evangelicalism, which incontestably manifests a Christian possibility, a limited one, no doubt, and excessive through certain of its features, but not intrinsically illegitimate, and consequently representative of certain theological, moral, and even mystical values. If Evangelicalism—to use the term favored by Luther—were situated in a world such as that of Hinduism, it would appear therein as a possible way, that is to say it would be, no doubt, a secondary *darshana* amongst others; in Buddhism it would not be more heterodox than is Amidism or the school of Nichiren, both of which, however, are quite independent with regard to the main tradition surrounding them.

To understand our point of view, one has to know that religions are determined by archetypes which are so many spiritual possibilities: on the one hand, every religion *a priori* manifests an archetype, but on the other hand, any archetype can manifest itself *a posteriori* within every religion. It is thus that Shiism for example is, quite evidently, not due to a Christian influence, but to a manifestation, within Islam, of the religious possibility—or the spiritual archetype—which affirmed itself in a direct and plenary fashion in Christianity; and this same possibility gave rise, within Buddhism, to Amidist mysticism, but accentuating another dimension of the archetype, namely that of a cosmic prodigy of Mercy, which requires, and at the same time confers, the quasi-charisma of saving Faith; whereas in the case of Shiism the accent is upon the practically divine Man who opens Heaven to earth.

It could be said analogously that the Germanic soul—treated by Rome in too Latin a manner, but this is another question—that this soul, which is neither Greek nor Roman, felt the need of a more simple and more inward religious archetype, one less formalistic there-

5

fore, and more "popular" in the best sense of the word; this in certain respects is the religious archetype of Islam, a religion based on a Book and conferring priesthood upon every believer. At the same time and from another point of view, the Germanic soul had a nostalgia for a perspective that integrates the natural into the supernatural, that is, a perspective tending towards God without being against nature; a piety that was non-monastic, yet accessible to every man of good will in the midst of earthly preoccupations; a way founded upon Grace and trust and not upon Justice and works; and this way incontestably has its premises in the Gospel itself.

*
* *

Here it is once again appropriate—for we have done so on other occasions—to define the difference between a heresy which is extrinsic, hence relative to a given orthodoxy, and another that is intrinsic, hence false in itself as also with respect to all orthodoxy or to Truth as such. To simplify the matter, we could limit ourselves to noting that the first type of heresy manifests a spiritual archetype—in a limited manner, no doubt, but nonetheless efficacious—whereas the second is merely human work and in consequence based solely on its own productions;[1] and this decides the entire question. To claim that a "pious" spiritist is assured of salvation is meaningless, for in total heresies there is no element that can guarantee posthumous beatitude, even though—apart from all question of belief—a man can always be saved for reasons which escape us; but he is certainly not saved by his heresy.

On the subject of Arianism, which was a particularly invasive heresy, the following remark ought to be made: it is unquestionably heterodox by the fact that it sees in Jesus merely a creature; this idea can have a meaning in the perspective of Islam, but it is incompatible with that of Christianity. However, the lightning-like expansion of Arianism shows that it answered a spiritual need—corresponding to the archetype of which Islam is the most characteristic manifestation—and it is precisely to this need or to this expectation that Evangelicalism finally

---

[1] Such as Mormonism, Bahaism, the Ahmadism of Kadyan, and all the "new religions" and other pseudo-spiritualities which proliferate in today's world.

responded,[2] not in humanizing Christ, of course, but in simplifying the religion and Germanizing it in a certain manner. Another well-known heresy was Nestorianism, which rigorously separated the two natures of Christ, the divine and the human, and by way of consequence saw in Mary the mother of Christ but not of God; this perspective corresponds to a possible theological point of view, and thus it is a question of an extrinsic, and not a total, heresy.

Rigorously speaking, all religious exoterism is an extrinsic heresy, evidently so with respect to other religions, but also, and above all, with respect to the *sophia perennis*; this perennial wisdom, precisely, constitutes esoterism when it is combined with a religious symbolism. An extrinsic heresy is a partial or relative truth—in its formal articulation—which presents itself as total or absolute, be it a question of religions or, within these, of denominations; but the starting point is always a truth, hence also a spiritual archetype. Altogether different is the case of an intrinsic heresy: its starting point is, either an objective error, or a subjective illusion; in the first case, the heresy lies more in the doctrine, and in the second, it is *a priori* in the pretension of the false prophet; but, needless to say, both kinds can combine, and even do so necessarily in the second case. Although there is no error possible without a particle of truth, intrinsic heresy cannot have any doctrinal or methodic value, and one cannot bring to bear on its behalf any extenuating circumstance, precisely because it projects no celestial model.

*

*   *

It is not difficult to argue, against the Reformation, that it is impossible that the traditional authorities and the councils, by definition inspired by the Holy Spirit, were mistaken; this is true, but does not exclude paradoxes that mitigate this quasi-evidentness. First of all—it is this that gave wings to the Reformers, starting with Wycliff and Huss—Christ himself repudiated many "traditional" elements supported by the "authorities" in calling them "prescriptions of men"; then, the excesses of "papism" at the time of Luther and well before

---

[2] Arius of Alexandria was not a German, but his doctrine went out to meet an aspiration of the German mentality, whence its success with the Visigoths, the Ostrogoths, the Vandals, the Burgundians and the Langobards.

then, prove if not that the papacy in itself is illegitimate, at least that it comprises excesses which the Byzantine Church is the first to note and to stigmatize. We mean to say that the Pope, instead of being *primus inter pares* as Saint Peter had been, has the exorbitant privilege of being at once prophet and emperor: as prophet, he places himself above the councils, and as emperor, he possesses a temporal power that surpasses that of all the princes including the emperor himself; and it is precisely these unheard-of prerogatives which permitted, in our time, the entry of modernism into the Church, like a Trojan horse and despite the warnings of the preceding popes; that popes may personally have been saints does not at all weaken the valid arguments of the Eastern Church. In a word, if the Western Church had been such that it could have avoided casting the Eastern Church into the "outer darknesses"—and with what manifestations of barbarism—it would not have had to undergo the counterblow of the Reformation.

Be that as it may, to say that the Roman Church is intrinsically orthodox and integrally traditional does not mean that it conveys in a direct, compelling, and exhaustive manner all aspects of the world of the Gospel, even though it necessarily contains them and manifests them occasionally or sporadically; for the world of the Gospel was Oriental and Semitic, and immersed in a climate of holy poverty, whereas the world of Catholicism is European, Roman, imperial; this is to say that the religion was Romanized in the sense that the characteristic traits of the Roman mentality determined its formal elaboration. Suffice it to mention in this respect its juridicism and its administrative and even military spirit; traits which are manifested, among others, by the disproportionate complication of rubrics, the prolixity of the missal, the dispersing complexity of the sacramental economy, the pedantic manipulation of indulgences; then by a certain administrative centralization—even a militarization—of monastic spirituality, without forgetting, on the level of forms—which is far from being negligible—the pagan titanism of the Renaissance and the nightmare of Baroque art. Still from the point of view of formal outwardness, the following remark could be made: in the Catholic world, and already by the end of the Middle Ages, the difference between religious and laical dress is often abrupt to the point of incompatibility; when the essentially worldly and vain, even erotic trappings of the princes are compared with the majestic garments of the priests, it is hard to believe that the former are Christians like the latter, whereas in the

Oriental civilizations the style of dress is in general homogeneous. In Islam, there does not even exist a dividing line between religious personages and the rest of society; at the level of appearances there is no laical society opposed to a priestly one. This being said, let us close this parenthesis, the point of which was simply to show that the Catholic world presents traits—on its surface as well as in its depths— which certainly do not express the climate of the Gospels.[3]

It has been argued to satiety that it is sacred institutions that count and not the human accidents that disfigure them; this is obvious, yet the very degree of this disfiguration indicates that in the institutions themselves part of the imperfection was due to some human zeal. Dante and Savonarola saw this clearly in their own way, and the very phenomenon of the Renaissance proves it. If we are told that the papacy, such as it was throughout the centuries, represents the only possible solution for the West, we agree, but then the risks which this inevitable adaptation fatally comprised should have been foreseen, and everything should have been done to diminish, not to increase them; if a strongly marked hierarchy was indispensable, the sacerdotal aspect of every Christian should have been insisted upon all the more.

Be that as it may, what permitted Luther to separate from Rome,[4] was his awareness of the principle of "orthodox decadence", that is of the possibility of decadence within the immutable framework of a traditional orthodoxy, an awareness inspired by the example of the scribes and the pharisees in the Gospel, with their "prescriptions of men"—by which is meant, objectively, the specifications, develop-

---

[3] For a Joseph de Maistre, whose intelligence otherwise had great merits, the reformers could not be other than "nobodies" who dared to set their personal opinions against the traditional and unanimous certitudes of the Catholic Church; he was far from suspecting that these "nobodies" spoke under the pressure of an archetypal perspective which, being such, could not but manifest itself in appropriate circumstances. The same author accused Protestantism with having done an immense evil in breaking up Christianity, but he readily loses sight of the fact that Catholicism did as much in rashly excommunicating all of the Patriarchs of the East; without forgetting the Renaissance, whose evil was, to say the least, as "immense" as those of the political and other effects of the Reformation.

[4] He separated from the Roman Church only after his condemnation, by burning the bull of excommunication; and moreover one should not lose sight of the fact that at the time of the Reformation there was no unanimity on the question of the Pope and the Councils, and even the question of the divine origin of the papal authority was not secure from all controversy.

ments, elaborations, clarifications, and stylizations which may be required by a particular temperament, but not by another.[5]

Another association of ideas which was useful to Luther and to Protestantism in general is the Augustinian opposition between a *civitas dei* and a *civitas terrena* or *diaboli*: the witnessing of the disorders of the Roman Church easily led him to identify Rome with the "earthly city" of Saint Augustine. There is also, and fundamentally, a tendency in the Gospel which answers with particular force the needs of the Germanic soul: namely the tendency towards simplicity and inwardness, and thus contrary to theological and liturgical complication, to formalism, to dispersion of worship, to the all too often insolently casual tyranny of the clergy. From another viewpoint, the Germans were sensitive to the nobly and robustly popular character of the Bible; which has no relationship with democracy, for Luther was a supporter of a theocratic regime upheld by the emperor and the princes.

Without question, the perspective of Evangelicalism is typically Pauline; it is founded on the so to speak gnostic dualism of the following elements: the flesh and the spirit, death and life, servitude and freedom, Law and Grace, justice through works and justice through faith, Adam and Christ. From another point of view, Evangelicalism is founded, like Christianity as such, on the Pauline idea of the universality of salvation answering the universality of sin or of the state of the sinner; only the redemptive death of Christ could deliver man from this curse; by the Redemption, Christ became the luminous head of all humanity. But the typically Pauline accentuation of the Message is the doctrine of justification through faith, which Luther made the pivot of the religion, or more precisely of his mysticism.

*

* *

After the failure of Wycliff and Huss—from whom it would have been proper to retain, if not the entire doctrine, then at least certain of its tendencies—the popes contributed by their impenitence to the

---

[5] Hinduism also—without mentioning the Mediterranean paganisms—furnishes an example of this kind, with the heavy and endless pedantry of the brahmans which, however, it was not too difficult to escape, given the plasticity of the Hindu spirit and the suppleness of its corresponding institutions.

Lutheran explosion;[6] after the failure—within the very framework of Catholic orthodoxy—of Dante, Savonarola, and other warners, Luther by the scathing nature of his denunciation caused the Catholic renovation; Providence willed both outcomes, the Evangelical Church as well as the Tridentine Church. Ideally speaking: after the Council of Trent, Catholicism should have assimilated—without disavowing itself—the essence of the message of Evangelicalism, just as Evangelicalism should have rediscovered the essence of the Catholic reality; instead, both parties hardened in their respective positions, and in fact, it could not have been otherwise, if only for the same reason that there are diverse religions; which is to say, it is necessary for spiritual perspectives, before being qualified, to be entirely themselves, all the more so in that their over-accentuation responds to racial or ethnic needs.[7]

Each denomination manifests the Gospel in a certain manner; now this manifestation seems to us to be the most direct, the most ample, and the most realistic possible in the Orthodox Church, and this can already be seen in its outer forms, whereas the Catholic Church offers an image that is more Roman, less Oriental, in a certain sense even more worldly since the Renaissance and the Baroque epoch, as we have pointed out above. Latin civilizationism has nothing to do with the world and the spirit of the Gospel; but, after all, the Roman West is Christian and in consequence Christianity has the right to be Roman. There remains the Evangelical Church; the question of its forms of worship does not arise, since in this respect it participates in the Catholic culture, with the difference however that it introduces into this culture a principle of rather iconoclastic sobriety, while having the advantage of not accepting the Renaissance and its prolongations; this is to say that Evangelicalism remained, artistically

---

[6] This is something which, within the Catholic camp, Cardinal Newman and others have acknowledged.

[7] In so saying, we do not lose sight of the fact that the Germans of the South—the Allamanis (the Germans of Baden, the Alsatians, the German Swiss, the Swabians) and the Bavarians (including the Austrians)—have a rather different temperament than that of the Germans of the North, and that everywhere there are mixtures; racial and ethnic frontiers in Europe are, in any case, rather fluctuating. We do not say that every German is made for Evangelicalism, for Germanic tendencies can obviously manifest within Catholicism, just as, conversely, Protestant Calvinism manifests above all a Latin possibility.

speaking and in the intention of Luther, with the forms of the Middle Ages, while simplifying them, and that it thus escaped that unspeakable aberration which was Baroque art. From the spiritual point of view, Protestantism retains from the Gospel the spirit of simplicity and inwardness while accentuating the mystery of faith, and it presents these aspects with a vigor whose moral and mystical value cannot be denied; this accentuation was necessary in the West, and since Rome would not take it upon itself, it is Wittenberg that did so.

In connection with Protestant quasi-iconoclasm, we will point out that Saint Bernard also wished to have chapels empty, bare, and sober, in short that "sensible consolations" be reduced to a minimum; but he wished it for the monasteries and not for the cathedrals; the sense of the sacred, in this case, was concentrated on the essential of the rites. We meet with this point of view in Zen as well as in Islam, and above all we meet with it several times in Christ, so much so that it would be unjust to deny any precedent in the Scripture to the Lutheran attitude; Christ wanted one to worship God "in spirit and in truth" and that in praying one not use "vain repetitions, as the heathen do"; this is the emphasis on faith, with the primacy of sincerity and intensity.

*

* *

The celibacy of priests, imposed by Gregory VII after one thousand years of the contrary practice—which has always been maintained by the Eastern Church—presents several serious drawbacks: it needlessly repeats the celibacy of the monks and separates the priests more radically from lay society, which becomes all the more laic thereby; that is, this measure reinforces in the laity the feeling of dependence and of lesser moral value, marriage being in practice belittled by yet another ukase. Next, the celibacy imposed upon an enormous number of priests—for society has all the more need of priests as it is numerous, and Christianity embraces all of the West—this celibacy then, imposed upon too large a collectivity, necessarily created moral disorders and contributed to the loosening of morals, whereas it would have been better to have good married priests than bad celibate priests; unless the number of priests be reduced, which is impossible since society is large and has need of them. Finally, the celibacy of the clergy prevents the procreation of men of religious vocation, and thus impoverishes society; if only men without religious vocation have children, the society will become more and more worldly and "horizontal", and less and less spiritual and "vertical".

However that may be, Luther lacked realism in his turn: he was astonished that during his absence from Wittenberg—this was the year of Wartburg—the promoters of the Reformation gave themselves up to all kinds of excesses; at the end of his life, he even went so far as to regret that the masses of the mediocre had not remained under the rod of the Pope. Hardly concerned about collective psychology, he believed that the simple principle of piety could replace the material supports which contribute so powerfully to regulate the behavior of the crowds; not only does it keep this behavior in equilibrium in space, but it also stabilizes it in time. He did not know, in his mystical subjectivism, that a religion has need of symbolism in order to subsist; that the inward cannot live in a collective consciousness without outward signs;[8] but, prophet of inwardness, he scarcely had a choice.

The Latin West had too often lacked realism and measure, whereas the Greek Church, like the East in general, knew better how to reconcile the demands of spiritual idealism with those of the everyday human world. From a particular viewpoint, we would like to make the following remark: it is very unlikely that Christ, who washed the feet of his disciples and who taught them that "the first shall be the last", would have appreciated the imperial pomp of the Vatican court: such as the kissing of the foot, the triple crown, the *flabelli*, the *sedia gestatoria*; on the other hand, there is no reason to think that he would have disapproved of the ceremonies—of sacerdotal and not imperial style—which surround the Orthodox Patriarch; he would no doubt have disapproved of the cardinalate, which on the one hand further raises so to speak the princely throne of the Pope, and on the other hand constitutes a dignity that is non-sacerdotal and more worldly than religious.[9]

We have spoken above of the celibacy of priests imposed by Gregory VII, and we must add a word concerning the Evangelical councils and the monastic vows. When one reads in the Gospel that

---

[8] This is, be it said in passing, what is forgotten even by most of the impeccable gurus of contemporary India, starting with Ramakrishna.

[9] "But be not ye called Rabbi: for one is your Master, even Christ; and all ye are brethren." "Neither be ye called masters: for one is your Master, even Christ" (Matthew 23: 8 and 10).

"there is no man that hath left house, or brethren, or sisters, or father, or mother, or wife, or children, or lands, for my sake, and the gospel's but he shall receive an hundredfold", one immediately thinks of monks and nuns; now Luther thought that it was solely a question of persecutions, in the sense of this saying from the Sermon on the Mount: "Blessed are they which are persecuted for righteousness' sake: for theirs is the kingdom of Heaven";[10] and he is all the more sure of his interpretation in that there were neither anchorites nor monks before the fourth century.

*

*   *

Viewed in its totality, Protestantism has something ambiguous about it, owing to the fact that, on the one hand it is inspired sincerely and concretely by the Bible, yet on the other hand it is bound up with humanism and the Renaissance. Luther incarnates the first kind: his perspective is medieval and so to speak retrospective, and it gives rise to a conservative pietism, tending at times towards esoterism. In Calvin, it is on the contrary the tendencies of humanism, hence of the Renaissance which, if they do not determine the movement, at least mingle with it rather strongly; no doubt, he is greatly inspired in his doctrine by Luther and the Swiss Reformers, but he is a republican in his own way—on a theocratic basis of course—and not a monarchist like the German Reformer; and it can be said on the whole that in a certain manner he was more opposed to Catholicism than was Luther.[11]

For some time already, the fundamental ideas of the Reformation had been "in the air", but it is Luther who lived them and who made of them a personal drama. His Evangelicalism—like other particular perspectives enclosed within a general perspective—is an overaccen-

---

[10] He says so in a marginal note of his translation: "Whosoever believes, must suffer persecution, and risk all" (*alles dran setzen*). And he repeats it in his song *Ein feste Burg ist unser Gott*: "Even if they (the persecutors) take body, goods, honor, child and wife, let them go (*lass fahren dahin*); they shall receive no benefit; the Kingdom (of God) shall be ours" (*das Reich muss uns doch bleiben*).

[11] As for Protestant liberalism, Luther, after a while, foresaw its abuses and he would in any case be horrified to see this liberalism such as it presents itself in our time; he who could bear neither self-sufficient mediocrity nor iconoclastic fanaticism.

tuated partitioning, so to speak, but sufficient and efficacious, hence "non-illegitimate".[12]

One cannot study the problem of Evangelicalism without taking into consideration the powerful personality of its real, or at least its most notable, founder. First of all, and this follows from what we have just said, nothing allows one to affirm that Luther was a modernist ahead of his time, for he was in no wise worldly and sought to please no one; his innovations were assuredly of the most audacious kind, to say the least, but they were Christian and nothing else; they owed nothing to any philosophy or to any scientism.[13]

He rejected Rome, not because it was too spiritual, but on the contrary because it seemed to him too worldly; too "according to the flesh" and not "according to the spirit", from his particular point of view.

The mystic of Wittenberg[14] was a German Semiticized by Christianity, and he was representative in both respects: fundamentally German, he loved what is sincere and inward, not clever and formalistic; Semitic in spirit, he admitted only Revelation and faith and did not wish to hear of Aristotle or the Scholastics.[15]

On the one hand, there was in his nature something robust and powerful (*gewaltig*), with a complement of poetry and gentleness (*Innigkeit*); on the other hand, he was a voluntarist and an individualist who expected nothing from either intellectuality or metaphysics. Unquestionably, his impetuous genius was capable of uncouthness— which is the least that can be said—but he lacked neither patience

[12] Evangelicalism properly so called, which is at the antipodes from liberal Protestantism, was perpetuated in pietism, whose father was De Labadie, a mystic converted to the Reformation in the seventeenth century, and whose most notable representatives were no doubt Spener and Tersteegen; this pietism or this piety exists always in various places, either in a diminished or quite honorable form.

[13] As is, on the contrary, the case in Catholic modernism. That this modernism is open not only towards Evangelicalism, but also towards Islam and other religions, gets us nowhere, since this same modernism is quite as open to no matter what, except to Tradition.

[14] For he was a mystic rather than a theologian, which explains many things.

[15] It could be objected that the Semites adopted the Greek philosophers, but that is not the question, for this adoption was diverse and graded, not to mention the many reticences. Besides, Luther—a cultivated man—was also a logician and could not not be one; in certain respects, he was Latinized of necessity—as was an Albert the Great or an Eckhart—but that was on the surface only.

nor generosity; he could be vehement, but not more so than a Saint Jerome or other saints who reviled their adversaries, "devoured" as they were by "zeal for the house of the Lord"; and no one can contest that they found precedents for this in both Testaments.[16]

The message of Luther is essentially expressed in two legacies, which attest to the personality of the author and to which it is impossible to deny grandeur and efficaciousness: the German Bible and the hymns. His translation of the Scripture, while conditioned in certain places by his doctrinal perspective, is a jewel both of language and piety; as for the hymns—most of which are not from his hand, although he composed their models and thus gave the impulse to all this flowering—they became a fundamental element of worship, and they were a powerful factor of expansion for Evangelicalism.[17]

The Catholic Church itself could not resist this magic; it ended by adopting several Lutheran hymns, become popular to the point of imposing themselves like the air one breathes. In summary, the whole personality of Luther is in his translation of the Psalms and in his famous hymn "A Mighty Fortress Is Our God" (*Ein feste Burg ist unser Gott*), which became the "war song" (*Trutzlied*) of Evangelicalism, and whose qualities of power and grandeur cannot be denied. But more gently, this personality is also in his commentary on the *Magnificat*, which attests to an inner worship of the Holy Virgin whom Luther never rejected; Pope Leo X, having read this commentary without knowing its author, made this remark: "Blessed be the hands that wrote this!" No doubt the German Reformer was not able to maintain the public worship of the Virgin, but this was because of the general reaction against the dispersion of religious sentiment and thus in favor of worship concentrated on Christ alone, which had to become absolute and consequently exclusive, as is the worship of Allah for Moslems. Besides, Scripture treats the Virgin with a somewhat surprising parsimony—which played a certain role here—but there are also

---

[16] When the reformer terms the "papist mass" an "abomination", we are made to think of the bonze Nichiren who claimed that it sufficed to invoke Amida once to fall into Hell; not to mention the Buddha who rejected the Veda, the castes and the gods.

[17] Among the composers of hymns, there were notably the pastor Johann Valentin Andrea, author of the "Chemical Marriages of Christian Rosenkreutz", and later Paul Gerhardt, Tersteegen and Novalis, whose hymns are among the jewels of German poetry; and let us add that the religious music of Bach testifies to the same spirit of powerful piety.

the crucial, and doctrinally inexhaustible, declarations that Mary is "full of grace" and that "all generations shall call me blessed".[18]

The German Reformer was a mystic in the sense that his progression was purely experimental and not conceptual; the pertinent demonstrations of a Staupitz were of no help to him. To discover the efficacy of Mercy, he needed first the "event of the tower": having meditated in vain on the "Justice" of God, he had the grace of understanding in a flash that this Justice is merciful and that it liberates us in and by faith.

*

*   *

The great themes of Luther are the Scripture, Christ, the Inward, Faith; the first two elements belong to the divine side, and the latter two to the human side. By emphasizing Scripture—at the expense of Tradition—Evangelicalism is close to Islam, where the Koran is everything; by emphasizing Christ—at the expense of the Pope, of hierarchy, of the clergy—Evangelicalism recalls devotional Buddhism which places everything in the hands of Amitabha; the worshiping and ritual expression of this primacy of Christ being Communion, which for Luther is as real and as important as for the Catholics. The Lutheran tendency towards the "inward", the "heart" if one will, is incontestably founded on the perspective of Christ; and likewise the emphasis on faith, which moreover evokes—we repeat—Amidist mysticism as well as Moslem piety. We would not dream of making these comparisons, at first glance needless, if they did not serve to illustrate the principle of the archetypes of which we have spoken above and which is of crucial importance.

As regards Christ made tangible in Communion, it is not true that Luther reduced the Eucharistic rite to a simple ceremony of remembrance, as did his adversary Zwingli;[19] quite to the contrary,

---

[18] As Dante said: "Lady, thou art so great and possesseth such power, that whosoever desireth grace and has not recourse to thee, it is as if his desire wished to fly without wings" (*Paradiso*, XXXIII, 13-15).

[19] Whose thesis has been retained by liberal Protestantism; Calvin attempted to bring it back more or less to that of Luther. The idea of a commemorative rite pure and simple is intrinsically heretical since "to do in memory of" is meaningless from the standpoint of sacramental efficacy.

he admitted the real Presence, but neither transubstantiation—which the Greeks also did not accept as such, although they ended by accepting the word—nor the bloodless renewal of the historical sacrifice; however, these sacramental realities perceived by the Catholics are implied in the Lutheran definition of the Eucharist—objectively but not subjectively—so much so that it could be said, even from the Catholic point of view, that Luther's definition is acceptable on condition of being conscious of this implication. For the Catholics, this implication constitutes the very definition of the mystery, which is perhaps disproportionate if one takes account of the somewhat dispersing and "glib" usage that Catholicism makes of its Mass;[20] certain psychological facts—human nature being what it is—no doubt would have required that the mystery be presented in a more veiled fashion and handled with more discretion. Certainly, the Lutheran Communion is not the equivalent of the Catholic Communion, but we have reasons for believing—given its context as a whole—that it nonetheless communicates to a sufficient degree the graces Luther expected of it,[21] which presupposes that the intention of the ritual change was fundamentally Christian—and free from all rationalist, let alone political, hindsight—as was the case in fact.

If the Lutheran Communion is not the equivalent of the Catholic Communion, it is because it does not comprise spiritual virtualities as extensive as those of the latter; but precisely, these initiatic virtualities are too lofty for the average man, and to impose them upon him is to expose him to sacrilege. From another point of view, if the Mass were always equal to the historical Sacrifice of Christ, it would become sacrilege due to its profanation by the more or less trivial manner of its usage: bungled low Masses, Masses attributed to this or that, including the most contingent and profane occasions. Certainly, the Mass coincides potentially with the event of Golgotha, and this potentiality,

---

[20] For one must not "cast pearls before swine" nor "give what is holy unto the dogs". With the Orthodox, the Mass is the center disposed of by the priests, whereas it could be said that with the Catholics it is the priest who is, in practice, the center who disposes of the Masses.

[21] The same could be admitted, with perhaps certain reservations which are difficult to make precise, for the Calvinist and Anglican Communions, but not for those of the Zwinglians or the liberal Protestants anymore than—and this will seem quite paradoxical at first sight—for the "conciliary" or "post-conciliary" masses, which are not covered by a valid archetype and which are, given their ambiguous intentions, merely the result of human arbitrariness.

or this virtuality, can always give rise to an effective coincidence;[22] but if the Mass had in itself the character of its bloody prototype, at each Mass the earth would tremble and would be covered with darkness.

One of the most aberrant arguments with which Zwingli, Karlstadt, Oekolampad, and others opposed to both the Catholic Church and Luther, was the following: if the bread is really the body of Christ, do we not, when communing, eat human flesh?[23]

To this there are four responses to make, and they are the following. Firstly, Christ said what he said, and one must take it or leave it; there is nothing to change in it, unless one wishes to leave the Christian religion. Secondly, Christ in fact offers neither flesh nor blood, but bread and wine, so wherefore the complaint? Thirdly, the crucial point is the question of knowing what signify this body which one has to eat and this blood which one has to drink; now this meaning, or this content, is the remission of sins, the Redemption, the restitution of the glorious human nature, innocence both primordial and celestial; man eats and drinks that which he must become, because he is that in his immortal essence; and to eat is to become united. Fourthly: that bread is not flesh, that wine is not blood we can see without difficulty; why then ask in what manner bread is the body and wine the blood? This does not concern us, this has no interest for us; it is God's concern. What alone is important for us is the transforming and deifying virtue of the sacrament: its capacity to grant us saving impeccability, that of Christ.[24]

*

*　*

The Lutheran doctrine is founded essentially upon the anthropological pessimism and the predestinationism of Saint Augustine: man is fundamentally a sinner, and he is totally determined by the Will of God.

[22] And this is independent of the intrinsic efficacy of the sacrament, notwithstanding that this efficacy is realized in proportion to the holiness, hence receptivity, of the communicant.

[23] This argument is supposed to allow us to conclude that the bread "signifies"—hence "is not"—the body of Christ; the weakness of the argument is at the level of its intention.

[24] In the mysteries of Eleusis too, bread and wine were used "eucharistically" and they communicated a divine power.

What, then, is the meaning in Saint Augustine of the idea that man is irremediably a sinner, that he is powerless so long as he is left to his own devices? It means that the "fall" has the effect of destroying the equilibrium between the inward and the outward, the vertical or the ascending and the horizontal or earthly; that the exteriorizing and worldly tendencies prevail over the interiorizing and spiritual tendencies, and that when taken alone, the horizontal tendency leads *ipso facto* to the descending tendency. Now works do not suffice to rectify the situation; faith alone can accomplish this prodigy, which does not mean that faith can do without works, that it could thus be perfectly itself in their absence.

As in Amidism, the first condition of salvation, according to Luther, is the awareness of abysmal and invincible sin, and hence the impossibility of vanquishing sin by our own strength. For Luther and for Christianity in general, man is practically sin;[25] on the part of God, there is Grace—which Luther identifies with the "Justice" of God the Redeemer—and between these two extremes, there is faith, in which the sinner and Grace meet. Luther declares in a lecture on the Epistles to the Romans that Christ "made his Justice mine, and my sin his", and he adds: "For him who throws himself body and soul into God's Will it is impossible to remain outside God". Likewise, he says in speaking of Justice that "faith raises the human heart so high, that it becomes one spirit with God (*dass er ein Geist mit Gott wird*) and acquires the very Justice of God".

The tormented mysticism of Luther—yet in its own way victorious in the final analysis—evokes all the tension between knowing and believing, or between knowledge and faith. For Luther, there is nothing but faith; nevertheless he could not deny that faith united with Grace to the point of being "one spirit with God", is a manner of knowing God through God, or in other words, that it is the divine Knowledge in us; for all certitude is knowledge, and there is no faith without certitude. To deny this would be to deny the Holy Spirit, and along with it, our deiformity.

"Blessed are those who have believed yet have not seen": this is the very definition of faith; faith is the key—or the anticipation—of knowledge; it is a kind of "sympathetic magic" toward transcendent

---

[25] In an analogous manner, Islam views every man as a "slave", and Asharism practically concludes from this that every man is capable only of fear and obedience—that he is intellectually a "villain", or a *shûdra* as the Hindus would say.

realities. But faith may also be viewed in another manner: when the starting point is metaphysical certitude or intellection—and this is a "naturally supernatural" mystery—faith will be the life of knowledge, in the sense that it will make knowledge penetrate into all of our being; for it is necessary to "love God with all of our strength", hence with all that we are.

A very important aspect of the problem of faith—we have already alluded to it—is the relationship between faith and works: for Luther, works do not contribute to salvation; to believe that they do would be to doubt the Redemption, it would be to imagine that our actions— intrinsically sinful—could take the place of the saving work of Christ, or that they could add anything whatsoever to it. Consequently, it is faith alone that saves, and this is acceptable if we specify—and Melanchthon did not omit to do so—that works prolong faith, that they are an integral part of faith in proportion to its sincerity; in short, that they prove faith. Without works, faith would not quite be faith, and without faith, works would be eschatologically inoperative.

If Luther, who despite his occasional violence was a virtuous man, underestimated the role of works, this could also have been because he included works in virtue and virtue in faith; virtue is in fact situated between these two poles, it is a dimension of sincere faith and at the same time it is expressed by works; but virtue is independent of works, and, needless to say, it is better to be virtuous without works than to accomplish works without virtue. Moreover, it is fitting to distinguish between works that are obligatory and those that are optional, and obviously, the man of little virtue ought to insist all the more upon meritorious actions, on the one hand in order to compensate for his moral indigence and on the other in order to remedy this indigence progressively.

For Luther, faith ennobles even insignificant actions, except for sins, of course; faith, according to him, is a kind of sanctity, and it is even the only kind of sanctity possible. But what his mystical subjectivity did not seem to be able to realize, at least not *a priori*, is that this mystery of faith could not constitute a rule of life for the masses; in this, the German reformer was as unrealistic as the Popes who wished to impose a kind of monastic perfection upon the clergy or even, practically—though to a lesser degree—upon the whole of Christianity.

All this brings us to the crucial question of asceticism and permits us to insert some parenthetical remarks on this subject. There is an ascesis that consists simply in sobriety, and which is sufficient for the naturally spiritual man; and there is another which consists in fighting against passions, the degree of this ascesis depending upon the demands of the individual nature; finally, there is the ascesis of those who mistakenly believe themselves to be burdened with all sins, or who identify themselves with sin through mystical subjectivism, without forgetting to mention those who practice an extreme asceticism in order to expiate the faults of others, or even simply in order to give a good example in a world that has need of it. Of these modes of asceticism, Evangelicalism retains only the first, and for two reasons: firstly, because it is faith which saves, and not works; secondly—and this reason coincides on the whole with the first—because it is not for us to add our insignificant merits to the infinite merits of Christ.

In summary: according to Luther, the grace obtained by and in faith regenerates the soul and permits it to become united with the divine Life; it enables man to resist and combat evil, and to exercise charity towards the neighbor. Works are useful when we do not consider them meritorious; in which case they become integrated into faith.

*

* *

In the Lutheran perspective the awareness of being a sinner is everything, since strength of faith depends upon this awareness; according to Luther, it is better to sin and to be aware of one's misery, than not to sin and not have this awareness.

But also, and in connection with the crucial idea of sin, there is the fear of damnation, and the scruple not to burden oneself with yet another sin by rashly yielding to the contrary certitude. The tensions and twists which are the result of this attitude are quite typical of voluntaristic and sentimental individualism, absent in other forms of piety; but it is a fact that with the Semites this attitude determines the entire perspective. Be that as it may, the solution of the problem is the following, and it is esoterism that furnishes it, since it always considers the simple nature of things: it is true that the individualistic sentiment of being saved can easily—although not necessarily—give rise to an almost narcissistic and morally paralyzing satisfaction, which is liable to compromise the tension towards God and above all the virtue of fear; now the healthy attitude here—the virtue of hope, if one prefers—consists in a conditional and almost unarticulated certitude, namely, that certitude of salvation is included in the certitude of God, in an eminent and sufficient manner. One should say: "thanks to the love and fear of God, no fear of damnation"; and not say: "thanks to good works, certitude of salvation"; for the latter conviction, by its very nature, or rather, by reason of the mechanism of the human soul, risks drawing us away from God to the very extent that it becomes rooted in one's consciousness; it draws one away from God by the fact that practically it takes the place of God.

In consequence, all of this means that the terrors and despairs of Luther were logically unnecessary, although mystically fruitful and necessary in fact; if Scripture has to contain threats of hell, it is because most men are wild beasts, and subtle considerations on the relation between cause and effect would be ineffectual, to say the least. On the one hand, a great number of souls have been saved thanks to the image of eternal suffering; on the other hand, this image has not sufficed to prevent innumerable crimes; if we wish to take pity on men, let us also take pity on Scripture.

As regards the scruples which we have mentioned above, it is appropriate to add the following precisions: when our starting point is the intellectual certitude of absolute Reality and its hypostatic dimensions, we will say that this certitude has as its consequence—and also in a certain manner as its condition—firstly, that we abstain from all that takes us away from the Supreme Reality in principle or in fact, and secondly, that we practice what brings us closer or what leads us to it; these two consequences are an integral part of metaphysical certitude, to the extent that it really is ours. It is in the certitude of the Sovereign Good, and not elsewhere, that we have the certitude of salvation—of salvation as such and not of our own salvation only—and we have it to the very extent that the second certitude is absorbed in the first.

Gnostically speaking, there are the "psychics" who can be saved or damned; then the "pneumatics", who by their nature cannot but be saved; and finally the "hylics", who cannot but be damned. Now Luther practically conceived only of this third category, and theoretically—with reservations and conditions—that of the "psychics", but in no wise that of the "pneumatics", hence all the tormentedness of his doctrine. In reality, all three seeds are found in every man, the "pneumatic", the "psychic" and the "hylic"; it remains to be seen which predominates. In practice, it suffices to know that to say "yes" to God, while abstaining from what takes one away from Him and accomplishing what brings one closer to Him, pertains to the "pneumatic" nature and assures salvation, all question of "original sin" and "predestination" aside; thus in practice there is no problem, save that which we conceive and impose upon ourselves.

The "pneumatic" is the man who so to speak incarnates "faith which saves", and thus incarnates its content, the "grace of Christ"; strictly speaking, he cannot sin—except perhaps from the point of appearances—because, his substance being "faith" and therefore "justice through faith", all that he touches turns to gold. This possibility is extremely rare, being "avataric" above all, yet, it exists, and cannot but exist.

Be that as it may, Luther does not seem to know what to do with good conscience, the one that Catholics obtain through confession and works; he confuses it with self-satisfaction and laziness, whereas it is the normal and healthy basis for the requirements of the love of God and the neighbor. Now the essential here is not the fact of this confusion, but the consequence Luther draws from it and the stimulation he obtains from it.

The question of knowing whether we are good or bad may be asked approximately, for we possess intelligence, but it cannot be asked in all strictness, for we do not dispose of God's measures; now to say that we cannot answer a question means that we do not need to ask it.

*

* *

On the subject of faith and works, let us insert the following parenthetical remarks. Just as Luther puts faith in place of moral works, so Shinran, well before him and on the other side of the globe, puts faith in place of spiritual means: one has to invoke Amida, not in order to obtain birth in the "Pure Land"—for this would be to rely on "self-power" to the detriment of "other-power"—but out of gratitude towards Amida who has saved us *a priori* by granting us faith. Shinran has but one concern, which is to avoid—or circumvent—the idea that we save ourselves thanks to our own merit. The notion of "gratitude" here is a euphemism intended to veil the fact that we cannot deprive ourselves of realizatory initiative; and besides, if faith is not ours, whose is it, and if it is Amida's, what proof is there that it belongs to us or that we benefit from it? One of two things must be true: either the act of gratitude is optional, in which case one may do without it, it being sufficient to believe instead of invoking Amida; or else the act of gratitude is obligatory, in which case there is no longer a question of gratitude, and the argument is merely a ruse in order to mask "self-power", which determines every act and which we, as free and responsible creatures, cannot escape.

Neither Luther nor Shinran can change the nature of man, which precisely entails a certain liberty and thus a possibility of "self- power", hence of merit; but like the Japanese mystic, the German reformer is in love with the experience of faith, and with the Scripture that nourishes it; and perish all the rest. There is also in Luther a part of Asharism: like the Arab theologian, Luther sacrifices intelligence to faith, and freedom to the Prescience and Omnipotence of God. And if an Ashari and a Shinran are "orthodox" in their fashion, as their respective traditions acknowledge, we do not see why we cannot grant Luther the same extenuating circumstances or the same approving evaluations, *mutatis mutandis*.

Luther believes, like Shinran, that in putting faith in place of works, he brings a certain consolation and liberation; but this is solely a question of spiritual temperament. For some, it is much more reassuring to base themselves upon works, which are something objective, concrete, tangible, and definable; whereas one can always torment oneself with the question of whether one really has faith, or whether one has understood faith.

Be that as it may, in the thought of Luther, like in that of Shinran—and this follows from certain of our preceding demonstrations—there are compensatory arguments that re-establish equilibrium, so that our objection has a merely relative import, except for minds that abuse the formulations in question. One thing is certain, and it is the essential in these formulations: it can happen that faith saves in the absence of outward works, but it never happens that works save without faith.

Man cannot escape the duty of having to do good, it is even impossible under normal conditions not to do good; but what matters is that he know that it is God who acts. A work of merit belongs to God, but we participate therein; our works are good—or better—to the extent that we are penetrated by this awareness.

*

* *

25

As for predestination, which is so important in Augustinian and then in Lutheran thought, it is at bottom none other than ontological necessity insofar as it refers to a determined possibility. Now God may displace or change the mode of a possibility, but He cannot make a possibility become impossible.

Predestination as such is situated in Relativity—in *Mâyâ*, if one prefers—since it concerns the relative or the contingent; but its root in the Absolute is reducible to Necessity. Absolute Being comprises both Necessity and Freedom; and in consequence, the same holds true for relative or contingent Being—the world; thus it is false to deny the possibility of freedom in the world, just as it is false to deny predestination. A work freely accomplished by man always contains, as a different dimension, predestination; but it could also be said, with a change of emphasis, that a freely done work is situated within predestination as within an invisible mold which pertains to another dimension, precisely; the difference being like that of space and time, in the sense that time is totally different from the three spatial dimensions and yet is always present. Space then corresponds to necessity, in the sense that things in it are what they are, and are found where they are found, whereas time corresponds to freedom, in the sense that things can change or move; all this being a purely symbolic, hence indirect and partial, analogy, for in reality necessity and freedom are found everywhere.

Be that as it may, the consequence of all this implies that it is an error to reduce works to predestination, thereby denying their freedom, and that it is no less an error to deny all predestination in works, thereby lending them an absolute freedom that belongs to God alone. For the principle is this: freedom as such is everywhere freedom, and necessity as such is everywhere necessity, but whereas Necessity and Freedom are absolute in God, they are relative in the world, in the sense that there is no manifested necessity that does not comprise an element of freedom on account of contingency, no more than there is manifested freedom that does not comprise an element of necessity by reason of predestination. To reduce our actions to predestination is to attribute absoluteness to them; to believe that they are free in regard to the Absolute is to attribute its Liberty to them. Ontologically, our actions are predestined, and we must know this in order not to believe that we are as sovereign as God, and that we could be situated outside His Will; but practically, our actions are free, hence meritorious, and we must know it in order to be able to act and merit.

*
*　　*

However, in theology there is not only the opposition between pre-destination and freedom, there is also the opposition between faith and knowledge; and just as some believe that freedom must be denied in the name of predestination, or conversely, so others believe that knowledge must be rejected in the name of faith, or on the con-trary—as is the case with rationalists—that faith must be rejected in the name of what they believe to be knowledge. In reality there is no incompatibility here, any more than there is with freedom and predestination; for if these two principles are the complementary dimensions of one and the same possibility of manifestation, the same holds true for knowledge and faith, in the sense that there is no faith without any knowledge, nor knowledge without any faith. But, it is knowledge that has precedence: faith is an indirect and volitive mode of knowledge, but knowledge suffices unto itself and is not a mode of faith; nevertheless, when situated in Relativity, knowledge requires an element of faith to the extent that it is *a priori* intellectual and not existential, mental and not cardiac, partial and not total; otherwise all metaphysical understanding would imply sanctity *ipso facto*. However, all transcendent certitude has something divine about it—but as certi-tude only, and not necessarily as the acquisition of a particular man.

In other words: in a Semitic climate much is made of the incom-patibility between knowledge and faith, and to the pre-eminence of the latter, to the point of holding the former in contempt and of forgetting that within Relativity the one goes hand in hand with the other. Knowledge is the adequate perception of the real, and faith is the conformity of will and sentiment to a truth imperfectly perceived by the intelligence; if the perception were perfect it would be impos-sible for the believer to lose his faith.

Yet theoretical knowledge, even if perfect and hence unshakable, always requires a volitive element which contributes to the process of assimilation or integration, for we must "become what we are"; and this operative element, or this element of intensity, stems from faith. Inversely, in religious faith there is always an element of knowledge that determines it, for in order to believe, it is necessary to know what one must believe; moreover, in plenary faith there is an element of certitude which is not volitive, and whose presence we cannot prevent, whatever be our efforts to refuse all knowledge in order to benefit from the "obscure merit of faith".

In God alone is knowledge dispensed from an element of realizatory intensity or of totalizing will; as for faith, its prototype *in divinis* is Life or Love; and in God alone are Life and Love independent of any motive justifying or determining them *ab extra.* It is by participation in this mystery that Saint Bernard could say: "I love because I love", which is like a paraphrase of the saying of the Burning Bush "I am that I am"; "That which is".

It is knowledge, or the element truth, which gives faith all of its value, otherwise we could believe no matter what, so long as we believe; it is only through truth that the intensity of our faith has meaning. And quite paradoxically, it is predestination which makes us freely choose truth and good; without freedom there is no choice. Predestination, in the final analysis, is all that we are.

But divine Freedom requires that, together with the predestination which is absolute, there be another predestination which is paradoxically relative, and which relates to modes and degrees. Likewise, divine Necessity requires that together with Freedom which as such is absolute, there be a relative freedom; and this latter freedom is ours, and while it cannot be anything other than freedom, it nevertheless falls within the framework of a necessity that surpasses it.

*

*   *

Just as the early Churches conceive a hierarchy which places the monks and priests above the laity and the worldly, so also Luther— who had nothing of the revolutionary or even of the democrat in him—conceives a hierarchy which places those who truly live by faith above those who have not yet reached this point, or who are simply not capable of it. He intended to appeal to those who "willingly do what they know and are capable of doing, with firm faith in the beneficence and favor of God", and to those "like unto whom others ought to become"; but not to those who "make ill use of this freedom and who rashly trust in it, so that they must be driven with laws, teachings, and warnings"; and other descriptions of the kind. All of this means that his intention comprised a kind of esoterism, at least in practice: "Faith does not suffice—he declares—except faith that takes shelter under the wings of Christ"; now Christ is love.

"Though I speak with the tongues of men and of angels. . . . though I have all faith, so that I could remove mountains, and have not love (*charitas, agape*), I am nothing. . . . And now abideth faith, hope, love, these three; but the greatest of these is love." This crucial passage of the First Epistle to the Corinthians seems to contradict all that the Apostle taught concerning justification through faith in his Epistle to the Romans; how to explain this paradox? The answer is, on the one hand, that love is the greatest thing since "God is Love" and since the most noble Commandment is the love of God and the neighbor; but on the other hand, faith has primacy, since it is the key to everything and since it is faith which saves. The mystic of Wittenberg would even say that in practice—not in principle—faith is greater, because love, being too great, is impracticable and cannot be attained except by and in Christ and through faith. That love is too great follows precisely from the passage of the Epistle to the Corinthians, wherein the Apostle deems it necessary to call for the intercession of the "tongues of angels", the "gift of prophecy", the understanding "of all mysteries, and all knowledge", and faith that "removes mountains". Luther not unreasonably—and basing himself on the doctrine of the Epistle to the Romans—deduces that love is realizable only indirectly or virtually by and in faith, except for the level which is accessible to us naturally, namely charity towards our neighbor. In a word, to affirm that love is the greatest thing does not amount to saying that it is the most immediately essential; one has to understand a given passage in Scripture in the light of another given passage which, while seeming to contradict it, in reality defines it and renders it concrete.

There is moreover in this famous passage to the Corinthians an element of Semitic stylization, in the sense that exaggeration, taken to the point of absurdity, serves to indicate the grandeur of the thing which is being spoken about; it is a "henotheistic" logic, so to speak, one which lends an absolute character to the thing whose excellence one wishes to demonstrate to the detriment of another thing, also presented in an almost absolute light, at another moment. Taken literally, however, it is clearly absurd to maintain that he whose faith can remove mountains, *et cetera*, is nothing if he does not have love, since a faith of such strength could lack nothing, otherwise it would not be so strong, precisely; this Luther rightly noticed in his own fashion.[26]

We could also say that the Apostle has slipped from one perspective to another, namely, from that of faith to that of love; or rather, that both points of view forced themselves upon his mind successively, independently of one another. Now a choice has to be made: Catholicism and Orthodoxy—which were one for more than a thousand years—accorded pre-eminence to love, whereas Evangelicalism wanted to emphasize faith; love with faith in the first case, faith with love in the second. In all justice, both accentuations ought always to have coexisted, and indeed they often did before the Reformation; but in fact, the Abrahamic and moreover somewhat "Quietistic" idea of the faith which saves had lain dormant during that age of mystical heroism and superstitious abuse that was the Middle Ages.

The proof of the primacy of love is that the supreme Commandment is to love God and one's neighbor; and the proof of the primacy of faith is that practically the creed is more imperative than charity, because it is better to believe in God without charity than to exercise charity without believing in God. Catholicism starts from the idea of the primacy of love and from the fact of our freedom, and it demands zeal in ascesis; Evangelicalism for its part starts from the primacy of faith and from the fact of our powerlessness, and it demands steadfastness in trust.

We could also mention an analogy which brings us back to our considerations on religious archetypes: Vishnuism distinguishes between *bhakti*, love properly so called and heroic if need be, and *prapatti*, confident abandonment to the divine Mercy; these are the two ways that it proposes to the faithful. Now the way of love corresponds analogically to the sacerdotal and monastic perspective of early and Patristic Christianity, whereas the way of trust or faith is found in Evangelicalism; analogy is not identity, but in the final analysis the fundamental attitudes and the celestial archetypes from which they derive are the same on both sides.

---

[26] Nevertheless, not all of his arguments are conclusive. Let us note at this point that in all inter-confessional controversies one meets with purely "functional" arguments which in themselves are inadequate; for example, the Epistle to the Romans attributes all vices to the pagans, whereas they cannot be attributed to the best of the Stoics or Neoplatonists. Some arguments are meant to clear the ground and not to serve the truth as such—and these are necessarily two-edged.

Love is on the one hand our tendency towards God—the tendency of the accident towards the Substance—and on the other hand our consciousness of "myself" in the "other", and of the "other" in ourselves; it is also the sense of beauty, above us and around us and in our own soul. Faith is to say "yes" to the truth of God and of immortality—this truth which we carry in the depths of our heart—it is to see concretely what appears as abstract; it is, to speak in Islamic terms, to "serve God as if thou sawest Him, and if thou seest Him not, He nonetheless seeth thee"; and it is also the sense of the goodness of God and trust in Mercy. He who has faith, has goodness; and he who has love, has beauty; but at the same time, each of the poles contains the other. We are the accidents, and the Substance is Beauty, Goodness, and Beatitude.

Love and faith: the one as well as the other is a door towards knowledge; and knowledge in its turn gives rise both to faith and love. Love opens onto gnosis because it tends towards union; faith opens onto it because it is founded upon truth; to love is to want to be united, and to believe is to acknowledge what is true and become what one acknowledges.

*
*   *

In drawing their swords the Apostles violated the Sabbath; it is the inward Sabbath that counts and takes primacy over the outward. Saint Paul suppressed "circumcision of the flesh" in the name of "circumcision of the Spirit"; Meister Eckhart teaches that if we knew that God is everywhere, we would take Communion even when eating ordinary bread. All this becomes clear in the light of this principle: outward means are necessary only because—or to the extent that—we have lost the access to their interior archetypes; a sacrament is the exteriorization of an immanent source of grace—the "living water" of Christ—exactly as Revelation is an outward and macrocosmic manifestation of Intellection. Luther was certainly unaware of this principle or mystery; nevertheless, his exclusive recourse to faith, his tendency to interiorize everything for the sake of the "spirit" and against the "flesh", hence also his reducing the sacraments as regards their form and number, all refer logically and mystically to the principle of inwardness or immanence which we have just spoken of.[27]

The Koran gives more than one example of the principle of abrogation (*naskh*): there are verses that annul others, and in most cases, the meaning of the one—whether it be the "nullifying" (*nâsikh*) or the "annulled" (*mansûkh*) verse—is more universal than that of the other. The profound meaning of this phenomenon is that every form can be abrogated by a more essential form, and with all the more reason by their common essence; a form is never a pure absolute, although it may be a "relatively absolute", as is precisely the case of sacred forms. In Hindu and Buddhist climate, this passage—gradual or abrupt—from the formal to the essential is an acknowledged possibility, whereas in the Semitic West, it is excluded; the notion of heresy does not admit of relativizing, or even justifying, reservations; this is the spirit of alternativism, which in many cases is right—in the East as well as in the West—but not in all cases. As for the principle of abrogation, we had to mention it in the context of Luther's audacities, in order to demonstrate, indirectly at least, that a spiritual perspective, assuming it is even a possibility as such may draw conclusions which exceed what one would normally expect, or which violate the bases of a given traditional criteriology.

If Luther rejects all that Catholicism understands by "tradition", it is by association of ideas connected with the "prescriptions of men" mentioned in the Gospel, as we have pointed out earlier; he allows only "Scripture" to remain, and it becomes everything; bibliolatry is the pivot of his religion, as is also the case in Judaism and Islam.

*

* *

---

[27] If this perspective, which could not but be manifested at a given moment of the Christian cycle, were intrinsically false and ineffectual, how to explain that an esoterist such as Jacob Boehme could flower in such a climate, not to mention other Rosicrucian and Hermetic Lutheran theosophists. Moreover, it is known that Luther's coat-of-arms features a rose with a heart and a cross in the center, which perhaps is more than chance. Let us also mention in this context such Anglican esoterists as John Smith the Platonist and William Law the mystical theologian, without forgetting the isolated mystic of the first half of the twentieth century who was the anonymous author (Lilian Stavely) of *The Golden Fountain, The Prodigal Returns,* and *The Romance of the Soul.*

Scholastic theology teaches that man can—and consequently must—obtain grace not only through a supernatural gift of God, but also by natural means, such as virtues and works. Luther was well aware that we cannot produce God's grace—and moreover no one has ever said the contrary—but he seems to be unaware that we can remove the obstacles separating us from grace, exactly as it suffices to open a shutter in order to let in sunlight; one does not attract light by magic any more than one can create it, rather one removes that which renders it invisible.

The mystic of Wittenberg is "more Catholic than the Pope" in feeling that it is pretension on man's part to believe in the almost theurgic virtue of certain actions: to believe that a good act can *ipso facto* entail a concordant grace, as if man had the power to determine the divine Will; and this feeling furnishes Luther with a reason, perhaps the main one, for rejecting the Mass. In reality, to believe that we can determine the divine Will by our comportment—*Deo juvante*—is in no wise pretentious, given that God created us for that; it is a normal or "supernaturally natural" effect of our theomorphism; thus there is no harm in the idea that our actions can be meritorious before God; and no one obliges us to become proud of them. Good conscience is a normal phenomenon; it is the normal climate within which man runs towards God; there is nothing in good conscience that attracts us towards the world, it being perfectly neutral in this respect, unless we be hypocrites. On the contrary, it attracts towards Heaven, since by its very nature it is a taste of Heaven.

What fundamentally constitutes the Lutheran message is the accentuation of faith within the awareness of our misery; or by this very awareness, but also in spite of it. All the limitations of this point of departure have indirectly the function of a key or a symbol; they are compensated, beyond the words, by the ineffable response of Mercy; the initial torment is resolved in the final analysis in the quasi-mystical experience of the faith that appeases, vivifies, and liberates.

*

* *

The idea that no work can be "justice" before God because all human work is tainted with sin, that is to say with concupiscence first and then with pride—as a result of the sin of Adam and Eve—this has its logical basis in the limitation of the human "I" in the face of the divine "Self", and in the impossibility of the "I" to liberate itself without the decisive concurrence of the "Self". Certainly, analogy is not identity, and theology is not metaphysics, in spite of points where they meet; but there where there is analogy, there can always be identity by way of exception and to some degree, as the spark can always flash forth from the flint. The Christian denominations as such could never be of the same order as gnosis, any more than some other exoterism could; and yet a Meister Eckhart and a Jacob Boehme manifest this perspective in their way, the first within the framework of Catholicism and the second within that of Evangelicalism.[28] Both saw the "immanent transcendence" of the pure Intellect: Eckhart in recognizing the *increatus et increabilis* character of the kernel of human intelligence, and Boehme in referring to "inward illuminations" (*innere Erleuchtungen*) of a sapiential, hence intellective, nature. Similarly, each was able to account for *Mâyâ*, the principle of universal Relativity: Eckhart in establishing the distinction between hypostatic differentiation and the "ineffable Depth" (*der Ungrund*), and Boehme in posing the principle of opposition or of contrasts, rooted in God and operating in the world in order to make God knowable in objective and distinctive mode.[29]

One recognizes in Luther tendencies quite analogous to those of the "friends of God" (*die Gottesfreunde*), a mystical society which flowered in the fourteenth century in the Rhineland, Swabia, and Switzerland, and whose most eminent representatives were Tauler and the blessed Suso. The former—known to Luther—made himself the spokesman of the Eckhartian doctrine of "quietude" (*Gelassenheit*)

---

[28] It is true that certain convictions of Boehme stray from Lutheran—or post-Lutheran—orthodoxy, but for all that he did not become a Catholic; he lived and died in the Evangelical Church, and his death was that of a saint. We could also mention Paracelsus—by whom Boehme was inspired, incidentally—who was at once Rosicrucian theosophist, mystic, and physician, and to whom is owed a "spagyric medicine", that is, one akin to Hermeticism and based upon the *solve et coagula* of the alchemists. It would be inexplicable that so eminent a mind would have chosen Evangelicalism if it were intrinsically heretical. As for Boehme, let us note in passing that his anthropology, like that of certain Fathers of the Church, was not immune from a kind of antisexuality and moralizing puritanism which sees the original fall in the form of the body and not in matter alone, whereas the Hindu doctrine for example takes seriously into account the sexual aspect of human theomorphism.

[29] In theology, the pure intellect is prefigured by the objectivizing notion of the Holy Spirit, and *Mâyâ* by the temporalizing notion of predestination; the Holy Spirit enlightens, strengthens, and inflames, and predestination makes creatures and things be what they are, and what they cannot not be.

and fought against "justice through works" (*Werkgerechtigkeit*) and against outward religiosity.

According to Tersteegen[30]—one of the saintly men of the Evangelical Church—"the true theosophers, of whom we know very few after the time of the Apostles, were all mystics, but it is very far from the case that all mystics are theosophers; not one amongst thousands. The theosophers are those whose spirit (not reason) has explored the depths of the Divinity under divine guidance, and whose spirit has known such marvels thanks to an infallible vision."[31]

What exoterism—Catholic, Orthodox, anymore than the Evangelical—does not say, and cannot say, is that the Pauline or Biblical mystery of faith is none other at its root than the mystery of gnosis: that is, gnosis is the prototype and the underlying essence of the former. If faith can save, it is because intellective knowledge delivers; this knowledge which, being transcendent, is immanent, and conversely. The Lutheran theosophers were gnostics within the framework of faith, and the most metaphysical Sufis accentuated faith on the basis of knowledge; no doubt there is a faith without gnosis, but there is no gnosis without faith. The soul can go to God without the direct concurrence of pure Intellect, but the latter cannot manifest itself without giving the soul peace and life, and without demanding from it all the faith of which it is capable.

---

[30] In an epistle entitled *Kurzer Bericht von der Mystik.*

[31] The theosopher Angelus Silesius would not perhaps have left the Lutheran Church had he not been expelled for his esoterism; in any case, Bernardine mysticism seemed to correspond best to his spiritual vocation. This makes us think somewhat of Shri Chaitanya who, as an Advaitin, threw out all of his books one fine day to think only of Krishna; and let us note at this point that this *bhakta*, while accepted as being orthodox, rejected the ritual of the brahmans and the castes in order to put the entire accent on faith and love, not on works.

THE VEIL OF THE TEMPLE: A STUDY OF CHRISTIAN INITIATION

Marco Pallis

"Jesus, when he had cried again with a loud voice, yielded up the ghost. . . . And, behold, the veil of the temple was rent in twain from the top to the bottom . . ." (Matt. 27:50, 61). This occurrence, which is attested by the three Synoptic Gospels, marks the end of Christ's human ministry, in the ordinary sense of the word, since all that follows, from the Resurrection till his final Ascension, is of a miraculous order. Like all sacred events, the portent at the moment of Christ's death on the cross can be regarded from both a historical and a symbolical angle, since the two views do not exclude one another; in the present case it is the symbolism of the occurrence that will chiefly be considered.

It is important to be reminded of what the veil of the temple of Jerusalem served to mark, namely the boundary between the main portion of the sacred building, where all Jews were admitted and which contained the seven-branched candlestick and the altar of sacrifice, and the Holy of Holies, which was quite empty and into which only the officiating priest could enter. When he did so, the priest had to divest himself of his clothes. Voidness of the place and nakedness of the man are both highly significant indications of what the Holy of Holies stood for in the Jewish tradition, namely "the mysteries" or, in other words, *that* of which the knowledge, formless and inexpressible, can be symbolized only "apophatically," by an emptying or divestment, as in the present case. Esoterically speaking, this knowledge can refer only to God in His suchness, the divine Selfhood transcending even being.

Whatever lay on the hither side of the veil, on the other hand, represented the tradition in its more exoteric aspects, which are multiple and formally expressible in various ways.

All three evangelists stress the fact that the veil parted "from the top to the bottom," as if to indicate that the parting was complete and irremediable and that henceforth no definable boundary would exist between the "religious" side of the tradition and the mysterious or, if one so prefers, between the exoteric and esoteric domains. As far as the human eye was able to discern they were to be merged—which does not mean, of course, that their interpenetration would in any way detract from the reality of each domain in its own order, but that any formal expression of their separation was precluded once and for all. For this to be true, it would mean, among other things, that the central rites of the tradition must be such as to serve this comprehensive purpose and that, with any spiritual "support," its context alone, and not its form, would provide the clue as to which domain it pertained to in given circumstances.

This gives the key to Christian spirituality as such; it starts from there. Moreover, it can be seen that if the unicity of revelation has needed to be given increasingly diversified expression parallel with the downward march of a cosmic cycle, each traditional form deriving from this necessity must affirm itself, above all, in those particularities that distinguish it from other comparable forms. Thus Islam remains the prophetic tradition par excellence; though the prophetic function itself is universal and though in other cases one may speak of such and such a prophet or prophets, whenever one refers to *the* Prophet without epithet, one means Mohammed and no one else. Similarly, if one speaks of Enlightenment with a capital E, it is of the Buddha one is thinking; which does not mean, however, that enlightenment does not belong to every avataric founder of a religion—obviously this function will always imply the supreme knowledge—but its presentation under the form of "supreme awakening," *samma sambodhi,* nevertheless remains the keynote of Buddhism in a sense not shared by other traditions. With Christianity it is *the* Incarnation that provides its specific note; in all other cases, one can only speak of such and such *an* incarnation; emphasis on the word will be relatively more diffuse. The particularity of the Christian tradition, namely its *eso-exoteric* structure, is closely bound up with this all-absorbing role of Christ as the Incarnate Word, in whom all essential functions are synthesized without distinction of levels.

Apart from this special character attaching to Christianity, it is evident that an authentic and integral tradition could at no time be equated solely with its collective and exoteric aspects. Whatever the nature of the formal framework, the presence (latent or explicit) of the esoteric element is necessary; otherwise the tradition in question would be—to use a common Tibetan expression—"without a heart." Similarly, a tradition is never reducible to an esoterism alone: hence the need to be firmly anchored in an orthodox exoterism, speaking its scriptural language and making use of such ritual and symbolical supports as it provides; an esoterism trying to function minus its normal exoteric framework would be like a heart without a body, to use the same comparison as before. Belief in the possibility of a quasi-abstract and wholly subjective spiritual life, one in which tradition and the formal expressions of revealed truth do not count, is a typical error of various neo-Vedantist and other kindred movements that have seen the light of day in India and elsewhere in recent times.

Different ways in which the relationship "mysteries-religion" or "esoteric-exoteric" can be given effect to may be profitably studied by comparing some of the principal traditions in this respect. For instance, in the Islamic tradition, where the two domains are defined with particular clarity, "the veil of the temple" has been present from the origins and remains intact to this day; both the law (*shariah*) and the esoterism (*tasawwuf*) are traceable back to the Prophet himself. This is why the Islamic arrangements have so often been quoted as a model when this subject has come up for consideration.

With Christianity, as we have seen, a rending of the veil previously extant in Judaism marks the final affirmation of the New Covenant in the face of the Old and, with it, the birth of a wholly independent tradition. In the case of Buddhism, on the other hand, the nonexistence of any such veil is laid down from the start. The Buddha's saying that "I have kept nothing back in my closed fist" means that in his tradition the purely spiritual interest alone really counts. Although in Buddhism, as elsewhere, an exoteric organization becomes unavoidable from the moment that the number of adherents begins to increase, the fact itself will always remain, from the Buddhist point of view, a matter for regret—something to be accepted *contre coeur*, under compulsion of events, but never in principle.

Something similar can also be said of Christianity: If Christ's kingdom, by his own definition, is "not of this world"[1] and if the penalty of casting the pearl of great price before swine is that they "will turn and rend you," then one of the consequences of the removal of the veil between the Holy of Holies and the more accessible part of the temple (to return to our original symbolism) has been a certain blurring of the distinction between the two domains even where it

---

[1] Islam says this in its own way, when it declares that Jesus was the bringer of an esoterism (*haqiqah*) only, whereas the Prophet Mohammed endowed his followers both with the things of this world and with the things of the other world.

really applies—the shadow, as it were, of an overwhelming grace. This confusion has expressed itself in the life of the Christian church under the twofold form of a minimizing of what, in spirituality, is most interior and of an excessive focusing of attention on the more exterior and peripheral manifestations of the tradition, and especially on the collective interest treated almost as an end in itself. Carried to extremes, this tendency amply accounts for the fact that it was within the Christian world, and not elsewhere, that the great profanation known as "the modern mentality" first took shape and became, as time went on, the vehicle of "scandal" among all the rest of mankind. If this happening, like everything else of a disastrous kind moreover, comprises its providential aspect, as bringing nearer the dark ending of one cycle and the bright dawning of another, it nevertheless does not escape—by force of *karma* as Buddhists would say—the curse laid by Christ Himself on all "those by whom scandal cometh." The pain of the cross, in which all must be involved, is there, in anticipation of its triumph.

To return to our original thesis: The special attention called by the evangelists to the fact that the temple veil was split "from top to bottom" shows that this feature of the great portent was an essential one; the veil once torn asunder can *never* be sewn together again. To attempt to do so, on any plea whatsoever, would amount to an arbitrary proceeding, one deserving the epithet "heretical" in the strictest sense of the word. The condemnation by the church of "gnosticism" has no other meaning.[2]

Moreover, the fact that the Christian revelation was, before all else, a laying bare of the mysteries had been widely recognized even by theologians having no pretensions to a particularly inward view of things. We have known an ordinary Greek priest say to his congregation that "the entire liturgy is a mystagogy," using a word belonging to the vocabulary of the ancient Hellenic mysteries and also figuring in

---

[2] It is probable that even in the early days of the church the label "gnostic" was sometimes applied to things not really meriting the intended reproach but appearing to do so by reason of superficial similarities that belied their true nature. In our time the accusation of new-fangled gnosticism has provided an all too convenient weapon against those who have suggested that the gift of intelligence is a vocational qualification for the fullest understanding of the Christian dogmas. This gratuitous confusing of intellectuality with "pride" marks a suicidal tendency of which the concordant reaction is the association, in the profane mind, of the word "religion" with an attitude of perfunctory conformism and credulity.

the text of the liturgy itself, which does not mean, however, that the man himself will have possessed clear notions of what it really stands for; nevertheless even such a passing reference is in its way significant. Nor is it devoid of interest to point out in the same connection that the Eastern Church, by comparison with the Latin Church, has preserved both in its rituals and in its usual mode of expression a certain "archaism" that anyone who has attended a celebration of the liturgy in a Greek or Russian church could hardly fail to notice; it is not surprising, then, that in the Eastern rite the sacraments are referred to as "the mysteries," a word that, here again, is charged with associations taken over from the esoteric side of the pre-Christian tradition in the ancient world.

For the sake of greater precision it will perhaps be useful at this point to refresh one's mind as to the characteristics that serve to delineate the esoteric realm and to distinguish it from the exoteric. One might also have said: those that delineate the initiatic realm, since in principle the two things make but one; this second term, however, represents a somewhat more particularized aspect of the same reality, since it is concerned with the methodic realization of what the esoterism represents in the realm of theory.[3]

In seeking an adequate definition one can safely turn to René Guénon when he said that whereas an exoteric view of things concerns itself with the individual human interest in the largest sense of the word but stops short there, an esoteric view reaches beyond the individuality in order to embrace all the superior states of the being and even aspires to the supreme state—if what really transcends all possibilities of comparison may be so described, by an unavoidable concession to the insufficiency of human language.

If we accept the above definition, then the touchstone of discernment, in the present case, is the *finality* respectively envisaged, whether individual and limited, that is to say, or else universal and unlimited by any condition whatsoever. In other words, the finality of a religious exoterism will be the realization (or "recovery," if one takes into

---

[3] According to its primitive meaning, the Greek word θεωρία (*theoria*) should be rendered as "contemplation"; but today this use of the word hardly survives outside the ranks of those following the Hesychast way. In modern Greek, as in other European languages, "theory" has become a sadly impoverished term, with purely mental associations and opposable, as such, to "practice" with a bias in favor of the latter; and as for "contemplation," this is well-nigh untranslatable into current speech.

account the Adamic doctrine of the Fall) of the state of "true man," *Chen-jen* of the Taoists;[4] whereas esoterism, for its part, will envisage as its ultimate aspiration the realizing of "transcendent man," goal of the Taoist way, or Universal Man, if one prefers the more familiar term taken from Sufism. It is noteworthy that the realization of the Two Natures, which is the goal of Christian endeavor, to be truly complete would have to include both of the above finalities after the model of Christ Himself, who was "true man" or "second Adam" at the same time as "true God"; the term "christification" might well be used to express this supreme ideal.

When it comes to "initiatic method," designed to foster spiritual realization at all its degrees, it is important not to lose sight of the very wide range of variation in initiatic practice, as between different traditions. In this field, no less than in others, each tradition exhibits its own peculiarities, a fact that does not affect the general principles governing initiatic life but that nevertheless forbids one to drive analogy, as from one to another, too far; and still less does it encourage one to systematize a given pattern of initiation to the point of making of that pattern an absolute test of authenticity or otherwise. Provided one does not exceed the limits of fair comparison, however, there is undoubted profit to be derived from a parallel study of initiatic procedure as found in different traditions; when doing so we shall chiefly be concerned with those features that have a direct or indirect bearing on the question of Christian initiation to which we have gradually been leading up.

Turning first to the Buddhist world: In Tibet it can be said that practically every spiritual activity, down to the smallest detail, is geared to an initiatic purpose, either directly or else indirectly as in the case of "scholastic" studies in the Gelugpa Order, for instance, to which the Dalai Lama belongs. Anything directly relating to *method*, however, will involve an initiatic act of some kind; even to open a book concerned with method requires its initiatory *lung* or ritual authorization imparted by a lama of the spiritual family to which the prospective initiate intends to be attached, and each subsequent stage in the process

---

[4] In practice, a point of view that *a priori* limits its own scope to a human finality is unlikely to realize the perfection of the human order itself, for a habit of taking the short view tends to restrict a man's horizon within ever narrower limits; the end of this road is an out-and-out profane mentality. The esoterist, on the other hand, through focusing his aim beyond all limitations, is able to take the finality of religious exoterism "in his stride," as it were, and this is the surest way to realize it.

will likewise be marked by its appropriate *lung*. In Tibet everything is calculated to foster and facilitate the initiatic life for those who aspire to it; the supremacy of this ideal is recognized by all, from the head of the government down to the beggar at the street corner.

Over and above the normal initiatic arrangements, which in essentials do not differ from what is to be found in India or other places, Tibetan spirituality includes a large number of special initiations known as *wang-kur* (from *wang* = power and *kur-wa* = to confer), each of which gives access to one particular form of methodic meditation focused on a *mandala* or symbolical diagram disposed around a central divinity, a combination of sacred geometry and traditional iconography of forms, colors, gestures, letters, and the like. Visualization of such a *mandala*, under the direction of one's guru, is one of the common features of tantric technique; it is not everyone, however, who, after receiving the *wang* empowering him to meditate on such and such a *mandala*, actively puts this into effect. Many try to amass such *wangs* simply as a means of stimulating their own pious fervor; such a "quantitative" attitude to the acquisition of *wangs*, though not contrary to the letter of the traditional rules, does evidently depart from the spirit of the institution, and for this reason it is condemned by informed opinion both on the score of "spiritual diffuseness" and also as liable to produce, in extreme cases, dissonances of an unpredictable order.

In any case, this shows that in Tibet, as elsewhere, a sharp distinction has to be made between the *mutabarrik* (to borrow a convenient Sufic term meaning "blessed"), the man who receives initiation from mixed motives not fully in tune with its intrinsic purpose, and the *salik* (traveler), namely the man who proceeds with full intent, keeping the end of the road in view. All one can say is that in Tibet prior to the Chinese Communist irruption the number of *salikun* was relatively high as compared with most other places; there was little sign of decadence in this respect.

Returning to the *mutabarrik* type as commonly found in the Tibetan world, an important thing to be noted is that the initiatic act, though clearly recognized as such and though its virtuality always remains what it is in an objective sense, is nevertheless envisaged subjectively in a *quasi-exoteric* sense and with a view to benefits that do not exceed the individual sphere—such as piety in this life and a "happy rebirth" in the next—a fact that by definition forbids one to apply the epithet "esoteric" to the religious manifestation in question. Yet the initiatic possibility is undeniably there, if unexploited.

This discrepancy of attitude is carried to its furthest point in the great mass *wang-kurs* that take place from time to time. At these gatherings, which thousands may attend, the initiating lama goes through the motion of conferring the *wang* and preaches the appropriate doctrine before the crowd, though few of the participants will be known to him personally either before or after the event; no question of "qualification" can possibly arise under these circumstances. A case in point was the conferring, by the Dalai Lama when he was staying close to the Indian border in 1950, of the "initiation of the Great Compassionate," an eleven-faced form of Avalokitesvara, whose *mandala* is specially associated with the Gelugpa, the "Yellow-Hat" Order of Monks. Vast numbers of people from all the country round and from both sides of the border journeyed to Dung-kar (White Conch) Monastery, where the sacred sovereign was staying, in order to receive the *wang* in question; I myself would gladly have accompanied them, but by that time the political obstacles had become insurmountable. The fervor aroused among the people was tremendous, and to this extent it was no small spiritual occasion. Nevertheless, it must be admitted that those who received the initiation were, almost without exception, simple *matabarrikun*; if an odd *salik* was to be found among them, his presence could not have been detected by any recognizable sign.

But even so, the initiation itself was perfectly regular according to all traditional canons; it was open to any of those who, on that occasion, received the *wang* of the Great Compassionate to present himself then or at any subsequent period to a competent lama in order to put into effect the method pertaining to that particular *mandala*. No question of validity could possibly arise in this connection, nor was even the humblest *mutabarrik* in the crowd unaware of the fact that this was an initiation and not something else and that the possibility existed of its being someday turned more fully to account. We have described this happening at considerable length, as shedding a certain light on the ambivalent use of an undoubtedly initiatic act and therefore also on certain aspects of the Christian tradition.

We must next consider one or two features of Japanese Buddhism that are of special interest from the point of view that concerns us here; but first we must notice a fact of a general nature, namely that in Japan, despite the obviously initiatic character of so much to be found there, it is only the tantric sects,[5] of which Shingon and Tendai are the chief, that administer an initiation under the form most familiar to us, specifiable, that is to say, in terms of time and occasion, of "before initiation" and "after." As regards method, Shingon is closely akin to Tibetan spiritual practice, a common feature being the use of *mandalas* composed of divine portraiture, Sanskrit letters, and other symbols also found in Tibet. Apart from the cases just mentioned, the remaining Japanese sects do not confer a formal initiation when attaching a new disciple to the line or subsequently; a spiritual master may admit or reject a prospective disciple, and he may also terminate his discipleship at any time if dissatisfied with his progress. Otherwise the disciple, once accepted, will be swept, as it were, into the spiritual current more or less quickly and completely but without this fact having to be confirmed by a set ritual act of any kind. It is the process as a whole that constitutes initiatic participation, the rest depending upon the aptitude of the disciple and the grace of his master, in which respect Japanese practice does not differ from that of other traditions.

Coming now to the best-known (and least understood by Europeans) of the Japanese sects, namely Zen, we find there a method in which an extreme stringency of discipline and the use of apparently senseless conundrums (*koans*) are combined for the purpose of ridding the mind of the habit of conceptualism, thus allowing the intuitive faculty to be released. That a spiritual training carried out on these lines constitutes an initiatic process, in the most rigorous sense of the word, will have become plainly apparent to anyone who has read, for instance, Herrigel's account of his own training in archery under a Zen master.[6]

The same applies to other forms of Zen training, as described in various books; they one and all display a character that by no stretch could be described as "exoteric," but without this entailing a rite of

---

[5] For much of the information to be found in this article we have to thank Miss Carmen Blacker, lecturer in Japanese at Cambridge and herself a Buddhist; through her kind help we were able to obtain directly from Japan authoritative answers to a number of questions that otherwise would have remained in doubt.

[6] One can contrast with this the initiatic practice in the Corporation of Archers in ancient Turkey. There initiation took a perfectly normal form according to the Sufic model, with the sheikh of the corporation whispering the Name in the ear of the disciple while at the same time placing his fingers on the "grip" of the bow, where the two halves from which the Tartar type of bow (including the Japanese) is constructed are "unified"; the symbolism needs no explaining!

access of the kind that would be deemed indispensable elsewhere—unless one is to regard acceptance by the master and the administering by him to the disciple of his first *koan* as tantamount to "initiation" as we know it; this, however, was not the view of my informant. Rather would it seem as if the whole process is to be described as "initiatic," without any particular incident in the course of it being singled out as being more essential than others. In a sense this absence of a specific initiation goes with the attitude of *jiriki* (own power) extremism apparent in Zen.[7]

Though the spiritual master and the method he imparts are everything in fact, the theoretical emphasis remains always on the personal effort of the pupil—hence the abysmal misunderstandings to which Zen so readily lends itself in the minds of Occidentals with their habitually individualistic bias. Privileged are those few who have found the way to becoming naturalized in Japanese wisdom to the point of overcoming their own congenital self-obsession as well as the ratiocinative habit that Zen in particular sets out to eradicate. We are not among those who believe that "Zen for the West" corresponds to a widespread possibility. Attempts to publicize Zen methods, by Westernized Japanese, have only resulted, in most cases, in an increase of the existing intellectual disorder in the West; while a number of earnest souls, lured into the pursuit of a, by them, unrealizable ideal, have been deterred thereby from seeking other ways, in Buddhism or in traditions nearer home, better suited to their own temperamental needs.

We must now consider the case of another Japanese sect that has still more to tell us than Zen in relation to the subject of the present article. We are referring to Jodo (Pure Land) and its associated sects, in which Invocation of the Buddha of Light, Amitabha (Japanese Amida) is the principal, and indeed the only essential, support used. Here again there is no formal initiation, though one would have expected that a conferring of the formula to be invoked, known as *nembutsu* and enshrining the Name of Amida, would be just the occasion for such an initiatic rite. In point of fact, however, any person may invoke with this formula at will whether he be resorting

---

[7] For the *jiriki* (own power) and *tariki* (other power) types of Japanese spirituality to which Zen and Jodo respectively belong see the appendix of my book *The Way and the Mountain* (London: Peter Owen, 1960).

for instruction to a guru of the line or not. On the doctrinal side, it is noteworthy that Jodo and its sister sect Jodo Shinshu (Pure Land true religion) of which Shinran was the Patriarch, have often been compared to Christianity because of their devotional character and because of the role of Savior attributed to Amida thanks to whose "vow" and by whose grace alone the disciple hopes to enter the Pure Land after his earthly life is over. Painted scrolls showing the Buddha Amida and his heavenly attendants on their way down to welcome his devotee into paradise rank among the most deeply moving examples of Japanese art.

Despite the fact that the Pure Land schools display this strongly devotional character, it would nevertheless be a mistake to label them without more ado as a way of *bhakti* (to use a well-known Hindu term), not only because all branches of Buddhism, whatever may be their outward form, remain in principle ways of knowledge, as laid down in the beginning but also because the Pure Land teachings, if one looks at them more closely, represent a synthesis of devotional and sapiential elements that fully satisfies the needs of a spirituality having an intellectual goal in view.[8]

The Pure Land itself, symbolizing the goal, admits of interpretation at two levels: In a more outward sense it is the Western Paradise of Amitabha, sojourn in which both is blissful and does not entail further wandering in the Round of Existence, *samsara*; what it envisages is a "deferred liberation" comparable to the *krama-mukti* of Hinduism. But the very name "Pure Land" and the fact that this was substituted for the more usual form "Western Paradise" shows that something more lies behind this first interpretation, for where total purity is to be found, there is *selfhood*—the two things are really identical. It is admixture with its resulting internal stresses that necessitates

---

[8] We have it on the authority of a distinguished priest of Jodo Shin, the Venerable Shojun Bando, that in Shin Buddhism the guru-*chela* relationship has been strongly upheld in the case of those who wish to proceed far along that road. For our benefit he quoted Rennyo, a saint of the fifteenth century, as saying: "Your faith is not consummated without the guru's guidance," and also, "Five factors are required for your rebirth in the Pure Land, namely anterior (good) *karma*, guru, light, faith, and Name." All the evidence, positive and negative, goes to show that in this branch of the Buddhist tradition the line of demarcation between a fully esoteric and initiatic and a bhaktic and even a frankly exoteric participation remains pretty indefinite; nevertheless, in any given case it would be easy to say to which category a man's spiritual activity really belongs.

samsaric existence. On this showing, the Pure Land can only mean Nirvana—anything less is excluded by the very form of the name.[9] Otherwise put, one can say that the Western Paradise represents a relative purity, which from the point of view of the impurity of the world appears quasi-absolute, whereas the Pure Land as such is pure in an unqualified sense.

This dual interpretation implicit in the name "Pure Land" inevitably evokes a similar possibility of transposition as applying to the Christian term "salvation," since this too is habitually described as a passage to paradise; this state beyond all suffering and in "proximity" to the Divine corresponds very closely to the Western Paradise of the Buddhists. Nevertheless, in the Christian case, as in the other and with equal logic, the "salvation" that is offered admits of two interpretations, the one indicating a state that is more or less conditioned (depending on which paradise the soul that has been "saved" is called upon to occupy) and the other referring to an entirely unconditional realization, one where it is no longer possible to think of an individual being at all, but only selfhood in the transcendent sense; this has been pointed out before by other writers. Admittedly, the word "salvation" for practically everyone nowadays, and probably for the majority even in primitive times, does carry a more or less restricted meaning in fact, but this does not authorize one to conclude that it does so in principle. It must be remembered that "salvation" is the term Christians have always used; its authority goes back to the Scriptures and to Christ Himself. It would be surprising indeed if it implied any restriction of finality in an absolute sense. There is really nothing to astonish us in the equivocal usage to which the idea of "salvation" has given rise, seeing that this agrees with the bivalency of the Christian spiritual language under all its forms consequent upon the rending of the temple veil.

We have referred to primitive times, but even in later times can one imagine a Meister Eckhart using the word "salvation" with any

---

[9] A single telling quotation from the Patriarch Shinran himself will suffice to clinch the point: "Rebirth (in the Pure Land] . . . is complete unsurpassed enlightenment." We have it on good authority that in Japan nowadays the intellectual level among Shin followers is, on an average, rather low; little more than worldly benefits is envisaged in many cases. Nevertheless, the highest possibility is there for the seeking; but men must have eyes to see and ears to hear or this ever-present opportunity will pass them by.

thought but its transcendent meaning? For such as he, a paradise would indeed be "the sage's prison," as the Sufis say. Those who have seen as far as Eckhart may have been comparatively few, but their mere existence is enough to prove the case. All one need say really, in this connection, is that for those for whom the veil is truly parted "from top to bottom" salvation will bear the sense of total deliverance, while for those (the many) whose more or less obscured minds still cause them to imagine a veil where none really is, the same word "salvation" will evidently bear the limited connotation we have become accustomed to take for granted as the only possible one—somewhat abusively, however, both because this restricts scriptural and traditional usage and also because we have thereby been led into systematizing what by rights should remain undefined, instead of allowing the context to tell us which meaning is the one intended. Spiritually this opportunity for discernment is beneficial by reason of the greater "mindfulness" it fosters (to use a favorite Buddhist term) by comparison with a more cut-and-dried solution.

With Hesychasm we find ourselves at last over the threshold of Christian initiation as such, by which we mean, not that this form exhausts the possibilities implied in the name to the extent of providing a single type to which all else can be referred, but that this spiritual current of the Eastern Church represents a perfectly normal "specification" of initiatic activity according to the Christian idiom, one that is neither the result of absorbing elements of foreign origin, as in the case of Hermetism for instance, nor confined to some exceptionally enclosed organization like the Fede Santa and certain other medieval initiations, nor yet the appanage of a vocational institution like the guilds of cathedral builders or the knightly orders. All these things have existed in the Christian world, but none of them conforms to conditions, in terms of finality, doctrine, and method, such as would allow one to identify it without further qualification with "Christian initiation" in an all-inclusive sense. Seeing that Hesychasm is the only extant example of something satisfying the required conditions in a sufficient degree to answer our present purpose, we are left no choice but to take this for our starting point and afterward to build from there.

The chief points to note about Hesychasm are as follows: (1) its basis in Scripture and the Fathers, (2) its invocative formula, (3) the position in it of the "geront" (Slavonic *staretz*), (4) its declared goal, and (5) the absence of any specifically initiatic rite.[10]

Let us take these headings in order and enlarge, where necessary, on various points of technical detail.

1. Scriptural and patristic authority: This has always been strictly maintained, thus providing all that was needed by way of theoretical foundation for the practices of Hesychasm from the earliest times of its existence under that name till nowadays. In the eighteenth century an anthology of extracts from the Greek Fathers was compiled, known as the *Philokalia*, and this is regarded as containing all the essential doctrinal material required by a follower of this way. This collection exists in both Greek and Russian.[11]

2. The short sentence known as the Jesus Prayer here provides the one and only formula to be invoked, though there is much to be said regarding the manner of its use. It runs as follows: "Lord Jesus Christ, Son of God, have mercy upon me." It will be immediately apparent that these words, as far as their rational understanding takes one, are the common property of all Christians without distinction; no ritual authorization is required, and it would indeed be surprising if such were the case. A precisely comparable case is the *nembutsu* in "Pure Land" Buddhism which also never has become an object of ritual communication to the disciple.

When it comes to a use of the Jesus Prayer as *mantram* in virtue of the presence in it of the Holy Name, its rational connotation, though still evident, takes second place. In Hesychasm, as in other traditions where the inherent power of a name becomes the operative factor in a method, the novice is warned from the outset against using the formula except under direction of a qualified master. To find his spiritual master is therefore, for him, an urgent task. If, however, after persistent searching he is unable to discover such a master, the would-be disciple is permitted to apply the prescribed method as best he can with the aid of books while casting himself on the mercy of Christ as the one unfailing source of instruction. The whole method is closely akin to the Hindu *japa-yoga* or the Sufi *dhikr,* if some Orthodox

---

[10] This and other facts relating to Hesychasm have been carefully checked in consultation with a follower of this way who has spent much time on Mount Athos and been in touch with some notable geronts belonging to the Greek islands.

[11] A selection from the *Philokalia* in two volumes, excellently translated into English by E. Kadloubovsky and G. E. H. Palmer, has been published by Faber and Faber (London).

apologists, out of a quite uncalled-for desire to safeguard a Christian originality no one threatens, have tried to deny this analogy, this only serves to show into what contradictory positions a perverted sense of loyalty is able to lead otherwise quite intelligent people.

3. The Hesychast "geront" (*staretz*) when found will discharge all the normal functions of a guru according to the Indian conception of the word. In Hinduism one's spiritual master is acknowledged as the direct representative of the supreme *Sad-guru*, the Divine Self. In Buddhism the same holds. The present writer was repeatedly told, in Tibet, that he should look on his lama as if he were "the Buddha himself." Hesychasm says the same: The disciple should behave toward his "geront" as if he were in the presence of Christ. One function only the "geront" will not assume—that of "initiator." According to the Christian spiritual economy Christ, as synthesizing the avataric function exclusively in his own person, is the only possible initiator[12]— hence the sacraments Christ instituted are the only conceivable supports in the initiatic, as well as the exoteric, path from its inception until the goal is reached. A man may envisage these supports with greater or lesser understanding—he may use the opportunity they provide to the full or only by halves—but in principle they remain objectively all-sufficing and indivisible at the level of form, and no subjective qualification or its absence can modify the fact. Hence a human teacher, though representing Christ in a certain way, will always efface himself in principle by stressing the indirect character of the function he exercises.

4. As regards the ultimate purpose of spiritual endeavor, Hesychasm makes use of a word found in the Fathers—namely, "deification." Plainly, this term stands for something far exceeding the individual realm and its possibilities; one is in undoubtedly esoteric country here. It must not be supposed, however, that deification is opposable in principle to the more usual word "salvation," for reasons already fully explained; rather should it be taken as throwing light on the highest possibilities that salvation intrinsically comprises.

---

[12] An exception, more apparent than real, might be made in the case of the Latin rosary, if this were ever taken as the support of a fully initiatic way, which it certainly could be by one endowed with the proper understanding and dispositions; in that case, it would be logical for the Holy Virgin, as original communicator of the rosary to Saint Dominic, to appear in the role of initiator, a privilege due to her in her capacity of *Coredemptrix*, and which no other creaturely figure can possibly share. Evidently, there is no departure from Christian principle here.

5. Concerning the absence of any special initiatic rite in Hesychasm, and in Christianity as such, we have already commented sufficiently, both in previous sections and in the present section under headings (2) and (3). All one can add to the above is to say that those who have searched for an initiatic rite supposed to operate over and above the sacraments have been losing their time. So far as Christianity is concerned, the hour that saw the veil of the temple rent in twain saw the end of any such possibility forever.[13] To complete the present survey, a brief discussion concerning the nature of the Christian sacraments is called for, regarded from the initiatic point of view.

Two of them, baptism and confirmation (called Chrismation in the Eastern rite), can conveniently be grouped together in this context,[14] if only for the reason that they are the ones that most evidently display the character of initiatic rites. In baptism there are two aspects to be noted, the first of which is essential and the second accessory. The essential purpose of baptism is to give back to "fallen" man the virtuality of "true man," or of Adam when still in Eden. This finality can hardly be accounted a purely exoteric interest, though treated thus in practice and even though admittedly it does not look beyond the plenitude of the individual possibility as represented by the state of Adamic innocence, which, moreover, corresponds to the human nature of Christ, the second Adam. The accessory aspect of baptism, which might also be called its "aggregatory" aspect, is its effect of making a man into a member of the Christian community, a plainly exoteric purpose when regarded in isolation from the higher possibility that goes with it.

Chrismation, on the other hand, the Pentecostal grace, though it includes the general purpose of confirming a man in all the functions pertaining to Christian life (questions of special vocation apart), is more predominantly turned in the direction of supra-individual aims; the gift of the Holy Ghost could not in principle envisage an individual realization only, even if it be treated perfunctorily in most cases, as a

---

[13] In the course of the present study of Christian initiation a number of unacknowledged references have been made to the work of Frithjof Schuon, several of whose books treat of the same subject in more extended form. I gladly acknowledge my indebtedness to this source.

[14] In the Eastern rite both sacraments are given together, one after the other, by the priest; the postponing of confirmation to a later age and its conferring by a bishop belongs to the Latin rite. Evidently, no doctrinal implication attaches to this difference.

means of increasing piety and no more. If Chrismation can be said to "amplify" the grace already received in baptism, it would be still more true to say that it transposes that grace in the sense of "exaltation"; in other words, its normal finality, despite exoteric shortsightedness, cannot but be the state of "transcendent man" or "deification," to give it its Christian label. Thus the two natures of Christ are covered, in intention, by the two sacraments jointly; the Eucharist is there to render operative this double fulfillment.

At this point it is advisable to answer a possible objection: In view of the fact that baptism has long been imparted to all without distinction and even imposed on them in infancy whether they wish it or not, it might be asked whether this is not *per se* contrary to the initiatic principle, since this normally will imply "qualification" in the recipient, therefore also a selective character to the imparting itself; the same objection would apply to Chrismation.

We think, however, that enough has already been said to show why this objection does not apply in the present case, because of the bivalent character attaching by definition to all essential elements in the Christian tradition as from the very outset. A baptized person may remain unaware of the fact that the rite he went through had more than an aggregatory meaning; the teaching he receives on the subject of baptism's power to neutralize "original sin" may mean to him little more than a quasi-moral benefit, in which case—this is the case of the majority—his participation in the fruits of baptism will necessarily remain exoteric and largely passive. Let, however, an awareness of the greater possibilities likewise comprised in the sacrament he has received but dawn on his mind and that man will be able, from that moment, to view his own baptism and confirmation retrospectively as having opened the gate to a realization far exceeding the exoteric domain. No one will have compelled him to do so, nor is there any presumption as to how many others will or will not follow suit, so that distinctions of qualification, as mentioned above, will not have been disregarded in any essential way, nor will the condition of intellectual aptitude for such a path have been disregarded either. The theoretical position should be clear enough; as for an effective realization of all that baptism and Chrismation offer between them, that is another matter, and it is that which constitutes initiatic life in the Christian sense.

Three of the remaining sacraments, matrimony, ordination, and unction, need not long detain us. In fact the only one of these three that might concern us here is unction, to which the Latin Church adds the epithet "extreme," since the other two explain themselves sufficiently by their form. The nature of unction, on the other hand, seems rather difficult to define from our present standpoint. Inasmuch as it is designed as an instrument of divine healing, it might be placed in a class of its own. In Eastern Christianity not only sick people but also all the faithful are able (but not obliged) to partake of this sacrament. This happens once a year, on the Wednesday in Holy Week, when all who so wish come to receive this medicine for their souls.

This brings us to the remaining two sacraments, penance, or confession, and the Eucharist; like baptism and Chrismation, they belong together, the one being a preparation for the other. The only description that seems to fit the sacrament of penance is by calling it a rite of psychic purification, in the highest sense of the word, and this is doubtless how a Hindu, for instance, would classify it. The Eucharist, on the other hand, would count for him as a sacrificial rite (*yajña*), which it is in the first instance, but it is many other things besides—every aspect of Christian spirituality finds its focus here, so that the Eucharist can justly be called "the axial mystery," the one that synthesizes all that the other mysteries have to offer. That it is not "an exoteric rite" (however human ignorance may treat it on occasion) is surely obvious—could anything conceivably be more "inward" than the body and blood of the *avatara*? Its partaking is, for a Christian, what the Tibetans describe as *lamai nendjor* (spelled *blamai rnalbyor*) = union (*yoga*) with the "guru," a sense that the word "communion" is also intended to convey.

The two elements, bread and wine, figuring in the rite correspond, as many are aware, to the two great "dimensions" of spiritual life, "the exterior" and "the interior,"[15] and therefore also to the two natures of Christ, human and divine, the realization of which the Eucharist is above all designed to bring about. When the bread is broken, the sacrifice is accomplished. When the elements are mingled in the chalice, exterior and interior become merged in a single overflowing of the divine compassion—fused but not confused, to quote Meister Eckhart's pregnant saying. The symbolical message is exactly the same as that of the temple veil and its parting, which the mixing of the

---

[15] The two names of God corresponding, in Islam, to these dimensions are *az-Zahir* and *al-Batin*.

consecrated elements reproduces here. That is why the Eucharist is food and drink unto salvation, taking this word not merely in its usual restricted sense but also in that unqualified sense that all authentic traditions give to whatever word they use to indicate the ultimate goal of man's spiritual voyage.[16]

This completes our attempted recapitulation of the evidence relating to "Christian initiation" within that "eso-exoteric" structure that the Christian form of tradition characteristically displays. The ambiguities that have revealed themselves in the course of Christian history are to a large extent traceable to this ambivalence of structure; this fact should not, however, be taken for a mere reproach, since it also translates a positive value in that "bursting of all bounds" by the mysteries, which the descent of Christ into the world marked from the outset. Its negative effects are also apparent enough, in the extreme exteriorization that took place later; for if the Holy of Holies, with the parting of the curtain, overflowed into the outer portion of the temple, the reverse was also true. It is a price that had to be paid in practice but which can still be neutralized by spiritual realization and by that alone.

One final message must be addressed to the Christian aspirant who, even when fortified with the assurance that his tradition has (human obtuseness notwithstanding) conserved the virtuality of its inner life, will yet not find his own spiritual problem solved over-night—indeed far from it. The Christian way, under today's conditions, is beset with difficulties for those who are not content to accept whatever an exoteric participation offers them and no more; not the least of these difficulties is an apparently total absence of qualified spiritual instruction—able, that is to say, to harness whatever resources are provided by the tradition to the service of an initiatic method. In a monotonously general picture of spiritual indigence, Hesychasm marks the one noteworthy exception, but this source of guidance too might one day dry up (God forfend it!) as a result of the increasing alienation from the contemplative ideal that has gone with the spread

---

[16] The withdrawing of the chalice from the laity in the Latin Church at a certain time in the Middle Ages, though it does not destroy the sacrament in a technical sense (each consecrated element implying the other as with the two natures of Christ), does in a certain symbolical sense appear to restrict man's spiritual finality to the "exterior"; it foreshadows the general exoterization that took place in practice. We are not the first to have pointed out this analogy.

of modern secularism in the Orthodox countries themselves, especially among the young.[17]

In the Catholic West, despite the relative popularity of monastic institutions, the situation is, if anything, still more difficult, since what passes nowadays for a "contemplative life" would hardly earn that epithet from the mouth of, say, an average Tibetan lama or Hindu *sannyasin*. We say this, not in order to discourage the devotee bent on getting his Christian virtuality turned into a reality—indeed the opposite is our purpose—but because when once a man is committed in intention to the "unseen warfare" under any form, for him to underrate the extent of the opposing forces is itself a danger. One has to size up a challenging situation accurately, but without dismay. This is a prior condition to any spiritual victory.

Without venturing on any slick solution to this vexed question of spiritual method and its adequate communication within the Christian world, one can at least say one thing (Hesychasm apart and without allowing for any as yet unverified possibilities in the Western tradition itself), namely that a Christian aspirant enjoys one particular advantage inasmuch as he is able to profit by any unexpected opportunity of spiritual guidance without needing to be provided, even when entering on the most inward quest, with any spiritual "support" beyond the ones he already possesses by right. One is thinking always of Christianity under its still traditional form and not of various residues of its fragmentation where the indispensable means of grace are evidently lacking. If on the one hand a Christian has a number of special difficulties to contend with—and no religious form can be wholly free from such—on the other hand he can confidently claim

---

[17] The eight hundredth anniversary of the founding of the Athonite community was to be marked, so we have read, by the construction of a motorable road onto the peninsula in order to render it more accessible to visitors wishing to attend the celebration. It is to this well-worn tune that the first big inroad into the privacy of the great monastic fastness is being inaugurated, a privacy that the Muslim Turks, in the days of their mastery, never failed to respect. All over Asia road making, by opening a way for hurried, thoughtless visiting by all and sundry, has been the means of depriving places of pilgrimage of their traditional *raison d'être*, the argument of facility is everywhere the same—*facilis descensus Averni!* If Christians only knew their own interest, the whole Christian world would be up in arms to defend the inviolability of Athos. According to a more recent report, the authorities of the Holy Mountain, alarmed by the fact that so many young tourists are coming there simply for the sake of a cheap holiday in romantic surroundings, have requested the Greek government to tighten the regulations for issuing permits of entry. A timely precaution, some will say; but then what becomes of the age-long freedom of pilgrimage itself?

for himself this unexpected fruit ripened from the original parting of the temple veil, a strange paradox in its way—but then spiritual life is full of paradoxical happenings. There is really nothing to be surprised at here.

MYSTICISM

William Stoddart

Except by those who reject it or are ignorant of it entirely, it is generally understood that mysticism claims to be concerned with "Ultimate Reality." The relationship in question is mostly taken to be of an "experiential" kind, and the phrase "mystical experience" is often used—the assumed object of the experience being, precisely, "Ultimate Reality," which is allegedly transcendent and hidden in regard to our ordinary senses. This mystical experience is held to be "incommunicable" and, particularly when doubt is cast on the alleged object of the experience, it is often said to be, in a pejorative sense, purely subjective.

Nevertheless, it would generally be admitted that, as well as "mystical experience," there is also "mystical doctrine." There is thus at least something that can be communicated (for this is what doctrine means), and at the same time something that is "objective," for whatever can be transmitted must needs be objective, even should the object in question prove to be illusory. The subjective as such cannot be transmitted,[1] but its object can—at least in conceptual terms. To say: "I have experienced something indescribable and incommunicable" is already a description and a communication. As such it can be considered objectively by a third party and, depending on the adequacy of the description, the sensitivity of the hearer, and the reality of the object, it can even stir within him a responsive chord. This means that in favorable circumstances it can, to a greater or lesser degree, stimulate in the hearer a similar intuition or "experience."

The assumed object of both "mystical experience" and "mystical doctrine" is Ultimate Reality. Mystical doctrine may call this the One, the Absolute, the Infinite, the Supreme Self, the Supreme Being, or some other name, and mystical experience is deemed to be union

---

[1] In modern subjectivism, what is expressed is only a subject that is already relative, namely the passional, sentimental, and imaginative ego; in order to express itself, it necessarily makes use of objective elements which it chooses arbitrarily, while separating itself arrogantly and foolishly from objective reality. The "purely subjective," in the modern world, can only announce its presence by gasps and howls, and this is the very definition of modern "avant-garde" poetry.

therewith, to whatever degree and in whatever mode. With this end in view, one also speaks of the "mystical way" or the "mystical path." This is the process of "unification" with the One, the Supreme Self, or the Supreme Being,—all of these being names given to Ultimate Reality.

From all of this, it clearly emerges that mysticism or mystical experience has two poles, namely mystical doctrine and the mystical way or path. Thus in mysticism, as in other spheres, it is a question of doctrine and method, or theory and practice. These twin elements of mysticism will be examined in detail in the course of this essay. The validity and justifiability of mysticism, let it be said right away, depend on the validity and justifiability of its object. If this be a reality, the experience is valid and, in the manner described, capable of being communicated to, and evoked in, a third party.

*
*　*

As is often done, I have spoken of mysticism in a manner that might give the impression that mysticism is an independent entity capable of existing in a vacuum. Such an impression would be false, however, since in practice mysticism only makes its appearance within the framework of one or other of the revealed religions. Indeed it would be true to say that mysticism constitutes the inward or spiritual dimension of every religion. Mysticism is esoterism, while the outward religious framework is the respective exoterism. The exoterism is for all, but the corresponding esoterism is only for those who feel a call thereto. Esoterism, unlike exoterism, cannot be imposed. It is strictly a matter of vocation.

It has been said that "all paths lead to the same summit." In this symbol, the variety of religions is represented by the multiplicity of starting-points around the circumferential base of a cone or mountain. The radial, upward, pathways are the mystical paths. The oneness of mysticism is a reality only at the point that is the summit. The pathways are many, but their goal is one. As they approach this goal, the various pathways more and more resemble one another, but only at the Summit do they coincide. Until then, in spite of resemblances and analogies, they remain separate, and indeed each path is imbued with a distinctive perfume or color—Islamic mysticism is clearly not Christian mysticism—but at the Summit these various colors are (still speaking symbolically) reintegrated into the uncolored Light. Islamic mysticism and Christian mysticism are one only in God.

58

It is this point of "uncolored Light," where the different religions come together, that is the basis of the *philosophia perennis* or *religio perennis*. This is the supra-formal, divine truth which is the source of each religion, and which each religion incorporates. The heart of each exoterism is its corresponding esoterism, and the heart of each esoterism is the *religio perennis*—or esoterism in the pure state.

In all the religions, the goal of mysticism is God, who may also be given such names as the One, the Absolute, the Infinite, the Supreme Self, the Supreme Being.[2] In sapiential or "theosophic" mysticism, the goal is said to be the Truth, conceived as a living Reality capable of being experienced. Mysticism thus has three components: the doctrine concerning God or Ultimate Reality ("mystical doctrine"), "oneness" with God or Ultimate Reality ("mystical experience"), and the movement that leads from the former to the latter ("the mystical path"). In other words: the doctrine of Unity, the experience of Union, and the path of Unification.

Mystical doctrine is one and the same as metaphysics or mystical theology. Mystical experience, when present in a total or at least sufficient degree, is salvation or liberation. And the purpose of the mystical path is "spiritual realization," i.e., the progression from outward to inward, from belief to vision, or (in scholastic terms) from Potency to Act.

*
* *

Many people are familiar with the three fundamental modes of spiritual realization proclaimed by Hinduism: *karma-mârga* (the "Way of Action"), *bhakti-mârga* (the "Way of Love"), and *jñâna-mârga* (the "Way of Knowledge"). These correspond to the three degrees or dimensions of Sufism: *makhâfa* ("Fear"), *mahabba* ("Love"), and *ma'rifa* ("Knowledge" or "Gnosis").[3]

---

[2] This also includes the "non-theistic" religion of Buddhism, since here too Ultimate Reality, variously referred to in different contexts as *Dharma* ("Law"), *Âtmâ* ("Self"), *Nirvâna* ("Extinction"), or *Bodhi* ("Knowledge"), is seen as transcendent and absolute.

[3] This word is used purely etymologically, and does not hark back to the current, in the early history of Christianity, known as "gnosticism." "Gnosis," from the Greek, is the only adequate English rendering for the Sanskrit *jñâna* (with which in fact it is cognate) and the Arabic *ma'rifa*.

Strictly speaking, it is only *bhakti* and *jñâna* (i.e., *mahabba* and *ma'rifa*) that constitute mysticism: mysticism is either a way of Love, a way of Knowledge, or a combination of both. One will recall the occasion in the life of Christ when he was received in the house of the sisters Martha and Mary. What has come to be known in Christianity as the "Way of Martha" is paralleled by the Hindu *karma-mârga*, the way of religious observance and good works. The contemplative or mystical way, on the other hand, is the "Way of Mary," which comprises two modes, namely, *bhakti-mârga* (the "Way of Love") and *jñâna-mârga* (the "Way of Knowledge"). *Karma* as such is purely exoteric, but it is important to stress that there is always a karmic component within both *bhakti* and *jñâna*. The Way of Love and the Way of Knowledge both necessarily contain an element of Fear or conformity. Likewise, the Way of Knowledge invariably contains within it the reality of Love. As for the Way of Love, which is composed of faith and devotion, it contains an indirect element of *jñâna* in the form of dogmatic and speculative theology. This element lies in the intellectual speculation as such, not in its object, the latter being limited by definition,[4] failing which it would not be a question of *bhakti*, but of *jñâna*. In spite of the presence in each Way of elements of the two others, the three Ways *karma*, *bhakti*, and *jñâna* (or *makhâfa*, *mahabba*, and *ma'rifa*) represent three specific and easily distinguishable modes of religious aspiration.

As for the question as to which of these paths a given devotee adheres to, it is overwhelmingly a matter of temperament and vocation. It is a case where the Way chooses the individual and not the individual the Way.

Historically speaking, Christian mysticism has been characterized in the main by the "Way of Love," whereas Hindu mysticism and Islamic mysticism comprise both the "Way of Love" and the "Way of Knowledge." The language of the "Way of Love" has a remarkably similar ring in whichever mysticism it crops up, but the more jñânic formulations of Hinduism and the more "gnostic" formulations of

---

[4] In the Way of Love (*bhakti* or *mahabba*), God is envisaged at the level of "Being" (which has as consequence that the Lord and the worshiper always remain distinct). In the Way of Knowledge (*jñâna* or *ma'rifa*), on the other hand, God is envisaged at the level of "Beyond-Being" or "Essence."

Sufism tend to strike a foreign note in the ears of those who are familiar only with Christian, or at any rate bhaktic, forms of spirituality.[5]

*

* *

The goal of religion, in all its varieties, is salvation. What, then, is the difference between exoterism and esoterism? Exoterism is formalistic, but faith and devotion can give it depth. Esoterism is "deep"—supraformal—by definition, and is the apanage only of those with the relevant vocation. Here forms are transcended, in that they are seen as symbolic expressions of the essence. In esoterism too faith is essential, but here it has the meaning of sincerity and total commitment—effort towards "realization." It means the acquisition of the essential virtues of humility and charity, and the opening of the soul to Divine grace. Metaphysically, the difference between exoterism and esoterism, or between formalism and supra-formalism, lies in how the final Goal is envisaged: in exoterism (and in esoterism of the "bhaktic" type), God is envisaged at the level of "Being" (the Creator and the Judge): no matter how deep, how sublime, the exoterist's fervor, Lord and worshiper always remain distinct. In "jñânic" esoterism, on the other hand, God is envisaged at the level of "Beyond-Being" (the Divine Essence). At this level, it is perceived that Lord and worshiper (the latter known to be created in the image of the former) share a common essence, and this opens up the possibility of ultimate Divine Union.

*

* *

Reference was made earlier to "subjective" and "objective," and it may be useful to indicate precisely whence these two concepts derive. The most direct key in this regard is the Hindu appellation for the Divinity: *Sat-Chit-Ânanda*. This expression is usually translated as "Being-Consciousness-Bliss." This is accurate, and enables one to see that "Being" is the Divine Object (God Transcendent or Ultimate

---

[5] Those who, by way of exception, have manifested the "Way of Knowledge" in Christianity include such great figures as Dionysius the Areopagite, Meister Eckhart, Albertus Magnus, and Angelus Silesius. It is precisely the works of *jñânins* such as these that have tended to cause ripples in the generally bhaktic climate of Christianity.

Reality), "Consciousness" is the Divine Subject (God Immanent or the Supreme Self), while "Bliss"—the harmonious coming-together of the two—is Divine Union. The most fundamental translation therefore of *Sat-Chit-Ânanda* is "Object-Subject-Union." This is the model, or origin, of all possible objects and subjects, and of the longing of the latter for the former.[6]

This trinitarian aspect of the Divinity is universal, and is found in all religions. In Christianity it is the central dogma: God the Father, God the Son, and God the Holy Spirit. The analogy between the Christian Trinity and "Being-Consciousness-Bliss" can be seen from certain doctrinal expositions of the Greek Fathers and also from St. Augustine's designation of the Christian Trinity as "Being-Wisdom-Life." In Islam, although it is above all the religion of strict monotheism, certain Sufi formulations evoke the selfsame trinitarian aspect of the Divinity. Reference will be made later to the question of spiritual realization, but in Sufism this is essentially mediated by the invocation (*dhikr*) of the Name of God. In this connection it is said that God is not only That which is invoked (*Madhkûr*), but also That within us which invokes (*Dhâkir*), and even the invocation itself, since, in the last analysis, this is none other than the internal Act (*Dhikr*) of God.[7] We thus have the ternary *Madhkûr-Dhâkir-Dhikr* ("Invoked-Invoker-Invocation"), which is yet another form of the basic ternary "Object-Subject-Union." This cardinal relationship is the very essence of the theory and practice of mysticism, for this "Union" *in divinis* is the prefiguration of and pattern for the union of man with God.[8] Hindu, Christian, and Sufi doctrine coincide in elucidating just why this is so.

*
*　*

One of the most significant characteristics of mystical doctrine stemming from several of the great religions—and made explicit, for example, in the treatises of jñânic or gnostic mystics such as Shankara,

---

[6] *Sat-Chit-Ânanda* may also be interpreted as "Known-Knower-Knowledge" or "Beloved-Lover-Love."

[7] That this Divine Act should pass through man is the mystery of salvation.

[8] It will easily be seen that it is also the prefiguration of every other union under the sun, for example, conjugal union.

Eckhart, and Ibn 'Arabî—is the distinction made, within God Himself, between God and the Godhead, between "Being" and "Essence," or between "Being" and "Beyond-Being."[9] In ordinary theological doctrine, the fundamental distinction is between God and man, or between the Uncreated and the created. Mystical or esoteric doctrine, on the other hand, makes a distinction within each of these two terms. Thus, within the Uncreated (viewed as the "Divine Essence" or "Beyond-Being"), there is already a *prefiguration* of creation, and this is God as "Being." "Beyond-Being" is the principle of "Being," and God as Being (the immediate Creator of the world) is the principle of existence or creation.

Within creation—itself relative—there is also a distinction to be made, for within creation there is a *reflection* of the Uncreated (the Absolute) in the form of Truth and Virtue, Symbol and Sacrament, Prophet or Redeemer. Once again mystical doctrine renders explicit the reality of mystical union, for it is by uniting himself with the "created" Symbol or Sacrament (for example, in truth, in beauty, in virtue, in the Eucharist, or in the Invocation of a Divine Name), that the mystic realizes his union with (or reintegration into) the uncreated Divinity. Only through the sacramental perfecting of the created, can one reach the Uncreated. This is what is meant in Christianity by "the imitation of Christ," or in Islam by the observance of the *Sunna*.

This exposition is taken from the writings of Frithjof Schuon,[10] who has explained how "Being" (the *prefiguration* of the relative in the Absolute) is the uncreated Logos, whereas the *reflection* of the Absolute in the relative (namely: truth, beauty, virtue, Prophet, Savior) is the created Logos. Without this "bridge" (the Logos with its created and uncreated aspects), no contact whatsoever between created and Uncreated, between man and God, would be possible:[11] the gulf between the two would be unbridgeable. This would be "dualism," not "Non-Dualism" (or *Advaita*, to use the term from Shankaran metaphysics), and the very opposite of mysticism.

---

[9] The same distinction is also made by St. Gregory Palamas in his doctrine of the Divine Essence and the Divine Energies.

[10] See especially *Esoterism as Principle and as Way* (Perennial Books, London, 1980).

[11] The error of deism is precisely that it has no concept of the role of the Logos and envisages no such bridge.

The doctrine of the Logos, and its cardinal relevance to the mystical path, can be summarized in diagrammatic form as follows:

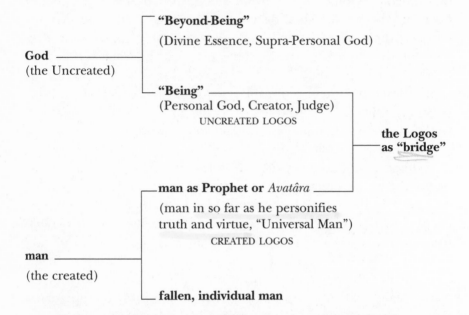

Within each religion, the Founder is the personification of the Logos, and his role as such is always made explicit. Christ said: "No man cometh to the Father but by me." The Prophet Mohammed said: "He that hath seen me, hath seen God." The Buddha said: "He who sees the *Dharma* sees me, and he who sees me sees the *Dharma*." Mystical union is realized only through the Logos.

This brings us directly to the three classical "stages" (*maqâmât* in Arabic) recognized by all mysticisms:

    I.   Purification (or Purgation),
    II.   Perfection (or Illumination), and
    III. Union.

The second stage, "Perfection," corresponds precisely to the aspirant's assimilation to the created Logos. In Christianity, this takes the form of the "imitation of Christ" and in Islam, the observance—inward and symbolically total—of the "Wont of the Prophet" (*Sunna*). Prayers such as the "Hail Mary" (*Ave Maria*) in Catholicism and the "Blessing on the Prophet" (*salât 'alâ 'n-Nabî*) in Islam, which contain

the names of the created Logos (*Jesus* and *Muhammad* respectively),
are instrumental to the end in view.

*

*   *

As we have seen, mysticism includes both mystical doctrine and mystical experience. Mystical experience is the inward and unitive "realization" of the doctrine. This is the domain of spiritual method. In
Hinduism spiritual method is represented by *yoga*—not the physical
exercises derived from *hatha-yoga* now widely experimented with in
the West, but *raja-yoga*, the "royal art" of contemplation and union.
If, in Hinduism, the *veda* (knowledge) is the *scientia sacra*, then *yoga*
(union) is the corresponding *ars sacra* or *operatio sacra*. Here the saying of the Medieval French architect Jean Mignot applies with fullest
force: *ars sine scientiâ nihil*. One cannot meaningfully or effectively
practice anything, if one does not know what one is doing. Above all,
one cannot practice a spiritual method except on the basis of previously comprehended spiritual doctrine which is both the motivation
and the paradigm for the spiritual work to be undertaken. If doctrine
without method is hypocrisy or sterility, then method without doctrine
means going astray, and sometimes dangerously. This makes clear why
doctrine must be "orthodox"—that is, in essential conformity with the
subtle contours of truth. Here it must be noted that pseudo-doctrine,
born of nothing more than human invention, is one of the most powerful causes of going astray.

These points have to be stressed, because in the present age
many of those attracted by mysticism are eager at all costs for "experience"—without caring to ask themselves: experience of what—and
without the safeguards either of conforming to the discipline of a religious tradition or of receiving permission and guidance from a spiritual authority. It is precisely this illegitimate wresting of method from
doctrine that is harmful. The more real and effective the spiritual
method appropriated, the more dangerous it can be for the appro-
priator. There are many recorded cases of psychological and spiritual
damage resulting from the unauthorized use (i.e., the profanation)
of religious rites and sacraments.

In the past, it was the opposite fault that was most likely: to know
the truth, but—through weakness, passion, or pride—to fail to put it
into practice; in other words, it was a question of hypocrisy, and not
the heresy—most commonly in the shape of a "false sincerity"—char-

acteristic of modern times. How typical of the age we live in that, here as elsewhere, it stands on its head! The new shortcoming is infinitely worse than the earlier one. It is forgotten that every "quest" inevitably has an object and, whether one cares to recall it or not, the object of a mystical or spiritual quest is Ultimate Reality or God. With such an object one cannot trifle with impunity.

Yoga is the way or method of union with God, through a dedicated concentration on Him. A particularly direct form of this is (in Hindu terms) *japa-yoga*, which involves the enduring invocation of a *mantra* (a Divine Name or a formula containing a Divine Name). *Mutatis mutandis*, this spiritual method plays a central role in all mysticisms. In Mahâyâna Buddhism, for example, it occurs in the form of the Tibetan *Mani* and the Japanese *Nembutsu*. In Islam, nothing is more enjoined on the spiritual aspirant than *dhikr Allâh*, the "remembrance of God" through the invocation of His Name. In Hesychasm (the mysticism of Eastern Christianity), invocation of the Divine Name takes the form of the "Prayer of Jesus," a practice vividly described in *The Way of a Russian Pilgrim*.[12] The analogous method in Western Christianity is the cult of the Holy Name. This flourished in the Middle Ages, and was also preached with poignancy and single-mindedness in the 15th century by St. Bernardino of Siena: "Everything that God has created for the salvation of the world is hidden in the Name of Jesus." The practice was revived, in the form of the invocation *Jesu-Maria*, in the revelations made to Sister Consolata, an Italian Capuchin nun, in the earlier part of this century.[13]

This method of concentrating on a revealed Divine Name indicates clearly that mysticism is the very opposite of giving free rein to man's unregenerate subjectivity. In fact, it is the exposing of his unregenerate subjectivity to the normative and transforming influence of the revealed Object, the Sacrament or Symbol of the religion in question. It was in this respect that St. Paul could say: "Not I, but Christ in me." At the same time, and even more esoterically, it is the exposing of our paltry egoism, seen in turn as an "object," to the withering and

---

[12] *The Way of a Pilgrim*, S.P.C.K., London, 1954.

[13] *Jesus Appeals to the World*, Alba House (Society of St. Paul), Staten Island NY 10314, 1971.

yet quickening influence of the divine Subject, the immanent Self.[14] This possibility is envisaged in Islam in the *hadîth qudsî* (a "Divine saying" through the mouth of the Prophet Mohammed): "I (God) am the hearing whereby he (the slave) heareth."[15] The vehicle of both processes is the Invocation of a Divine Name (which is both Subject and Object), within a strictly traditional and orthodox framework, and with the authorization of an authentic spiritual master. In this domain, there is no room for curiosity and experiment.

*

* *

In the mysticisms of several religions, the soul's quest for God is symbolized in terms of the mutual longing of the lover and the beloved. St. John of the Cross, for example, makes use of this symbolism in his mystical poetry, from which the following verses are quoted:

> *Oh noche que guiaste*
> *Oh noche amable más que el alborada:*
> *Oh noche que juntaste*
> *Amado con amada*
> *Amada en el Amado transformada!*

> O night that led'st me thus!
> O night more winsome than the rising sun!
> O night that madest us,
> Lover and lov'd as one,
> Lover transformed in lov'd, love's journey done!
>   (translated by Professor E. Allison Peers)

> *Descubre tu presencia,*
> *Y máteme tu vista y hermosura;*

---

[14] This synthesis of the dual aspect of realization or method is taken from the writings of Frithjof Schuon. See especially *Eye of the Heart* (World Wisdom Books, Bloomington, Indiana, 1997), chapter "Microcosm and Symbol."

[15] A similar thought is echoed in the words of St. Theresa of Ávila: "Christ has no body now on earth but yours, no hands but yours, no feet but yours; yours are the eyes through which is to look out Christ's compassion on the world; yours are the feet on which he is to go about doing good, and yours are the hands with which he is to bless us now."

> *Mira que la dolencia*
> *De amor que no se cura*
> *Sino con la presencia y la figura.*
>
> Reveal your presence clearly
> And kill me with the beauty you discover,
> For pains acquired so dearly
> From love, cannot recover
> Save only through the presence of the lover.
> (translated by Roy Campbell)

As a child of the 16th century, St. John of the Cross sought to convey his "subjective" experiences rather than objective doctrine, as the mystics of a few centuries earlier had done. And yet he never wavered from the Divine Object of all mystical striving. At the practical level, in an instruction for aspirants, he said, for example: "All goodness is a loan from God." The soul's subjectivity is uncertain; only the objective reality, that comes from beyond it, is absolutely certain.

*

* *

Mysticism was earlier defined as the inward or spiritual dimension contained within every religion—each religion being understood as a separate and specific Divine Revelation. Religion comprises a "periphery" and a "center," in other words, an exoterism and an esoterism. The exoterism is the providential expression or vehicle of the esoterism within it, and the esoterism is the supra-formal essence of the corresponding exoterism. This is why mysticism or esoterism—erroneously regarded by some as "unorthodox"—can in no way subvert the religious formalism of which it is the sap.

On the other hand, "essence" so far transcends "form," that inevitably it sometimes "breaks" it. Conflicts have at times occurred between the purest mysticism and the respective exoteric authority; the cases of Meister Eckhart in medieval Christendom and Al-Hallâj in Islam—the one leading to condemnation and the other to martyrdom—provide striking examples. Nevertheless Eckhart enunciated this shattering of forms in a positive way when he said: "If thou wouldst reach the kernel, thou must break the shell." It is hardly necessary to add that such a "transcending" of forms is at the very antipodes of heresy, which is a crude violation of the forms of a religion at their own level. Forms can be transcended only "from above" (or "from within"). To violate—or even simply to neglect—forms "from below" (or "from without") is the very opposite of transcending them. Outwardly man must observe traditional forms as perfectly as possible. This is required for the aspirant's assimilation to the created Logos, as has been explained above. Man can only offer to God—and so transcend—what he has perfected.

Mysticism is the reality of man's love for God and man's union with God. It is a hymn to Subjectivity, a hymn to Objectivity, a hymn to Joy or Union—these three Divine Hypostases being one. It has been stressed how, contrary to certain appearances and contrary to a commonly heard opinion, mysticism is always a flowering within an orthodox framework. But, since mysticism transcends forms "from above" (or "from within"), mysticism knows no bounds. Its essence is one with the Absolute and the Infinite. Let us therefore give the last word to Jalâl ad-Dîn Rûmî, one of the greatest mystics of Islam and one of the greatest mystical poets of all time:

> I am neither Christian nor Jew nor Parsi nor Moslem. I am neither of the East nor of the West, neither of the land nor of the sea. . . . I have put aside duality and have seen that the two worlds are one. I seek the One, I know the One, I see the One, I invoke the One. He is the First, He is the Last, He is the Outward, He is the Inward.

11

Spirituality

"Men ought always to pray and not to faint."—Luke 18:1

"Pray without ceasing."—I Thessalonians 5:17

"How great is the power of prayer! It can be likened unto a queen, who has constant access to the king, and who can obtain from him anything she asks for!"—St. Therese of Lisieux (1873-1897)

"Bless the Lord, O my soul, and all that is within me, bless his holy Name."—Psalm 103:1

"It is ordained that man must put before all things the universal commandment—to remember God—of which it is said: 'thou shalt remember the Lord thy God' (Deut. 8:18). For, by the reverse of that which destroys us, we may be secure. What destroys us is forgetfulness of God, which shrouds the commandments in darkness and despoils us of all good."—St. Gregory of Sinai (1265-1346)

"Let no one think, my brother Christians, that it is the duty only of priests and monks to pray without ceasing, and not of laymen. No, no; it is the duty of all of us Christians to remain always in prayer."—St. Gregory Palamas (1296-1359)

"For the sake of saving your souls, do not neglect the practice of the unceasing prayer. At first it may appear difficult to you, but be assured, as it were from Almighty God, that this very Name of Our Lord Jesus Christ, constantly invoked by you, will help you to overcome all difficulties, and in the course of time you will become used to this practice and will taste how sweet is the Name of the Lord."—St. Gregory Palamas (1296-1359)

"A mind which is not dispersed among external things, returns to itself, and from itself it ascends to God by an unerring path."—Basil the Great (329-379)

"A man who is deeply wounded in his heart by provocation and abuse shows thereby that deep in himself he harbors the old serpent. If he bears the blows in silence or answers with great humility, he will render this serpent weak and powerless. But if he argues with bitterness or speaks with arrogance, he will give the serpent an added strength to pour poison into his heart and mercilessly to devour his entrails."—St. Symeon the New Theologian (949-1022)

"We must understand, then, that even though God doesn't always give us what we want, He gives us what we need for our salvation."—St. Augustine (354-430)

"I cannot communicate continuously, as is my need, but I have come to understand that an act of love [the invocation] brings Jesus into the soul, that is, it increases grace and is like a Communion.

"The will of God, my vocation to attain sanctity, is one continuous [invocation] 'Jesus, Mary, I love you, save souls!' [*Jesu-Maria, vos amo, salvate animas!*] Every effort, every force and activity of the soul must be aimed at not interrupting the act of love. Nothing else, this alone! For this is the way.

"Spiritually, Jesus demanded of me an absolute silence of thoughts and words, and of the heart an unceasing 'Jesus, Mary, I love you, save souls!' The more faithful I am to this little way of love, the more is my soul flooded with joy and a true peace that nothing is able to disturb, not even my continuous falls. For, when I bring these to Jesus, He makes me remedy them through acts of humility, and these in turn increase the peace and joy in my heart.

"How happy, active, and vigilant ought the certainty to make me that my very act of love endures to all eternity!

"Oh Jesus, grant that I may live entirely concealed in Thee, in complete self-effacement, so that Thou mayest always do what Thou wilt with me. Thou alone must remain, and an unceasing 'Jesus, Mary, I love you, save souls!' Grant that in the seventeen hours in my day, I may not lose one!

"The unceasing act of love keeps the soul always in peace. I believe that it has a strong ascendancy over suffering and helps one to suffer joyfully. . . . The act of love is stronger than any pain. . . . I feel that the unceasing act of love maintains, and will continue to maintain, my little bark steady through all confusion, boredom, and tediousness.

"'Tell all souls, Consolata, that I [Jesus] prefer an act of love and a Communion of love to any other gift which they may offer Me! Yes, an act of love is better than the discipline, for I thirst for love, poor souls! They think that in order to reach Me it is necessary to live an austere, penitential life! See how they misrepresent Me. They make Me out as one to be feared, whereas I am kindness itself! See how they forget the precept which I have given them, the very essence of the entire Law: "Thou shalt love the Lord thy God with thy whole heart, with thy whole soul, with thy whole mind, and with thy whole strength (Mark 12:30)"'. . . ."—Sister Consolata Betrone (1903-1946)

THE POWER OF THE NAME:
THE JESUS PRAYER IN ORTHODOX
SPIRITUALITY

Bishop Kallistos Ware

[handwritten: hesychia silence]

Prayer and Silence

"When you pray," it has been wisely said by an Orthodox writer, "you yourself must be silent. . . . You yourself must be silent; let the prayer speak."[1] To achieve silence: this is of all things the hardest and the most decisive in the art of prayer. Silence is not merely negative—a pause between words, a temporary cessation of speech—but, properly understood, it is highly positive: an attitude of attentive alertness, of vigilance, and above all of *listening*. The hesychast, the man who has attained *hesychia*, inward stillness or silence, is *par excellence* the one who listens. He listens to the voice of prayer in his own heart, and he understands that this voice is not his own but that of Another speaking within him.

The relationship between praying and keeping silent will become clearer if we consider four short definitions. The first is from *The Concise Oxford Dictionary*, which describes prayer as ". . . solemn request to God . . . formula used in praying." Prayer is here envisaged as something expressed in words, and more specifically as an act of asking God to confer some benefit. We are still on the level of external rather than inner prayer. Few of us can rest satisfied with such a definition.

Our second definition, from a Russian *starets* of the last century, is far less exterior. In prayer, says Bishop Theophan the Recluse (1815-94), "the principal thing is to stand before God with the mind in the heart, and to go on standing before Him unceasingly day and night, until the end of life."[2] Praying, defined in this way, is no longer merely to ask for things, and can indeed exist without the employment of any words at all. It is not so much a momentary activity as a continuous

---

[1] Tito Colliander, *The Way of the Ascetics* (London, 1960), p. 79.

[2] Cited in Igumen Chariton of Valamo, *The Art of Prayer: An Orthodox Anthology*, translated by E. Kadloubovsky and E.M. Palmer (London, 1966), p. 63.

state. To pray is to *stand before God,* to enter into an immediate and personal relationship with Him; it is to know at every level of our being, from the instinctive to the intellectual, from the sub- to the supra-conscious, that we are in God and He is in us. To affirm and deepen our personal relationships with other human beings, it is not necessary to be continually presenting requests or using words; the better we come to know and love one another, the less need there is to express our mutual attitude verbally. It is the same in our personal relationship with God.

In these first two definitions, stress is laid primarily on what is done by man rather than God. But in the personal relationship of prayer, it is the divine partner and not the human who takes the initiative and whose action is fundamental. This is brought out in our third definition, taken from St. Gregory of Sinai (d. 1346). In an elaborate passage, where he loads one epithet upon another in his effort to describe the true reality of inner prayer, he ends suddenly with unexpected simplicity: "Why speak at length? Prayer is God, who works all things in all men."[3] *Prayer is God*—it is not something that I initiate but something in which I share; it is not primarily something which *I* do but which *God* is doing in me: in St. Paul's phrase, "not I, but Christ in me" (Gal. 2:20). The path of inner prayer is exactly indicated in St. John the Baptist's words about the Messiah: "He must increase, but I must decrease" (John 3:30). It is in this sense that to pray is to be silent. "You yourself must be silent; let the prayer speak"—more precisely, let God speak. True inner prayer is to stop talking and to listen to the wordless voice of God within our heart; it is to cease doing things on our own, and to enter into the action of God. At the beginning of the Byzantine Liturgy, when the preliminary preparations are completed and all is now ready for the start of the Eucharist itself, the deacon approaches the priest and says: "It is time for the Lord to act."[4] Such exactly is the attitude of the worshiper not only at the Eucharistic Liturgy but in all prayer, public or private.

---

[3] *Chapters,* 113 (PG 150, 1280A). See Kallistos Ware, "The Jesus Prayer in St. Gregory of Sinai," *Eastern Churches Review* iv (1972), p. 8.

[4] A quotation from Psalm 118 [119]:126. In some English versions of the Liturgy this is translated, "It is time to do [sacrifice] unto the Lord," but the alternative rendering which we have used is richer in meaning and is preferred by many Orthodox commentators. The original Greek uses the word *kairos:* "It is the *kairos* for the Lord to act." *Kairos* bears here the special meaning of the decisive moment, the moment of opportunity: he who prays seizes the *kairos*. This is a point to which we shall return.

4. Our fourth definition, taken once more from St. Gregory of Sinai, indicates more definitely the character of this action of the Lord within us. "Prayer," he says, "is the manifestation of Baptism."[5] The action of the Lord is not, of course, limited solely to the baptized; God is present and at work within all men, by virtue of the fact that each is created according to His divine image and likeness. But this image has been obscured and clouded over, although not totally obliterated, by man's fall into sin. It is restored to its primal beauty and splendor through the sacrament of Baptism, whereby Christ and the Holy Spirit come to dwell in what the Fathers call "the innermost and secret chamber of our heart." For the overwhelming majority, however, Baptism is something received in infancy, of which they have no conscious memory. Although the baptismal Christ and the indwelling Paraclete never cease for one moment to work within us, save on rare occasions most of us remain virtually unaware of this inward presence and activity. True prayer, then, signifies the rediscovery and "manifestation" of this baptismal grace. To pray is to pass from the state where grace is present in our hearts secretly and unconsciously, to the point of full inward perception and conscious awareness when we experience and *feel* the activity of the Spirit directly and immediately.

"In my beginning is my end." The purpose of prayer can be summarized in the phrase, "Become what you are." Become, consciously and actively, what you already are potentially and secretly, by virtue of your creation according to the divine image and your re-creation in Baptism. Become what you are: more exactly, return into yourself; discover Him who is yours already; listen to Him who never ceases to speak within you; possess Him who even now possesses you. Such is God's message to anyone who wants to pray: "You would not seek Me unless you had already found Me."

But how are we to begin? How can we learn to stop talking and to start listening? Instead of simply speaking to God, how can we make our own the prayer in which God speaks to us? How shall we pass from prayer expressed in words to prayer of silence, from "strenuous" to "self-acting" prayer, from "my" prayer to the prayer of *Christ in me?*

One way to embark on this journey inwards is through the Invocation of the Name.

---

[5] *Chapters*, 113 (PG 150, 1277D).

"Lord Jesus . . ."

It is not, of course, the only way. No authentic relationship between persons can exist without mutual freedom and spontaneity, and this is true in particular of inner prayer. There are no fixed and unvarying rules, necessarily imposed upon all who seek to pray; and equally there is no mechanical technique, whether physical or mental, which can compel God to manifest His presence. His grace is conferred always as a free gift, and cannot be gained automatically by any method or technique. The encounter between God and man in the kingdom of the heart is therefore marked by an inexhaustible variety of patterns. There are spiritual masters in the Orthodox Church who say little or nothing about the Jesus Prayer. But, even if it enjoys no exclusive monopoly in the field of inner prayer, the Jesus Prayer has become for innumerable Eastern Christians over the centuries the standard path, the royal highway. And not for Eastern Christians only:[6] in the meeting between Orthodoxy and the West which has occurred over the past sixty years, probably no element in the Orthodox heritage has aroused such intense interest as the Jesus Prayer, and no single book has exercised a wider appeal than *The Way of a Pilgrim.* This enigmatic work, virtually unknown in pre-revolutionary Russia, has had a startling success in the non-Orthodox world and since the 1920s has appeared in a wide range of languages. Readers of J.D. Salinger will recall the impact of this "small pea-green cloth-bound book" on Franny.

Wherein, we ask, lies the distinctive appeal and effectiveness of the Jesus Prayer? Perhaps in four things above all: first, in its simplicity and flexibility; secondly, in its completeness; thirdly, in the power of the Name; and fourthly, in the spiritual discipline of persistent repetition. Let us take these points in order.

Simplicity and Flexibility

The invocation of the Name is a prayer of utmost simplicity, accessible to every Christian, but it leads at the same time to the deepest mysteries of contemplation. Anyone proposing to say the Jesus Prayer for lengthy periods of time each day undoubtedly stands in need of a *starets*, of an experienced spiritual guide. Such guides are extremely

---

[6] There existed, of course, a warm devotion to the Holy Name of Jesus in the medieval West, and not least in England. While this displays certain points of difference from the Byzantine tradition of the Jesus Prayer, there are also obvious parallels.

rare in our day. But those who have no personal contact with a *starets* may still practice the Prayer without any fear, so long as they do so only for limited periods—initially, for no more than ten or fifteen minutes at a time—and so long as they make no attempt to interfere with the natural rhythms of the body.

No specialized knowledge or training is required before commencing the Jesus Prayer. To the beginner it is sufficient to say: Simply begin. "In order to walk one must take a first step; in order to swim one must throw oneself into the water. It is the same with the invocation of the Name. Begin to pronounce it with adoration and love. Cling to it. Repeat it. Do not think that you are invoking the Name; think only of Jesus Himself. Say His Name slowly, softly and quietly."[7]

The outward form of the prayer is easily learnt. Basically it consists of the words "Lord Jesus Christ, Son of God, have mercy on me." There is, however, no strict uniformity. The verbal formula can be shortened: we can say "Lord Jesus Christ, have mercy on me," or "Lord Jesus," or even "Jesus" alone. Alternatively, the form of words may be expanded by adding "a sinner" at the end, thus underlining the penitential aspect. Sometimes an invocation of the Mother of God or the saints is inserted. The one essential and unvarying element is the inclusion of the divine Name "Jesus."

There is a similar flexibility as regards the outward circumstances in which the Prayer is recited. Two ways of using the Prayer can be distinguished, the "free" and the "formal." By the "free" use is meant the recitation of the Prayer as we are engaged in our usual activities throughout the day. It may be said, once or many times, in the scattered moments which otherwise would be spiritually wasted: when occupied with some familiar and semi-automatic task, such as dressing, washing up, mending socks, or digging in the garden; when walking or driving, when waiting in a bus queue or a traffic jam; in a moment of quiet before some especially painful or difficult interview; when unable to sleep, or before we have gained full consciousness on waking. Part of the distinctive value of the Jesus Prayer lies precisely in the fact that, because of its radical simplicity, it can be prayed in conditions of distraction when more complex forms of

[7] "A Monk of the Eastern Church" [Lev Gillet], *On the Invocation of the Name of Jesus* (The Fellowship of St. Alban and St. Sergius, London, 1950), pp. 5-6. (Reprinted by SLG Press, 1970, pp. 2-3.)

prayer are impossible. It is especially helpful in moments of tension and grave anxiety.

This "free" use of the Jesus Prayer enables us to bridge the gap between our explicit "times of prayer"—whether at church services or alone in our own room—and the normal activities of daily life. "Pray without ceasing," St. Paul insists (1 Thess. 5:17): but how is this possible, since we have many other things to do as well? Bishop Theophan indicates the true method in his maxim, "The hands at work, the mind and heart with God."[8] The Jesus Prayer, becoming by frequent repetition almost habitual and unconscious, helps us to stand in the presence of God wherever we are. So we become like Brother Lawrence, who "was more united with God during his ordinary activities than in religious exercises." "It is a great delusion," he remarked, "to imagine that prayer-time should be different from any other, for we are equally bound to be united to God by work at work-time as by prayer at prayer-time."[9]

The "free" recitation of the Jesus Prayer is complemented and strengthened by the "formal" use, when we concentrate our whole attention on the saying of the Prayer, to the exclusion of all external activity. Here, again, there are no rigid rules, but variety and flexibility. No particular posture is essential. In Orthodox practice the Prayer is most usually recited when seated, but it may also be said standing or kneeling—and even, in cases of bodily weakness and physical exhaustion, when lying down. It is normally recited in complete darkness or with the eyes closed, not with open eyes before an icon illuminated by candles or a votive lamp. *Starets* Silouan of Mount Athos (1866-1938), when saying the Prayer, used to stow his clock away in a cupboard so as not to hear it ticking, and then pull his thick woolen monastic cap over his eyes and ears.[10]

Darkness, however, can have a soporific effect! If we become drowsy as we sit or kneel reciting the Prayer, then we should stand up for a time. We may even make a prostration each time, touching the ground with our forehead. The Prayer may also be recited standing.

---

[8] *The Art of Prayer*, p. 92.

[9] Brother Lawrence of the Resurrection (1611-91), Barefooted Carmelite, *The Practice of the Presence of God*, ed. D. Attwater (Paraclete Books, London, 1962), pp. 13, 16.

[10] Archimandrite Sofrony, *The Undistorted Image: Staretz Silouan* (London, 1958), pp. 40-41.

A prayer-rope or rosary, normally with a hundred knots, is often employed in conjunction with the Prayer, not primarily in order to count the number of times it is repeated, but rather as an aid to concentration and the establishment of a regular rhythm. Quantitative measurement, whether with a prayer-rope or in other ways, is not encouraged. It is true that, in the early part of *The Way of a Pilgrim*, great emphasis is laid by the *starets* on the precise number of times that the Prayer is to be said daily. Possibly the point here is not the sheer quantity but the inward attitude of the Pilgrim: the *starets* wishes to test his obedience and readiness to fulfill an appointed rule without deviation. More typical is the advice of Bishop Theophan: "Do not trouble about the number of times you say the Prayer. Let this be your sole concern, that it should spring up in your heart with quickening power like a fountain of living water. Expel entirely from your mind all thoughts of quantity."

The Prayer is sometimes recited in groups, but more commonly alone; the words may be said aloud or silently. There should be nothing forced or labored in the recitation. The words should not be formed with excessive emphasis or inward violence, but the Prayer should be allowed to establish its own rhythm and accentuation, so that in time it comes to "sing" within us by virtue of its own intrinsic melody. *Starets* Parfenii of Kiev likened the flowing movement of the Prayer to a gently murmuring stream.[11]

From all this it can be seen that the invocation of the Name is a prayer for all seasons. It can be used by everyone, in every place and at every time. It is suitable for the "beginner" as well as the more experienced; it can be offered in company with others or alone; it is equally appropriate in the desert or the city, in surroundings of recollected tranquility or in the midst of the utmost noise and agitation. It is never out of place.

Completeness

Theologically, as the Russian Pilgrim rightly claims, the Jesus Prayer "holds in itself the whole gospel truth"; it is "a summary of the Gospels."[12] In one brief sentence it embodies the two chief mysteries

---

[11] *The Art of Prayer*, p. 110.

[12] *The Way of a Pilgrim*, tr. R.M. French (London, 1954), p. 29.

81

of the Christian faith, the Incarnation and the Trinity. It speaks, first, of the two natures of Christ the God-man (*Theanthropos*): of His humanity, for He is invoked by the human name, "Jesus," which His Mother Mary gave to Him after His birth in Bethlehem; of His eternal Godhead, for He is also styled "Lord" and "Son of God." In the second place, the Prayer speaks by implication, although not explicitly, of the three Persons of the Trinity. While addressed to the second Person, Jesus, it points also to the Father, for Jesus is called "Son of God"; and the Holy Spirit is equally present in the Prayer, for "no man can say 'Lord Jesus,' except in the Holy Spirit" (1 Cor. 12:3). So the Jesus Prayer is both Christocentric and Trinitarian.

Devotionally, it is no less comprehensive. It embraces the two chief "moments" of Christian devotion: the "moment" of adoration, of looking up to God's glory and reaching out to Him in love; and the "moment" of penitence, the sense of unworthiness and sin. There is a circular movement within the Prayer, a sequence of ascent and return. In the first half of the Prayer we rise up to God: "Lord Jesus Christ, Son of God . . ."; and then in the second half we return to ourselves in compunction: ". . . have mercy on me a sinner."

These two "moments"—the vision of divine glory and the consciousness of human sin—are united and reconciled in a third "moment" as we pronounce the word "mercy." "Mercy" denotes the bridging of the gulf between the righteousness of God and the fallen creation. He who says to God, "Have mercy," laments his own helplessness, but voices at the same time a cry of hope. The Jesus Prayer contains not only a call to repentance but an assurance of forgiveness and salvation. The heart of the Prayer—the actual name "Jesus"—bears precisely the sense of salvation: "Thou shalt call His name Jesus, for He shall save His people from their sins" (Matt. 1: 21).

Such are among the riches, both theological and devotional, present in the Jesus Prayer; present, moreover, not merely in the abstract but in a vivifying and dynamic form. The special value of the Jesus Prayer lies in the fact that it makes these truths come alive, so that they are apprehended not just externally and theoretically but with all the fullness of our being. To understand why the Jesus Prayer possesses such efficacy, we must turn to two further aspects: the power of the Name and the discipline of repetition.

The Power of the Name

"The Name of the Son of God is great and boundless, and upholds the entire universe." So it is affirmed in *The Shepherd of Hermas*,[13] nor shall we appreciate the role of the Jesus Prayer unless we feel some sense of the intrinsic power and virtue of the divine Name. If the Jesus Prayer is more effective than other invocations, this is because it contains the Name of God.

In the Old Testament, as in other ancient cultures, there is a virtual identity between a man's soul and his name. His whole personality, with all its peculiarities and all its energy, is present in his name. To know a person's name is to gain a definite insight into his nature, and thereby to acquire an established relationship with him—even, perhaps, a certain control over him. That is why the mysterious messenger who wrestles with Jacob at the ford Jabbok refuses to disclose his name (Gen. 32:29). The same attitude is reflected in the reply of the angel to Manoah, "Why askest thou thus after my name, seeing it is secret?" (Judg. 13:18). A change of name indicates a decisive change in a man's life, as when Abram becomes Abraham (Gen. 17:5), or Jacob becomes Israel (Gen. 32:28). In the same way, Saul after his conversion becomes Paul (Acts 13:9); and a monk at his profession is given a new name, usually not of his own choosing, to indicate the radical renewal which he undergoes.

In the Hebrew tradition, to do a thing *in the name* of another, or to *invoke* and *call upon his name*, are acts of the utmost weight and potency. To invoke a person's name is to make that person effectively present. Everything that is true of human names is true to an incomparably higher degree of the divine Name. The power and glory of God are present and active in His Name. The Name of God is *numen praesens*, God with us, *Emmanuel*. Attentively and deliberately to invoke God's Name is to place oneself in His presence, to open oneself to His energy, to offer oneself as an instrument and a living sacrifice in His hands. So keen was the sense of the majesty of the divine Name in later Judaism that the *tetragrammaton* was not pronounced aloud in the worship of the synagogue: the Name of the Most High was considered too devastating to be spoken.[14]

---

[13] *Similitudes*, ix, 14.

[14] For the veneration of the Name among medieval Jewish Kabbalists, see Gershom G. Scholem, *Major Trends in Jewish Mysticism* (3rd ed., London, 1955), pp. 132-3; and compare the treatment of this theme in the remarkable novel of Charles Williams, *All Hallows' Eve* (London, 1945).

This Hebraic understanding of the Name passes from the Old Testament into the New. Devils are cast out and men are healed through the Name of Jesus, for the Name is power. Once this potency of the Name is properly appreciated, many familiar passages acquire a fuller meaning and force: the clause in the Lord's Prayer, "Hallowed be Thy Name"; Christ's promise at the Last Supper, "Whatever you shall ask the Father in My Name, He will give it you" (John 16:23); His final command to the Apostles, "Go therefore, and teach all nations, baptizing them in the Name of the Father, and of the Son, and of the Holy Spirit" (Matt. 28:19); St. Peter's proclamation that there is salvation only in "the Name of Jesus Christ of Nazareth" (Acts 4:10-12); the words of St. Paul, "At the Name of Jesus every knee should bow" (Phil. 2:10); the new and secret name written on the white stone which is given to us in the Age to Come (Rev. 2:17).

It is this biblical reverence for the Name that forms the basis and foundation of the Jesus Prayer. God's Name is essentially linked with His Person, and so the Invocation of the divine Name possesses a genuinely sacramental character, serving as an effective sign of His invisible presence and action. For the believing Christian today, as in apostolic times, the Name of Jesus is power. In the words of the two Elders of Gaza, St. Barsanuphius and St. John (sixth century), "The remembrance of the Name of God utterly destroys all that is evil." "Flog your enemies with the Name of Jesus," urges St. John Climacus, "for there is no weapon more powerful in heaven or on earth. . . . Let the remembrance of Jesus be united to your every breath, and then you will know the value of stillness."[15]

The Name is power, but a purely mechanical repetition will by itself achieve nothing. As in all sacramental operations, man is required to co-operate with God through his active faith and ascetic effort. We are called to invoke the Name with recollection and inward vigilance, confining our minds within the words of the Prayer, conscious whom it is that we are addressing and who responds to us in our heart. St. Gregory of Sinai speaks repeatedly of the "constraint and labor" undergone by those who follow the Way of the Name; a "continual effort" is needed.

This faithful perseverance takes the form, above all, of attentive and frequent repetition. Christ told His disciples not to use

---

[15] *Ladder*, 21 and 27 (PG 88, 945C and 1112C).

"vain repetitions" (Matt. 6:7); but the repetition of the Jesus Prayer, when performed with inward sincerity and concentration, is most emphatically not "vain." The act of repeatedly invoking the Name has a double effect: it makes our prayer more unified and at the same time more inward.

Unification

As soon as we make a serious attempt to pray in spirit and in truth, at once we become acutely conscious of our inward disintegration, of our lack of unity and wholeness. In spite of all our efforts to stand before God, thoughts continue to move restlessly and aimlessly through our head, like the buzzing of flies (Bishop Theophan) or the capricious leaping of monkeys from branch to branch (Ramakrishna). To contemplate means, first of all, to be present where one is—to be *here* and *now*. But usually we find ourselves unable to restrain our mind from wandering at random over time and space. We recall the past, we anticipate the future, we plan what to do next; people and places come before us in unending succession. We lack the power to gather ourselves into the one place where we should be—*here*, in the presence of God; we are unable to live fully in the only moment of time that truly exists—*now*, the immediate present. This interior disintegration is one of the most tragic consequences of the Fall. The people who get things done, it has been justly observed, are the people who do one thing at a time. But to do one thing at a time is no mean achievement. While difficult enough in external work, it is harder still in the work of inward prayer.

What is to be done? How shall we learn to live in the present, in the eternal Now? How can we seize the *kairos*, the decisive moment, the moment of opportunity? It is precisely over this that the Jesus Prayer can help. The repeated invocation of the Name can bring us, by God's grace, from dividedness to unity, from dispersion and multiplicity to singleness. "To stop the continual jostling of your thoughts," says Bishop Theophan, "you must bind the mind with one thought, or the thought of One only."[16]

The ascetic Fathers distinguish two ways of combating thoughts. The first method is for the "strong" or the "perfect." These can

---

[16] *The Art of Prayer*, p. 97.

"contradict" their thoughts, that is, confront them face to face and repel them in direct battle. But for most of us such a method is too difficult and may, indeed, lead to positive harm. Direct confrontation, the attempt to uproot and expel thoughts by an effort of will, often serves merely to give greater strength to our imagination. Violently suppressed, our fantasies tend to return with increased force. Instead of fighting our thoughts directly and trying to eliminate them by an effort of will, it is wiser to turn aside and fix our attention elsewhere. Rather than gazing downwards into our turbulent imagination and concentrating on opposing our thoughts, we should look upwards to the Lord Jesus and entrust ourselves into His hands by invoking His Name; and the grace that acts through His Name will overcome the thoughts which we cannot obliterate by our own strength. Our spiritual strategy should be positive and not negative: instead of trying to empty our mind of what is evil, we should fill it with the thought of what is good. "Do not contradict the thoughts suggested by your enemies," advise Barsanuphius and John, "for that is exactly what they want and they will not cease from troubling you. But turn to the Lord for help against them, laying before Him your own powerlessness; for He is able to expel them and to reduce them to nothing."[17]

The Jesus Prayer, then, is a way of turning aside and looking elsewhere. Thoughts and images inevitably occur to us during prayer. We cannot stop their flow by a simple exertion of our will. It is of little or no value to say to ourselves, "Stop thinking"; we might as well say, "Stop breathing." "The rational mind cannot rest idle," says St. Mark the Monk; thoughts keep filling it with ceaseless chatter, as in the dawn chorus of birds. But while we cannot make this chatter suddenly disappear, what we can do is to detach ourselves from it by "binding" our ever-active mind "with one thought, or the thought of One only"—the Name of Jesus. In the words of St. Diadochus (fifth century), "When we have blocked all the outlets of the mind by means of the remembrance of God, then it requires of us at all costs some task which will satisfy its need of activity. Let us give it, then, as its sole activity the invocation *Lord Jesus . . .*"[18]

[17] *Questions and Answers*, ed. Sotirios Schoinas, 91; tr. L. Regnault and P. Lemaire, 166.

[18] *A Hundred Texts on Knowledge and Discernment*, 59 (ed. E. des Places, *Sources chretiennes*, 5bis [Paris, 1955]), p. 119.

"Through the remembrance of Jesus Christ," states Philotheos of Sinai (?ninth-tenth century), "gather together your disintegrated mind that is scattered abroad."[19] Instead, then, of trying to halt the *sequence* of thoughts through our own power, we *rely* on the power that acts through the Name.

According to Evagrius of Pontus (d. 399), "Prayer is a laying aside of thoughts."[20] *A laying aside*: not a savage conflict, not a furious repression, but a gentle yet persistent act of detachment. Through the repetition of the Name, we are helped to "lay aside," to "let go," our trivial or pernicious imaginings, and to replace them with the thought of Jesus. But, although the imagination and the discursive reasoning are not to be violently suppressed when saying the Jesus Prayer, they are certainly not to be actively encouraged. The Jesus Prayer is not a form of meditation upon specific incidents in the life of Christ, or upon some saying or parable in the Gospels; still less is it a way of reasoning and inwardly debating about some theological truth such as the meaning of *homoousios* or the Chalcedonian Definition.

As we invoke the Name, we should not deliberately shape in our minds any visual image of the Savior. This is one of the reasons why we say the Prayer in darkness, rather than with our eyes open in front of an icon. "Keep your mind free from colors, images and forms," urges St. Gregory of Sinai; beware of the imagination (*phantasia*) in prayer—otherwise you may find that you have become a *phantastes* instead of a *hesychastes*![21]

Inwardness

The repeated invocation of the Name, by making our prayer more unified, makes it at the same time more inward, more a part of ourselves—not something that we *do* at particular moments, but something that we *are* all the time; not an occasional act but a continuing state. Such praying becomes truly prayer of the *whole man*, in which the words and meaning of the prayer are fully identified with the one who prays. All this is well expressed by the late Paul Evdokimov

---

[19] *Chapters*, 27 (*Philokalia*, vol. ii [Athens, 1958], p. 283).

[20] *On Prayer*, 70 (PG 79, 1181C).

[21] *How the hesychast should persevere in prayer*, 7 (PG 150, 1340D).

(1901-70): "In the catacombs the image that recurs most frequently is the figure of a woman in prayer, the *Orans*. It represents the only true attitude of the human soul. It is not enough to *possess* prayer: we must *become* prayer—prayer incarnate. It is not enough to have moments of praise; our whole life, every act and every gesture, even a smile, must become a hymn of adoration, an offering, a prayer. We must offer not what we *have* but what we *are*."[22] That is what the world needs above all else: not people who *say* prayers with greater or less regularity, but people who *are* prayers.

The kind of prayer that Evdokimov is here describing may be defined more exactly as "prayer of the heart." In Orthodoxy, as in many other traditions, prayer is commonly distinguished into three categories, which are to be regarded as interpenetrating levels rather than successive stages: prayer of the lips (oral prayer); prayer of the mind (mental prayer); prayer of the heart (or of the mind in the heart). The invocation of the Name begins, like any other prayer, as an oral prayer, in which words are spoken by the tongue through a deliberate effort of will. At the same time, once more by a deliberate effort, we concentrate our mind upon the meaning of what the tongue says. In course of time and with the help of God our prayer grows more inward. The participation of the mind becomes more intense and spontaneous, while the sounds uttered by the tongue become less important; perhaps for a time they cease altogether and the Name is invoked silently, without any movement of the lips, by the mind alone. When this occurs, we have passed by God's grace from the first level to the second. Not that vocal invocation ceases altogether, for there will be times when even the most "advanced" in inward prayer will wish to call upon the Lord Jesus aloud. (And who, indeed, can claim to be "advanced"? We are all of us "beginners" in the things of the Spirit.)

But the journey inwards is not yet complete. A man is far more than his conscious mind; besides his brain and reasoning faculties there are his emotions and affections, his aesthetic sensitivity, together with the deep instinctive layers of his personality. All these have a function to perform in prayer, for the whole man is called to share in the total act of worship. Like a drop of ink that falls on blotting paper, the act of prayer should spread steadily outwards from the

---

[22] *Sacrement de l'amour. Le mystère conjugal à la lumière de la tradition orthodoxe* (Paris, 1962), p. 83.

conscious and reasoning center of the brain, until it embraces every part of ourselves.

In more technical terms, this means that we are called to advance from the second level to the third: from "prayer of the mind" to "prayer of the mind in the heart." "Heart" in this context is to be understood in the Semitic and biblical rather than the modern sense, as signifying not just the emotions and affections but the totality of the human person. The heart is the primary organ of man's being, the innermost man, "the very deepest and truest self, not attained except through sacrifice, through death."[23] According to Boris Vysheslavtsev, it is "the center not only of consciousness but of the unconscious, not only of the soul but of the spirit, not only of the spirit but of the body, not only of the comprehensible but of the incomprehensible; in one word, it is the absolute center."[24] Interpreted in this way, the heart is far more than a material organ in the body; the physical heart is an outward symbol of the boundless spiritual potentialities of the human creature, made in the image and likeness of God.

To accomplish the journey inwards and to attain true prayer, it is necessary to enter into this "absolute center," that is, to descend from the mind into the heart. More exactly, we are called to descend not from but *with* the mind. The aim is not just "prayer of the heart" but "prayer of the mind in the heart," for our conscious forms of understanding, including our reason, are a gift from God and are to be used in His service, not rejected. This "union of the mind with the heart" signifies the reintegration of man's fallen and fragmented nature, his restoration to original wholeness. Prayer of the heart is a return to Paradise, a reversal of the Fall, a recovery of the *status ante peccatum*. This means that it is an eschatological reality, a pledge and anticipation of the Age to Come—something which, in this present age, is never fully and entirely realized.

Those who, however imperfectly, have achieved some measure of "prayer of the heart," have begun to make the transition about which we spoke earlier—the transition from "strenuous" to "self-acting" prayer, from the prayer which I say to the prayer which "says

---

[23] Richard Kehoe, OP, "The Scriptures as Word of God," *The Eastern Churches Quarterly* viii (1947), supplementary issue on "Tradition and Scripture," p. 78.

[24] Quoted in John B. Dunlop, *Staretz Amvrosy: Model for Dostoevsky's Staretz Zossima* (Belmont, Mass., 1972), p. 22.

itself" or, rather, which Christ says in me. For the heart has a double significance in the spiritual life: it is both the center of man's being and the point of meeting between man and God. It is both the place of self-knowledge, where man sees himself as he truly is, and the place of self-transcendence, where man understands his nature as a temple of the Holy Trinity, where the image comes face to face with the Archetype. In the "inner chamber" of his own heart he finds the ground of his being and so crosses the mysterious frontier between the created and the Uncreated. "There are unfathomable depths within the heart," state the Macarian Homilies. ". . . God is there with the angels, light and life are there, the kingdom and the apostles, the heavenly cities and the treasures of grace: all things are there."[25]

Prayer of the heart, then, designates the point where "my" action, "my" prayer, becomes explicitly identified with the continuous action of Another in me. It is no longer prayer *to* Jesus but the prayer *of* Jesus Himself. This transition from "strenuous" to "self-acting" prayer is strikingly indicated in *The Way of a Pilgrim*: "Early one morning the Prayer woke me up as it were."[26]

Hitherto the Pilgrim has been "saying the Prayer"; now he finds that the Prayer "says itself," even when he is asleep, for it has become united to the prayer of God within him.

Readers of *The Way of a Pilgrim* may gain the impression that this passage from oral prayer to prayer of the heart is easily achieved, almost in a mechanical and automatic fashion. It needs to be emphasized that his experience, while not unique,[27] is altogether exceptional. More usually prayer of the heart comes, if at all, only after a lifetime of ascetic striving. It is the free gift of God, bestowed as and when He will, and not the inevitable effect of some technique. St. Isaac the Syrian (seventh century) underlines the extreme rarity of the gift when he says that "scarcely one in ten thousand" is counted worthy of the gift of pure prayer, and he adds: "As for the mystery

---

[25] *Hom.* xv, 32 and xliii, 7 (ed. Dörries/Klostermann/Kroeger [Berlin, 1964], pp. 146, 289).

[26] *The Way of a Pilgrim*, p. 14.

[27] *Starets* Silouan of Mount Athos had only been practicing the Jesus Prayer for three weeks before it descended into his heart and became unceasing. His biographer, Archimandrite Sofrony, rightly points out that this was a "sublime and rare gift"; not until later did Father Silouan come to appreciate how unusual it was (*The Undistorted Image*, p. 24).

that lies beyond pure prayer, there is scarcely to be found a single man in each generation who has drawn near to this knowledge of God's grace."[28] One in ten thousand, one in a generation: while sobered by this warning, we should not be unduly discouraged. The path to the inner kingdom lies open before all, and all alike may travel some way along it. In the present age, few experience with any fullness the deeper mysteries of the heart, but very many receive in a more humble and intermittent way true glimpses of what is signified by spiritual prayer.

The Journey's End

The aim of the Jesus Prayer, as of all Christian prayers, is that our praying should become increasingly identified with the prayer offered by Jesus the High Priest within us, that our life should become one with His life, our breathing with the Divine Breath that sustains the universe. The final objective may aptly be described by the Patristic term *theosis*, "deification" or "divinization." In the words of Archpriest Sergei Bulgakov, "The Name of Jesus, present in the human heart, confers upon it the power of deification." "The Logos became man," says St. Athanasius, "that we might become god." He who is God by nature took our humanity, that we men might share by grace in His divinity, becoming "partakers of the divine nature" (2 Peter 1:4). The Jesus Prayer, addressed to the Logos Incarnate, is a means of realizing within ourselves this mystery of *theosis*, whereby man attains to the true likeness of God.

The Jesus Prayer, by uniting us to Christ, helps us to share in the mutual indwelling or *perichoresis* of the three Persons of the Holy Trinity. The more the Prayer becomes a part of ourselves, the more we enter into the movement of love which passes unceasingly between Father, Son, and Holy Spirit. In the Hesychast tradition, the mystery of *theosis* has most often taken the outward form of a vision of light. This light which the saints behold in prayer is neither a symbolical light of the intellect, nor yet a physical and created light of the senses. It is nothing less than the divine and uncreated Light of the Godhead, which shone from Christ at His Transfiguration on Mount Tabor and which will illuminate the whole world at His second coming on the Last Day. Here is a characteristic passage on the Divine Light taken

---

[28] *Mystic Treatises by Isaac of Nineveh*, translated by A.J. Wensinck (Amsterdam, 1923), p. 113.

from St. Gregory Palamas. He is describing the Apostle's vision when he was caught up into the third heaven (2 Cor. 12:2-4): "Paul saw a light without limits below or above or to the sides; he saw no limit whatever to the light that appeared to him and shone around him, but it was like a sun infinitely brighter and vaster than the universe; and in the midst of this sun he himself stood, having become nothing but eye."[29] Such is the vision of glory to which we may approach through the invocation of the Name.

The Jesus Prayer causes the brightness of the Transfiguration to penetrate into every corner of our life. Constant repetition has two effects upon the anonymous author of *The Way of a Pilgrim*. First, it transforms his relationship with the material creation around him, making all things transparent, changing them into a sacrament of God's presence. He writes: "When I prayed with my heart, everything around me seemed delightful and marvelous. The trees, the grass, the birds, the earth, the air, the light seemed to be telling me that they existed for man's sake, that they witnessed to the love of God for man, that everything proved the love of God for man, that all things prayed to God and sang His praise. Thus it was that I came to understand what *The Philokalia* calls 'the knowledge of the speech of all creatures'. . . . I felt a burning love for Jesus Christ and for all God's creatures."[30] In the words of Father Bulgakov, "Shining through the heart, the light of the Name of Jesus illuminates all the universe."[31]

In the second place, the Prayer transfigured the Pilgrim's relation not only with the material creation but with other men. "Again I started off on my wanderings. But now I did not walk along as before, filled with care. The invocation of the Name of Jesus gladdened my way. Everybody was kind to me, it was as though everyone loved me. . . . If anyone harms me I have only to think, 'How sweet is the Prayer of Jesus!' and the injury and the anger alike pass away and I forget it all."[32] "Inasmuch as you have done it unto one of the least of these My brethren, you have done it unto Me" (Matt. 25:40): the Jesus Prayer helps us to see Christ in all men, and all men in Christ. The

---

[29] *Triads in Defense of the Holy Hesychasts*, I, iii, 21 (ed. Meyendorff, vol. i, p. 157).

[30] *The Way of a Pilgrim*, pp. 31-2, 41.

[31] *The Orthodox Church*, p. 171.

[32] *The Way of a Pilgrim*, pp. 17-18.

Jesus Prayer, therefore, is not escapist and world-denying but, on the contrary, intensely affirmative. It does not imply a rejection of God's creation, but the reassertion of the ultimate value of everything and everyone in God.

"Prayer is action; to pray is to be highly effective."[33] Of no prayer is this more true than of the Jesus Prayer. While it is singled out for particular mention in the office of monastic profession as a prayer for monks and nuns,[34] it is equally a prayer for laymen, for married couples, for doctors and psychiatrists, for social workers and bus conductors. The invocation of the Name, practiced aright, involves each one more deeply in his or her appointed task, making each more efficient in his actions, not cutting him off from others but linking him to them, rendering him sensitive to their fears and anxieties in a way that he never was before. The Jesus Prayer makes each into a "man for others," a living instrument of God's peace, a dynamic center of reconciliation.

---

[33] Tito Colliander, *The Way of the Ascetics*, p. 71.

[34] At the clothing of a monk, in both the Greek and the Russian practice, it is the custom to give him a prayer-rope. In the Russian use the abbot says the following as it is handed over: "Take, brother, the sword of the Spirit, which is the Word of God, for continual prayer to Jesus; for you must always have the Name of the Lord Jesus in mind, in heart, and on your lips, ever saying: Lord Jesus Christ, Son of God, have mercy on me a sinner." See N.F. Robinson, SSJE, *Monasticism in the Orthodox Churches* (London/Milwaukee, 1916), pp. 159-60. Note the usual distinction between the three levels of prayer: lips, mind, heart.

THE ROSARY AS SPIRITUAL WAY

Jean Hani

For a majority of today's Christians there is an undeniable disaffection with and, at times, even a disdain for the saying of the Rosary. The reason is that, over the years, whether through neglect or ignorance, its true meaning and import have tended to be so obscured as to become—at least in appearance, for the Rosary itself remains what it always has been—an anodyne devotion and—a supreme disqualification for the modern mind—outdated. Thus one of their more powerful ritual means is lost sight of and, in fact, withdrawn from Christians. But the practice of the Rosary constitutes, and there should be no hesitation here, an authentic way to spiritual realization; it is actually based, as we shall see, on that which is the essential operative exercise of all ways.[1]

The object utilized, a rosary or chaplet, is basically nothing but a "prayer-counter." And yet, like every traditional instrument, it possesses a symbolic meaning to be shown later. Its simplest form is a cord fashioned with as many small knots as one likes to count prayers. Wherever there are "repetitive" prayers, there are rosaries or chaplets for this use. I know of a Brahman chaplet, the *aksha-mala*, upon which is repeated the sacred formula *AUM* or a litany of divine names, the names of Vishnu for example; Buddhists recite, upon a chaplet of 108 beads, the formula *Namomitabhaya Budhaya* (in Japan *Namu Amida Butsu*), which means: "Hail to Amida Buddha." In Islam there are two types of chaplets, both formed of 99 beads. A chaplet of the first type has three series of 33 beads; for the first series one says: *Subhan Allah*, "Glory to God," for the second: *al-hamdu li'Llah*, "God is praiseworthy," and for the third: *Allahu akbar*, "God is great." With the second type one recites in sequence the litany of the 99 divine Names: the Compassionate, the Merciful, the King, the Holy One, the Peacemaker, the Powerful, the Creator, etc.

---

[1] Essential pages on this subject are those of Frithjof Schuon, *Gnosis, Divine Wisdom*, 2nd ed., trans. G. E. H. Palmer (Pates Manor, Bedfont: Perennial Books Ltd., 1990), pp. 118-23. Then read François Chenique's fine book *Le Buisson ardent, Essai sur la métaphysique de la Vierge* (Paris: La pensée universelle, 1972), its last chapter in particular.

For Christianity, the origin of the chaplet goes far back in time. The Greek chaplet, which is called a *kombologion*, a word composed of *logos*, "word," and *kombos*, "knot," goes back to St Pachomius and St Basil. In the West the names "chaplet," which means "little hat," and "rosary," "rose garden," date from the Middle Ages; at origin, they designate the crown or hat of roses worn in certain processions of the Virgin, and relate to the custom of plucking roses while reciting the *Ave*, or to the custom of crowning statues of the Virgin. The chaplet of the Christian East numbers 100 beads upon which are recited the formula "Lord Jesus Christ, Son of God, have mercy on me" or simply "Jesus."

The recitation of the chaplet constitutes a prayer of a particular nature, that of repetitive prayer, which is defined by these two basic elements: the divine Name, either alone or enshrined in a formula, and the rhythmic repetition of this Name; correlatively, but as a natural and almost indispensable consequence, a meditational activity is added.

The first element, which is also the essential one, is the divine Name. Chaplet prayer can be defined as an invocation of the divine Name. By this very fact it is to be distinguished from prayer as understood in the current sense, namely asking or petitionary prayer. It in fact goes back to the category of incantation, which also emphasizes, as we shall see, the repetitive aspect. Incantation follows a movement that differs from ordinary asking prayer; the latter calls out to the grace from On High to descend upon the one praying with a view to obtain a clearly defined object, whether temporal or spiritual. Incantation is itself somewhat like the prayer of praise, an uplifting movement of the soul towards God with an intent to also praise, but equally and above all with a meditative intent, with a view to the soul's union with God. It is an aspiration of the being toward the universal to obtain a quite spiritual grace, and therefore an interior illumination. It is also a quite interior labor, but one most often expressed by words which serve it as support and have been formed, in the vast majority of cases, as I have said, by a formula enshrining a divine Name, called a *mantra* in India. I use this word intentionally, a word that has no corresponding term among Western languages, for it has a very precise significance by likewise including within itself the idea of a rhythmic repetition.

The essential element of this prayer is therefore the divine Name itself, so much so that it is often reduced to the pronunciation of this

Name. This Name actually has an unlimited power, for it is identical to God Himself. In fact, as Meister Eckhart says, "the Father neither sees, nor hears, nor speaks, nor wishes anything but His own Name. It is by means of His Name that the Father sees, hears, and manifests Himself. The Name contains all things. Essence of the Divinity, it is the Father Himself. . . ."[2] Under these conditions we see the whole import and efficacy of the divine Name, that which is called the "remembrance of God" and the "remembrance of His Name" so often mentioned in the Psalms: "The sufficient reason for the invocation of the Name," writes Frithjof Schuon,

> is the remembering of God; and this, in the final analysis, is not other than consciousness of the Absolute. The Name actualizes this consciousness and, in the end, perpetuates it in the soul and fixes it in the heart, so that it penetrates the whole being and at the same time transmutes and absorbs it. Consciousness of the Absolute is the prerogative of the human intelligence, and also its aim.[3]

Meister Eckhart will also add, shortly after his lines cited above: "The Father gives thee His eternal Name, and it is His own life, His being, and His divinity that He gives thee in one single instant by His Name."

In the recitation of the chaplet the divine Name is invoked under two different forms in the *Pater* and the *Ave*, that is to say in revealed prayers. This is of prime importance, for revealed names and formulas are laden with a power those invented by man cannot possesses naturally. In the *Pater* the formula is "Hallowed be Thy Name!" ("hallowed" in the biblical sense, that is "proclaimed holy"); in the *Ave* the Name is that of Jesus and the first part, the only revealed part, constitutes the basic formula, for the second part, comprised of an asking prayer, is an addition made rather late in the Middle Ages. Its first part is composed of the salutation of the angel Gabriel, which amounts to saying that it is pronounced by God: "Hail Mary, full of grace, the Lord is with thee" (Luke 1:28) and the salutation addressed to the Virgin by her cousin Elizabeth: "Blessed art thou amongst women, and blessed is the fruit of thy womb Jesus" (Luke 1:42); a salutation that can also

---

[2] Meister Eckhart, *Commentary on the Gospel of John*, cited by Frithjof Schuon, *Stations of Wisdom* (Bloomington: World Wisdom Books, 1995), p. 128.

[3] *Stations of Wisdom*, p. 127.

be said to be addressed by God, since, when Elizabeth pronounces it, she is, the Gospel tells us, "filled with the Holy Spirit."

The name of Jesus in Hebrew—*Yeshou'a* for *Yehoshou'a*—clearly means "Savior"; but if we examine the way that it is written, where, as we know, only consonants and semi-consonants appear, we have YHShW'(a) and immediately we see that this word secretly contains the divine Name YH, pronounced *Yah*, which we will soon encounter again and which is the first element and the basis for the great divine Name YHWH. All Christians pronounce it, often unawares, when they sing *Alleluia*, that is to say *Hallelu-Yah*, "Praise ye the Lord."

On the other hand and of capital importance there is the Name of Mary in the *Ave*. But let me immediately point out that, although the two names, Jesus and Mary, have been placed by the Church in the definitive text of the *Ave*, they have been in truth reinserted, for they are to be found in the same Gospel context, Mary one line before and Jesus a few lines later (Luke 1:28 and 31). The fact that they were reinserted for recitation—not without inspiration from On High—shows the great importance that the Church attaches to the invocation of the Name. A variety of interpretations have been given to the name of Mary; according to some, it would have had a reverential meaning, that of "Lady"; according to St Jerome it meant *stella maris*, "star of the sea,"[4] adopted by the Latin liturgy in the hymn *Ave maris stella*. But these meanings are not its most important one. Its most important meaning lies hidden and revealed at one and the same time by the manner in which it is written in Hebrew. In Hebrew this name is not Mary but *Mariam*, which was retained intact in the Greek of St Luke (1:28 and 30), and it is a pity that this manner of writing her name was thereafter neglected, for its already mentioned secret sense only becomes apparent in the Hebrew form. Mariam, in Hebrew, is written MRIM, since vowels are omitted (I or Y is a semi-consonant). The word itself is divided up in this way: MIM on the one hand and R on the other. By articulating the vowel A in the first component, we obtain *Maim*, which means "the waters." The M (mem) is the hierogram for universal passivity, pure receptivity, symbolized by water and the waters in Jewish cosmogony, as elsewhere in nearly all traditions; the I or Y (yod) is the hierogram for divine activity, the principle of manifested activity, and the R (resh) the deployment of energy, energy in motion. The Hebrew character corresponding to R was, originally,

---

[4] St Jerome, *Nomina Hebraica*, s.v.

the hieroglyph of a serpent raised to strike forward. Thus the name MaRIaM is nothing less than a translation of the creative act: RI is the *ad extra* emission of the divine creative energy which is unleashed on cosmic Substance, that is to say on the totality of potentialities and their receptive surroundings, represented by the primordial Waters as brought out in the first verses of Genesis: "The Spirit of God was moving over the face of the waters." And so the Name of Mary is, in its way, a divine Name, one connected with the *ad extra* divine activity, which means that Mary is a manifestation of what this divine Name represents. Jean Borella has given an excellent description of this mystery which is that of the Immaculate Conception: Mary is the human manifestation of universal Possibility, that is to say, on the highest level, a conception of the divine Essence, a conception *per force* "immaculate," and with which the Virgin is identified, as she herself has proclaimed to Bernadette. At the level of Being, universal Possibility becomes universal Substance (*Prakriti*), the *Materia prima* or "universal Mother" out of which unfold the possibilities of manifestation under the activity of the divine Spirit (*Purusha*); at the cosmic level, this is the Spirit of God upon the primordial Waters (a "maternal" symbol); at the primal human level, it is the couple Adam-Eve, the primordial androgyne, and, at the present human level, man and woman.

The conception of God Incarnate, the earthly manifestation of the divine Word, the archetype of Creation and the Universal Man, could not have happened according to any other process than that of Creation itself. This is why the Mother of God Incarnate could not herself be anything other than the human manifestation of the All-Possibility and universal Substance, the universal Mother and *Materia prima* quickened, like the primordial Waters, by the divine Spirit.[5]

In this respect it is remarkable that the words of the angel Gabriel: "The Holy Spirit will come upon thee and the power of the Most High will overshadow thee" (Luke 1:35) is almost a carbon copy of the Genesis text: "The Spirit of God covered the waters with his shadow." I have modified the usual translation, for the term used by the angel (*episkiasei*) has the sense of "to cover," with the connotation of "incubate" or "fecundate," just like the verb *merakhepheth* in the text of Moses, a verb inexactly translated by "hovered." The complete verse is: *rouah elohim merakhepheth' al phenel ha-maim.*

[5] Jean Borella, *La Charité profanée* (Bouère, France: Ed. Dominique Martin Morin, 1979), pp. 341-53; also see: Abbé Henri Stéphane, *Introduction à l'ésotérisme chrétien*, t. 1 (Paris: Dervy Livres, 1979), pp. 89-100.

It is at the level of the God-Man, the Universal Man, that the "mystery of the Virgin Mother" takes root. But there, by the same token, the mystery of fallen man's reintegration also takes root; fallen man: he who, on his own behalf, should live the "mystery of the Virgin." Actually, to rediscover its eternal archetype, its "principial possibility" and its purest reality *in divinis*, manifested being has to realize within itself this "mystery of the Virgin"; All-Possibility is a manifested being's exemption from all limit, enabling it to rediscover the Purity, Beauty, Poverty, and Goodness, the principal qualities of the Virgin in her primordial indifferentiation, those qualities which have shone with such brightness in her earthly manifestation. In this return to the archetype, the "mystery of Redemption" or "spiritual regeneration," the couple "Spirit/Virgin Mary," or again "New Adam/New Eve," or "Christ/Church" makes its appearance, a couple presiding over this new birth, as do Adam and Eve over ordinary birth. By this we see how such titles given to Mary as "co-redemptrix," "mediatrix of graces," and "mother of men" are to be explained.

To enter into this process of reintegration, the task set before the individual soul is a self-transformation identifying it with the universal Soul, for the Holy Spirit can act only in that soul which participates in the qualities of Substance, as in the pattern of the Incarnation.[6] This kind of spiritual alchemy is effected by the Sacraments and contemplation. And with this we return to our line of thought on prayer and incantation, the role of which is to create in the soul a state of total submission, a state of ontological plasticity which puts the soul in harmony with the Virgin and her virtues.

Such is the goal of reciting the Rosary. During this exercise the soul, as Frithjof Schuon remarks, applies to itself the angel's words to Mary; it identifies itself with the virginal womb in order to become a place for the generation of the Word within itself. To the extent that the soul is identified with the Virgin, the microcosmic mystery of the Incarnation is accomplished within it. The repetition of the angel's words ends up transforming the soul into its virginal archetype.[7] Actually the words of the incantation are pronounced by God, and their power is such that, when Mary gives her consent, that is to say acquiesces to their meaning, she conceives. The divine Name is the

---

[6] Henri Stéphane, *ibid.*, p. 52 seq.

[7] *Ibid.*, pp. 97-8.

vehicle of grace, making real a presence in the soul which is a power for transformation.

To those who would object that this is just autosuggestion, I reply that it is nothing of the sort, for no purely personal act of imagination is involved here. This exercise is performed within the framework of the Church and is only effected by divine grace; and yet our mental activity does have a role to play: by picturing to oneself the virginal condition, we create a psychic ambiance conducive to the activity of grace, we approach the envisaged state by somehow infusing its Marian image into ourselves. Also, let me hasten to describe in what spirit anyone who recites the Rosary should apply the words of the angel, that is to say God, to himself. This involves what I would like to call a "prophetic affirmation" in which we affirm, "by anticipation," that what should be realized is realized, somehow compelling it, with God's help, to be realized. This is a method to be found in all spiritual ways: hence, in Hindu incantatory practice, the repetition of the *mantra* "I am That" proceeds in the same fashion. We can see, then, how appropriate it is to recite with sentiments of profound humility and self-detachment. This is no doubt also why, so as to avoid any premature conviction in anyone who recites, the Church has added, after the angelic salutation, the prayer of the *Ave*'s second part in which the individual confesses himself a "sinner," a term which refers, not so much to a particular state of culpability, but to that of "creature" and "creaturely nothingness."

In his invaluable book on the Virgin, François Chenique has developed a meditation arising from the words of the *Ave Maria*. By the initial salutation, he says, the soul enters into a relationship with the Virgin, the manifestation of universal Substance. The soul's desire is to realize Mary's perfections and the very Name of Mary acts in this direction; the expression "full of grace" refers to the Immaculate Conception, who is necessarily filled with divine grace, and the soul asks to receive this grace. "The Lord is with thee" reminds us that God is always with Mary because He is always present in universal Substance, it being a given that He acts through it and within it to make it produce; God will be likewise present in the soul which conforms itself, as an individual substance, to the qualities of universal Substance from which it was separated by the Fall. "Blessed are you amongst women" because the Woman is a manifestation of Substance and Mary, the preeminent Woman, the New Eve, is so to an altogether superior degree; therefore she is *per force* blessed, and likewise the soul will be blessed if the divine image is reestablished in it, for it is God who is blessed and blesses, as is affirmed in the last formula: "and blessed is the fruit of thy womb, Jesus." Substance quickened by the divine presence of the Spirit, engenders a blessed fruit; and likewise the virginalized soul will engender within itself the image of the Word. Thus, through Mary's Name, the *Ave* attunes us to the universal Mother and her virginal qualities; the soul becomes virgin and God can be reflected therein. After this the Name of Jesus actualizes the Christic qualities within us.[8]

We see by this that the saying of the Rosary is not just one devotion among other more or less anodyne devotions; it is as Frithjof Schuon has stated, "the Jesus Prayer of the Western Church." And so we begin to understand the importance given to the two Names "Jesus-Mary," an invocation often mentioned in numerous mystical writings, but whose vast import is not always perceived. It constitutes an authentic *mantra* and could, by itself alone, play the same role as the *Ave* of which it is both core and compendium.

The efficacy of saying the Rosary rests essentially in the operative virtue of these divine Names. However, it would be wrong to consider the form of recitation secondary, namely the repetitive form which, without being essential, is nonetheless vital. Besides and as already mentioned, it is common to all analogous recitations contained in the category of what is called *japa yoga* or *mantra yoga*, the first designation rightly signifies "yoga by repetition," that is the repetition of sacred formulas on a chaplet; hence this definition already shows the importance of this repetitiveness since it is associated with the very word "yoga" which means "union," indicating that this union is effected somewhat at least through repetition.

What is more, I should hasten to say that, without repetition, there is no incantation, this last term implying, besides the invocation of the Name, the idea of the conditioning of the psychism, making it apt for receiving a spiritual influence from On High. Now it is precisely the role of repetition which can be traditionally referred back to the prayer of the "importunate widow" of the Gospel parable. Repetition constitutes a salutary automatism in as much as a discipline imposed with words and gestures; its regular rhythm channels the feelings,

---

[8] François Chenique, *op. cit.*, p. 148.

reduces mental dispersion, facilitates attention, recollection, and concentration, thus creating the ambiance needed for receiving spiritual energy. It is also a kind of "rumination" of the words of prayer, a rumination which facilitates their total absorption.

Rhythm has a major role to play in this. I no longer remember who, but someone has compared the repetitive movement of incantation in the Rosary to that of a spiral, the variable elements being situated on the outside, on the turns of the spiral, while the divine Names are identical to the immobile axis around which the spiral fans out.

But we need to go even further. If we consider, not only the saying of the *Aves* themselves, but the saying of the entire chaplet, we notice that its rhythm is profoundly structured by a quite significant number symbolism. And yet what is so surprising in that? The Rosary, as is known, has a supernatural origin and God creates everything "with number, measure, and weight" (Wisd. of Sol. 11:20) and He has even "numbered wisdom" (Eccl. 10:9).

The chaplet is built upon a combination of the numbers 1, 2, 3, 5 and 10.[9] The small "stem" which carries the cross is formed by a 1-3-1 design (1 *Pater*, 3 *Aves*, 1 *Pater*) which symbolizes the divine Unity, the divine Trinity and the return to Unity on the one hand, and, on the other, the evolving of the world from the Creation: the 3, symbol of the ternary of evolution, signifies then the binary, the division of unity, and the return to this unity $(1 \rightarrow 2 + 1)$, which means that everything should return to God, from whom everything has issued forth, after the cycle of evolution.

This symbolism is also that of the decades and ultimately, as we shall see, that of the entire Rosary. The numerical design of the decade is 1-10: 1, divine Unity, and 10, the perfection of the created at the climax of its evolution; the 10 is even called "multiple unity," that is to say the deployment of unity. This is the Pythagorean decad, at the root of which is the famous Tetraktys (the sum of the first four numbers: $1 + 2 + 3 + 4$). What we have here is the sign of the return to the One once evolution has been accomplished.

The 10 is repeated 5 times to form the chaplet: $10 \times 5 = 50$. Five is a cipher for man (earthly man), and 10×5 is a repetition of the idea of evolution and return to unity, evoking the state of the "perfect man"

[9] On this subject see the small book by the Abbé E. Bertaud, *Études de symbolisme dans le culte de la Vierge*, 1947, pp. 33-63.

(Eph. 4:16) toward whom the reciter of the Rosary should tend. At the same time the number of 50 *Aves* refers to Pentecost (the Feast 50 days after Easter), that is to say the union of the Virgin with the Holy Spirit and once again, by way of consequence, perfection, the union of the soul with the Spirit, obtained by Mary the Pneumatophore.

Lastly, the Rosary is comprised of 15 (10 + 5) decades and 150 (15 x 10) *Aves.* The 15, which plays here the primary role, possesses an altogether exceptional value, for it represents nothing less than the divine Name *Yah*, the first element, as already mentioned, of the great Name Yahweh; 15 is in fact the numerical value of the two letters which form this Name: Y (= 10) and H (= 5). This means that the divine Name is mysteriously enclosed in the saying of the Rosary, but also that, ritually and however indirectly, it is invoked by whoever recites it.

To close, notice that, if we add to the 150 *Aves* of the decades the 3 beginning *Aves*, we obtain the number 153 which is surely counted as among the most important for Christianity, since it is the number of fishes in the miraculous catch (John 21:1-14). A long discussion by St Augustine in his 122nd treatise on St John's Gospel, a discussion I have alluded to elsewhere, shows that this number was the sign of the regeneration of men by the Spirit of Jesus.[10] This regeneration is even signified by the very name of the Rosary, a name derived from "rose" which is a symbol of knowledge, of Christian initiation, and of Mary herself, whom the Latin liturgy has compared to this flower: "She is like a rose planted beside the water courses," chants the Office of the Virgin, and the litanies name her *Rosa mystica*.[11]

Not only do numbers make the Rosary a symbol of Creation in its dual movement of issuing from God and returning to Him. This symbolism is also connected to the chaplet's very form, composed as it is of small spheres—the beads arranged in a circle upon the string that holds them. René Guénon has aptly described this symbolism by referring to the Hindu text which defines the meaning of every kind of chaplet. This text is drawn from the *Bhagavad Gita* (VII, 7) where Krishna, who is here the supreme God (*Atma*), says: "Upon Me (*Atma*) all things have been strung like a row of pearls on a thread." Here we have the *sutratma*, that is to say *Atma* seen as the "thread" which penetrates and binds all beings and all worlds to each other, at the same

[10] Jean Hani, *La Divine Liturgie*, pp. 115-6.

[11] St Peter Damian called Mary the "Rose of Paradise." On this question see M. Gorce,

time that it is the "breath" which causes them to subsist. Each world, each state of existence can be represented by a sphere traversed by this thread so as to form an axis joining together the poles of this sphere. The "chain of worlds" would be, then, a series of spheres threaded like pearls on a necklace; this "chain" is generally depicted as circular in shape, each world being a cycle and the whole chain the cycle of cycles. The chaplet is a symbol of this "chain of the worlds," a symbol where the thread is ultimately the essential component since it represents Divinity. Nor is this symbolism without rapport to "breath" (*atma*): the formula pronounced over each bead corresponds in principle to a kind of respiration. Now respiration includes two phases which symbolize the production and reabsorption of a world; the interval between two respirations, the passage from one bead to the following one, is a silence which symbolizes *pralaya* or a state of emptiness between two universal manifestations.[12]

Thus the chaplet, a static cosmic symbol in its basic form, becomes, by recitation, a dynamic one, the latter being punctuated by those significant numbers analyzed above; and this remark brings us to the just alluded to image of the spiral, another version of the chaplet's circular symbolism, a version in which the different circles or spirals described correspond to the spherical beads and the immobile axis with the thread or *sutratma*. These two symbols are so much the more congruent since the spiral in question is one of the most remarkable representations of the totality of creation's universal vortex starting with the divine Principle.[13]

And so we see what an extraordinary substructure for invocation, if we can call it that, the instrument of the chaplet represents. Through its dual symbolism it places whoever recites it in rapport with the entire universe, with the movement of the entirety of divine Creation into which whoever recites it is integrated; it "immerses" us, so to say, in the divine process that sustains the world, reconciling

La Rosaire et ses antécédents historiques, Paris, 1931 (summarized in his edition of *Roman de la Rose* (the initiatic meaning of which is well known), Paris, 1933, p. 30.

[12] René Guénon, "The Chain of the Worlds," in *Fundamental Symbols* (Bartlow, Cambridge: Quinta Essentia, 1995), pp. 249-56, who also points out that the number of beads, 108 in the Buddhist chaplet and 99 in the Muslim chaplet, are cyclic numbers and expressions of the cycle of cycles.

[13] On this subject see Matgioi, *La Voie métaphysique*, 1936, p. 94 ff., referred to and developed by René Guénon in *The Symbolism of the Cross*, pp. 141-4.

the rhythm of the individual soul with the rhythm of the "Soul of the World," to borrow a Platonic expression, that Soul where the creating Word resonates, and finally takes him up into that ascensional movement which mounts from multiplicity to Unity.

The recitation of the *Aves* with this just described sacred rhythm should already be quite enough to make of the Rosary a "spiritual way." Western tradition has, however, since its very beginnings enriched it even more by proposing, for each decade, a supplementary meditation having to do with what is called the "Mysteries of the Virgin": the "Joyful Mysteries" for the first chaplet, the "Sorrowful" for the second, and the "Glorious" for the third. Although well known, I will list them so as to facilitate an understanding of what I am saying:

1. The Joyful Mysteries: Annunciation, Visitation, Nativity, Presentation in the Temple, and Finding in the Temple.

2. The Sorrowful Mysteries: Agony in the Garden, Scourging at the Pillar, Crowning with Thorns, Carrying of the Cross, and Crucifixion.

3. The Glorious Mysteries: Resurrection, Ascension, Pentecost, Assumption of the Blessed Virgin, and the Coronation of the Blessed Virgin in Heaven.

These "mysteries" are stages in the life of the Blessed Virgin; but this life is the model for the life of the Christian who therefore has to follow these stages, which are like so many spiritual "stations"; for "the Blessed Virgin," as Jean Borella has written, "the symbol and prototype of the human soul, is that pure mirror where God can be reflected, the 'Mirror of Justice' which is also the 'Gate of Heaven.'"[14] These "mysteries" are in fact contained in the two Names of Jesus and Mary, and their meditation accompanies the invoking of these Names, a meditation which displays, so to speak, the inner riches of these Names before the eyes of the soul. Meditation and invocation mutually sustain each other: thus the soul tends to "realize" the mysteries of that which should be its own spiritual life from beginning to end.

François Chenique, in his previously cited book, gives an excellent commentary on these Mysteries of the Rosary, which I will summarize very briefly. In the Joyful Mysteries, he says, the soul opens itself to

---

[14] Jean Borella, *op. cit.*, p. 145.

the Divine: in the Annunciation, it receives the seed of the Word; in the Visitation, it focuses itself on the divine presence and acts in conformity with it;[15] in the Nativity, the soul gives birth to the Word and expresses it. The Blessed Virgin, writes Frithjof Schuon in this connection, has the Word issue from her womb, while the one reciting utters it through the formula by which the Word became incarnate.[16] In the Presentation, the soul declares itself subject to the exterior law, a precondition for any realization of the spiritual order; in the Finding, we find the joy of God in the temple of our heart. The Sorrowful Mysteries recall the Incarnate Word's tribulations, in which the Blessed Virgin has participated directly and which we ourselves should personally traverse, following Christ and Mary. For God to grow in us so that we might be resurrected, we have to "scourge" our very self, "crown it with thorns," so that we make it "carry the cross," and finally "crucify" it, put to death the "old man." Françoise Chenique has rightly stated that this involves what Islamic mysticism calls "extinction" (*al-fana*).[17] The Glorious Mysteries describe the soul's transformation. In the Resurrection, the "mortified" soul is revivified after its "extinction" and rediscovers true life; in the Ascension, it is raised aloft, leaves the created to be united with the divine nature; with Pentecost it is deified by the power of the Holy Spirit; in the Assumption it is, like Mary, elevated through "all the heavens," that is to say through the superior states of being, and finally, in the Coronation, it attains to Divinity within which it becomes "that which it is" for all eternity, the divine aspect from which it had been separated, its archetype.[18]

This meditation on the Mysteries, which is a traversing of the stations of the spiritual way, can be unfolded according to different formal modalities, while remaining, quite naturally, identical in its depths.

---

[15] Jean Borella writes (*ibid.*, pp. 415-7), in connection with the Visitation, that it is as if a second Annunciation and contains the *mysterium caritatis*: the Blessed Virgin transmits to the world, in the person of Elizabeth, the divine Word.

[16] Cited by François Chenique, *op. cit.*, p. 162.

[17] Jean Borella, *op. cit.*, p. 382, relates the Crowning with Thorns to the death of reason, the Carrying of the Cross to the death of the will, and the Crucifixion to the death of the body (the "flesh").

[18] François Chenique, *op. cit.*, pp.161-3 and 178-84.

THE VIRGIN

James S. Cutsinger

The cause of what preceded her, the protectress of what came after her, and the patroness of things eternal.—St Gregory Palamas

It is now widely known that Frithjof Schuon, recognized throughout the second half of the twentieth century as one of the world's most prolific and authoritative writers on religion and spirituality and as its most important expositor of the *Sophia Perennis*, was in his private life a Sufi master, the Shaykh 'Îsâ Nûr al-Dîn Ahmad al-Shâdhilî al-'Alawî al-Maryamî. It has also become public knowledge that the *tarîqah* or spiritual order which Schuon founded and guided, a branch of the *Shâdhilîyyah* lineage, is of a Marian provenance, a fact indicated by the last of his Islamic names. Known as the *Tarîqah Maryamîyyah*, this order has been blessed with the celestial patronage of the Virgin Mary, Sayyidatnâ Maryam in Islam—a patronage, Schuon has explained, which was bestowed freely by Heaven, and not by virtue of any initiative or intention of his own. "The coming of Sayyidatnâ Maryam did not depend upon my own will," he writes, "but upon the will of Heaven; it was a totally unexpected and unimaginable gift."[1]

This information will come as no great surprise to careful readers of Schuon's books, especially those written after 1965 when he first experienced what he would refer to in later years as the Marian Grace. Those who are sensitive to such things will have noticed that there is something almost palpably feminine or shaktic about the substance of much of his work, a quality which can be sensed on occasion even in his very mode of expression. It is difficult to say in just what this consists. One commentator has suggested that his writing exhibits a

---

[1] From a letter of September 1981. "There are Sufis who claim a mystical connection with a particular Prophet: they are *Ibrâhîmî*, *Mûsâwî*, *Îsâwî*—that is, of Abraham, of Moses, of Jesus—"as may be seen from the *Fusûs al Hikam* of Ibn 'Arabi. It is thus," Schuon continues, that "our *Tarîqah* is *Maryamî*—the Shaykh Al-'Alawî having been unquestionably *Îsâwî*" (unpublished Text 275). The Shaykh Al-'Alawî is the celebrated Algerian master of whom Schuon was first the disciple and later the *muqaddam* or representative in Europe.

107

"spherical quality" in the sense that the sphere contains the greatest volume for a given area, and I have elsewhere noted that Schuon's words seem "connected somehow, as if organically, to the realities he describes."[2] The distinctive shape and texture of his style are of course something that must be discerned by each reader firsthand, and I hope in what follows to provide an opportunity for those who may still be unacquainted with Schuon to experience these qualities for themselves. But whatever one's impressions with respect to the form of his writings, and however it may be best described, one soon discovers with respect to their matter that they contain numerous explicit references to the Blessed Virgin, with additional allusions and indications often tucked away into notes. In a recent review of the entire *corpus*, I could not find a single book containing no mention of the Virgin at all, and most of them seem replete with her presence. As is often the case with Schuon's teaching on a given subject, however, these references are for the most part occasional in nature, and they are almost always rather brief; in fact, only two chapters in his published writings are specifically devoted to Marian topics.[3] What this means is that one must read persistently and extensively in order to piece together the elements of a distinctively Schuonian Mariology.

This has been my aim precisely in preparing this article. From the very beginning of my acquaintance with Schuon's books, and later more profoundly when I had the privilege of meeting him and reading certain documents of a more personal kind, I have been deeply affected by the Virginal dimensions of his teaching, both doctrinal and methodic, and it has seemed to me for some time that I could perhaps perform a useful service for other like-minded readers and

---

[2] Seyyed Hossein Nasr, ed., *The Essential Writings of Frithjof Schuon* (Rockport, Mass.: Element Books, 1991), 54; James S. Cutsinger, *Advice to the Serious Seeker: Meditations on the Teaching of Frithjof Schuon* (Albany: State University of New York Press, 1997), 6. None of this is to suggest, of course, that there is not a more rigorous and masculine side to his work as well; I have also written of Schuon that while "the message he brings is a good one, it is a goodness that produces a shock, as if one were swallowing light" (James S. Cutsinger, "A Knowledge that Wounds Our Nature: The Message of Frithjof Schuon," *Journal of the American Academy of Religion*, LX/3, 465).

[3] "The Wisdom of Sayyidatnâ Maryam," *Dimensions of Islam*, trans. P. N. Townsend (London: Allen and Unwin, 1969), and "*Sedes Sapientiae*," *In the Face of the Absolute* (Bloomington, Ind.: World Wisdom Books, 1989). Even in these chapters, however, the topic announced by the title does not prevent Schuon from expounding a variety of other subjects as well. While there are certainly systematic elements in his teaching, it is not itself a system—or not at least in the usual sense of the word—and this fact can be seen in part in his mode of presentation.

friends by endeavoring to follow the thread which connects a representative sampling of Marian quotations, gathered from a wide variety of his writings. It will be understood, I hope, that in no sense have I presumed to exhaust a topic so infinitely rich in implication and resonance, nor of course does space allow me to cite explicitly any but a small number of passages. What follow are hints, indirections, openings.

Another, rather different, caveat should be inserted before I begin, and that is to say that this article is not meant for just anyone. It is certainly not intended for skeptics or cynics—for those who may come looking to argue about the very legitimacy of the spiritual life, or who may have more particular quibbles concerning the role of the Virgin or the temperament of those who are drawn to her. Attending to their complaints is a task for quite another occasion; all I can do here is to register my agreement with Schuon that whether one knows it or not, the Marian mysteries have "absolutely nothing to do with fairy tales, let alone with 'depth psychology.'"[4] If a critic objects that the following meditations are merely so much "romanticism" or "aestheticism" or "folklore," I gladly respond in Schuon's own words that

> far from disclaiming any affinity with these things, we adopt them in the precise measure that they have a relationship either with tradition or with virgin nature, restoring to them in consequence their legitimate and, at the very least, innocent meanings. For "beauty is the splendor of the true"; and since it is possible to be capable of perceiving this without lacking "seriousness," to say the least, we do not feel obliged to offer excuses for being particularly sensitive to this aspect of the Real.[5]

I must explain here at the outset as well that although I am myself a Christian, and by profession a Christian theologian, I am not in fact writing for Christians *per se*. Protestants in particular will be little

[4] *In the Face of the Absolute*, 89. Schuon has pointed out that "one of the most odious effects of the adoption of the psychoanalytical approach by believers is the disfavoring of the cult of the Holy Virgin; only a barbarous mentality that wants to be 'adult' at all costs and no longer believes in anything but the trivial could be embarrassed by this cult" (*Survey of Metaphysics and Esoterism*, trans. Gustavo Polit [Bloomington, Ind.: World Wisdom Books, 1986], 199).

[5] *Logic and Transcendence*, trans. Peter N. Townsend (London: Perennial Books, 1984), 6.

helped by these comments; if this article were mainly for them, then yet another, though of course very different, set of explanations and defenses would be in order, defenses serving to justify, on scriptural grounds, the position and role of the Blessed Virgin in Schuon's life and teaching, and the extraordinary degree of veneration which he exhibits towards her. As it happens there are several passages in the Bible which have proven to be especially important keys to his Mariology, and we shall examine them shortly. But he would be the first to admit that taken on their own, apart from the context provided by their use in the traditional liturgies and the expositions afforded in the orthodox commentaries, these texts provide no decisive support for his teaching.[6]

As for those Christians, on the other hand, who celebrate these liturgies and who rely on those commentaries—Christians in other words of the Apostolic communions, whether of the East or the West—they, too, are not really my primary audience, for such readers would also require, at least in most cases, something very different from what I intend to provide. It is certainly true that Roman Catholics and Orthodox understand much better than Protestants the decisive role of the Virgin in the Christian economy, and yet I know from experience that they are still often puzzled, if not scandalized, when they first learn about Schuon's teachings on Mary. Even when they study his words with great care, many still come away unconvinced by the greater part of his doctrine, and I am under no illusions that my own merely supplemental remarks will be sufficient in addressing their fundamental objections. As we shall find, Schuon himself actually went to some lengths in helping Christians to under-

---

[6] I should perhaps add here in passing that Schuon regarded the traditional Protestant perspective, firmly based on the Bible, as a perfectly legitimate and saving *upâya* or spiritual means, and he knew that Protestant suspicions concerning Catholic and Orthodox veneration of the Virgin are, from one point of view, a natural and understandable part of a "general reaction against the dispersion of religious sentiment and thus in favor of worship concentrated on Christ alone" (*Christianity/Islam: Essays on Esoteric Ecumenicism*, trans. Gustavo Polit [Bloomington, Ind.: World Wisdom Books, 1985], 29). This may also be the place to point out that I shall make no attempt to respond to the arguments of the Muslim exoterist, who is of course *a fortiori* suspicious of anything bordering on the divinization or worship of a human being, including Christ Himself. The Koran speaks with great respect concerning the Virgin and includes a *sûrah* with her name; indeed hers is the only feminine name to occur in the Book, and as we shall see later, the exposition of Schuon's Mariology rests in part on Koranic texts. But it is no part of his aim, or mine, to convince every Muslim that his Marian teachings are valid.

stand the deeper significance of traditional Marian teachings, and in highlighting their consistency with his own expositions—whether one finds these teachings in the works of great saints, or in the liturgies and iconography of the Church, or in such dogmatic titles of the Virgin as *Theotokos* or "Mother of God," a title, promulgated by the third of the Ecumenical Councils, which my fellow Orthodox above all willingly acknowledge as essential to their faith.[7] And yet he knew very well in so doing that the Church, in its efforts to formulate the truth in a way that will be intelligible to as many people as possible, "cannot recognize Mary's Divine Reality without entering into insoluble contradictions—although it admits this Reality implicitly at least when, for example, it defines the Virgin as 'Co-Redemptress,' 'Mother of God,' 'Spouse of the Holy Ghost.'"[8]

Here, as some of my readers will realize, we anticipate the very heart of my topic, and here of course, too, we can see very clearly, in just a single short phrase, one of the most important reasons that Schuon presents a problem for many traditional Christians. For in speaking so candidly of the Virgin's Divinity, her "Divine Reality," he has evidently, and very consciously, transgressed a certain traditional boundary. As my co-religionists know, it is a boundary long established by theologians, who, while insisting on the Divinity of Mary's Son, "begotten by the Father before all ages" (Nicene Creed), have at the same time been loath, however exalted the words of the liturgical hymns that are sung in her praise, to think of His mother

---

[7] In response to the Nestorian heresy, the Third Council (Ephesus) proclaimed that the Virgin is to be called, not simply *Christotokos* or "Mother of Christ," but *Theotokos* or "Mother of God." Schuon's standpoint with respect to this title will be considered more fully below.

[8] *Treasures of Buddhism* (Bloomington, Ind.: World Wisdom Books, 1993), 92. The term "Co-Redemptress"—in Latin *Co-Redemptrix*—is used only in the Western Church, and then explicitly only since the fourteenth century. But the idea thus expressed, that the Blessed Virgin participates in the redeeming work of her Son, is quite ancient and is common to the Eastern Church as well. According to St Anselm, "God is the Father of all created things, and Mary is the Mother of all re-created things. God is the Father of the constitution of all things, and Mary is the Mother of the restitution of all things" (*Oratio* VII). Among the Orthodox, the holy hierarch St Theophanes of Nicaea says, "It cannot happen that anyone, of angels or of men, can come otherwise, in any way whatsoever, to participation in the Divine gifts flowing from what has been divinely assumed, from the Son of God, save through His Mother" (*The Life of the Virgin Mary, the Theotokos* [Buena Vista, Colorado: Holy Apostles Convent and Dormition Skete, 1989], 516). The term has never been defined as dogma, but it has been used by many popes.

as sharing in this principial stature. Even though she is called "more honorable than the Cherubim and beyond compare more glorious than the Seraphim,"[9] it has been the judgment of the Church that the Virgin even so is no more than a creature, and it is not surprising therefore if the Schuonian Mariology should be considered too "high"—too high in where it places Mary in relation to God—even as his Christology is often considered too "low" in what it says about the status of Jesus.[10] It is not surprising, in other words, that even the most serious of Christian devotees of Our Lady should be offended by the claim that the Blessed Mother is herself of an avataric substance, a "Divine descent," and thus like her Son an incarnation of God. And yet this is precisely Schuon's fundamental perception of Mary, and the consistent teaching of all his books and unpublished writings.

In seeking to understand this perception, it is clear that we shall be entering what Schuon admits is "an extremely subtle domain, in which definitions are always hazardous." And yet, as he himself adds at once, "the nature of the problem leaves us no choice; there are things one can only express imperfectly, but which nevertheless cannot be passed over in silence."[11] The Virgin is clearly one of those things, one of those mysteries—perhaps indeed the most important of all—which the Church has for so long been so good at protecting that Christians seem themselves nearly to have forgotten its deepest significance.[12] I do not pretend to have understood it fully myself, but to the extent that I have an inkling at least, some intuition of the

---

[9] According to St Dionysius the Areopagite, the Seraphim and Cherubim are the two highest ranks of the Celestial Hierarchies, above whom there is only God. The phrase comes from the *Megalynarion*, a well-known hymn of the Orthodox Church, sung in every Divine Liturgy of St John Chrysostom: "It is truly meet to bless thee, O *Theotokos*, who art ever blessed and all-blameless, and the Mother of our God. More honorable than the Cherubim and more glorious beyond compare than the Seraphim, thou who without stain barest God the Word, and art truly *Theotokos*: we magnify thee."

[10] I have endeavored to respond to this common, but ill-conceived, objection to Schuon's teaching on Christ in a recent article, "The Mystery of the Two Natures," *Sophia: The Journal of Traditional Studies*, 4/2 (Winter 1998), also published in French as "Le Mystère des deux Natures," *Connaissance des Religions*, Numéro Hors-Série (Juillet-Octobre 1999).

[11] *Christianity/Islam*, 243.

[12] The Eastern Church has always drawn a line, more or less solid, between its *kerygmata*, teachings codified as dogmas and proclaimed to all and sundry, and its *mysteria*, the inner mysteries of the faith, reserved in their fullness for initiates illumined by Baptism and Chrismation; Christology has traditionally been placed on the first, Mariology on the second, side of that line.

Virgin's presence and message, I have Frithjof Schuon to thank, and it is in part as a way of expressing my gratitude that I have attempted to describe here the lineaments of his Mariology. As I have tried to emphasize, I do not intend to argue with those who have no use for these teachings, whether skeptical critics or Christian exoterists. But if with this small beginning I can somehow assist the esoterist, who is *a priori* open to the depth of this mystery, to see Mary more truly in her intrinsic reality, and to become in this way more fully conformed to her substance, then I shall consider myself profoundly satisfied.

Christianity and the Bible

The first level of the teaching which I propose to discuss takes the form of a spiritual or anagogical commentary on certain Marian passages in the Bible.[13] Of course, as we have noted already, this is not to imply that the sacred texts offer proof of Schuon's doctrine, or not at least in its fullness, and certainly not at the level of their literal meanings; but then neither can they be said to "prove" the Mariology of the Church, which goes well beyond what the Bible explicitly records regarding Mary. Indeed, when one considers the extraordinary prerogatives accorded her by the exoteric tradition, one realizes that "scripture treats the Virgin with a somewhat surprising parsimony."[14] And yet as Schuon points out, this can easily be explained by the fact that she "lived in effacement and refused to perform miracles; the almost complete silence of the Gospel in regard to her illustrates this effacement." But it illustrates as well, he continues—however indirectly and allusively—something of the Virgin's true greatness, for in their very reticence the scriptures provide us with a first and most important hint that "Maryam is identifiable with esoteric Truth (*Haqîqah*) inasmuch as she is a secret Revelation."[15]

This identification of Mary with pure esoterism is one of the most important dimensions of the Schuonian doctrine, and we shall have occasion to return to it near the end of these reflections. For the

---

[13] First, that is, in the order in which it shall be treated here. I do not mean to imply that this is Schuon's own priority, nor that his Mariology is dependent on these scriptures, or on their interpretation in the traditional commentaries. One cannot stress too often that Schuon was not a theologian, but a metaphysician and esoterist, whose doctrine was based simply on the nature of things.

[14] *Christianity/Islam*, 30.

[15] *Dimensions of Islam*, 84.

moment it is worth noting, however, that many Christian authorities have rendered a similar interpretation, seeing in the relative silence of scripture a sign of the Virgin's surpassing amplitude and dignity. Writing in the earliest years of the Church, St Ignatius of Antioch, for example, describes Mary's virginity and her giving birth to the *Logos* as "secrets crying to be told, but wrought in God's silence,"[16] and many centuries later St Louis Marie de Montfort could teach in a similar vein that "even though Mary was His faithful spouse, God the Holy Spirit willed that His apostles and evangelists should say very little about her, and then only as much as was necessary to make Jesus known." Otherwise, the saint explains, "men as yet insufficiently instructed and enlightened concerning the person of her Son might wander from the truth by becoming too strongly attached to her," an attachment owing to "the wondrous charms with which the Almighty had endowed even her outward appearance."[17] The understatement in scripture is thus by no means a sign of the Virgin's unimportance or insignificance. One must admit that "the Gospel says nothing about the daily life of Mary," but at the same time, says Schuon, it is surely obvious that "the life of a co-redeeming *Mater Dei* could not in any event be 'ordinary' in the stupidly conventional sense of the word."[18]

---

[16] *Letter to the Ephesians*, 19.

[17] *True Devotion to the Blessed Virgin* (Bay Shore, New York: Montfort Publications, 1980), 1, 20. This is apparently what nearly happened to St Dionysius the Areopagite, who, having visited Jerusalem where he met the Blessed Virgin in person, writes to St Paul his teacher, "I bear witness before God, who dwelt in that most honorable virginal womb, that I would have taken her for the true God, and would have honored her with the adoration due to God alone, if my newly-enlightened soul had not retained thy Divine instructions and laws" (*The Life of the Virgin Mary, the Theotokos*, 441).

[18] *Sufism: Veil and Quintessence*, trans. William Stoddart (Bloomington, Ind.: World Wisdom Books, 1981), 77. Schuon writes elsewhere of "the strange case of Fâtimah. Embodying, according to unanimous tradition, the purest sanctity, she was put aside, frustrated, and forgotten. On occasion she was treated in a hard way even by the Prophet her father. Herein is the whole drama of a celestial soul predestined to be the martyr of terrestrial life. Her abasement is, as it were, the shadow cast by her spiritual elevation, human individuals appearing in her destiny as the cosmic instruments of her painful alchemy. There is something of this likewise in the case of the Blessed Virgin, treated not without a certain coldness by the Gospels and passed over largely in silence by most of the New Testament, to reappear afterwards in all the greater splendor" (*Islam and the Perennial Philosophy*, trans. J. Peter Hobson [London: World of Islam Festival Publishing Company, 1976], 92-93). I have noted that on this point

Although references to a variety of Biblical texts can be found in his work when he is speaking of Mary, Schuon returns again and again to four sets of verses in particular, three in the Old Testament and one in the New. The first of the Old Testament passages is Genesis 3:15, called by the Church Fathers the *protoevangelium*, or primordial Gospel, insofar as it prophesies, in its Christian interpretation, the coming of Christ. Speaking to the serpent in the Garden, God says, *And I will put enmity between thee and the woman, and between thy seed and her seed; it shall bruise thy head, and thou shalt bruise his heel.* In the immediate and literal context, the woman of course is Eve, who is tempted by the serpent, or Satan, and disobeys God. But at the same time it is obvious that the woman whose seed will eventually bruise, while being bruised by, the devil is Mary, and for this reason, beginning in the second Christian century, the Church has often taught that the wife of the first Adam and the mother of the Second Adam are spiritually linked to each other as antitypes. St Irenaeus of Lyons is representative in this respect:

> As Eve was seduced by the word of an angel to flee from God, having rebelled against the Word, so Mary by the word of an angel received the glad tidings that she would bear God by obeying His Word. The former was seduced to disobey God, but the latter was persuaded to obey God, so that the Virgin Mary might become the advocate of the virgin Eve. As the human race was subjected to death through a virgin, so was it saved by a Virgin.[19]

Schuon has the support of saints; it should be added, however, that when occasion demanded he was not averse to disagreeing with them. On this very question, for example, he criticized St Thérèse de Lisieux—"despite her angelic nature," which he was among the first to honor—for "diminishing the Blessed Virgin in order to bring her 'nearer.'" For Thérèse, he continues, "the Blessed Virgin is 'mother' more than 'queen,' as if Mary were not great and mysterious before making herself little and intimate; and it is for the queen, not her subjects, to decide when and how she intends to be mother, the worth and the charm of the maternal intimacy residing here precisely in its combination with majesty" (*Sufism: Veil and Quintessence,* 77).

[19] *Against Heresies,* V, 19; see also III, 22. A similar symbolic pairing can be found in St Justin the Philosopher, *A Dialogue with Trypho,* 100, and in Tertullian, *On the Flesh of Christ,* 17. The western tradition observes that *Ave,* the first word of the Angelic Salutation in Latin, being the palindrome of the Latin for Eve, *Eva,* indicates that the reversal of the Fall was effected in Mary. Thus, in the *Ave Maris Stella,* used since the ninth century as the Vesper hymn for the Common of Feasts of the Blessed Virgin, the Church addresses her with these words: *Sumens illus Ave/Gabrielis ore/Funda nos in pace/Mutans Evae nomen*—"Receiving that Ave from the mouth of Gabriel, establish us in peace, changing the name of Eve."

Schuon calls attention to the profound theological implications of this pairing many times in his writings. Noting, for example, that the two women are complementary opposites in the order of their relation with the corresponding masculine figures, he writes that "if Eve, issued from Adam, symbolizes the fall, the Holy Virgin, from whom Christ issued, symbolizes victory over the serpent."[20] Or again, highlighting yet another contrast, he stresses that Mary, "by her purity as also by her mercy, conquers the sin of the demiurgic Eve, the bringer forth of creatures and of passions; Eve, who brings forth, seduces, and attaches, is 'eternally' conquered by the Virgin, who purifies, pardons, and sets free."[21]

At the level of these formulations, no exoterist should have cause for objection. But Schuon soon takes a further step, beyond the familiar typological coupling, when he undertakes to explain the metaphysical relationship between the two sides of *the woman* in terms of the Hindu conception of *Mâyâ*. In the Schuonian doctrine, as his readers know, *Mâyâ* is a dimension of the Divine Principle; rooted in God's infinitude, it is what "causes" the Divinity to radiate outside of itself into Manifestation. *Mâyâ* is thus the principle of every theophany, and yet at the same time, since what is "outside" the Divinity is not really Divine, it is the principle of all obscurity and the cause of man's forgetfulness. It is the reason that God is able to appear to man, but paradoxically it is also the reason that man does not see Him.[22] Now according to Schuon, this ambivalent character of the Divine Relativity can be seen in two distinct aspects of the feminine, which are manifest in the persons of Eve and the Virgin:

> As the universal archetype of femininity, *Mâyâ* is both Eve and Mary: "psychic" and seductive woman and "pneumatic" and liberating woman; descendent or ascendant, alienating or reintegrating genius. *Mâyâ* projects souls in order to be able to free them, and projects evil in order to be able to overcome it; or again: on the one hand, She projects her veil in order to be able to manifest the potentialities of the Supreme Good; and, on the other, She veils good in

[20] *The Eye of the Heart* (Bloomington, Ind.: World Wisdom Books, 1997), 95.

[21] *Gnosis: Divine Wisdom*, trans. G. E. H. Palmer (London: Perennial Books, 1990), 75.

[22] See "The Doctrine of Illusion" in my *Advice to the Serious Seeker*.

order to be able to unveil it, and thus to manifest a further good: that of the prodigal son's return, or of Deliverance.[23]

The last part of this passage is crucial, for it might otherwise be thought that the relationship between the two aspects of *the woman* is a merely reciprocal one. Schuon makes it very clear, however, that even though the sin of Eve—that is, the tendency of the cosmogonic projection to move in the direction of nothingness—"confers on *Mâyâ* an ambiguity," this ambiguity "is quite relative and, far from being symmetrical, cannot tarnish *Mâyâ*." For "the glory of Mary totally effaces the sin of Eve, which is to say that with regard to the total extent of Existence and above all with regard to its Divine Summit, there is no longer any ambiguity, and evil is not."[24] After all, everything but the Supreme Principle is only a seeming; only God truly is, and thus "Eve is infinitely forgiven and victorious in Mary."[25]

For centuries, Christians have turned to the Song of Songs, or Canticles, in celebrating the life of the Virgin, and like the fathers before him, Schuon refers to it, too. Two verses have been especially prominent in the traditional commentaries of such saints as Bernard of Clairvaux, and in the festal antiphons, *stichera*, and other propers for the Virgin's Conception, her Nativity, her Entrance into the Temple, the Annunciation, and other Marian Feasts of the liturgical year: namely, Canticles 1:5, *I am black, but beautiful*; and Canticles 4:7, *Thou art all fair, my love; there is no spot in thee*. The figure who is speaking in the first of these passages, and who is addressed in

---

[23] *Survey of Metaphysics*, 73-74.

[24] *Face of the Absolute*, 59.

[25] *Face of the Absolute*, 61. "The key to the mystery of salvation through woman, or through femininity, if one prefers, lies in the very nature of *Mâyâ*. If *Mâyâ* can attract towards the outward, she can also attract towards the inward. Eve is life, and this is manifesting *Mâyâ*; Mary is Grace, and this is reintegrating *Mâyâ*. Eve personifies the demiurge under its aspect of femininity; Mary is the personification of the *Shekhînah*, of the Presence that is both virginal and maternal. Life, being amoral, can be immoral; Grace, being pure substance, is capable of absorbing all accidents" (*Esoterism as Principle and as Way*, trans. William Stoddart [London: Perennial Books, 1981], 143). Elsewhere Schuon calls our attention to yet another, in this case methodic, correlation between the two women within *the woman*: "The discriminative and contemplative abstraction from the world could not exclude our natural contacts with our ambience, which is not merely Eve, but also Mary. There is parallelism, not incompatibility, between the 'remembrance of God' and contingent life" (*The Play of Masks* [Bloomington, Ind.: World Wisdom Books, 1992], 52).

the second—in both cases a woman—is variously interpreted in the Christian tradition, depending on the level of meaning emphasized, as standing allegorically either for the people of Israel, or for the Church, or for the human soul in a state of grace. But whichever of these meanings is stressed, it is agreed that the Blessed Virgin—whose soul is understood to be spotless, who is the Mother of the Church, and in whom culminate the promises of God to His people—is the supreme type of the figure in question, and hence that this sacred text is fundamentally a dialogue between God and His Virginal Bride.

Again and again in his writings, Schuon returned to the first of these verses, *Nigra sum sed formosa*, helping to plumb the depths upon depths of its meaning. I would venture to say, in fact, that there may well have been no other passage in the Bible with which he was more endlessly fascinated, and this fascination can be seen in the evident delight with which he reveals its application to Mary.[26] Recalling, for example, her cosmic role in relation to *Mâyâ*, he explains that the Virgin "manifests the universal Veil in its function of transmission; she is Veil because she is a form, but she is Essence by her content and consequently her message. She is both closed and open, inviolable and generous," and it follows therefore, he continues, that "she is 'black but beautiful' because the Veil is both closed and transparent, or because, after having closed by virtue of inviolability, it opens by virtue of mercy."[27] Not only, however, is the Virgin "at first obscure and sacrificial, and then luminous and beatific"; she is also, and yet more profoundly, "luminous and beatific in the obscurity." She is, Schuon adds in a typically powerful coda, "divinely obscure—that is, unmanifest and infinite—in her very beauty."[28] Stressing on the other hand her mode of action, rather than her state of being, he indicates in another place that the Blessed Mother is like her Son in bringing a message of inwardness. But hers is an inwardness—that is, a blackness—which is more "welcoming" than rigorous, and it is in this sense

---

[26] Another verse in the Song of Songs which he often cites, and which is intimately linked not only to the doctrine of the Virgin, but to the method of quintessential prayer, is Canticles 5:2: *I sleep, but my heart waketh.*

[27] *Esoterism*, 62. "The Russian Church," he adds, "celebrates a 'feast of the Veil' in remembrance of an apparition of Mary at Constantinople, in the course of which the Virgin lifted her luminous veil and held it, in a miraculous fashion, above those present. The Russian word *pokrov* means both 'veil' and 'intercession': the *Mâyâ* which dissimulates Essence is at the same time the *Mâyâ* which communicates graces."

[28] Unpublished Text 511.

that "one can attribute to her, as does the Song of Songs, the quality of being 'black but beautiful'; she does not tear us away from the outward world, but draws us gently towards the inward."[29]

Of course the fact that the Virgin is gentle does not take anything away from her majesty or transcendent dignity. Although we are grateful for her beauty and mercy, we must not forget that like Christ she is "not of this world" (John 18:36).[30] She is black, Schuon writes, "because she transcends and thereby negates our all too human plane"; or again: "the black color of the beloved in the Song of Songs, and of many images of the Blessed Virgin, expresses not so much the very relative ambiguity of Existence as its 'self-effacement.'"[31] And yet this last symbolism is not exclusive either, for from still another point of view the Virgin's color also serves to remind the esoterist of the end of his Path. Her darkness betokens the struggles of the spiritual battle, but also the cooling shade to be enjoyed by the victor. In this case, "black represents the secret and supra-formal character of *gnosis*."[32] Speaking, for example, of the "supreme spiritual state" which is the aim of the Christian hesychast, Schuon notes that the goal of "'holy silence' (*hesychia*)" is "symbolized by the black color given to certain Virgins,"[33] and in this respect there is clearly a beauty within the blackness—even as there is a *yang* in the *yin* in the familiar emblem of the Far Eastern tradition. For even though "knowledge is exclusive and separative at the exterior," it is "inclusive and unitive at the interior." The final goal of the spiritual journey is thus like Mary herself: it "is

---

[29] *Christianity/Islam*, 145-46. It is characteristic of Schuon to contrast the predominantly "inward" and spiritual function of Christ, called in Islam the "Seal of Sanctity," with the more outward and social function of the Prophet Muhammad.

[30] Schuon observes that the *Magnificat* (Luke 1:46-55) "is impregnated with elements of Mercy and Rigor, and it thus reflects an aspect of the nature of the Virgin herself: the mildness of the Virgin is accompanied by an adamantine purity, also by a strength of soul which evokes such Biblical figures as Miriam and Deborah, and which represents a dimension inseparable from the greatness of her who was called *O Clemens, O Pia, O Dulcis Virgo Maria*"—words, Schuon notes, which were "added spontaneously by St Bernard to the *Salve Regina* on the occasion of a solemn gathering at Speyer Cathedral" (*Dimensions of Islam*, 89).

[31] *Face of the Absolute*, 220, 60.

[32] *Dimensions of Islam*, 15.

[33] *The Transcendent Unity of Religions*, trans. Peter Townsend (London: Faber and Faber, 1953), 180-81.

virginal because the ego cannot violate it, and it is maternal because it welcomes, adopts, and reintegrates; it is Beauty and Goodness; it is at once Night and Wine."[34]

In addition to the *protoevangelium* of Genesis and the Song of Songs, traditional Christians have always made considerable use of the Wisdom books of the Old Testament as inspired sources for their understanding of the Virgin. Two texts have been especially important, Proverbs 8:22-30 and the Wisdom of Solomon 7:22-30, both of which speak of a feminine being named *Sophia* or Wisdom, who is very clearly of a celestial, if not a principial, order. In Proverbs she says of herself that she was *set up from everlasting, from the beginning, or ever the earth was*. Even as God *prepared the heavens, I was there: when He set a compass upon the face of the depth. Then I was by Him, as one brought up with Him: and I was daily His delight, rejoicing always before Him.* As for the book of Wisdom, it is said there of *Sophia* that *she is the breath of the power of God, and a pure influence flowing from the glory of the Almighty. She is the brightness of the everlasting light, the unspotted mirror of the power of God, and the image of His goodness. She can do all things: and remaining in herself, she maketh all things new. For she is more beautiful than the sun, and above all the order of stars: being compared with the light, she is found before it.* These and other similar passages have for centuries been read by the Church in celebration of its Marian feasts, and they can be found incorporated in many Christian hymns and litanies in honor of the Virgin. Thus in the western Mass for the Feast of the Immaculate Conception, it is said of Mary, as it was said of *Sophia*, that she "was begotten before all the worlds, set up from of old before the earth." And in the Akathist Hymn of the Eastern Church, among a dazzling array of other titles, the Virgin is described as the Space of

---

[34] Unpublished Text 448. "Spiritual truth, a Moroccan shaikh has said, is more beautiful when it is veiled like a fiancée. This opinion suggests—apart from a solicitude for dialectic breadth—an almost liturgical attitude of respectful distance, or even reverential awe, with regard to the truth" (*Dimensions of Islam*, 13). Schuon points out that these two aspects of the Virginal substance are given a concrete and very powerful expression in the iconography of the Eastern Church. "In many icons the Holy Virgin expresses mercy by the inclined and spiral-like movement of her posture, while the severity of her facial expression indicates purity in its aspect of inviolability; other icons express solely this purity, emphasizing the severity of the features by a very upright position; others again express mercy alone, combining the inclination of the body with sweetness of expression" (*Stations of Wisdom* [Bloomington, Ind.: World Wisdom Books, 1995], 135).

the Spaceless God, an epithet which reflects the fact that *Wisdom alone compassed the circuit of Heaven* (Ecclesiasticus 24:5).[35]

To my knowledge, Schuon never comments in detail on these particular sophianic prerogatives, nor does he single out any specific verse from these sacred texts, but he certainly affirms the essential connection between Wisdom and Mary, and in doing so it is evident that he is well aware of the long tradition of Christian meditation and devotion which is based on this relationship. He is also aware that the Church has often associated Divine Wisdom with the *Logos*, the Word which was incarnate in Christ, and for this reason he teaches, in many places, that this *Logos* must contain in some fashion a feminine dimension or aspect, which was personified or incarnate in Mary. Thus

> the Blessed Virgin personifies the pre-existential and existentiating *Sophia*: the *Logos* inasmuch as it "conceives" creatures, then "engenders" them, and finally "forms" or "embellishes" them; if Mary thus represents the unmanifested and silent *Logos*—*nigra sum sed formosa*—Jesus is the manifested and law-giving *Logos*.[36]

In 1 Kings, the Bible speaks of the great Throne of Solomon or Throne of Wisdom, and like many Christian authorities, it is common for Schuon to explain the Virgin's relationship with the *Logos* by identifying her with this Throne. She herself, he insists—with St Bernard and others—is the *Sedes Sapientiae*, of which *there was not the like made in any kingdom* (1 Kings 10:20). "This is first of all because she is the Mother of Christ who, being the Word, is the 'Wisdom of God'; but it is also, quite obviously, because of her own nature, which results from her quality as 'Spouse of the Holy Spirit' and 'Co-Redemptress.'" And since she is such a Throne, he continues—a "'Throne quickened by

---

[35] The phrase points as well, of course, to the doctrine of the Incarnation, for it was in the space of the Virginal matrix or womb that God the Infinite dwelt. In the apse of an Orthodox church, one often sees an icon called Our Lady of the Sign, or the *Platytera*. Seated in majesty, with the Child enthroned on her lap, the Virgin holds her hands outstretched, as if embracing the universe, and there is often an inscription which reads *Platytera Tôn Ouranôn*: "She who is more spacious than the Heavens." As for the Akathist and other traditional "litanies of the Virgin," including that of Loreto, Schuon writes that they "are in a certain respect concerned with Existence insofar as it is the first manifestation of the Self and the substance of all existential perfections" (*Dimensions of Islam*, 134). This observation should help to cast a new light for many readers on the relationship between God and the Wisdom of Mary.

[36] *Esoterism*, 62.

the Almighty' according to a Byzantine hymn—Mary is *ipso facto* identified with the Divine *Sophia*, as is attested by the Marian interpretation of some of the eulogies of Wisdom in the Bible. Mary could not
have been the locus of the Incarnation did she not bear in her very
nature the Wisdom to be incarnated."[37]

Now it is important to pause for a moment with this formulation, because it anticipates certain ideas that I shall be commenting
on more carefully later. As this passage indicates, Schuon's teaching
about the Divinity of Mary—based in this case on her identification
with uncreated Wisdom—does not mean, despite what a superficial
reading might lead one to assume, that he wished to deny her humanity, which was obviously essential in order that she might become a
true *locus* for Christ's Incarnation. On the contrary, it is only by fully
respecting the fact that the Virgin was a genuine woman that it is possible to understand in what way she can at the same time be *Sophia*
or the *Logos* incarnate. "The human femininity of the Blessed Virgin,
and thus her subordination," he writes, far from being opposed to
Divinity, indicate "a real celestial superiority in a particular connection: femininity appears here—in view of the spiritual and cosmic
supereminence of the personage—as the inverted reflection of pure
essentiality," and it is in this way precisely that "she is thus identified
with Divine Femininity, or with the Wisdom 'which was at the beginning.'"[38] Elsewhere, speaking more particularly concerning her virtues, Schuon calls attention to the fact that "the Virgin, despite her
supreme sanctity, remains woman and aspires to no other role; the
humble soul is conscious of its own rank and effaces itself before what
surpasses it. It is thus that the *Materia Prima* of the Universe"—that is,
the underlying Substance of things, which the Schuonian perspective
identifies with the immanent Wisdom of God—"remains on its own
level and never seeks to appropriate to itself the transcendence of
the Principle."[39] And yet here is the wonder, of course: that it is precisely in not desiring to emulate God that Mary shows herself to be so
organically a part of Him, so fully Divine. According to St Louis Marie

---

[37] *Face of the Absolute*, 137-38.

[38] *Logic and Transcendence*, 119. Readers familiar with Schuon's work will notice that
this is yet another application of the Law of Inverse Analogy. See my *Advice to the
Serious Seeker*, 114.

[39] *Gnosis*, 121. Although it is true for Schuon that "a being such as the Virgin appears
only once every one or two millennia" (unpublished "Summary of an Audience with
the Shaykh" [Spring 1985]), her greatness is in no way inconsistent with her humble

de Montfort, the Blessed Virgin made a practice of "hiding herself in the depths of nothingness during her whole life," and as a result, says the saint, "Mary is entirely relative to God. Indeed I would say that she is relative only to God."[40]

St Louis, of course, does not intend simply to provoke our awe; he would have us strive to become ourselves conformed to this Virginal model, and so too would Schuon. He knows that so great a mystery cannot but have profound implications for understanding our own nature as we proceed in the Path, and he is quick to help us see what they are:

> The Divine *Mâyâ*—Femininity *in divinis*—is not only that which projects and creates; it is also that which attracts and liberates. The Blessed Virgin as *Sedes Sapientiae* personifies this merciful Wisdom which descends towards us and which we too, whether we know it or not, bear in our very essence; and it is precisely by virtue of this potentiality or virtuality that Wisdom comes down upon us. The immanent seat of Wisdom is the heart of man.[41]

In turning to the New Testament, Christians have taken note of two important passages in the Apocalypse in their efforts to fathom the full significance of the Mother of God: Revelation 12:1, which speaks of *a great wonder in Heaven: a woman clothed with the sun, and*

submission to the role for which she was destined as a human woman within the spiritual economy instituted by her Son. Thus, while "no man can be more holy than the Blessed Virgin," nonetheless "any priest can celebrate the Mass and preach in public, which she could not do . . . in the framework of a traditional Christian world" (*Castes and Races*, trans. Marco Pallis and Macleod Matheson [Pates Manor, Bedfont, Middlesex: Perennial Books, 1982], 34).

[40] *True Devotion*, 9, 116. It is clear why Schuon was so fond of this work and why he recommended it so heartily to Christian seekers. In precisely the same spirit, he himself writes: "The soul of the Blessed Virgin, prototype of every sanctified soul, is made of inborn worship, and this actualizes the Real Presence as a mirror reflects the sun; the virginal soul is consubstantial with this Presence just as space coincides with the ether that it contains" (*Esoterism*, 114).

[41] *Face of the Absolute*, 144. I am reminded of G. K. Chesterton's words: "Men are men, but Man is a woman." One also notes the following words of Schuon: "If Mary is seated upon the Throne of Solomon and is even identified with that Throne—with the authority it represents—this is not only by Divine right but by human right as well, in the sense that, being descended from David, she is heiress and queen in the same way that Christ, in like respect, is heir and king. One cannot but think of this when one sees the crowned Romanesque Virgins seated with the Child on a royal Throne" (*Face of the Absolute*, 139-40).

the moon under her feet, and upon her head a crown of twelve stars; and Revelation 21:11, which describes *the bride* of the Lamb, shining with the very *glory of God: and her light was like unto a stone most precious, even like a jasper stone, clear as crystal.* But more often they have turned to St Luke, where even at the literal level of meaning the Christian is offered two extremely important insights into the Virginal nature—first, in the narrative of the Annunciation: *And the angel came in unto her and said, Hail, thou that art highly favored, the Lord is with thee: blessed art thou among women* (Luke 1:28); and second, in the description of Mary's meeting with St Elizabeth: *And Elizabeth was filled with the Holy Ghost: and she spake out with a loud voice, and said, Blessed art thou among women, and blessed is the fruit of thy womb* (Luke 1:41-42). It is of course upon the inspired combination of these verses that the *Ave Maria*, or Angelic Salutation, of the western Rosary is based, and it is not surprising that Schuon, who was so keenly interested in the practice of methodic prayer in all traditions, frequently spoke of the *Ave*, nor that his Mariology was expressed in part in numerous comments on these Gospel verses.

According to Schuon, two things are made clear in these sacred texts: on the one hand, that the Virgin is perfectly sinless, as the Old Testament had prophesied,[42] and as the Catholic Church has dogmatically affirmed in its doctrine of the Immaculate Conception; and on the other hand, that she is in her own right a Divine incarnation. As to the first of these points, he notes that when Gabriel first addresses Mary, he says *Ave gratia plena*. "The angel did not say *Ave Maria*, because to him *gratia plena* is the name that he gives to the Virgin; this amounts to saying that *Maria* is synonymous with *gratia plena*."[43] It follows for the Schuonian, as it does for the Church, that "the Virgin is holiness"; since she is utterly filled with God's grace, there is no room in her for the presence of sin. She therefore possesses in her very nature "the entirety and quintessence of all the spiritual qualities or attitudes and of all the virtues which accompany or condition them."[44] Not surprisingly, Schuon links

[42] We have noted already a verse from the Song of Songs, *Thou art all fair, my love; there is no spot in thee* (4:7). Among a host of other Old Testament texts which have been adduced by the tradition in proof of the Virgin's perfection, the following provides an especially eloquent testimony: *Thou art fairer than the children of men: grace is poured into thy lips: therefore God hath blessed thee forever* (Psalm 45:2).

[43] *Esoterism*, 143.

[44] Unpublished Text 251. Schuon adds in the same place that "the snow placed by the angels in the breast of the Prophet-child is Virginity."

this personal, moral perfection of the Virgin's human nature to the primordial harmony of pure Existence, and he does so in such a way as to encourage us to look to her as a model. "*Maria* is the purity, the beauty, the goodness, and the humility of the cosmic Substance," and "the microcosmic reflection of this Substance is the soul in a state of grace." The Virgin's blessing, therefore, "is on him who purifies his soul for God."[45]

In underscoring these preliminary points, Schuon's reflections on the Angelic Salutation are perfectly consistent with what is affirmed by the exoteric Christian tradition, at least in principle. But as I have already mentioned, he takes the additional step of insisting that the Virgin's immaculate nature, as announced by the angel, is owing to her own Divinity. According to the Roman constitution *Ineffabilis Deus,* "The Blessed Virgin Mary, at the first instant of her conception, by a singular privilege and grace of the omnipotent God, was preserved free from all stain of original sin"—but only, it is added at once, "in consideration of the merits of Jesus Christ, the Savior of mankind."[46] In this way the Catholic Church, well aware of the direction in which popular piety might otherwise develop—and in which it has developed in any case—has attempted to forestall the deflection of worship away from Jesus. But in the esoteric perspective, "whatever the self-imposed limitations that exoteric theology may have to assume here for reasons of expediency,"[47] there is really no reason not to admit what this extraordinary prerogative of Mary in truth implies:

> On the one hand, the Gospel says of the Holy Virgin that she is "full of grace" and that "the Lord is with thee," and that "henceforth all generations shall call me blessed"; on the other hand, Christ inherited from the Virgin his entire human nature, from the psychic as well

[45] *Gnosis*, 119. Schuon continues, "This purity—the Marial state—is the essential condition, not only for the reception of the sacraments, but also for the spiritual actualization of the Real Presence of the Word. By the word *Ave*, the soul expresses the idea that, in conforming to the perfection of Substance, it puts itself at the same time in harmony with it, whilst imploring the help of the Virgin Mary, who personifies this perfection."

[46] It was with these words that Pope Pius IX proclaimed the Dogma of the Immaculate Conception (8 December 1854).

[47] *Treasures of Buddhism*, 92. As Schuon writes elsewhere, "Christianity in practice deifies the Mother of Christ, despite exoteric reservations, namely the distinction between *latria* and *hyperdulia*"—that is, between worship, properly speaking, and the highest form of veneration (*Face of the Absolute*, 227).

as physical point of view, so that his sacramental body and blood are fundamentally those of the Virgin. Now a person who possesses such prerogatives—to the point of being called "Mother of God"—necessarily has an "avataric" quality, expressed theologically by the idea of "Immaculate Conception." Thus the cult of Mary is not merely a matter of tradition; it clearly results from Scripture.[48]

When we recall that "Immaculate Conception" is the name which Mary gave herself in speaking with St Bernadette at Lourdes, it is understandable why, according to Schuon, the dogma must refer to "an intrinsic quality of the Virgin": since it is a quality which by definition she possessed from the very start, from her conception, it obviously pertains to her nature, for it would be absurd to suppose that a "nature" might have existed in some other form before benefiting from an extrinsic addition. Therefore, he concludes, "Mary is 'Divine' not only through Jesus, but also, and *a priori*, by her receptivity proportionate to the Incarnation," and this being so, we must admit that "the Logos 'was incarnated' in her already before the birth of Christ, which is indicated by the words *gratia plena* and *Dominus tecum*."[49]

I might briefly note before leaving this subject that Schuon was perfectly aware of the divergence between the eastern and western churches on the question of Mary's conception. Like Roman Catholics, the Orthodox teach that the Virgin was sinless, readily

---

[48] *To Have a Center* (Bloomington, Ind.: World Wisdom Books, 1990), 122-23. "As Jesus had no human father, His body and blood came to Him from Mary, which is also true for the eucharistic species and reveals a new aspect of the quality of 'Co-Redemptress'" (*Esoterism*, 38).

[49] *The Transcendent Unity of Religions* (London: The Theosophical Publishing House, 1984), 154. It will be understood, I trust, that this is one of those cases where the Schuonian logic will inevitably seem less than conclusive to "a dogmatism that is too intent upon dotting every 'i'"; as Schuon sees it, however, we are here faced with "a context in which holy indetermination would do no harm and in any case would be more appropriate" (*Christianity/Islam*, 122). Commenting elsewhere on the implications of Mary's immaculate nature, he says that the Virginal "Substance is not only filled with the Divine Presence in an ontological or existential manner, in the sense that it is impregnated with it by definition, that is to say by its very nature"—as is signified by the words *gratia plena*—"but it is also constantly communicating with the Word as such. So, if *gratia plena* means that the Divine Mystery is immanent in the Substance as such, *Dominus tecum* signifies that God, in his metacosmic transcendence, is revealed to the Substance, just as the eye, which is filled with light, sees in addition the sun itself." He concludes, as so often, with a concrete application: "The soul filled with grace will see God" (*Gnosis*, 119).

confessing her to be the *Panagia* or "All-Holy One," and believing her to have been so from the very beginning. But in their understanding, the guilt of man's "original sin" is not inherited: every newborn is innocent, and the dogma of the Immaculate Conception is therefore at best superfluous; at worst it runs the risk of diluting our admiration for the Virgin's perfection, for if she were by nature and necessarily virtuous, one could not attribute to her the excellence of spiritual victory. As is so often the case, Schuon's perspective not only sheds new light on the dispute, but has the effect of resolving it on a higher level:

> Was Mary *a priori* delivered from the capacity for sin, or was she sinless through the superabundance of her virtue? In other words, was she impeccable because of the absolute holiness of her nature, or was she holy as a result of the absolute impeccability of her intelligence and her will? Those who maintain the first thesis seek to avoid attributing to Mary an imperfection of substance; those of the second seek to avoid depriving her of the perfection of merit; but both sides seem to lose sight of the fact that at the degree of the Blessed Virgin the alternative loses all its meaning. The "immaculate conception"—attributed to Mary also by the Islamic tradition—admits of every meritorious attitude by its very nature, rather as a substance contains in synthesis all its possible accidents; and inversely, perfect impeccability—out of the question for the ordinary man—is *ipso facto* equivalent to the absence of "original sin."[50]

Islam and the Koran

Having been brought up as a Christian, and remaining his entire life an adamant defender of the Divinity of Christ and the other essential truths of this tradition, it was only natural for Schuon to formulate his understanding of the Blessed Virgin in terms of the Christian scriptures. But having decided as a young man to enter Islam—

---

[50] *Face of the Absolute*, 65-66. "Greek theology," he writes, "in conformity with its prudence in matters of dogmatic definition and its fidelity to scriptural symbolism, sought to avoid crystallizing, on the plane of outward doctrine, a truth closely relating to the highly delicate question of 'human divinity,' if we may call it that. Whatever the case, if the Catholic dogma of the Immaculate Conception means that the Virgin is 'the perfect creature,' the absence of this dogma with the Greeks means in the last analysis that 'there is none good but God,' according to the Gospel words themselves" (*The Eye of the Heart*, 100). It is evident, for Schuon, that both perspectives are true.

"without being converted," of course, but "for reasons of esoteric and therefore spiritual expediency"[51]—and having fulfilled within this framework, for over sixty years, the function of a Sufi Shaykh, it was also very natural that his Mariology should rest in part on references to Sayyidatnâ Maryam which one finds in the Koran, as well as on certain traditions of the Prophet Muhammad.

Christians are often surprised to discover that the sacred Book of Islam is sometimes even more explicit than the Bible in its praise of Mary, and that it too—as Schuon notes—teaches a doctrine of the immaculate conception. It is said, for example, that when the Virgin was born, her mother, *the wife of 'Imrân*—known to Christians as St Anne—prayed to God on behalf of the child, *I entrust her and her offspring to Thy protection from Satan the outcast* (Sûrah 3:35, 36), and the fact that this prayer was answered is proven by the saying of the Prophet: "Satan toucheth every son of Adam the day his mother beareth him, save only Mary and her son." Elsewhere, in a passage reminiscent of the words of Gabriel and St Elizabeth in the Gospel of Luke, *blessed art thou among women*, the Koran affirms of Mary that *Allah hath chosen thee and made thee pure, and hath preferred thee above all the women of creation* (Sûrah 3:42), a teaching which was confirmed, according to another *hadîth*, when the Prophet told his daughter Fâtimah, "Thou art the highest of the women of the people of Paradise, excepting only the Virgin Mary, daughter of 'Imrân." Furthermore, one entire *sûrah* bears the Virgin's name, in which it is revealed—in confirmation of a Christian tradition found in the Book of St James, where we learn of Mary's early years in the Temple—that even as a child she *had withdrawn from her family to a place facing the East, and she placed a veil between her and her people* (Sûrah 19:16-17). In another passage, the Koran teaches that Allah *made the son of Mary and his mother a sign* (Sûrah 23:50),[52] and elsewhere again that when God *citeth an example for those who believe*, mention is made of *Mary, the daughter of 'Imrân, who kept chaste her womb, and We breathed therein of Our Spirit. And she testified to the truth of the words of her Lord and His scriptures, and was of those who are absorbed in prayer* (Sûrah 66:12). So

---

[51] *Transcendent Unity* (1984), 83. See in this regard a recent article by Martin Lings, "Frithjof Schuon and René Guénon," *Sophia: The Journal of Traditional Studies*, 5/2 (Winter 1999), 13.

great was the Prophet's own respect for Mary that upon returning in conquest to Mecca, he ordered that all of the images in the Ka'bah be destroyed, excepting only two icons: one of an old man, said to be Abraham, and another of the Virgin and Child, which he protected with his own hands.

Schuon was deeply interested in the implications for Marian doctrine and method which can be discovered in two Koranic passages in particular. The first, the Verse of the *Mihrâb* or "Prayer-niche," speaks of the Virgin's presence in the Temple, where she had been brought as a child of three, and where she lived until her betrothal to Joseph—Zachariah, the husband of her cousin Elizabeth, being high priest in those years. *Her Lord accepted her with full acceptance and vouchsafed to her a goodly growth; and made Zachariah her guardian. Whenever Zachariah went into the sanctuary [Mihrâb] where she was, he found that she had food. He said: O Mary! Whence cometh unto thee this food? She answered: It is from Allah. Verily Allah provideth sustenance beyond all reckoning for those whom He will* (Sûrah 3:37).[53] It is the belief of Islam, as it is of Christianity, that the Blessed Virgin was miraculously sustained during these years by celestial food which was regularly brought to her by the angels. According to the Orthodox Patriarch Photius, Mary "gave an example of an immaterial life on earth, having been nourished, so to speak, from the very swaddling clothes, on the virtues alone,"[54] and the Schuonian Mariology is in perfect accord with this teaching: not only does her life in the Temple help to instruct us as to the Virgin's own stature in the Divine economy;

---

[52] "It will be noted," writes Schuon, "that the 'sign' is not Jesus alone, but He and His Mother" (*Sufism*, 155).

[53] Orthodox Christians and traditional Catholics agree in teaching that the Blessed Virgin spent her youth in the Temple as one of the Temple virgins. Orthodoxy remembers this fact in its Feast of the Entrance, recalling how her parents, St Joachim and St Anne, had brought her there in fulfillment of a vow to God. The Church sings in one of its hymns, "Thy wise parents, O undefiled one, brought thee, who art the 'Holy of Holies,' as an offering to the House of the Lord, there to be reared in holiness and made ready to become His Mother" (Matins Canon for the Nativity of the Blessed Virgin, Ode Six, Plagal of the Fourth Tone). St John of Damascus writes of her, "Transplanted into the Temple of God, and enriched by the Spirit like a fruitful olive tree, Mary became the dwelling of every virtue, and a holy and admirable temple, worthy of the Most High God" (*On the Orthodox Faith*, IV, 14).

[54] "Homily II on the Annunciation." The Metropolitan George of Nicomedia adds, "The heavenly food which the Immaculate Virgin received enriched her with Divine

it provides the spiritual pilgrim with a powerfully attractive model of what his own state of life should be like.

On the one hand, writes Schuon, since "the *Mihrâb* is equivalent to the Holy of Holies of the Temple," it follows that "at the time of the presence of the Virgin in the Temple, she was the high priest," and since esoterically "the *Mihrâb* is the heart," she herself was "the Holy of Holies."[55] Recalling *the East* which she faced (Sûrah 19:16) as she performed her priestly function, Schuon adds, "It is noteworthy that the Virgin is *Stella Matutina*, an allusion to the East, which in our symbolism denotes fervor. Aside from this particular meaning, the East expresses the coming of light, and it is thus that the Christian tradition interprets the Marian title 'Morning Star'; now fervor derives from light just as in principle light and heat go together."[56] On the other hand, Mary's seclusion and piety become in turn an example for others; indeed "Maryam is the inner soul which invokes and which, by that fact, is withdrawn from the world."[57] According to certain Koranic commentators on the phrase *she placed a veil between her and her people* (19:17), the sanctuary of the Temple was separated from the outer court by a series of veils, seven in number, which "become seven

grace. But it did not bring about a cleansing from sins in her, because she who partook of it had no sin; she was pure and free from any stain" ("Homily on the Entrance of the Blessed Virgin into the Temple").

[55] Unpublished Text 328. Calling attention to the Virgin's Koranic epithet "daughter of 'Imrân," and specifically to the name 'Imrân itself, Schuon writes that "the triliteral root of this name comprises amongst others the meanings 'prosperity' and 'flowering,' which are most appropriate for her whom God 'caused to grow with a goodly growth' and to whom He gave 'His sustenance beyond measure.'" He adds that "the words 'daughter of 'Imran' link Mary not only to her direct father but also to her ancestor, the father of Moses and Aaron, whence the description 'sister of Aaron' which the Koran likewise employs, wishing thus to stress that the priestly and esoteric super-eminence of the brother of Moses is remanifested in Mary" (*Dimensions of Islam*, 93-94). It should be understood, of course, that the Schuonian teaching on this point goes well beyond what exoteric Islam is willing to accept; indeed, "when the Koran declares that 'God hath chosen thee (O Mary) and hath purified thee, and hath raised thee above all women,' there are commentators who find a way of having it say merely that Mary was 'the most pious woman of her time,' no more, no less; an absurd minimalizing," Schuon continues, "which is explainable by the fear of mariolatry; it is always a case of *ad majorem Dei gloriam* which, in the climate of a sensitive monotheism, is theologically and psychologically decisive" (*Survey of Metaphysics*, 98). It goes without saying that exoteric Christianity, in its own way, is no less sensitive on this score.

[56] *Face of the Absolute*, 218.

[57] Unpublished Text 328.

doors," Schuon writes, "which Zachariah had to open with a key each time he visited Mary in the Temple."[58] What this veiling signifies for the spiritual traveler is that "the Holy Virgin represents the *khalwah* or spiritual retreat." Combining this symbolic meaning of the Koranic passage with the text which we discussed from Canticles, Schuon continues, "'I am black, but beautiful': this verse likewise expresses the mystery of the *khalwah*; and it follows that if the *khalwah* is *a priori* obscure, it subsequently transforms itself into a golden light."[59] Thus, together with the Song of Songs, the Verse of the *Mihrâb* serves to show that

> what Sayyidatnâ Maryam asks of us is that we always remain in *khalwah,* in the midst of the world and of life; not so much in the *khalwah* which is obscure as in the one which is golden, which accompanies us everywhere like a protecting and blessed aura, as soon as we surrender ourselves to the Celestial Ray. In this state, man no longer feels any curiosity for the dissipating things of this world; he is no longer interested in things that are useless for him, and he is only concerned about remaining in the little golden garden of spiritual poverty. For Sayyidatnâ Maryam is like crystal, into which nothing senseless or impure penetrates; that is why the Koran says that she kept her virginity intact, meaning her heart.[60]

As for the food with which Mary was nourished during her time of retreat, Schuon teaches that what it refers to finally is God Himself, whose Names she invoked without ceasing. "Sayyidatnâ Maryam was nourished in the Temple (the *Mihrâb*) by celestial foods. Now for man

---

[58] *Esoterism,* 61.

[59] Unpublished Text 838. Schuon adds in the same text, "One speaks also of the protecting mantle of the Holy Virgin, which springs from the same symbolism; and one may say the same of her long hair, which is her natural mantle."

[60] Unpublished Text 838. Commenting in another place on the Virgin's response to Zachariah, Schuon observes that "by this saying—or this teaching—Maryam invites us to do what she does, to be what she is; to enter into her, so to speak, to be carried by her; for it is the function of the Divine man to be the intermediary between us and Heaven" (Unpublished Text 344). The Muslim exoterist will object to this language, pointing out that in the Koran the Virgin is addressed with the words, *O Maryam, be in prayer before thy Lord and prostrate thyself and bow with those who bow* (Sûrah 3:43). Schuon explains this verse, however, by saying that "the order given to the avataric creature does no more than express the nature of this creature, cosmic perfections always deriving from a Divine order; in pronouncing His order in eternity, God created the nature of the Virgin. The angels only repeat this order to the glory of Mary.

to live, he has need of food and drink." It therefore makes perfect sense, says Schuon, that the Christian and Muslim traditions should concur in believing that the Virgin was given fruit by the angels, for "fruits combine the two, the solid and the liquid; they nourish by their flesh and give drink by their juice." The Christian will naturally think of the Bread and Wine of the Eucharist, themselves the very substance of God, but in this case Schuon chooses to emphasize the link with the sacrament of the Name and the method of *Dhikr* or Invocation. "One can say that the supreme Name is at once Food and Drink; it is the Divine Fruit which combines all the gifts which make us live. To say that the Holy Virgin received diverse fruits means that she lived by Divine Names, according to the double relationship of Ambrosia and Nectar."[61]

Another important Koranic text which Schuon often comes back to is a passage in which Christians are reproached for their belief in a Divine trinity—not, however, the Trinity dogmatically proclaimed by the Church, but a trinity composed of Allah, Jesus, and Mary: *They surely disbelieve who say: Lo! Allah is the third of three, when there is no God save the One God. The Messiah, son of Mary, was no other than a messenger, the like of whom had passed away before him, and his mother was a saintly woman* (Sûrah 5:73, 75). The burden of these verses is of course to stress, in a way characteristic of the Muslim economy, that nothing may be associated with Allah, and that Jesus and His mother must therefore be regarded as no more than creatures. According to Schuon, what is being censored in this passage is thus a trinity resulting from "the deification of Jesus and Mary," a trinity which is "indirectly attributed to the Christians by the Koran," but which at the same time, contrary to what many exoterists of both traditions have assumed, "this Book nowhere identifies with the Trinity of Christian doctrine."[62] As Schuon sees it, however, there is nonetheless an important, underlying connection between these two trinities, which the revealed text helps the esoterist to discern, even while stressing

It is worthy of note," he concludes, that the Virgin serves as a model even here, at the level of external practice, for "this verse in effect indicates that the movements of the Moslem prayer pertain to the Marian nature" (*Dimensions of Islam*, 85).

[61] Unpublished Text 640.

[62] *Transcendent Unity* (1984), 24.

"the exoteric incompatibility of Christian Trinitarianism with Islamic Unitarianism."[63]

"The trinity which the Koran attributes to Christianity—the Father, the Son, and the Virgin—is altogether logical in its way,"[64] writes Schuon, and he explains this logic on three distinct levels. First of all, by putting Mary in the "place" of the Holy Spirit in its formulation of the Trinity, the Islamic revelation was intended to take into account certain "heretical worshipers of the Virgin" who lived at the time of the Prophet, whose "very existence" serves to show "what the Christian dogmas would have become through an inevitable fault of adaptation had they come to be adopted by the Arabs, for whom they were not intended."[65] Second, the Koranic trinity "expresses a psychological situation *de facto*"[66] by seeking to address "the Marianism which existed in practice" among orthodox Christians at the birth of Islam, and which, while being perfectly consistent with the Christian spiritual economy, "from the Islamic point of view constituted a partial usurpation of the worship due to God."[67] Finally, on yet a third level, which is the most important for our purposes here, Schuon joins ranks with the Sufi 'Abd al-Karîm al-Jîlî in explaining the text esoterically, and this he does by insisting, in numerous places, that it makes perfect sense for the Blessed Virgin to be identified with the Holy Spirit, even as Jesus is with the *Logos* or Son, for "Mary incarnates either the Spirit considered in its feminine aspect or the feminine complement of the Spirit."[68] The Koranic text is completely "justified," he writes, "in the sense that the Holy Virgin is by her nature, and not by adoption, the human receptacle of the Holy Spirit (whence *gratia plena* and *Dominus*

---

[63] *Logic and Transcendence*, 106.

[64] *Survey of Metaphysics*, 21.

[65] *Transcendent Unity* (1984), 24. Writing in the late fourth century A.D. in the *Refutation of All Heresies*, St Epiphanius describes two opposite sects: on the one hand the "opponents of Mary," who denied her perpetual virginity, and on the other hand the "Collyridians," who practiced a kind of Marian eucharist, offering her cakes (*kollyrides*) as a goddess (see Jeremiah 7:18, 44:15-28). There is evidence that the latter group persisted and had spread to Arabia by the sixth century, and Islam, says Schuon, was "bound to react" against this form of "Mariolatry" insofar as "it bore a close resemblance to Arab paganism" (*Transcendent Unity* [1984], 24).

[66] *Logic and Transcendence*, 106.

[67] *Transcendent Unity* (1984), 24.

[68] *Christianity/Islam*, 147.

tecum); as 'Immaculate Conception,' she is *a priori* the vehicle of the Spirit and thereby personifies it."[69] By "bringing the Virgin Mary into the Christian Trinity," the Islamic revelation thus provokes "an interpretation which is not theological in fact but is so by right and finds its support in the Scriptures"—an esoteric interpretation which is closely "linked to the feminization, in certain ancient texts, of the Divine *Pneuma*."[70]

As surprising as this may be to some, a connection between Mary and the Holy Spirit is well established in a number of Christian sources. We do not, of course, find it at the level of dogma, and yet there are sufficient formulations to this effect, both in ancient texts and in the devotional and speculative writings of modern saints and theologians, to suggest that it can be entertained as a *theologoumenon* or pious opinion even in exoteric circles. A fragment from an early Coptic life of the Virgin is exemplary in this respect. Jesus said, "I will not leave you desolate; but if I go, I will send the Spirit, the Comforter, unto you in My place, after not many days, but when Pentecost cometh." Up to this point, the ancient source is simply recapitulating the words of Christ in the Gospel (John 14:16-18). But the text then continues, showing those who are listening to Jesus precisely where they might discover that promised Spirit: "And behold, she who was My dwelling place, and I was her Son in the flesh and in the Godhead, even she the expression of whose image is like Mine according to flesh, behold she is with you now."[71] Depending on the language in which they were

---

[69] *Sufism*, 161. "It follows," he continues, "that an invocation of Mary, such as the *Ave*, is practically, implicitly, and quintessentially an invocation of the Holy Spirit, which in Islam pertains to the hypostatic mystery of *Rahmâniyah*, Divine 'Generosity,' which is Life, Radiation, Light; the Virgin, like the Spirit, is the 'womb' (*rahim*), both inviolable and generous, of all graces" (*Sufism*, 161). Elsewhere we learn from Schuon that "a Maghribi shaykh, who had no knowledge of Christianity except through the Koran, told us that Maryam personifies Clemency-Mercy (*Rahmah*) and that our age is especially dedicated to her for that very reason; the essence of Mary—her 'crown'—are the Names *Rahmân* and *Rahîm*, and she is the human manifestation of the *Basmalah* ('in the Name of God the Clement, the Merciful')" (*Dimensions of Islam*, 93). It is noteworthy that in the *Trisagion* prayer of the Orthodox Church, the Spirit is described in words which suggest these two aspects of the Koranic formula: "O Heavenly King, the Comforter, the Spirit of Truth, who art everywhere present and fillest all things: Treasury of Blessings and Giver of Life, come and abide in us, and cleanse us from all impurity, and save our souls, O Good One." As Treasury the Holy Spirit is *Rahmân*, while as Giver it is clearly *Rahîm*.

[70] *Christianity/Islam*, 95.

[71] *Sahidic Fragments of the Life of the Virgin*, IV, 45-50.

writing, it was more or less likely for ancient writers to emphasize this relationship. Schuon calls attention to the fact that "the Hebrew word *Rûah*, 'Spirit,' is feminine,"[72] and so also, we may note, is the term for Spirit in Syriac, which explains why among certain Syrian fathers—the "Persian sage" Aphraates, for example—the Third Person of the Trinity is often described in distinctly feminine terms.

As for more recent Christian writers, Schuon notes that "according to the blessed Fr Kolbe"—now canonized by the Catholic Church as St Maximilian Kolbe—"Immaculate Conception" is one of the Names of the Holy Spirit." It can be said, the saint adds, that "in espousing Mary, the Spirit was as if incarnated in her," that she is "united with the Holy Spirit to the point of being able to present herself in his Name," and that "the Immaculate One personifies the Mercy of God."[73] One must admit, of course, that Schuon often expressed himself on this point in words which such a Christian would never have chosen, and yet his teaching is essentially the same. Making use of the Hindu term for the underlying cosmic potency which is informed by the Spirit, he explains that the Virgin "personifies the receptive or passive perfections of universal Substance; but she likewise incarnates—by virtue of the formless and occult nature of the Divine *Prakriti*—the ineffable essence of wisdom or spirituality, the both virginal and maternal *materia prima* of all formal coagulations of the Spirit."[74]

As this last passage helps to show, the Schuonian doctrine often associates the Holy Spirit with the uncreated Wisdom of the Old Testament texts which were examined earlier, seeing in both an expression of the Divine femininity manifested in Mary on the human plane. In this respect the teaching is not unlike that of Vladimir Solovyov, Sergei Bulgakov, Paul Evdokimov, and other Eastern Orthodox writers who are associated with the Russian school of sophi-

---

[72] *Christianity/Islam*, 95. He adds in the same place, "Let us likewise note that one finds in the Epistle to the Hebrews the expression 'My Mother the Holy Ghost' (*Matêr mou to hagion pneuma*)."

[73] *Esoterism*, 38.

[74] *Dimensions of Islam*, 92-93. The following is instructive in this context: "In the Catholic sign of the cross a ternary is superimposed on a quaternary; the content of the sign is in fact the Trinity, but the gesture itself consists of four stations; the fourth coincides with the word *Amen*." According to Schuon, "This fourth station belongs to the Blessed Virgin as Spouse of the Holy Spirit and Co-Redemptress, that is, ultimately, as *Mâyâ* at once human and Divine. This is moreover what is betokened by the *Amen* itself, for it expresses the *Fiat Voluntas Tua* of Mary" (*Face of the Absolute*, 60).

ology. Like the Catholic saint Fr Kolbe, these theologians also draw a close connection between the Holy Spirit and the Blessed Virgin, but they insist as well on an additional link with *Sophia*. On the one hand, according to Bulgakov, Wisdom is a name for what all three Persons of the Trinity share: she is "the silence and mystery of the Godhead."[75] But at the same time, in her very mystery and elusiveness, *Sophia* maintains a special intimacy with the Holy Spirit, which *bloweth where it listeth* (John 3:8), and it is through this same Spirit that the Divine Wisdom becomes embodied in Mary, who was herself—as we noted earlier—elusively hidden from the public gaze.[76] The Spirit, says Bulgakov, "abides in the ever-virgin Mary as in a holy temple, while her personality seems to become transparent to Him and to provide Him with a human countenance." Indeed Mary—who made herself as it were "entirely transparent"—"is, in personal form, the human likeness of the Holy Ghost."[77] Speaking in much the same way about the "Primordial Femininity" which "was there when God prepared the Heavens" (Proverbs 8:27), and bringing us back in so doing to the Book of Islam, Schuon points out that "the qualities of this *Materia prima* or this *Prakriti* are purity and transparence, and receptivity with regard to Heaven and intimate union with it," and that Sayyidatnâ Maryam—who is the emptiness precisely in which the Spirit may move—is for this reason described in the Koran as "'chosen and purified,' 'submissive,' and 'believing the Words of her Lord.'" The reader is then offered this image:

> The manifested Divine Spirit is in certain respects comparable to the
> reflected image of the sun on a lake. In this image there is a feminine
> or "horizontal" element, and this is the potential luminosity which

---

[75] Sergei Bulgakov, *Sophia, the Wisdom of God: An Outline of Sophiology* (Hudson, New York: Lindisfarne Press, 1993), 51.

[76] According to the Orthodox theologian Paul Evdokimov, "There is a mysterious coincidence in the theological silence that surrounds both the Holy Spirit and the Virgin during the first three centuries, but their double *kenôsis* ends with a radiant and simultaneous proclamation, during the fourth and fifth centuries. The *Theotokos* appears as the pre-established center of the world, the thrice-holy place of the Divine Advent. . . . As the New Eve, she contains in herself all of humanity, as Adam did; and her flesh, which she gives to her Son, is that of the 'mother of all the living' (Gen 3:20)" (*Woman and the Salvation of the World*, trans. Anthony P. Gythiel [Crestwood, New York: St Vladimir's Seminary Press, 1994], 195).

[77] Bulgakov, 116-117, 122.

is inherent in water, and the perfect calm of a surface unruffled by any wind; and since these qualities permit the perfect reverberation of the "solar" body, they are already something of it. So it is that the Primordial Recipient is a providential projection . . . of the Divine Content.[78]

Now of course, none of this is in any way to suggest that the Blessed Virgin as a human woman is somehow herself to be equated with the Divine Spirit. I paused once before at a similar point in this exposition, and I should do so again lest we make a very serious mistake in our reading of Schuon. As I have elsewhere explained, not even Jesus *is* God in the much too simplistic sense with which this pious ellipsis is often interpreted by traditional Christians, for the Divine and human natures of Christ are not the same, and the Ecumenical Councils of the Church explicitly forbid their confusion.[79] Precisely the same distinction is in order here. When Schuon tells us that Mary "is the personification of the Holy Spirit"[80] or that "the Spirit 'as creation' is none other than the Virgin,"[81] or again—speaking in terms of *Sophia*—that "the Virgin Mother personifies supraformal Wisdom,"[82] he does not wish to imply that there is no difference between her human reality and the Divinity which she contains and makes present. Commenting on a verse which we have already cited from the *sûrah* "The Prohibition" (Sûrah 66:12), he takes note of the words *We breathed into her of Our Spirit*—words with which the Koran describes the Annunciation—and he observes that "the image of breath evokes both the intimacy and subtlety of the gift, its depth or infinitude, if one will," in this way underscoring the avataric relation between the Virgin and God. At the same time, however, the preposition in the phrase *of Our Spirit* reminds us that "no Divine manifestation can

---

[78] *Dimensions of Islam,* 85-86.

[79] See my article "The Mystery of the Two Natures" (note 10 above). "God and man have been united in Jesus Christ, but unless we choose to be heretics, the Christian tradition forbids us to think that the manhood in question was merely that of a historical individual, or that the Divinity was that of the pure Absolute" (132).

[80] Schuon teaches that Mary is "*la personnification de l'Esprit Saint, comme l'indiquent clairement les expressions* gratia plena *et* Mater Dei" (*Du Divin à l'humain* [Paris: Le Courrier du Livre, 1981], 47).

[81] *Gnosis,* 106.

[82] *Christianity/Islam,* 124.

involve the Divine Spirit in itself and in its intrinsic totality; otherwise the Spirit would henceforth be in the manifestation in question, and no longer in God."[83]

In any case, to sum up these last observations: according to Schuon, the trinity which we find mentioned in the Koran, although it is not the same as the Trinity of the Christian creeds, nevertheless is not lacking in truth—*quod absit*—even from an exoteric Christian point of view, while for the esoterist, by calling attention to the Blessed Virgin's "incarnational" relationship with the Holy Spirit, it has the effect of opening a door as it were onto her avataric substance and stature. From the point of view of exoteric Islam, of course, such an opening is altogether beside the point, to say the least, for it is in the nature of the Muslim spiritual economy to emphasize the Divine transcendence to the exclusion of every human theophany. And yet even here, Schuon notes—even in terms of what the traditional Muslim may be prepared to allow for in his considerations of Mary—it is possible to follow the lead suggested by this same Koranic text in such a way as to

---

[83] *Dimensions of Islam*, 94. What Schuon says here is true of every "Divine descent." For "in the *Avatâra* there is quite obviously a separation between the human and the Divine—or between accident and Substance; then there is a mixing, not of human accident and Divine Substance, but of the human and the direct reflection of the Substance in the cosmic accident; relatively to the human this reflection may be called Divine, on condition that the Cause is not in any way reduced to the effect" (*Esoterism*, 63). Any adequate exposition of the Schuonian doctrine of the *Avatâra* would obviously take us too far afield, but one should point out at the very least that like that of the Hindus, it differentiates between a number of avataric modalities. "One may distinguish broadly speaking four categories of incarnation," Schuon writes, "two of them 'major' and two 'minor,' each of the two groups comprising a 'plenary' and a 'partial' incarnation. The major *Avatâras* are the founders of religions or, in circumstances where the question of a renewal of form could not arise, the supreme dispensers of a grace, such as Rama and Krishna; among these founders or dispensers, some are 'solar' and others 'lunar' manifestations of the Divinity, depending on the form of the Message, and so also on the nature of the collectivity receiving it. The minor *Avatâras* are also subdivided into plenary or solar and partial or lunar; they are the great sages or saints who, within the framework of a given tradition and consequently on a lesser scale, repeat the function of the major *Avatâras* in a manner either solar or lunar; there are also feminine incarnations, but their role—that of *shakti*—is always relatively secondary, whatever the level of their manifestation" (*Stations of Wisdom*, 86). Insofar as she is the feminine complement of Christ, Mary may be described as a major "descent" of the lunar type, though as we shall see below the avataric reciprocity which she shares with her Son does not fully exhaust her reality. In any case, the point to underscore at the moment is that every *Avatâra*, whatever the level or scope, "is 'man as such,' while being at the same time 'such and such a man'" (Unpublished Text 919).

glimpse something of the exceptional nature of the Virgin. It is true of course that the Muslim exoterist will never be persuaded to accept the idea of a Divine incarnation, but he will readily admit even so that the Spirit of God makes itself present in the messages which it brings and thus through the person of its messengers.[84] Thus, where the Christian speaks in terms of a God-man, the Muslim will describe the greatest of men by saying that such a one is a prophet, and according to Schuon, this is precisely what can and must be said in Islamic terms about Mary.

He directs our attention, on the one hand, to the similar positions which the Blessed Virgin and the Prophet of Islam occupy in the formal economies of the two traditions. "The function of the Prophet," he writes, is "analogous and symbolically even identical to that of the Virgin Mary, who was likewise the 'ground' for the reception of the Word." Mary, "fecundated by the Holy Ghost, is 'Co-Redemptress' and 'Queen of Heaven,'" while the Prophet Muhammad, "inspired by the same Paracletic Spirit, is 'Messenger of Mercy' (*Rasûl ar-Rahmah*) and 'Lord of the Two Existences' (*Sayyid al-Kawnayn*), this world and the next." In a memorable observation often borrowed by other traditionalist writers, Schuon points out that "the Virgin is 'immaculate' and, from the merely physical standpoint, 'virgin,' while the Prophet, like the Apostles, is 'illiterate' (*ummî*), that is to say, pure from the taint of human knowledge or knowledge humanly acquired."[85]

These very suggestive correspondences might alone entitle us to describe the Blessed Mother as having the stature of Prophetess, but other reasons can be brought forward as well. For example, "Maryam is mentioned, together with other Messengers, in the *sûrah* 'The Prophets'; furthermore," Schuon adds—still speaking of the Koran—"her story is related with care and praise, which would be inconceivable for an ordinary saint (*waliyah*),"[86] but which accords perfectly with what the Prophet himself said in describing her as the "Queen

---

[84] It is said in Islam that when Jesus told his disciples of "another Comforter" whom He would send, "even the Spirit of truth" (John 14:16, 17), He was speaking of the Prophet Muhammad.

[85] *Transcendent Unity* (1984), 120-121.

[86] Unpublished Text 430.

of the women saints in the Muslim paradise."[87] Surely "all this would prove," says Schuon, "if proof were necessary, the supereminent rank of Maryam, that is to say her quality of Prophetess (*Nabiyah*)."[88] We are not to forget, he admits—considering the matter with his usual thoroughness—that "according to a *hadîth*, no woman was ever a prophet." But in this case, he asserts, "it is a question exclusively of law-giving prophecy."[89] In other words, the saying "refers, not to intrinsic dignity, but to extrinsic function,"[90] and hence "there is no reason for thinking, Islamically speaking, that the term 'prophetess' (*nabiyah*) could not fit the Virgin Maryam."[91]

Gnosis and the Primordial Norm

It is only natural, I have said, that Schuon sought to express his Marian doctrine in terms borrowed from the scriptures of the Abrahamic traditions and in light of their orthodox commentaries. He was after all a traditionalist, who always insisted that an operative spirituality must be grounded in one of the great revelations bestowed by Heaven, and as one who had lived in the two worlds of Christianity and Islam, his continual fascination with what the Bible and the Koran have to say about Mary is not unexpected. But he was at the same time a metaphysician and master of *gnosis*, whose message was that of pure esoterism, and it also makes perfect sense that his perception of the Virgin's presence and meaning would not have been confined to those worlds.[92] Unlike the exoteric authorities of a given religion, whose perspectives are

---

[87] *Dimensions of Islam*, 81. This teaching comes from a tradition of the Prophet mentioned earlier.

[88] Unpublished Text 430.

[89] *Face of the Absolute*, 104. Schuon is referring to the distinction in Islam between the *Nabi* (feminine: *Nabiyah*) or prophet as such and the "law-giving prophet" or *Rasûl*. The latter is an apostle or messenger, sent by God as the founder of a given tradition, in accordance with the Koranic verse *And for every nation there is a messenger* (Surâh 10:48). Every *Rasûl* is a *Nabi*, but not every *Nabi* is a *Rasûl*.

[90] Unpublished Text 430.

[91] *Face of the Absolute*, 105. Speaking directly to his disciples, Schuon adds, "Maryam is the *Nabiyah* of the *khalwah*" (Unpublished Text 337).

[92] While "it is in the nature of esoterism," Schuon writes, "to base itself externally" on certain elements in a given exoterism, those elements are "precarious and often almost imperceptible" from the point of view of the corresponding exoteric mentality (*Gnosis*, 36).

determined by certain confessional loyalties—and in fact unlike even the masters of what he sometimes called "average Sufism"[93]—Schuon was utterly free in his fidelity to the "nature of things," to the *fitrah* or primordial norm, and within the inward space of that freedom he realized that the Virgin's intrinsic reality transcends the doctrinal boundaries of the traditions which honor her, manifesting something that is truly universal and Divine. It was for this reason that he called himself *Maryamî*, and it is in this light that one may understand the Marian character of the spiritual order he founded. It is indeed "our insistence upon the nature of things," he writes, "that explains and justifies our connection with Sayyidatnâ Maryam; it is because our perspective is *a priori* metaphysical, esoteric, primordial, and universal that our *Tarîqah* has the right to be named *Tarîqah Maryamîyah*, in perfect accordance with the teachings of Sufic tradition."[94]

It is possible to glimpse at least something of the universal scope and plenitude of the Blessed Virgin by considering first the implications of a title accorded her in Islamic mysticism. As we have just noted, there is good reason—even on exoteric grounds—for calling Mary a Prophetess, but among certain Sufis a further "paracletic" step is sometimes taken in which she is referred to as the "Mother of Prophecy and of all the Prophets," a phrase to which Schuon returns a number of times in his writings. What this formulation helps to make clear, he explains, is a dimension of the Marian reality which might not otherwise have been discerned at the level of scriptural exegesis—namely, that "the message of the Blessed Virgin," understood in its essence, "contains all the prophetic forms possible in their universal and primordial indifferentiation."[95] On the one hand, of course, her message has to do with her Son; theologians have pointed out that the only time she speaks publicly in the Gospel is on the occasion of the wedding feast in Cana of Galilee,

---

[93] In a chapter entitled "The Quintessential Esoterism of Islam," Schuon anticipates the obvious question: "Is not esoterism quintessential by definition?" He answers, "It is so 'by right,' but not necessarily 'in fact,' as is amply proved by the unequal and often disconcerting phenomena of average Sufism," in which "metaphysics is treated according to the categories of an anthropomorphist and voluntaristic theology and of an individualistic piety above all obediential in character" (*Sufism*, 131).

[94] Unpublished Text 745. See note 1 above.

[95] *Sufism*, 155. "Thus it is that the Virgin is considered, by certain Sufis as well as by Christian authors, as Wisdom-Mother, or as Mother of Prophecy and of all the Prophets."

when, referring to Jesus, she tells the servants, *Whatsoever He saith unto you, do it* (John 2:5).[96] But in the Schuonian perspective, *He*—the Son—must be understood as applying not simply to "Jesus as founder of a religion," but to the Divine *Logos* or Word, which was incarnate in Him, and hence not to "such and such a *Rasûl*, but the *Rasûl* as such."[97] As the Mother of that supra-temporal Word, Mary is thus the "matrix of all the sacred forms," a truth expressed, "according to a symbolism common to Christianity and Islam," when it is said that she "has suckled her children—the Prophets and sages—from the beginning and outside of time." This implies, continues Schuon, that "the domain of Mary" pertains to "a level where these systems as such lose much of their importance, and where by way of compensation the essential elements they have in common are affirmed," elements which, he adds—"whether they like it or not"—"give the systems all their value."[98]

---

[96] In the Koran, what amounts to the same message is delivered even more laconically, in fact in utter silence. When the Virgin returns to her family holding the one she has borne, and they, incredulous, say, *O Mary! Thou hast come with an amazing thing*, her response is to give place to the child: *Then she pointed to him*, and it is he who speaks: *Lo! I am the slave of Allah. He hath given me the Scripture and hath appointed me a Prophet* (Surâh 19:27, 29, 30).

[97] *Sufism*, 155. "The Prophets bring Laws; the Holy Virgin brings that which is at the root of all Laws; it is thus that she is the Mother of all the Prophets" (Unpublished Text 344). Schuon observes in this same source that Mary also bears the epithet "'Mother of the Book' [*Umm al-Kitâb*]," indicating that she is "the supra-formal essence of all Books, or the *Logos* as first Substance, pure Mercy." This is why "she personifies and teaches the quintessential orison, the Invocation: the spiritual nourishment, which is infinite. On earth she was the hidden and unknown mother of a Prophet; in Heaven she is the radiant Mother of all the Prophets; it is for this reason that she was, on earth, the wife of the Holy Spirit, not of a man." In another place, Schuon adds that "each Messenger—Sayyidatnâ Maryam included—is identified with the *Logos*, and at the same time, inasmuch as he is a human individual, he is a door to the *Logos*. Every Messenger has a Message, and the Message of Maryam is on the one hand her Son, and on the other hand the unexpressed Substance of all Messages" (Unpublished Text 400). I said above that the Son is fundamentally the *Logos* "in the Schuonian perspective," but it should be added that the Church teaches precisely the same—that the *hypostasis* or personal subject of Christ is the eternal Word. According to traditional patristic Christology, what Jesus was, "was both Divine and human, but who He was, was the *Logos*—His Person in fact being none other than the eternal second Person of the Trinity, who had existed from before the foundation of the world" ("The Mystery of the Two Natures," 117).

[98] *Christianity/Islam*, 147. Schuon quotes—"according to the revelations of Sister Mechthild of Magdeburg (13th century)"—the words of the Virgin Mother herself:

On an initial and most obvious level, this "Marian universality"[99] can be seen in the fact that the Virgin serves as a providential link between the western or Semitic traditions. "Precisely because, in the world of the Semitic monotheists, Maryam is the only feminization of the Divine," Schuon writes—"the only avataric *Shakti* of Vishnu, in Hindu terms"—"she had to appear in all three monotheistic religions at once."[100] For she was indeed "unique and incomparable both in Judaism, by her concrete personality as Prophetess— whether understood or not—and in Christianity, by her function as Co-Redemptress," and she was therefore "*ipso facto* unique and incomparable in Islam and was 'at home' in it, like all the Semitic prophets up to and including Christ."[101] If one objects that a being of so great a stature, so important to the religious worlds in question,

---

"'There I was the single betrothed of the Holy Trinity and mother of the Sages, and I took them before the eyes of God lest they fall, as so many others did. And as I was thus mother to many noble children, my breasts were filled with the pure and unmixed milk of true, sweet Mercy, in such wise that I nurtured the Prophets, and they prophesied before God (Christ) was born' (*Das fliessende Licht der Gottheit*, 1, 22)" (*Face of the Absolute*, 60). In another connection he notes that St Bernard of Clairvaux was among the saints who knew that "Mary is the 'milk' which flows from the Holy Ghost" (*Christianity/Islam*, 146) and who himself had experienced "the Marian mystery of *lactatio*" (*Face of the Absolute*, 225).

[99] *Dimensions of Islam*, 95. Schuon calls attention in this same place to other examples of Mary's universality. He notes that "at the time of the persecution of Christianity in Japan, the Christians did not hesitate to make their devotions in front of the statues of Kwannon, the Buddhist goddess of Mercy"; that "the basilica of Our Lady of Guadalupe, near Mexico City—a famous place of pilgrimage—is built on a hill which in ancient times was consecrated to the mother-goddess Tonantzin, a divinity of the Earth and the Moon," who "appeared herself, in the form of an Aztec princess of great beauty, to a poor Indian, telling him that she was the 'Mother of God' and that she wished to have a church on this spot"; that "above the principal gate of Córdoba, now no longer extant," there was an "image of a Roman goddess identified by the Christians as Mary" and respected as well by the Muslims, who "in their turn venerated the statue of the Virgin-Mother as the patroness of Córdoba"; and finally that "the town of Ephesus, where Mary was assumed into Heaven, was dedicated to Artemis, goddess of light," who as "the protectress of virginity and the beneficent guardian of the sea," is "thus both *virgo* and *stella maris*."

[100] *Dimensions of Islam*, 96. To turn the formulation around—for the sake of those who might be assisted by dialectic—the very fact that the Blessed Virgin did radiate across the boundaries of three distinct major traditions can be taken as an indication or sign that she is nothing less than an *Avatâra*.

[101] *Dimensions of Islam*, 96. Schuon refers to a *hadîth* at this point which "places Mary alongside Adam and above Eve, because of the privilege of having been breathed into by the Divine Spirit." As for the Virgin's prophetic stature in Judaism, this is above all

would surely have appeared at an earlier and more foundational moment and in a more incontrovertible form, manifesting herself among the ancient Jews even before the coming of their promised Messiah, Schuon replies that in taking a feminine form, the Divinity "is necessarily the *Shakti* of an *Avatâra* and thus necessarily appears along with Him," and as it were in His shadow. Mary "could thus appear neither in isolation nor, needless to say, in a spiritual climate" like that of Judaism or Islam, "whose perspective providentially excludes the notion of 'Divine Descents.'" Instead, "in view of her incomparability, she had to be linked with a masculine manifestation of 'human Divinity,'" and this "manifestation, in the Semitic world, is precisely Christ."[102]

But this is just the beginning. According to Schuon, if one wishes to enter into the Virgin's deepest reality, it is necessary to look beyond the role which she plays in the Abrahamic sector of humanity, and

---

evident in the *Magnificat*, whose words are an inspired synthesis of such Biblical texts as Genesis 17:7, 1 Samuel 2:1-10, 2 Samuel 22:28, Job 5:11-12, Isaiah 40:3-5 and 41:8-10, and Habakkuk 3:18, not to mention several Psalms, including 89:10, 98:3, 103:13, 17-18, 107:9, 111:9-10, 113:5-7, 126:3, 5, and 147:6. Schuon adds, "That the Blessed Virgin, speaking spontaneously, should express herself in Biblical terms is a matter of course for anyone with an inkling of what must be the relationship between infused knowledge and formal Revelation in the soul of such a being as Mary" (*Dimensions of Islam*, 98). The Venerable Mary of Agreda writes of the Virgin that "even in the years of her tender infancy it was noticeable that she understood the Scriptures, and she spent much time in reading them. As she was full of wisdom, she conferred in her heart what she knew from the Divine revelations made to her own self with what is revealed to all men in the Holy Scriptures" (*The Mystical City of God: The Divine History and Life of the Virgin Mother of God*, trans. Fiscar Marison [Rockford, Ill.: Tan Books and Publishers, 1978], 163).

[102] *Dimensions of Islam*, 97. Schuon writes extensively about "the complementarity of the holy personages" (*Christianity/Islam*, 146), that is the relationship between the Virgin and her Son, and he does so in a way which stresses its universal, and not only Christian, significance. We have already discussed the relationship between Mary and Wisdom, the supraformal *Sophia*, a relationship closely linking her to the Spirit as well, and from this point of view, notes Schuon, it is clear that the Mother must be regarded as "greater than the Child, who here represents formal wisdom, hence the particular revelation" of Christianity. But if we consider instead "the adult Jesus"— who said of Himself that *he that hath seen me hath seen the Father* (John 14:9)—then "on the contrary, Mary is not the formless and primordial essence, but his feminine prolongation, the *shakti*: she is then, not the *Logos* under its feminine and maternal aspect, but the virginal and passive complement of the masculine and active *Logos*, its mirror, made of purity and mercy" (*Christianity/Islam*, 124). Understood from this point of view, the Virgin is the dimension of *yin* in all things, even as Christ, by whom *all things were made* (John 1:3), is the *yang*, for "she personifies," says Schuon, "the passive and receptive qualities of the Divine Substance" (*Logic and Transcendence*, 110).

therefore beyond the providential relationship which she was destined to have with the incarnate Word of the Christian tradition. It is true, of course, that as the *woman* of the Apocalypse who is *clothed with the sun* (Revelation 12:1), Mary must not be confused with that Sun; she is veiled instead like the moon in its light, and from this point of view her role, a receptive and passive one, is to be the feminine complement of the redeeming *Logos*, hidden—as we have seen more than once—for the sake of His operative eminence. But this fact in no way excludes another, and yet higher, truth—a truth which is hinted at even in the letter of scripture. For it is said of this very same *woman* that the *moon* is *under her feet*, and *upon her head*, we are told, there is *a crown of twelve stars* (Revelation 12:1). From this point of view it is clear that the Virgin is more than the *Shakti* of a masculine *Avatâra:* she is also *Laylâ*, the supremely silent and indeterminate Night, *black but beautiful*, and embracing the suns of all the worlds.[103] "In addition to her celestial personality," which is already evident in the

Continuing in the same place, he writes that "if Christ is the 'spirit,' she is the 'soul,' and this means that man cannot be integrated in Christ without first being integrated in the Virgin, for there is no 'vertical' illumination without the corresponding 'horizontal' perfection." Elsewhere he adds that "if Christ is 'the Way, the Truth, and the Life,' the Blessed Virgin, who is made of the same substance, enfolds graces which facilitate access to these mysteries, and it is to her that this saying of Christ applies in the first place: 'My yoke is easy, and My burden is light'" (*Roots of the Human Condition* [Bloomington, Ind.: World Wisdom Books, 1991], 78). Schuon goes on to link the same complementarity with the account of creation in Genesis 1 and with Canticles, providing as he does so an important methodic insight. "Water represents Perfection according to Maryam, whereas Spirit is Perfection according to 'Isâ, their cosmogonic prototype being 'the Spirit of God moving on the Waters'; in the Song of Solomon there is an analogous reference in the words of the Beloved: 'I sleep, but my heart wakes.' Holy sleep, or *apatheia*, refers to the first of these two mysteries, and holy wakefulness to the second; their combination gives rise to a spiritual alchemy which is found in a variety of forms in all initiatory methods" (*Dimensions of Islam*, 86-87). One final point should be made in this context: insofar as she functions "economically" as the shaktic counterpart of her Son, Mary prepares for His "descent" according to her own, inverse avataric modality. Returning once again, as so often, to the language of Advaita Vedanta, Schuon observes—in one of his frequent paraphrases of the well-known Patristic formula—that in Christ "*Âtmâ* became *Mâyâ* so that *Mâyâ* might become *Âtmâ*." In the case of His mother, however, "*Mâyâ* (Mary) became *Âtmâ* (through the Immaculate Conception) so that *Âtmâ* (the Word) might become *Mâyâ* (through Christ's human nature)." In other words—putting the matter "in Tibetan terms"—"Mary the Immaculate is *Padme*, and Jesus the Incarnate is *Mani*; 'the Jewel in the Lotus'" (Unpublished Text entitled "Intrinsic Esoterism in Christianity").

[103] A woman's name in Arabic, *Laylâ* (or *Lailâ*) means "night," and in view of her mystery and darkness, she is often celebrated among the Sufis as representing the Divine Essence. The following, from a poem by the Shaykh Al-'Alawî, is exemplary in

exoteric perspective, and beyond even "her Divine Prototype" in the Holy Spirit and Wisdom, the Blessed Virgin is finally "the underlying Divine Substance," the "attracting, dilating, and gentling transmuting infinitude of inward and transcendent Reality."[104]

In order to understand what is meant by this teaching, it is important to realize that in the Schuonian doctrine the Supreme Principle is at once the Absolute and the Infinite. By virtue of its absoluteness, it is so far beyond everything else that it alone is to be regarded as truly real, and yet by virtue of its infinitude it is so intimately present within everything that whatever truly exists is itself. According to the first relationship, "the reality of the Substance annihilates that of the accident; according to the second, the qualities of the accident—starting with their reality—cannot but be those of the Substance."[105] As his readers know, Schuon returns to this fundamental polarity numerous times, and in doing so he often connects the first of the two poles with the masculine, and the second with the feminine. "In the first case, the accent is put on the symbolism of virility" or masculinity, for absoluteness means rigor, strength, and sovereignty, while in the second case, it is put on intimacy, fecundity, and nourishing mercy, for infinitude means the radiation of goodness, and thus one may say that "the Infinite is Divine Femininity."[106] Depending on which aspect of Reality one intends

---

this respect: "Full near I came unto where dwelleth / Lailâ, when I heard her call. / That voice, would I might ever hear it! / She favored me, and drew me to her, / took me in, into her precinct, / With discourse intimate addressed me. / She sat me by her, then came closer, / Raised the cloak that hid her from me, / Made me marvel to distraction, Bewildered me with all her beauty. / She took me and amazèd me, / And hid me in her inmost self, Until I thought that she was I, / And my life she took as ransom" (Martin Lings, *A Sufi Saint of the Twentieth Century: Shaikh Ahmad Al-'Alawî: His Spiritual Heritage and Legacy* [Berkeley, Cal.: University of California Press, 1973], 225). Commenting on this poem Schuon writes, "The 'Divine dimension' is called *Laylâ*, 'Night,' for its *a priori* non-manifested quality; this makes one think of the dark color of Parvati and of the black Virgins in Christian art and also, in a certain sense, of the nocturnal encounter between Christ and Nicodemus" (*Roots of the Human Condition*, 42).

[104] Unpublished Text 251. "No perfection," he adds, "is situated outside of her." Elsewhere he writes, "The Substance contains all that we love, and She is what we are" (Unpublished Text 683).

[105] *Esoterism*, 44.

[106] *Esoterism*, 49, 178.

to emphasize, "the Supreme Divinity is either Father or Mother."[107] It is of course primarily with a masculine "face" that God has willed to look upon the worlds of the Abrahamic traditions,[108] where He is understood to be the Father and the Sovereign Lord of all things, but even there it is evident that the Divinity is equally feminine in its intrinsic or inward reality, for *God created man in His own image, male and female created He them* (Genesis 1:27).

In Schuon's perspective, however, there is something more than just equality or symmetry here; there is also hierarchy. The symmetry is not surprising, for the principial aspects of Reality are like two sides of one coin, the Divine being no more absolute than it is infinite, and no more infinite than it is absolute: "Beyond-Being is the Absolute or Unconditioned, which by definition is infinite and thus unlimited; but one can also say that Beyond-Being is the Infinite, which by definition is absolute."[109] As for the existence of hierarchy, or at least a certain kind of hierarchy, those whose theology has been informed by the Semitic traditions will have been led to expect such a teaching, and they will readily understand what Schuon means in writing that "virility refers to the Principle, and femininity to Manifestation," and they will see why he places the masculine at the higher level when considering the cosmogonic relationship between God and creation. But unless they are already careful students of his books, what they may well be surprised to discover is that there is a second hierarchy in the Schuonian doctrine, a metaphysical and esoteric hierarchy intrinsic to the Principle itself, and that within this other and more inward order, it is the Divine Femininity which is the superior pole.

---

[107] *Esoterism*, 49-50. We must not forget, of course, that the Divine is finally beyond all categories, and that in Himself "God could be neither masculine nor feminine, for it would be an error of language to reduce God to one of two reciprocally complementary poles." Insofar as each requires the other to be what it is, Reality is obviously neither alone, nor even both as a synthesis, for its perfect simplicity is prior to all such pairs or syzygies. On the other hand, if "each sex represents perfection," and if we attend to that perfection as such, "God cannot but assume the characteristics of both" (*Dimensions of Islam*, 129).

[108] "There is not only a personal God—who is so to speak the 'human' or 'humanized' Face' of the suprapersonal Divinity—but there is also, 'below' and resulting from this first hypostatic degree, what we may term the 'confessional Face' of God: it is the Face that God turns towards a particular religion, the Gaze He casts upon it, and without which it could not even exist" (*Survey of Metaphysics*, 91).

[109] *Esoterism*, 49.

Thus he continues:

> Even though *a priori* femininity is subordinate to virility, it also comprises an aspect which makes it superior to a given aspect of the masculine pole; for the Divine Principle has an aspect of unlimitedness, virginal mystery, and maternal mercy, which takes precedence over a certain more relative aspect of determination, logical precision, and implacable justice.[110]

Indeed, as one reads more closely, it becomes apparent that the feminine "aspect" of the Principle is rather more than an aspect—more, in other words, than a particular quality or attribute with a value that is strictly *pro nobis*—for what Schuon is talking about in this and other similar passages is nothing less than the very Essence of God. He points out that "a Sufi, probably Ibn 'Arabî, has written that the Divine Name 'She' (*Hiya*), not in use but nevertheless possible, is greater than the Name 'He' (*Huwa*), and this refers," he explains, "to the Indetermination or Infinitude, both virginal and maternal, of the Self or 'Essence' (*Dhât*),"[111] an Essence which inwardly transcends the relative fixity and "masculinity" of the Divine Person, even as that Person transcends in turn the "femininity" of His creation. It is thus no accident that the Arabic word *Dhât* should be feminine, for it refers esoterically to "the superior aspect of femininity," which "surpasses the formal, the finite, the outward; it is synonymous with indetermination, illimitation, mystery, and thus evokes the 'Spirit which giveth life' in relation to the 'letter which killeth.'" For "femininity in the superior sense comprises a liquefying, interiorizing, liberating power: it liberates from sterile hardnesses, from the dispersing outwardness of limiting and compressing forms,"[112] and thus it gives access to a transcendent and supra-formal domain where, in the words of St

---

[110] *From the Divine to the Human*, trans. Gustavo Polit and Deborah Lambert (Bloomington, Ind.: World Wisdom Books, 1982), 95.

[111] *Logic and Transcendence*, 119.

[112] *Roots of the Human Condition*, 40-41. As I have written elsewhere, "The impassibility, integrity, and sovereignty of the exoteric western Deity are seen here to be the veils or projections of something other and higher, which, utterly unlike all manifested qualities and insusceptible to every category, remains in its very fluidity and indeterminacy rather more like the feminine than like anything else." Hence "the femininity of Non-Being or Beyond-Being can thus be considered, at least in this

Dionysius the Areopagite, "the dazzling obscurity of the secret Silence outshines all brilliance with the intensity of its darkness."[113]

As I have pointed out several times before, this is precisely for Schuon the Virgin Mary's "domain," the primordial and universal domain of pure esoterism.[114] *Nigra sed formosa*, she is in fact, he says, both the domain itself and the key to its entrance. On the one hand, she is a "feminine *Avatâra* of supreme degree,"[115] who like every incarnation of God is "at once created and uncreated,"[116] and who as her special vocation "personifies 'original Sanctity,'"[117] manifest-

---

context, as the Principle of the Principle, as constituting and deploying the very Divinity of God Himself" ("Femininity, Hierarchy, and God," *Religion of the Heart: Essays Presented to Frithjof Schuon on His Eightieth Birthday*, ed. Seyyed Hossein Nasr and William Stoddart [Washington, D.C.: The Foundation for Traditional Studies, 1991], 126).

[113] *The Mystical Theology*, Chapter 1.

[114] Orthodox writer Philip Sherrard draws an explicit connection between the apophatic silence of the supra-formal domain and the Divine Femininity: "The Feminine is the pure potentiality that transcends even Being. . . . she is 'beyond Being,' 'that which is not,' the *Nihil* or totally occluded state that is a precondition of God being able to be at all, or to know and affirm Himself at all. As such she is the principle of the masculine principle itself" (*Human Image, World Image: The Death and Resurrection of Sacred Cosmology* [Ipswich, England: Golgonooza Press, 1992], 178-79.

[115] *To Have a Center*, 119. "'Whoever has seen me has seen God': these words, or their equivalent"—Schuon is here paraphrasing Christ's teaching in the Gospel that *He that hath seen me hath seen the Father* (John 14:9)—"are found in the most diverse traditional worlds, and they apply especially also to the 'Divine Mary,' 'clothed in the sun' because reabsorbed in it and as it were contained therein" (*Esoterism*, 62).

[116] *Treasures of Buddhism*, 92. According to the Palamite doctrine, "The Virgin Mother dwells on the frontier between created and uncreated natures" (St Gregory Palamas, "Homily 14").

[117] "A Sufi has said that Sayyidatnâ Maryam personifies 'original Sanctity,' hence 'naturally supernatural' Sanctity, which implies no effort with a view to realization, no method, no constraint; there are certainly, with the Virgin, efforts which result from her Sanctity, but the latter is not the fruit of any effort; it is substantial and existential. Now Sanctity is essentially Contemplativity: it is the intuition of the spiritual nature of things; profound intuition, which determines the entire soul, hence the entire being of man. . . . Sanctity in itself coincides with the Plenitude of Grace (*gratia plena*) which calls forth the Presence of God (*Dominus tecum*)" (Unpublished Text 894). According to St Andrew of Crete, "When the Mother of Him who is Beauty itself is born, [our] nature recovers in her person its ancient privileges, and is fashioned according to a perfect model, truly worthy of God. And this fashioning is a perfect restoration; this restoration is a divinization; and this divinization is an assimilation to the primordial state" ("Homily I on the Nativity of the Blessed Virgin").

ing "the universal soul in her purity, her receptivity towards God, her fecundity, and her beauty."[118] At an operative or methodical level, she is thus the paragon of contemplative prayer and the *khalwah*, and a human embodiment of "the Divine Music that melts hearts and renders infinite."[119] But at the same time she is also, in her most inward depths, this Infinitude itself. For Mary "is not one particular color or one particular perfume," writes Schuon; "she is colorless light and pure air," and hence "in her essence she is identified with that merciful Infinitude which, preceding all forms, overflows upon them all, embraces them all, and reintegrates them all."[120] As the perfect type of cosmic equilibrium and "the model of every holy soul,"[121] "she equally personifies the *Haqîqah*, the naked and living Truth, which is hidden behind the veil of symbols." Thus, when a man comes to know the Blessed Virgin, she having condescended to let her veil fall, what he knows is precisely What is, surpassing every confusion between *Âtmâ* and *Mâyâ*, for "she expresses the *Dhât*, the Essence, which is beyond all form and all determination and which thereby liberates from limitations." This, Schuon adds, "is the supreme aspect of the feminine Principle,"[122] and it is this which the heart may discern, concretely but inexpressibly, in the Virgin Mother.

---

[118] *Christianity/Islam*, 67. Schuon continues by pointing out that these several attributes "are at the origin of all the angelic and human virtues, and even of every possible positive quality, as for example the purity of snow or the incorruptibility and luminosity of crystal." Speaking in another place about the Virgin's beauty, he writes, "Just as Sayyidnâ 'Îsâ took upon himself all the sorrow of the world, so Sayyidatnâ Maryam encompasses all the beauty of the world. With her beauty she places herself before the world so that it can no longer seduce us; it is thus that she delivers us through her beauty. It is through her beauty that she causes us to love God and to forget the world; she is a ray of the Beauty and of the Love of God" (Unpublished Text 312).

[119] Unpublished Text 448.

[120] *Christianity/Islam*, 147-48. Indeed, "all the qualities of Mary can be reduced to the perfumes of Divine Infinitude" (*Esoterism*, 38). According to St Gregory Palamas, "Those who know God recognize in her the habitation of the Infinite" ("Homily 14").

[121] In fact, Schuon adds, "she is as it were sanctity itself, without which there is neither Divine revelation nor return to God" (*Christianity/Islam*, 68-69). And again: "The Virgin personifies Equilibrium, since she is identifiable with the Substance of the Cosmos, which is both maternal and virginal—a Substance of Harmony and Beauty, and thereby opposed to all disequilibriums" (*Dimensions of Islam*, 89).

[122] Unpublished Text 796.

I have stressed more than once, beginning at the very outset of this article, that there can be no question of proving the validity of this highest and most inward of Schuon's Marian teachings from the starting point of the Semitic exoterisms—or not at least on the basis of their scriptures and dogmas.[123] In the case of Christianity, specifically theological thought, the aim of which is "to concentrate solely on the Christ-Savior"[124] in a way which suits the needs of the exoteric majority, is clearly ill-suited for grasping the avataric complementarity between the Son and His mother,[125] to say nothing of the existence of a hierarchy within the Principle or the idea of a supreme Femininity *in divinis,* and for this reason, says Schuon, "it is scarcely possible for theology to accept this mystery of Mary."[126] It is true, of course, that

[123] One feels obliged to add this last phrase, for "in spite of every theological precaution," and "whether one likes it or not," it is nonetheless true that "in Christianity the Blessed Virgin assumes the function of the feminine aspect of the Divinity" (*Dimensions of Islam,* 129) at the level of pious practice—a case, one is tempted to say, where extremes meet and *vox populi, vox Dei.* Schuon continues, not surprisingly: "This observation, far from being a cause for reproach in the eyes of the writer, has on the contrary for him the most positive of meanings." Elsewhere he points out that in the Semitic religions, "the Divinity is conceived in a masculine aspect," though "with a certain exception in the case of Christianity, which, without granting the Blessed Virgin the worship of 'latria,' does grant her, and to her alone, the worship of 'hyperdulia,' which practically, in spite of everything, amounts to a kind of divinization, if not by 'right,' at least 'in fact'" (*To Have a Center,* 119). In the piety of the Eastern Church, one is expressly asked to acknowledge Mary's share in the salvific work of God, as in the Akathist Hymn, where the invocations of the Virgin by her many names are punctuated by the refrain "O Most Holy Mother of God, save us." Indeed, the oldest known prayer to the Virgin, recited in the West as the *Sub tuum praesidium* and first found in a Greek papyrus fragment dating from the late third century A.D., is altogether explicit in this connection: "We turn to thee for protection, O Holy Mother of God: Despise not our petitions, but help us in our necessities. Save us from every danger, O Glorious and Blessed Virgin."

[124] *To Have a Center,* 123. Schuon is speaking specifically here about "Evangelicalism" and Protestant theology, but what he says applies just as much to every form of Christian exoterism.

[125] There are very occasional exceptions in certain speculative works. Bulgakov, for example, is able to write that the "Divine-humanity is to be found . . . in a double, not only a single, form: not only that of the God-human Christ, but that of His Mother, too. Jesus-Mary—there is the fullness of Divine-humanity." The Virgin, he adds, is her Son's "feminine counterpart" (*Sophia, the Wisdom of God,* 123). But such exceptions serve only to confirm the rule.

[126] *Face of the Absolute,* 60. Theological reflection, Schuon continues, "can function only with simple notions, precisely defined and concretely useful; its philosophical dimension can refine this structure, but it cannot transcend it."

if one is willing to look "along" certain theological doctrines, the spiritual and symbolic elaboration of their meaning can provide a kind of trajectory, suggesting a direction in which intellection might move, and this is precisely what I have endeavored to show in earlier parts of this article. And yet, for Schuon, it is only by attending to the very nature of things that one can hope to find any final and lasting proof of this greatest of the Virginal mysteries. Even when the most suggestive scriptures are read anagogically and in the light cast by the most exalted of traditional Marian titles, they still can only take us so far.

This is the case in fact even when we consider the most important of all the Virgin's dogmatic titles, namely, *Theotokos* or "Mother of God."[127] Such a reservation will perhaps surprise the Christian reader, who may have supposed, in view of all I have said, that the Schuonian would be quick to make use of so crucial and so suggestive a title; for here, if nowhere else, there appears to be an "opening" to Mary's ultimate stature, and hence to the principial and esoteric priority of the Divine Femininity. Moreover, the term *Theotokos* comes with the full weight of dogmatic tradition; unlike such epithets of liturgical hymnody as "Ark of the Covenant" and "Gate of Heaven," or "Celestial Ladder" and "Cause of the Deification of Men,"[128] which have the support merely of pious convention and traditional usage, this is a name which was formally bestowed on the Virgin by an Ecumenical Council of the Church, and as such its acceptance is obligatory for all the faithful. Historically, the title is *a priori* Christological, of course, having been promulgated in order to underscore the unity of the two natures in the single Person of Christ, and yet its implications for an esoteric Mariology are obvious. When Gregory the Theologian insisted that "if anyone does not accept the Holy Mary as *Theotokos*, he is without the Godhead,"[129] there is no reason to think that the saint meant to identify the Virgin with this Godhead, or that he himself would have accepted the doctrine that the Principle of the

[127] See above note 7.

[128] The first two of these titles are from the Litany of Loreto, and the second two from the Akathist Hymn. Other notable descriptions include "Mystical Rose," "Mirror of Justice," "Shrine of the Spirit," "Burning and Unconsumed Bush," "Hidden Sense of the Ineffable Plan," and "Restoration of the Fallen Adam."

[129] *Epistle* 101. Not only is Mary "the protectress of what came after her," being "the glory of the earthborn" and "the adornment of all creation"; she is also, says St Gregory Palamas, "the cause of what preceded her," and thus "the head and

Principle is a feminine Substance; but the very fact that his words may be so interpreted is not without significance. Surely, one imagines, Schuon must have placed considerable emphasis on this dogmatic definition of Mary's role. As it happens, however, he expressed serious reservations concerning Christian use of this title, and as we near the end of this article it is important to underscore what they were, for they provide a valuable key to the fundamentally esoteric nature of his Marian perspective, and an essential corrective to certain one-sided interpretations which might otherwise seem to follow from my exposition.

When I say that Schuon had reservations concerning this doctrinal formulation, I do not of course mean that he disagreed with the teaching as such, nor *a fortiori* that he disapproved of the idea of Divine Motherhood. Here as always he was a traditionalist, who would never have challenged the intrinsic orthodoxy of so important a religious dogma. Indeed, God being "not only 'the Father,' but also 'the Mother,'" Schuon himself explicitly says that "it is Mary who embodies her on the human plane," and that she may therefore be regarded as "the 'Mother' of the Divine Perfection or of the Supreme Good."[130] In this sense, if no other, the Virgin is certainly the Mother of God. Schuon's concerns were based instead, not on the legitimacy or value of the expression as such, but on the potential danger involved in mixing two very different categories or levels of spiritual doctrine, and he had in mind specifically the disequilibrating effects which may result when one attempts to give dogmatic form to ideas which are of an essentially closed or initiatic character, ideas normally reserved for an oral and symbolic transmission. The term *Theotokos*, he writes, is a "purely esoteric expression," and for this reason it is "by no means accessible to everyone."[131] In becoming a *de fide* dogma, however, the idea was necessarily inserted into a domain where all and sundry would be required to accept it, whether esoterists or not. Hence, while agreeing that the meaning contained in the title is "metaphysically plausible,"[132] Schuon knew even so that it remained

consummation of all that is holy." She is, in fact, "the beginning and the foundation and the root of all these ineffable good things" ("Homily on the Dormition").

[130] *Survey of Metaphysics*, 33-34.

[131] *Transcendent Unity* (1984), 132. See above note 12.

[132] *Christianity/Islam*, 79.

a "rather problematical epithet"[133] in its present dogmatic and ecclesiastical context, for "on the exoteric level and in the absence of subtle commentaries which would compensate for its audacity or imprudence," it can easily result for some in "an overshadowing of the metaphysics of the Absolute."[134]

Given the extraordinary depth to which his Mariology reaches, it is most instructive to see how thorough and balanced Schuon's observations are on this point. Although he himself had a profound affinity for the primordial mysteries of inwardness and immanence, willingly acknowledging a spiritual kinship with Abhinavagupta as well as with Shankara, they did not blind him to the importance of a preparatory and counterbalancing stress on transcendence, and one can see clear evidence of that fact in this case, precisely at a point where those whose love of the Eternal Feminine is less discerning might be tempted to exaggeration. Again and again one finds that the Schuonian message is one of pure objectivity. "It is useless," he cautions, "to seek to realize that 'I am *Brahma*' before understanding that 'I am not *Brahma*'; it is useless to seek to realize that '*Brahma* is my true Self' before understanding that '*Brahma* is outside me'; it is useless to seek to realize that '*Brahma* is pure consciousness' before understanding that '*Brahma* is the Almighty Creator.'"[135] By analogy,

---

[133] *To Have a Center,* 119. The phrase "Mother of God," says Schuon, is "actually highly elliptical" (*Roots of the Human Condition,* 38); indeed it is an ellipsis of "the most daring kind" (*Logic and Transcendence,* 117).

[134] *Christianity/Islam,* 79. Schuon goes so far as to say that the Nestorian "protest against the expression *Mater Dei,*" which originally precipitated the declaration of the dogma, "can be defended seriously and honestly," for the expression "unquestionably entails a certain 'neutralization' of the perspective of transcendence to which Nestorius had a sacred right to be deeply attached" (*Survey of Metaphysics,* 128). Elsewhere Schuon explains that "the esoteric nature of the Christian dogmas and sacraments is the underlying cause of the Islamic reaction against Christianity. Because the latter had mixed together the *Haqîqah* (the esoteric Truth) and the *Sharî'ah* (the exoteric Law), it carried with it certain dangers of disequilibrium that have in fact manifested themselves during the course of the centuries," dangers which Christ Himself indicates with the words *Give not that which is holy unto the dogs, neither cast ye your pearls before swine, lest they trample them under their feet, and turn again and rend you* (Matthew 7:6). If one asks, however, "whether things might have been otherwise," Schuon answers at once, "assuredly not," for "the inward and esoteric truth must of necessity sometimes manifest itself in broad daylight, this being by virtue of a definite possibility of spiritual manifestation and without regard to the shortcomings of a particular human environment" (*Transcendent Unity* [1984], 133-34).

[135] *Spiritual Perspectives and Human Facts,* trans. P. N. Townsend (Bedfont, England: Perennial Books, 1987), 115-16.

we could say in the present context that it is useless to seek to realize that the Virgin Mary is the Mother of God, and hence that she corresponds esoterically to the Divine Essence, before understanding outwardly, on the plane of exoteric doctrine, that from another and logically prior point of view she is at the same time a human woman and creature.

Twice before we have paused in order to stress this crucial paradox, and if we do so again it is because the matter seems to have been such an important one for Schuon—so important in fact that he felt obliged to distance himself, in spite of all we have seen, from the most exalted of all Christian names for the Virgin. As a metaphysician he knew very well that since the infinitude of the Divine Essence transcends the Divine Person, "Mary" is indeed God's Mother; but he also knew that they alone have a right to speak of such mysteries who have first distinguished not just between *Âtmâ* and *Mâyâ*, but between the Principle and its Manifestation, and who thus have enough discernment to realize that "either a phenomenon is God—which is a contradiction—in which case it has no mother, or it has a mother, and then it is not God, at least in respect of its having a mother, and setting aside the initial contradiction of the hypothesis."[136] Whatever else she might be, and however great the Reality which she manifests, whether on earth or in Heaven, the *Theotokos* remains, at the level of that manifestation, ontologically less than the One whom she bears. Only those who know at least this can hope to know that it is precisely in this way that she is also much more.

Experiencing the Marian Mystery

So it is that Schuon taught; but how, it might be asked, did he know? For many readers, the doctrine discussed in this article will doubtless seem merely speculative, and it is understandable, as we draw to a close, if some are wondering precisely where lies the authority for these varied and provocative insights. As I explained near the start, it has not been my aim to respond to the skeptical cavils of cynics, nor at this point is that surely necessary, for such critics will have dropped away many pages ago. On the other hand, I fully expect that even among those readers who remain, and who may find themselves attracted to Schuon's Marian teaching, the question I have raised

---

[136] *Christianity/Islam*, 79.

will persist. How could he have known these things? From one point of view, a perfectly sufficient answer has been provided already, for in describing the esoteric character of his message, and its essential difference from a strictly theological standpoint, I have several times emphasized its foundation in the very "nature of things." In order to verify what Schuon has said, we must therefore exercise our powers of discernment, for the truth of these matters is to be apprehended by the heart, and by virtue of the "metaphysical transparency" of phenomena.[137] But there is a second answer that can be given as well, one to which I alluded in beginning this article—an answer that concerns certain very particular experiences granted to Schuon by Mary herself.

Schuon has written that his spiritual relationship with the Virgin actually began in his childhood. As a lad of thirteen, he had composed a short poem in honor of the Divine Femininity, which he would later describe as a "presentiment" of certain graces to come: "Doth thy velvet arm bear me aloft to thee? Doth thy mantle silently descend upon me? Devoutly do I contemplate thy holy all; I dissolve in the fragrance of thy soul. To my heart dost thou softly ope a door; a quiet faith doth ripple gently down."[138] Having been a Protestant as a very young boy, he soon thereafter became a Roman Catholic, and he recalls in his memoirs that he "met Mary in two ways" in this new ambience: first through a "large and beautiful image of Our Lady of Perpetual Help, the famous Byzantine icon on a gold background," which hung in the monastery chapel where he attended Mass; and second through reciting the Rosary, in which he "spoke to Mary, which I had never done before."[139] When in his twenties he later entered Islam, this practice was of course abandoned, and his spiritual

---

[137] As his readers know, this is a frequently recurring phrase in the Schuonian writings. The following is representative: "There has been much speculation on the question of knowing how the sage—the 'gnostic' or the *jnâni*—'sees' the world of phenomena, and occultists of all sorts have not refrained from putting forward the most fantastic theories on 'clairvoyance' and the 'third eye'; but in reality the difference between ordinary vision and that enjoyed by the sage or the gnostic is quite clearly not of the sensorial order. The sage sees things in their total context, therefore in their relativity, and at the same time in their metaphysical transparency" (*Light on the Ancient Worlds*, trans. Lord Northbourne [Bloomington, Ind: World Wisdom Books, 1984], 116).

[138] From his unpublished memoirs, "Memories and Meditations" (1982), 10.

[139] "Memories and Meditations," 264. Although his parents were both of Roman Catholic background, they did not practice their religion, and Schuon was sent

attention became otherwise occupied for many years—though even then there were hints as to the continuing benediction of Sayyidatnâ Maryam. He recalls a time, for example, when he was invoking the Koranic Names of Mercy, "the Divine Names *Rahmân* and *Rahîm*":

> I invoked the two Names quite independently of any doctrinal perspective and thinking only of God. Then all at once I felt a powerful Presence: in it there was golden warmth, beauty, love, mercy, and I—who had not in the least been thinking of the Holy Virgin—suddenly knew that it was she. For a long while this state of grace continued, and I was as if inebriated from it.[140]

This experience seems to have been only a foreshadowing of something greater to come, however, for in March of 1965, at a time when he was faced with particular difficulties and sufferings, Mary came to him, he writes, in a yet more profound and decisive way. He was on his way to Morocco, and the ship had called at Port-Vendres along the French coast. Alone in his cabin, gazing into a bouquet of flowers, "I sought to explain to myself certain difficulties," and "to imagine, with regard to Paradise, what is imaginable; it was as if I were in a waking dream; in my consciousness nothing remained save images of Paradise. Then all at once," he continues, "the Divine Mercy overwhelmed me in a special manner; it approached me inwardly in a feminine form which I cannot describe, but which I knew to be the Holy Virgin; I could not think otherwise."[141] Later during the same trip, when he was staying in the Moroccan city of Tetuán, "the undreamt-of grace came to me anew," once again in the form of an inner vision—"the heavenly consolation, streaming forth from the primordial femininity"—and as with all truly celestial experiences, it left him feeling "a new man," forever changed for the better. "I was as if marked by Heaven. It was as though I lived in a special protective aura belonging already to Heaven, which at the same time carried with it an obligation."[142] He would later describe these moments as

---

instead to a Lutheran school. Shortly before dying in 1920, however, his father had encouraged him to enter the Catholic Church.

[140] "Memories and Meditations," 265.

[141] "Memories and Meditations," 266.

[142] "Memories and Meditations," 267, 268. "In retrospect," says Schuon, "I can describe the event on the ship and in Tetuán in these words: The heavenly Beauty is

having afforded him "a mystical contact" with Mary and as signs of his "heavenly adoption" by her[143]—an adoption and protection, he affirmed, through which the Virgin had become the patroness of his disciples as well. Hence the name of his Sufi order, which we noted earlier: the *Tarîqah Maryamîyyah.*[144]

I mention this decisive occasion in Schuon's life for two reasons. First, as already indicated, knowing at least something about his experiences can be of assistance when questions are posed by otherwise sympathetic interlocutors concerning his authority. If someone asks in good faith how he could have come to know what he taught, the answer in part is that he was instructed by the Blessed Virgin herself, for there can be little doubt that had it not been for these miraculous encounters, his understanding of the Divine Femininity would have been less intimate and his Mariology correspondingly less profound. On the other hand, it is very important that a note of caution be sounded; Schuon was a metaphysician, after all, and not a mystic, and it is therefore characteristic of him to insist that "instead of being governed by phenomena and following inspirations," one should "submit to principles and accomplish actions." For this reason, he

both remedy and sacrament. For its sweetness heals; it dissolves all melancholy and all bitterness. And its holiness transforms; it overcomes all consuming thoughts and all seductive curiosity. It bestows the motionless light of recollection and the inebriating draught of fervor; it is luminous gold and singing wine. May I be the mirror, wherein its saving image resounds" (270).

[143] Unpublished text entitled "On the Subject of a Pneumatic Personality." Although further details would be out of place in this context, it should be added, and emphasized, that these experiences were not the last. Indeed Schuon was to benefit from Mary's presence and graces throughout the rest of his life, though he remained circumspect in speaking about them, even in his unpublished writings. Describing a certain state in his memoirs, he writes very typically, "All at once she was there—a tall apparition, like snow and sun. But to say more would not become me" ("Memories and Meditations," 269). We do know, however, that he was granted additional visual experiences, that the Virgin would speak to him in his native German, and that he sometimes received presentiments of a tactile order when Mary clasped his hand.

[144] Martin Lings recently recounted his experience of being led to the *Tarîqah*, in the late 1930s, in response to his prayers to the Virgin, though it was only years later that he came to realize what the connection had been all along. He and other disciples in Europe had asked Schuon to add a further name to that of his own shaykh, the Shaykh Al-'Alawi, in order to distinguish their spiritual community from 'Alawiyyah Sufis in North Africa. "To our surprise [Schuon] said, 'Our *Tarîqah* is *Maryamiyyah*,' that is, of Mary; and he told us that more than once she had made it clear to him that she had chosen us for herself, and that she was our protective patroness. He went so far as to say: 'It is not we who have chosen her; it is she who has chosen us.' And so, after all, my *Ave Maria*, repeated such a multitude of times, had not been out of

would have been quick to discourage us from supposing that the truth of his Marian doctrine, or indeed any doctrine, depends exclusively upon certain spiritual states or gifts. For "what counts in the eyes of God," he goes on to warn, "is not what we experience, but what we do. Doubtless we may feel graces, but we may not base ourselves upon them. God will not ask us what we have experienced, but He will ask us what we have done."[145]

This being so, one hesitates to talk at all about Schuon's own experiences. Indeed it might have been preferable to pass them over in silence—at least in the present article, where the interest is not primarily of a biographical kind—were it not for the fact that he soon found a way to transpose what he had been given into an objective form, a form which could in turn become for others a support for intellection, and thereby an opportunity for their own discernment of principles. I spoke at the outset about a certain shaktic quality which can be detected in those of Schuon's books published after 1965, and it is noteworthy, too, that he began at this time to compose Arabic *qasîdahs* or poems in honor of the Virgin.[146] But there is something else as well—something of an even greater significance—which must also be mentioned. It seems that his contact with Mary had provided him with the inspiration for a level or modality of concrete expression quite different from what one finds in his writing, whether prose or verse, for shortly after these initial experiences, Schuon, who had

line with my final orientation" ("Frithjof Schuon: An Autobiographical Approach," *Sophia*, 4/2 [Winter 1998], 19).

[145] Unpublished Text 982.

[146] These verses vary from one or two quatrains to somewhat lengthier litanies, and in them the Virgin is addressed by such titles as "Full Moon of Full Moons," "Well-spring in the Garden of the All-Bountiful," "Flood of Graces," "Laylâ, Abode of the Ever-Merciful," "Nectar of Paradise," "Light-filled Crystal," "Repose of the Spiritual Travelers," "Gate of the Infinitely Good," and "Bride unto the Gnostics." In later years Schuon came to write a series of poems in English, the first of which, "*Regina Coeli*," was also addressed to Mary: "Thou art more than a symbol; Thou art near / To me as blood and heart; Thou art the air / That makes me live, that makes me pure and wise; / A sweet and tender air from Paradise. / Thou art more than the words describing Thee / And more than all the sacred songs that we / Sing in Thy praise; my ecstasy was Thine / Before God's very making of the vine" (*Road to the Heart: Poems* [Bloomington, Ind.: World Wisdom Books, 1995], 8). Later still, during the last three years of his life, Schuon wrote over three thousand lyric poems in German, and once again he had occasion to celebrate the great Marian Grace. "Port-Vendres, where the ship lay at anchor— / I will never forget that golden day. / I was alone in my room; the others / Wanted to walk a little on the shore. / They had brought me a bunch

been a gifted artist since childhood, began to express his perception of the Marian mysteries through paintings of the Virgin and Child, and this he continued to do until the early 1980s, producing numerous very beautiful icons.[147]

As those who have had the privilege of seeing them know, these paintings reflect very clearly something of the extraordinary insight which the manifestation of the Virgin Mother had brought him. At the same time, however—and more importantly—they have made it possible for others to share in the grace she bestowed, and in this way an experience which might have otherwise remained a strictly personal or individual *hâl* has become instead the vehicle for transmitting and evoking a like discernment. This in fact, says Schuon, was his very object in producing the icons. "If I were asked why I paint images of the Holy Virgin," he writes, "I should answer: to transmit, thus to make accessible to others, an inward vision," and thus "to make possible a participation in this vision."[148] It is therefore not necessary to depend exclusively on what he has said about Mary in his writings, for in this altogether unexpected fashion, he had provided the means of verifying the truth of his doctrine in the depths of one's own inward perception.

It has seemed to me obvious that any adequate account of the Schuonian teaching must at least acknowledge the existence of this aesthetic dimension, and yet having done so it is very difficult to know quite what to say, how to convey the many subtle particulars, especially when addressing readers who may have never seen his paintings before. The discursive formulation of any beauty is of course finally impossible, and this is all the more true when we are presented with beauty of a sacred and maieutic order—one which

---

of flowers— / I gazed into their bright splendor / And thought of Paradise like a child; / Then came—a waking dream—the Virgin sweet, / And remained, hidden deep within me / With her grace, which never left me— / Holy presence, luminous remembrance. / A picture come from Heaven; I gladly call it / The *Stella Maris*—my morning star."

[147] I use the term "icons" to underscore the hieratic and translucent quality of the images, their function as "windows to Heaven," but it should be understood that Schuon's paintings are not in a Byzantine style, nor are they meant to serve the same didactic purpose as Eastern Christian works of sacred art. It should also be stressed that Schuon was above all a metaphysician and a spiritual master, not an artist, and that it was for his books, not his art, that he wished to be known.

[148] From a letter of December 1982.

operates, says Schuon, by means of an "initiatic dis-illusion."[149] A Catholic writer, having admitted that "it is difficult to express in words the gratitude I feel for Schuon's beautiful pictures," nonetheless struggled to call attention to certain of their distinguishing features, seeing in the images "the timelessness and immobility of traditional American Indian art; the luminosity and hieratic attitude of the figures of Byzantine art; and the color, sensuality, and majesty— even sumptuousness—of Persian and Indian Islamic art."[150] Such observations do little more than touch the surface, however, and in some ways they may even mislead, for Schuon certainly did not set out to imitate any existing convention or to blend various styles, but simply to communicate what he saw when the Virgin came to him. "I painted her, not as she is portrayed in Christian religious art," he writes—nor for that matter in any other art—"but as I had inwardly experienced her, as virginal Mother or as motherly Virgin, and beyond all theological forms; as the embodiment of the Divine Mercy and at the same time of the *Religio Perennis*."[151]

[149] Schuon is actually describing the Egyptian Isis, "a well-known example of Divine Femininity," but his words apply equally to the Blessed Virgin as she appears in his paintings. "By drawing back the veils, which are accidents and darkness, she reveals her Nudity, which is Substance and Light; being inviolable, she can blind or kill, but being generous, she regenerates and delivers" (*Esoterism*, 50).

[150] The author is Ramon Mujica, a Peruvian scholar, and the words are taken from a copy of an undated letter. Referring to Schuon's own words above, Mujica writes that "for someone like myself who has been brought up in a Catholic background, Mr Schuon's representations of the Holy Virgin are . . . a source of 'initiatic dis-illusion.' The Virgin's Nudity—her naked immaculate earth, her transparent body of glory, her flower of virginity—scorches the lids of our hearts. An epiphany of light, a garden of resurrected suns, is food for the inner eye." On the subject of nudity in sacred art, Schuon notes that "according to the Catholic criteriology, total nudity is excluded so far as the messengers of Heaven are concerned"—"even partial nudity probably," he adds, "so far as women are concerned, except in the case of *lactatio*, as indicated by St Bernard's vision and also by certain icons"—"whereas in Hinduism it has either a neutral or a positive character. The reason for the Catholic attitude is that Heaven can neither wish to excite concupiscence nor to offend against modesty." And yet, he concludes, "even in the climate of Christianity there exists here a certain margin" (*Esoterism*, 217; see above note 98). In a private audience, Schuon once told me, "One loves Christ for His words, but one loves the Virgin for her body" (July 1996). In view of everything we have discussed in this article, I trust that the profoundly sober meaning of this remark will be evident.

[151] "Memories and Meditations," 268. It is true that when writing privately to friends he would himself sometimes speak about the stylistic content of the images, explaining for example that "in my paintings of the Virgin, a tendency towards Hinduism, towards Shaktism if you will, manifests itself, and towards the *Krita-Yuga*,

As I have already confessed, I am at a loss to know even how to begin describing this dimension of the Schuonian message, how to convey in words even a small portion of its transformative power, and it therefore seems best in conclusion if the icons are left to "speak" for themselves, offering as they do a kind of wordless summation, in color and contour, of the entire range of Schuon's Marian doctrine. For there indeed is the Blessed Virgin herself, "black but beautiful": on the one hand a very particular woman, often dark-skinned and in many cases bejeweled, clothed like primordial man with the air—the hidden model of the *khalwah* and of contemplative prayer, in herself strictly nothing; but at the same time a feminine *Avatâra* of supreme degree and the very Mother of God, the Priest in the Temple and that Temple itself, a Prophetess and the Mother of Prophets, merciful *Mâyâ* and *Sophia* incarnate, the *Shakti* of her Son and the elusive Spouse of the Spirit—and ultimately the ineffable *Dhât*, the inward bliss of the transpersonal Essence, through whose radiance we are invited to return to the Self.

How can we know that what Schuon tells us is true? How can we ever hope to fathom these mysteries? We need not, it seems, only listen to him; with his help we may gaze in wonder upon Mary herself.

and finally towards the proto-Semitic world, which is echoed in the Song of Songs." But he was quick to add in such contexts that "this was not my prior intention; it lies simply in the nature of things and likewise in the very kernel of my being"; for it was precisely there, it seems—in his heart—that he had been blessed with "a particular manifestation of the *Rahmah*, the *Sakînah*, the *Barakah*, the mystical *Laylâ*, determined by the end of time; and, from a metaphysical point of view, the self-determining of the *Haqîqah*" (from a letter of September 1981).

III

Sacred Art

—⚬⊙⊙⚬—

"As above, so below."—Hermetic formula

"Make all things according to the pattern which was shown thee on the mount."—Exodus 25:40; cf. Hebrews 8:5

"Beauty is the splendor of the Truth."—Plato (427-347 B.C.E.)

"Our dull understanding can only grasp the truth by means of material representations."— Suger, Abbot of St. Denis (1081-1151)

"[Material] form is a revelation of [spiritual] essence."—Meister Eckhart (1260-1327)

"She [the Blessed Virgin] was so beautiful that, when one has seen her once, one would wish to die in order to see her again."—St. Bernadette of Lourdes (1844-1879)

"We do not make obeisance to the nature of wood, but we revere and do obeisance to Him who was crucified on the Cross."—Leontius of Neapolis (d.c.650)

"The respect that is paid to the image passes over to its archetype"—Basil the Great (329-379)

"The church is an earthly heaven in which the heavenly God dwells and moves."—St. Germanus (d.733)

"To decorate their houses with religious pictures is a custom as old as Christianity itself, for the true Christian has always considered his home as nothing less than a temple of God, and the religious pictures as means to extend and preserve the spirit of Christianity in the home."—St. John Vianney, the Cure d'Ars (1786-1859)

"The best inscription of the Name of Jesus is the one that is in the heart, then the one that is spoken, and then the one that is painted. Everything that God has created for the salvation of the world is contained in the Name of Jesus."—St. Bernardino of Siena (1380-1444)

"If the stars should appear one night in a thousand years, how would men believe and adore, and preserve for many generations the remembrance of the City of God which had been shown! But every night come out these envoys of beauty, and light the universe with their admonishing smile."—R.W. Emerson (1803-1882)

—⚬⊙⊙⚬—

"We knew not whether we were in heaven or on earth, for surely there is no such splendor or beauty anywhere upon earth. We cannot describe it to you: only this we know, that God dwells there among humans, and that their service surpasses the worship of all other places. For we cannot forget that beauty."—Words of Vladimir, Prince of Kiev's (pagan) Russian emissaries upon witnessing the Divine Liturgy in the Hagia Sophia church in Constantinople (c.988)

"When, in my joy over the beauty of the House of God through the loveliness of the many-colored jewels, I am withdrawn from outward cares and a worthy meditation leads me, through transposition of the material into the spiritual, to perceive the various holy virtues, it seems to me as if I dwelt in a strange part of the universe, such as exists neither in the mire of the earth nor in the purity of Heaven, and then, with God's grace, it may happen that in anagogical [spiritual] manner, I am raised up from this lower to that higher world."—Suger, Abbot of St. Denis (1081-1151)

"Of old God the incorporeal and uncircumscribed was not depicted at all. But now that God has appeared in the flesh and lived among humans, I make an image of the God who can be seen. I do not worship matter but I worship the Creator of matter, who for my sake became material and deigned to dwell in matter, who through matter effected my salvation."—St. John of Damascus (c.675-c.749)

"Writings are to be understood and should be expounded chiefly according to four meanings. The first is called literal. . . . The second is called allegorical. . . . The third is called moral. . . . The fourth is called anagogical, that is to say, that which surpasses the senses [sovrasenso]; this occurs when one expounds spiritually a Scripture which, though true in the literal sense, also signifies the higher things belonging to the eternal glory, as one may see in the Psalm of the Prophet where it is said that when the people of Israel departed out of Egypt, Judea was made holy and free. Although this was clearly true according to the letter, the spiritual meaning is no less true, namely, that when the soul departs from sin, it is rendered holy and free in its powers."—Dante (1265-1321)

THE ROYAL DOOR

Titus Burckhardt

Between the years 1140 and 1150 the three-part doorway on the west front of Chartres cathedral was constructed. This has always been called the Royal Door, because the upright figures on the door-supports in part represent kings and queens of the Old Covenant.

The style of this door is still Romanesque in its reposeful equilibrium, and yet it is already Gothic in that the repose of its parts no longer strives earthwards, but upwards, as if these parts rose aloft like lights burning motionlessly. The forms are still austere and enclosed within themselves; they deliver themselves up as little to the uncertain light that changes constantly from morning to evening, as to the uncertain movements of the human soul. Bright and dark areas are created by smooth and rough surfaces (themselves fluted, jagged, or broken up by ornaments), with an effect rather like colors, and indeed, at one time, they were actually coated with gold and other colors. The original coating has now gone, but a still extant enamel—a mild, melodic brightness encasing the rawness of the stone—covers the surfaces and articulations.

From the point of view of their deepest meanings, the images on the three-fold Royal Door represent the most complete expression of doctrine that has ever been incorporated in the walls and supports of a doorway. Christ appears three times, each time in the middle of a tympanum: above the right-hand entrance, we see Him freshly descended to earth, sitting on the lap of His enthroned Mother; above the left-hand entrance, He ascends to Heaven, surrounded by angels; and on the central tympanum, He reveals Himself in His eternal majesty. The Nativity seems to indicate Christ's human nature, and the Ascension His Divine nature; but the immediate reference is simply to His coming and His going, to the fact that He is the alpha and omega of earthly existence, between which two extremes His eternal majesty stands, like the present moment between yesterday and tomorrow. These are the three different meanings of the Door—the Door that is Christ Himself.

The lower portion of the whole doorway represents earth, and the upper portion Heaven. For the figures on the door pillars, though their names are unknown, are certainly representatives of the Old Covenant, and the earthly forefathers of the Divine Incarnation. Like the Incarnation, they bear the Heaven of the tympanums. Between these lower and upper domains, and interrupted only by the entrance doors themselves, runs the exquisite row of capitals, on which all the main incidents in the life of Christ are successively portrayed: it is like the demarcation line between two worlds.

That the figures on the door pillars seem so tall and narrow signifies that they themselves are the "pillars of the Church," to which St. Paul refers in the Scripture. Durand de Mende writes: "The pillars of the Church are the bishops and the learned divines who keep the Church upright. . . ." Strictly speaking, the door pillars and the figures associated with them represent a kind of ante-chamber, just as does the Old Covenant with regard to the New. In a similar doorway at Le Mans, this division into ante-chamber and main body of the church is overt: the forward wall pillars are all decorated with Old Testament personalities, while the doorposts themselves are decorated with statues of the Apostles. The latter alone belong to the "body" of the Church.

In the pictorial or sculptural decoration of a building, Medieval art—especially Romanesque and early Gothic—bases itself on the meaning that inheres in each of its constituent parts as a result of its structural role. At the beginning, on the doors of some Romanesque churches, the spiritual meaning of the supporting pillars was indicated only by flat chiseled figures; one hesitated to bestow three dimensions on a human representation, and thus to detach it from the body of the building; a free-standing statue resembled too much the ancient idols. As, however, the figures carved on the door-posts or pillars began to take on from them their round or multi-faceted form, they became as if round figures themselves, and finally emerged from out of the building structure, without however detaching themselves from it completely. In this way the pillar, thanks to its spiritual meaning, gave birth to the statue, just as had also occurred in ancient times.

As a sign that the sculpted Old Testament patriarchs or prophets are incorporated in the eternal edifice of the Heavenly Jerusalem, one can see over their heads—not over all of them but over those on the right- and left-hand doors—a small building crowned with a tower.

The feet of the sculpted figures rest either on a calyx of petals (which gives them an astonishing similarity to the sacred statues of the Far East) or on monsters, seen as the vanquished might of the passions and of the devil.

The unusually large number of female figures amongst these Old Testament personages—eight have been preserved—points to the redemptive role of the Virgin Mary, the Protectress of the Church. She appears herself in the right-hand tympanum with the Divine Child, whose Nativity is represented there. On the lowest panel of the tympanum are depicted the Annunciation, the Visitation, the Nativity, the Adoration of the Shepherds, and, on the middle panel, the Presentation of Jesus in the Temple. In the Nativity scene, the Virgin rests on a bed that resembles a chest; a table covers this, like the sky or the heavens. On top of this table lies the Child in a basket, and an ox and an ass (of which only traces now remain) stretch out their heads towards Him. The table is not only the crib in which the newly born Christ-child lies, but also the altar on which the body of the Savior is forever sacrificed.[1] At the same time He is present on the other altar, portrayed immediately above, on which the mother offers her Child to the priest. The resting mother in the lowest panel, the temple altar in the middle panel, and the Virgin and Child in the uppermost panel (surmounted by a baldachin) are all situated centrally; for it is the same mystery expressed three times over: the Blessed Virgin is the foundation, the altar, and the throne of the manifestation of God in human form. The way in which the artist has expressed the theological truths by the very geometry of the representation bears witness to his mastership: in the lowest panel, the horizontal, resting position of the mother, with the Child portrayed above her, represents passive resignation, by means of which the Virgin, affirming the will of God, becomes the "substantial cause" of salvation. In her pure receptivity, open to grace, she is comparable to the *materia prima* of both the world and the soul. On the middle panel, the altar rises vertically, and on it the Child stands upright as His mother offers Him to the priest of God: she offers herself in the form of her Child, just as the soul must offer itself. In the figure of the Queen of Heaven in the topmost section, two concentric circles may be inscribed: the larger one surrounds the mother, the smaller one the Child on her lap, just as the nature of the mother surrounds on all sides the nature of the Child, and just as the soul that has reached true knowledge contains in its center the Divine Light, Emmanuel.

[1] See Émile Male, *L'Art religieux du XIIIe siècle en France*, Paris 1931, p. 188 et seq.

As the lowest and the highest in creation the Virgin appears in the manner described by Dante in the famous verses that he puts in the mouth of St. Bernard: *Vergine madre, figlia del tuo figlio, ùmile ed alta più che creatura* ("Virgin mother, daughter of thy son, lowly and exalted more than any creature").

St. Albert the Great wrote of the Virgin: "Her son is King of Kings and Lord of Lords; so she must be called Queen of Queens and Lady of Ladies. . . . Her son is called God of Gods; so she must be called Goddess of Goddesses."[2] This is the meaning expressed by the representation of Mary with her Child sitting on the throne, which, taken from a Byzantine model, has an even more peaceful and inaccessible aura because of the two angels swinging censers, who, like doves beginning their flight, rush to the center represented by the figures. Their blazing deportment contrasts with that of the other two angels, on the tympanum of the left-hand door, who bear Christ aloft in a cloud and, in so doing, fall back overpowered by the Divine Light.

According to the Medieval theologians the Virgin Mary, by virtue of the innate perfection of her soul, possessed in natural fashion all the wisdom of which man is capable. A direct reference to this wisdom is to be found in the allegories of the Seven Liberal Arts which, just outside an inner circle of adoring angels, decorate the tympanum of the Door of the Virgin. In the Medieval context the seven sciences—which were classified as the *trivium* of grammar, dialectic, and rhetoric and the *quadrivium* of arithmetic, music, geometry, and astronomy—were not exclusively empirical sciences, as are those we know today. They were the expression of so many faculties of the soul, faculties demanding harmonious development. This is why they were also called arts.

Following an ancient tradition, Dante, in his *Convivio*, compares the Seven Liberal Arts to the seven planets, grammar corresponding to the moon, dialectic to Mercury, rhetoric to Venus, arithmetic to the sun, music to Mars, geometry to Jupiter, and astronomy to Saturn. The creators of the Royal Door of Chartres were certainly aware of this correspondence. It is thus doubly significant that on the tympanum of the left of the three doors the signs of the zodiac are displayed. These belong to the unchanging heaven of the fixed stars and

---

[2] St. Albert the Great, Mariale, CLXII, 13-14 (Collection *Les Maitres de la Spiritualité chrétienne*, translated by Albert Carreau, Paris 1942).

thus represent the kingdom of the Divine Spirit, to whom this door, with its representation of the ascension of Christ, is dedicated. The seven planets, on the other hand, govern, according to the ancient viewpoint, the world of the soul. And Mary is the human soul in all its perfection.

By means of the signs of the zodiac—not all of which, incidentally, appear on the same door, Pisces and Gemini having had to be transposed, for want of room, to the Door of the Virgin—the arches surrounding the representation of Christ's ascension (on the left-hand door) can be seen to represent the firmament. Beside each of the twelve signs of the zodiac the corresponding month is represented pictorially in the form of its natural activity.

These natural activities—one for each month—are the terrestrial reflections of the twelve signs of the zodiac. From them one learns to what extent the course of human existence depends upon the heavens: in seedtime and harvest, in work and leisure; for the heavens, in their cycle, bring heat after cold, dry after wet, and thus keep life in being.

This is significant for Medieval art: in two tympanums, and in the arches surrounding them, the whole cosmos is represented, in its three great divisions: spiritual, psychic, and corporeal. Medieval man always kept the profounder order of things in mind.

The tympanum of the central door is wider and higher than those of the right- and left-hand doors and has only two zones, whereas the lateral doors have three. On the right-hand tympanum, the successive images of the human mother, of the sacrificial presentation in the temple, and of the Heavenly Queen are positioned one above the other; on the left-hand tympanum, where Christ ascends, a host of angels, like so many flashes of lightning from out of a storm-cloud, descend upon the disciples gathered below.

On the tympanum of the main door, the image of the eternal majesty of Christ, which has been portrayed on so many Romanesque church doors, finds its most harmonious representation. One can inscribe every geometrical figure into this tympanum; it will always be in consonance with the ordering of the five figures and with the wave of movements which go out from the central figure and return to it. Between the curve of the arch and the almond-shaped aureole surrounding Christ—these forms which separate and re-unite—a breath or spiration goes back and forth, giving the whole image its life.

Christ is surrounded by the four creatures described by Ezechiel and John: the lion, the ox, the eagle, and the winged man. These are interpreted as the eternal prototypes of the four evangelists and their fantastical animal form symbolically extends beyond the purely human the anthropomorphic representation of God situated between them.

On the innermost of the three arches angels surround the majesty of Christ, and the twenty-four elders of the Apocalypse, who appear on the two outer arches, look up towards Him. On the lintel, the twelve apostles are present in groups of three, and to their right and left are two prophetic witnesses, perhaps Elias and Enoch, who are to come again at the end of time.

Why is the birth of Christ portrayed over the right-hand entrance, which lies south of the main axis of the church, and the ascension of Christ over the left-hand entrance, north of the main axis, given that north and south, according to their liturgical interpretation, correspond to the Old and New Covenants respectively? Presumably the physical positioning of the doors harbors an allusion to the ancient cosmic symbol of the *januae coeli*, the two doors of the heavens, known to the later Roman period.[3] Heaven has two doors, namely the two solstices; through the "door of winter," the "new sun" enters the world, and through the "door of summer," the fullness of light leaves the world. According to an ancient view of things mentioned by Plato, the gods enter this world by the first door, and leave it through the second. The location of the winter solstice, which occurs during the Christmas season, is in the southern heavens, and the location of the summer solstice in the northern; it would seem that the representational order in the west door of Chartres Cathedral is a direct reference to this: through the southern door the Divine Light descends into the world; through the northern it returns into the invisible. Between the two gates of Heaven stands the immutable axis of the world; to this the central door corresponds.

We can now return to the Seven Liberal Arts. The order in which they are listed, when properly understood, testifies to a Pythagorean view of things, and this was not without influence on Medieval art. The division of these sciences—and all their elements—into *trivium*

---

[3] René Guénon, "Les Portes solsticiales," in *Études Traditionnelles*, Paris, May 1938 [Editor's Note: an English translation appears in René Guénon, *Fundamental Symbols*, Chapter 37, "The Solstitial Gate," (Cambridge, UK: Quinta Essentia, 1995)].

and *quadrivium* came into Christian culture from Greek antiquity in a late and simplified form. The Medieval spirit, however, was able to reanimate the integral vision originally inherent in it.

"Philosophy has two main instruments," writes Thierry of Chartres, "namely intellect (*intellectus*) and its expression. Intellect is illumined by the *quadrivium* (arithmetic, music, geometry, and astronomy). Its expression is the concern of the *trivium* (grammar, dialectic, and rhetoric)."[4]

In fact the *trivium* was a schooling in both language and thought. It is language that makes man, man; and that is why grammar comes at the beginning. Not without humor, the sculptor of the door of the Virgin has portrayed this art as a woman threatening with a rod two young children who are writing. The figures of the famous grammarians Donat and Priscian stand beside her. Dialectic, whose feminine representation in Chartres carries a scorpion and has Aristotle as a companion, is none other than logic. Rhetoric is the art of speaking, or rather, speaking in so far as it is an art; Cicero accompanies its allegorical figure.

The four members of the *quadrivium* are likewise represented in a feminine form in Chartres. They are: arithmetic, with a reckoning board; music, with a glockenspiel; geometry with a drawing-board; and astronomy, contemplating the heavens and accompanied by Boethius, Pythagoras, Euclid, and Ptolemy. These four arts or sciences refer to the four conditions of corporeal existence: number, time, space, and motion. Music, of course, is not only concerned with time, but also with sound; but it is in the realm of sound that time manifests itself most immediately and characteristically; otherwise we can grasp it only in movement, in which it is united with space.

"Everything proceeding from the profound nature of things," writes Boethius, the great transmitter of the *quadrivium*, "shows the influence of the law of number; for this is the highest prototype contained in the mind of the Founder. From this are derived the four elements, the succession of the seasons, the movement of the stars, and the course of the heavens."[5]

---

[4] Thierry of Chartres, *Handbook of the Seven Liberal Arts*, quoted in *Das Königsportal von Chartres* by Wolfgang Schöne, Reclam, Stuttgart, 1961.

[5] A. M. S. Boethius, *De Arithmetica libri duo*.

THE SEVEN LIBERAL ARTS

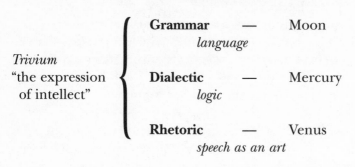

Trivium
"the expression
  of intellect"

Grammar — Moon
   language

Dialectic — Mercury
   logic

Rhetoric — Venus
   speech as an art

Quadrivium
"intellect"

Arithmetic — Sun
   number

Music — Mars
   time (harmony)

Geometry — Jupiter
   space (proportion)

Astronomy — Saturn
   motion (rhythm)

It is a qualitative, and not quantitative, conception of number that lies at the basis of Medieval arithmetic. It is thus less a method of reckoning than a way of understanding the nature of number, its properties, and the uniqueness of numerical series obtained by certain constant relationships.

That each individual number does not merely represent a sum of elements, but is in itself an expression of an essential unity, appears most clearly when one transposes each number into its corresponding geometrical form: three into an equilateral triangle, four into a square, five into a regular pentagon, etc. In each of these figures innumerable relationships occur, which variously exploit and demonstrate the law inherent in the figure concerned.

The connection between arithmetic, geometry, and music can be seen from the fact that the relationship of musical notes to one another is rendered visible in the mutual relationship of the variously long strings which produce them. This can be easily demonstrated on a monochord, which has a single string and a movable bridge.

Following Greek tradition, Boethius distinguishes three kinds of proportions: the arithmetic, in which the same interval obtains between all members of the series, as, for example: 1, 2, 3, 4, 5, 6. . . ; the geometric, which progresses by means of a constant multiplication (a:c = c:b); and the harmonic, which unites the preceding two, according to the formula a:c = a-b:b-c. The harmonic is the most perfect proportion: in music it appears as harmony, and in geometry as the "golden section."

The regular relationship of different movements to one another is rhythm. The day, the year, the lunar cycle, are the great rhythms which measure all change, and in this regard astronomy, the last member of the *quadrivium*, is the science of cosmic rhythms.

Number, proportion, harmony, and rhythm are clear manifestations of unity in diversity, and also clear indications of the way of return from diversity to unity. According to Boethius, the essence of things is intimately connected with unity: the more unity a thing possesses in itself, the more profoundly it participates in being.

In Medieval science, it is less a question of knowing many things, than of having a "whole" view of existence. Its method was anything but designed for the investigation of the material world and the furthering of technology. On the contrary: it possessed the means to open the spiritual eye to the beauty of mathematical proportions, and the spiritual ear to the music of the spheres.

When today we say "form," we mean only the visible and measurable aspects of a thing, especially its spatial contours. For the Medieval masters, on the other hand—for the scholars and, in a certain sense, also for the artists—"form" was the sum total of the essential properties or qualities of a thing; it was what constituted the inner unity of a manifested object. "The forms of things," writes Thierry of Chartres, "are, outside and beyond matter, contained in the Divine Spirit. There, in its simple and immutable fullness, true forms exist. But those which, in a certain and not fully explicable way, are impregnated into matter, are so to speak ephemeral and not forms in the true sense. They are only something like the reflections or representations of true forms."[6]

---

[6] J. M. Parent, *La doctrine de la création dans l'École de Chartres*, Paris, 1938 (Tierry: Librum hunc).

True form is thus neither limitable nor mutable; it is like a ray of the creative Spirit which, descending into matter, fleetingly lends it form. An analogy for this is artistic creation: just as the artist may more or less completely, depending on his humility, imprint on a material the spiritual picture that he carries within himself, so the essence of a thing may manifest itself more or less perfectly in that particular thing.

This way of looking at things is generally called Platonic, and so the men who taught in Chartres at the beginning of the twelfth century—such as Bernard, Gilbert de la Porée, William of Conques, and Thierry (who, at the very time that the Royal Door was being constructed, was chancellor of the Cathedral school)—were all Platonists. Yet it would do them an injustice simply to attribute their thought to a philosophical school; in their works there is an element that transcends thinking as such, namely a genuine spiritual contemplation which, though far from being dependent upon words, nevertheless has to make use of words in order to communicate itself.

According to the Platonic point of view, all existence emanates hierarchically from the one Divine Source, which is neither diminished nor altered thereby. Can this perspective be reconciled with the creation story as related in the Bible? There is indeed a contradiction between envisaging a light which shines because it is in its nature to shine (and which one can conceive of in no other way than as shining), and envisaging a creative act which, at a given moment, calls into existence something that previously was not there. The masters of Chartres asked themselves this question and also answered it. When, with William of Conques,[7] one regards time itself as something created, the apparent contradiction disappears. Before the creation of the world, God was not in time: he was in Eternity, which lies beyond all time, in the eternal Now. One cannot say that God created the world at a given time, for time itself began with the world; from the standpoint of this world, existence (which shines or radiates forth from God) appears as if it began in time. In such a bridging of two apparently incompatible images, the more than merely mental character of spiritual contemplation can be seen.

The art of the Royal Door, in its inimitable and unsurpassed reconciliation of stellar farness and living nearness, is born of the same spirit.

---

[7] William of Conques, *Philosophia mundi. Patrologia latina*, Migne, CLXXII, 39-115.

SHAKESPEARE IN THE LIGHT OF SACRED ART
Martin Lings

In the last few decades there has been a considerable increase of interest in the Middle Ages, which is no doubt partly due to a reaction, but
it is also, much more, a case of ignorance giving way to knowledge.
In another sense, it is simply a rising to the surface of something that
has always been there and is always being rediscovered. Could it not
be said that wherever the Middle Ages have not ceased to be accessible, wherever despite the barrier of the Renaissance they have always
remained with us, as in the poetry of Dante, for instance, or—to take
a more immediately accessible and inescapable example—as in their
architecture, their superiority has always been felt at heart? This
feeling implies also, if only subconsciously, the acknowledgement of
a more general superiority, for it is quite impossible that the great
Norman and Gothic cathedrals should have sprung from an age that
had no inward excellence to correspond to these superlative outward
manifestations.

One of the particular reasons for the present increase of interest
in the Middle Ages is in itself highly significant: during the last fifty
years Europeans have taken much more interest in the art of other
civilizations than ever before, and this has no doubt uprooted many
prejudices and opened the door to a certain freshness and objectivity of judgment. Having come to know some of the best examples of
Hindu, Chinese and Japanese art and then as it were returning to their
own civilization, many people find that their outlook has irrevocably
changed. After looking at a great Chinese landscape, for example,
where this world appears like a veil of illusion beyond which, almost
visibly, lies the Infinite and Eternal Reality, or after having been given
a glimpse of that same Reality through a statue of the Buddha, they
find it difficult to take seriously a painting such as Raphael's famous
Madonna, or Michelangelo's fresco of the Creation, not to speak of
his sculpture, and Leonardo also fails to satisfy them. But they find
that they *can* take very seriously, more seriously than before, some of
the early Sienese paintings such as Simone Martini's Annunciation,
for example, or the statuary and stained glass of Chartres Cathedral,

or the twelfth- and thirteenth-century mosaics in St. Mark's at Venice, or the icons of the Orthodox Church.

The reason why medieval art can bear comparison with Oriental art as no other Western art can is undoubtedly that the medieval outlook, like that of the Oriental civilizations, was intellectual. It considered this world above all as the shadow or symbol of the next, man as the shadow or symbol of God; and such an attitude, to be operative, presupposes the presence of intellectuals, for earthly things can only be referred back to their spiritual archetypes through the faculty of intellectual perception, the insight which pierces through the symbol to the universal reality that lies beyond. In the theocratic civilizations, if an artist himself was not an intellectual, he none the less obeyed the canons of art which had been established on an intellectual basis.

Sacred art in the full sense of the term is art which conforms to canons laid down not by individuals but by the spiritual authority of the civilization in question, as was the case with medieval Christian architecture, Gregorian chant, ancient Greek drama, Japanese No plays, Hindu temple dancing and music—to name only a few examples—and such art is always something of a criterion and also a potential source of inspiration for other less central works of art.

A medieval portrait is above all a portrait of the Spirit shining from behind a human veil. In other words, it is as a window opening from the particular on to the universal, and while being enshrined in its own age and civilization as eminently typical of a particular period and place, it has at the same time, in virtue of this opening, something that is neither of the East nor of the West, nor of any one age more than another.

If Renaissance art lacks an opening onto the universal and is altogether imprisoned in its own epoch, this is because its outlook is humanistic; and humanism, which is a revolt of the reason against the intellect, considers man and other earthly objects entirely for their own sakes as if nothing lay behind them. In painting the Creation, for example, Michelangelo treats Adam not as a symbol but as an independent reality; and since he does not paint man in the image of God, the inevitable result is that he paints God in the image of man. There is more divinity underlying Simone Martini's painting of St. Francis than there is in Michelangelo's representation of the Creator Himself.

Shakespeare was born less than three months after Michelangelo's death, and the two are often spoken of in the same breath as being among "the greatest geniuses of the Renaissance." Yet how does Shakespeare stand in the light of an intellectual approach which enhances, if possible, our respect for Dante, but which greatly diminishes our estimate of several others whose pre-eminence had long gone unquestioned? Let us quote, as touchstone, a masterly summing up of the difference between Renaissance art and medieval art: "When standing in front of a Romanesque or Gothic cathedral, we feel that we are at the center of the world; when standing in front of a Renaissance, Baroque or Rococo church we are merely conscious of being in Europe."[1] Now without trying to give Shakespeare so essential a place in the art of Christendom as the place which is held by the medieval cathedrals or by *The Divine Comedy*, could it not be said that to be present at an adequate performance of *King Lear* is not merely to watch a play but to witness, mysteriously, the whole history of mankind?

But this remark could not possibly be made about the majority of Shakespeare's writings, and if we wish to form any estimate of the mature dramatist whose outlook bestowed on him a universality that is a prolongation of the universality of the Middle Ages, the first thing to be done is to set most of the plays on one side for the moment so as not to confuse the issue. Few writers can have developed so much during their period of authorship as Shakespeare did. By the end of the sixteenth century he had written some twenty-two plays; but none of these can be said to represent his maturity, though some of them,[2] in various ways, give an unmistakable foretaste of what was to come.

There can no longer be any doubt that already at the age of thirty[3] or before, Shakespeare was familiar with the various doctrines—some truly esoteric, others merely occultist—which so passionately interested the London dramatists and other writers of the day, as well as the aristocrats who sustained, protected and encouraged them, including two successive patrons[4] of the players for whom Shakespeare wrote

---

[1] Frithjof Schuon, *The Transcendent Unity of Religions*, Harper and Row, 1984, p. 61, note.

[2] *Romeo and Juliet*, for example, *A Midsummer Night's Dream*, *Henry IV*, *As You Like It*, and *Twelfth Night*.

[3] In 1594; it was probably in this year that he wrote *Love's Labour's Lost*, and in the following year *Romeo and Juliet* and *A Midsummer Night's Dream*.

[4] See Paul Arnold, *Esotérisme de Shakespeare*, Mercure de France, 1955, pp. 60-1.

his plays and with whom he acted. Needless to say, the mainstream of the mystical legacy of the Middle Ages was Christian; but by the end of the sixteenth century it had been swelled by many tributaries— Pythagorean, Platonic, Cabalistic, Hermetic, Illuminist, Rosicrucian, Alchemical. In the margin of some of these traditional currents were sciences such as astrology and magic, and many minds were captivated and even monopolized by side-issues of this kind.

But centrally, the non-Christian traditions coincided with Christian mysticism, despite differences of terminology and perspective. They were concerned firstly with the means of purifying the soul of its fallen nature, and finally with the fruit of that restoration of the primordial state, the soul's beatific reunion with God. Shakespeare, like Lyly, Spenser, Chapman and Ben Jonson—to name only a few—was well aware that the result of the chemical marriage of sulfur and quicksilver, or of "the King and the Queen," the *magnum opus* of the Alchemists, is the perfected and resurrected soul, and that the alchemical work is thus an indispensable first stage on the path that leads finally to the mystic union of the perfect soul with the Divine Spirit. This union is in fact the theme of Shakespeare's alchemical poem *The Phoenix and the Turtle,* as Paul Arnold has demonstrated in his detailed commentary;[5] and if it be objected that this poem strikes too profound a note of maturity to be counted as a work of the mid nineties,[6] the same union, a marriage preceded and conditioned by trial and purification, is none the less the theme of more than one of Shakespeare's earlier plays. In this connection the reader has only to glance at Arnold's well-documented chapters on *Love's Labour's Lost* and *The Merchant of Venice*[7] or at Jean Paris' chapter on "the alchemical theater" in *Shakespeare.*[8]

The point to be made here is not that many of the earlier plays trace out symbolically the way of the Mysteries, but that they are too merely theoretical to be fully and "concretely" mysterial. On the esoteric path doctrinal knowledge has to be acquired by the mind before it can be existentially assimilated by the man as a whole; and this pro-

---

[5] *Ibid.,* pp. 130-39.

[6] It was first published only in 1601.

[7] *Ibid.,* Chapters II and IV.

[8] Evergreen Books, 1960.

cess of development is outwardly reflected in the chronological order of the plays. It is one thing to make use of an assemblage of symbols, but it is another thing to enter into that symbolism totally.

Let us suppose, to bring home our meaning, that Shakespeare had not lived to reach his maturity, or, in other words, that we had to build our estimate of his greatness on the basis of *Romeo and Juliet, A Midsummer Night's Dream, The Merchant of Venice, Richard II, Henry IV, Much Ado About Nothing, As You Like It, Julius Caesar* and *Twelfth Night,* these being probably the best of his earlier plays. The difference between that estimate and the one we are happily able to make would differ considerably from judge to judge, but it could not fail in any case to be vast. For it was only after these plays had been written, that is, just after the turn of the century, that there came a sharp and last-ing change, not in orientation but in intensity. It was as if Shakespeare had suddenly come to grips with the universe after having contem-plated it for some time with a half-detached serenity. From being in earnest, he had come to be in very deadly earnest.

*

* *

It is too often said that the marvelous variety of Shakespeare's charac-ters makes it impossible to divine anything about the author himself. About his temperament this may be true to a certain extent, but as regards his outlook and ideals it is altogether false. We can learn much about him indirectly even from his villains, and from his heroes we can learn much more, especially towards the end of a play, after he has fully developed them.

But when the hero, in a manifest state of undevelopment, at the beginning or in the middle of a play, gives vent to his ideas about this and that, he is perhaps revealing his own immaturity and may well even be saying the very opposite of what Shakespeare himself thinks. A striking example of this is in *King Lear* when Gloster, who has an important part in the sub-plot, says, before Shakespeare has fully developed him:

> As flies to wanton boys, are we to the gods;
> They kill us for their sport. (IV, 1, 222-25)

It is when Edgar hears these words that he decides to set upon his strange course of action for the purpose of saving his father from despair and suicide. Thanks to his efforts, Gloster is able to say eventually:

> Henceforth I'll bear
> Affliction till it do cry out itself
> "Enough, enough," and die. (IV, 6, 75-7)

and later still:

> You ever-gentle Gods, take my breath from me:
> Let not my worser spirit tempt me again
> To die before you please! (V, 2, 11)

The great weakness of Gloster, which he eventually overcomes, is lack of faith in Providence. Hamlet also has to make good a certain shortcoming in this respect. The "To be or not to be" soliloquy, from which so much has been deduced about Shakespeare's own views, does not merely not express the maturity of Hamlet but it shows him in the process of discovering his immaturity.

It is always possible that Shakespeare may have drawn on his own past experience for this soliloquy. But we can be certain that it does not represent in any way his settled convictions because its whole tenor is completely contradicted in the last scene of the play by the fully developed, perfectly balanced Hamlet voicing the maturity which Shakespeare has gradually shaped and built up for him. In this scene we find that he has altogether overcome his doubts with which, unlike Gloster, he had never fully identified himself. His now full-grown royalty of nature causes Horatio to exclaim, half in admiration, half in surprise: "Why, what a king is this!" (V, 2, 229-30); and his faith in Providence is unshakeable. He says to Horatio:

> There's a divinity that shapes our ends,
> Rough-hew them how we will. (V, 2, 10-11)

Shortly after this in connection with his premonition of his own imminent death, he reminds Horatio, in Gospel terms, of man's obligation to possess the virtue of trust: "There's a special providence in the fall of a sparrow" (V, 2, 229-30). This is no doubt as near as Shakespeare dare come to quoting, on the stage, the well known passage of St. Matthew:

Are not two sparrows sold for a farthing? And one of them shall not
fall on the ground   without your Father. But the very hairs of your
head are all numbered. Fear ye not   therefore, ye are of more value
than many sparrows. (10:29-31)

The gist of what Hamlet says could be summed up: All that matters is
to be ready for death when its moment comes. His actual words "the
readiness is all" have their equivalent in an equally significant passage
in the last act of *King Lear*. The news of the defeat and capture of
Lear and Cordelia plunges Gloster once more into "ill thoughts" as
they are called by Edgar, who pulls him out of them by reminding him
that just as a man has to submit to Providence as regards the time and
manner of his birth, so also he must submit as regards the time and
manner of his death and not seek to pluck the fruit before it is ripe.

> Men must endure
> Their going hence, even as their coming hither.
> Ripeness is all. (V, 2, 9-11)

It will be noticed that in these two speeches of Hamlet and Edgar, as
also elsewhere, Shakespeare is concentrating on the most universal
aspect of religion. He is concerned with man's having the right attitude of soul towards Providence rather than with any particular mode
of worship. Nor do we believe that this springs in the main from the
extreme religious soreness and sensitivity of his times which made
Christianity a dangerous topic. But we will come back shortly to the
question of his universality. Meantime there are some other clarifications to be made.Before the end of his period of authorship it was
even forbidden by law to mention the name of God on the stage. But
one could always refer to "the gods"; and if he deliberately chose to set
many of his maturer plays in a pre-Christian setting, it is to be noticed
none the less that his attitude to Greece and Rome is not typical of
the Renaissance. He does not merely borrow the surface of classical
antiquity. He places himself at the very center of the ancient world.
For him, and for Dante, just as for the ancient priests and priestesses
at Delphi, Apollo is not the god of light but the Light of God.

In the form of his drama Shakespeare belongs to his age. Marlowe's
Dr. Faustus is outwardly in some respects more medieval than anything
Shakespeare wrote. But in outlook Marlowe was altogether a man of
the Renaissance, whereas Shakespeare seems in a sense to go back

as time goes forward and by the turn of the century he had become, unlike many of his fellow dramatists, the continuer and the summer-up of the past, the last outpost of a quickly vanishing age. To say this is not really to say anything new; it is rather a case of putting two and two together. Bradley says of *King Lear*: "It does not appear to disclose a mode of imagination so very far removed from the mode with which we must remember that Shakespeare was perfectly familiar in the Morality plays and in *The Faerie Queene*." Of *Othello* Wilson Knight says: "Othello, Desdemona and Iago are Man, the Divine and the Devil," and he remarks in general that Shakespeare's heroes are "purgatorial pilgrims." Of *Macbeth* Dover Wilson says: "*Macbeth* is almost a morality play," and he says much the same of the two parts of *Henry IV*. Moreover, in this last connection, and with regard to Shakespeare as a continuer of past tradition, he reminds us: "Before its final secularization in the first half of the sixteenth century, our drama was concerned with one topic and one topic only: human salvation. It was a topic that could be represented in either of two ways: (i) historically, by means of miracle plays which in the Corpus Christi cycles unrolled before the spectators' eyes the whole scheme of salvation from the Creation to the Last Judgment; or (ii) allegorically, by means of morality plays, which exhibited the process of salvation in the individual soul on its road between birth and death, beset with the snares of the World or the wiles of the Evil One."[9] Dover Wilson does not define the word "salvation" and for the purpose of his book it is not necessary to do so. But as regards medieval art in general it is important to distinguish between what may be called esoteric works, which look beyond salvation to sanctification, and exoteric works, in which sanctification is at best no more than a remote ideal. If Shakespeare is a continuer of the past, which of these two categories does his art belong to, the exoteric or the esoteric?

An example of what may be called an exoteric work which stops short at salvation in the lowest sense is *The Castle of Perseverance*. In this morality play mankind (*humanum genus*) is represented as having led a very questionable life, and he is saved from Hell in the face of justice by operation of the Divine Mercy. A supreme example of an esoteric work is *The Divine Comedy* which presupposes salvation and deals with man's purification and his ultimate sanctification or in

---

[9] *The Fortunes of Falstaff*, Cambridge University Press, 1964, p. 17.

other words his regaining of what was lost at the Fall. It may be said that in the Middle Ages the mass of the laity was considered as following the path of salvation, whereas the monastic orders, and the lay orders attached to them, and one or two other brotherhoods such as those of the Freemasons and the Companions, aimed at following the path of sanctification. In other words they aimed at passing through Purgatory in this life. It is now known that Dante belonged to a brotherhood which was affiliated to the Order of the Temple,[10] and which was more or less driven underground when the Order of the Temple was abolished. Some have supposed that Shakespeare was a member of the brotherhood of the Rosie Crosse; others believe him to have been a Freemason. This is a part of his secret which will probably never be known, and in any case it is not within the scope of these pages to dwell on anything that is not obvious from what he wrote. What *is* obvious, however, is that his plays far transcend the idea of salvation in its more limited sense; and it may be remarked in passing that this does suggest that their author was following a spiritual path, which itself implies attachment to an order.

At the beginning of Act V of *The Winter's Tale*, with reference to the long penance done by King Leontes during the sixteen years which elapse between the two parts of the play, the priestlike Cleomenes says:

> Sir, you have done enough, and have perform'd
> A saint-like sorrow: no fault could you make,
> Which you have not redeem'd; indeed, paid down
> More penitence than done trespass: at the last,
> Do as the heavens have done, forget your evil;
> With them forgive yourself. (V, 1,1-6)

In *King Lear* the blind Gloster, recognizing the King's voice, asks to kiss his hand. Lear replies: "Let me wipe it first; it smells of mortality" (IV, 6, 137). This remark contains not only the very essence of the play but also of most of Shakespeare's other maturer plays; for in the course of them what does Shakespeare do but wipe away mortality, that is, the sin of Adam, from the hand of the hero? The hand must be altogether clean: there is no question of more or less. In *Hamlet* the Prince says of himself in the middle of the play that he

---

[10] See René Guénon, *The Esoterism of Dante*, Sophia Perennis et Universalis, 1996, p. 7.

is fairly virtuous: "I am myself indifferent honest"; but Shakespeare's purpose goes far beyond such mediocrity. The porter to the Gate of Purgatory, that is, the gate of salvation, is by definition of unfathomable mercy. Hamlet could have passed by him at the beginning of the play: so could Leontes at the moment of repentance, sixteen years before the speech just quoted; and so could Lear long before the end of the play. But the porter to the Gate of Paradise, that is, the gate to sanctification, is relentlessly exacting; and for his heroes and heroines, Shakespeare stands as that porter. He will let nothing pass except perfection; and so he makes Hamlet add to the above quoted words: "but yet I could accuse me of such things that it were better my mother had not borne me" (III, 1, 123-26).

Character after character is developed to a state of virtue which is pushed, one feels, to the very limits of human nature, until each could say, with Cleopatra:

Give me my robe, put on my crown; I have
Immortal longings in me. (V, 2, 279-80)

Even those who refuse to admit that Shakespeare himself speaks through any of his characters cannot escape from the fact that it is Shakespeare himself, and no one else, who is the architect of his plays. And when, after a certain maturity has been reached, play after play follows the same quest for human perfection, each play in its totality (over and above the marvelous variety of detail) hammering home the same message, we have no alternative but to conclude that Shakespeare was altogether preoccupied, at any rate for the last fifteen years of his life or more, by the same question which preoccupied Dante.

It was, however, Dante's privilege to establish for Christendom, one of those summits of art that every theocracy is bound to have, and this cannot possibly be said of Shakespeare. Christendom is indeed the nearest traditional civilization to his art, and providentially he was born just in time to be able to endow his plays with the mediaeval grandeur drawn from that world. But he does not speak in its terms. We have already given two examples of his universal manner of expression: Hamlet's "the readiness is all" and Edgar's "ripeness is all," but these are merely two of a multitude. Again and again throughout his plays we are reminded of what Sophocles has called "the unwritten and unassailable statutes of the Gods . . . not of today nor yesterday but from all time, and none knoweth when they were ordained."[11] These words are often taken as a reference to what is generally known as the Perennial Philosophy or *religio perennis*; and it is in this all-underlying religion and not in any particular religious form that Shakespeare's sacred art is rooted. That does not mean that he was not a devout practicing Christian.[12] Prereligious piety cannot be adopted in exchange for the particular religion of any time and place. Moreover, an essential factor of that piety is the mediation between Heaven and earth, a spontaneous characteristic of primordial man in virtue of his, as it were, organic access to the Spirit. But failing this, mediation can only be by the performance of rites that *religio perennis* does not bestow, and that those who have regained that liberating access still continue to perform for more than one reason.

"This deep-seated heredity [*religio perennis*] is like the remembrance of the lost Paradise and it can erupt in the soul by a kind of providential atavism."[13] We believe Shakespeare to have been an outstanding example of this possibility. Not that we would deny the same atavism for Dante, but from him it shines through a veil. He was a gift from Heaven to Christianity wherein he had a function to perform, whereas Shakespeare was a gift to the increasingly secularized closing centuries of this cycle of time, that is, to the seventeenth century onwards, and to no period more than the present. All the different traditions are in agreement that we are nearing the end of a temporal cycle, and that this is not old age any longer overlaid, as it was some five hundred years ago with the relative youth of Christianity and Islam, which are already now, especially the former, showing distinct signs of decrepitude—so quickly do developments take place when the end is near. And what is true of the traditions is also true of men: everything on the Earth is now in a sense old, which means that everyone is somehow faced with the question "Is it to be, for me, the wisdom of age or senility?" We have considered this situation at greater length elsewhere.[14] It is mentioned here because the vast majority have opted without knowing it for the negative alternative.

[11] *Antigone*, 454-7.

[12] Hamlet's reference to the sparrow is one of many indications that the Gospel is often present in Shakespeare's mind.

[13] Frithjof Schuon, *The Essential Writings*, Amity House, 1986, p. 531.

[14] *The Eleventh Hour*, ch. 5. Archetype, 2002.

There are inevitably some who have not; and the terminal wisdom that they represent has a close affinity with *religio perennis*. So, be it repeated, does Shakespeare: he is in fact clearly too much in his element in that outlook for it to have been forced upon him just by the religious problems of his day. Those problems served to compel him to lift the veil through which Dante was obliged to speak.

If it be asked, in connection with our title, whether we have the right to place any of Shakespeare's plays, even the mature one's, in the category of sacred art, a powerful plea for *yes* is implicit in the fact that the central theme of these plays is not merely religion, which in itself would be insufficient, but the very essence of religion, namely the Mysteries. Let us add to this a remark from Schuon's masterly chapter on the degrees of art: "The distinction between a sacred and profane art is inadequate and too precipitate when one wishes to take account of all artistic possibilities; and it is therefore necessary to have recourse to a supplementary distinction, namely that between a liturgical and an extraliturgical art."[15] This has the advantage of safeguarding the already mentioned category of sacred art in the traditional sense, while at the same time not labeling as profane certain extraliturgical manifestations of the Divine Spirit which "bloweth where it listeth."

---

[15] *Esoterism as Principle and as Way*, Perennial Books, 1981, p. 186.

THEOLOGY OF THE ICON
Jean Biès

The icon not only has its aesthetic; it also has its theology. The icon includes an *alchemic* aspect concerning the spiritualization of matter: its transfiguring function; a *symbolic* aspect concerning the transposition of the archetypes into visible images: its purifying function; and finally a *liturgical* aspect concerning the "descent from heaven to earth," which is its cultural function.

Plotinus had already glorified a vision of Nature that, aimed at the "inner eye," neglected the appearance of forms in order to reveal their essence. Orthodox Christianity adopted this philosophy while at the same time adapting it. Origen would outline the study of the five spiritual senses and the organ used for contemplating incorporeal objects, in other words the "eye of the heart." This is not analytical and discursive learning, it is an immediate intuitive knowledge offered by the spiritual core, from *logos* to the heart of sensitive things. The job of the artist will be to successively peel away the bark that covers them to let the being emerge. This explains the disappearance of all perspective, shortcuts, external lighting, and earthly horizons in the icon; this also explains the translucent aspect of the characters and objects, which is comparable to petals arranged around and throughout a luminous source. These coats, these tunics whose folds retain the memory of gowns, drape the souls more than the bodies.

The icon foreshadows, here and now, the glorification of mankind of the Eighth Day—not only mankind but all of Creation. The small wooden board, the egg yolk base paint,—symbol of the triple world—holy water diluting colored paste are the humble beginnings of the substantial Redemption that should operate during the Apocatastasis. For by becoming flesh, Christ made the metamorphosis and the deification of the physical world itself possible. If the Fall was not only Adam's, but the occultation covering the entire universe, the paradisiac modality, likewise, the final Salvation concerns not only humanity but all the atoms of the cosmos. A precious idea in Orthodoxy: by descending into Jordan, Christ sanctified the waters in advance; stretched on the cross, he sanctified the wood (this wood which also designates the cosmic substance); buried, he sanctified the earth; by breathing our air, he sanctified the air; and by manifesting himself in Hades, the fire. This is what the first aspect of the icon eloquently teaches.

Its second aspect recalls that the icon is a mirror in which Eternity, Paradise, the future Century are reflected; a window onto the Absolute, by which Essence, the supraterrestrial Beauty descends. The gold of the background suggests the deifying Grace penetrating every-thing. Its light arouses things more than it illuminates them since things illuminate themselves; it is the vehicle of archetypical presence. The icon procures the "sensation of divine things" by revealing them; it purifies the place where it mysteriously shines and attesting to the presence of the Transcendent there, it is as such, *theophany*. It is the point of convergence of a precipitate and a concentration of energy, the expression that Ramakrishna consecrated to the divine image: "a condensation of conscious" could be attributed to it without syncre-tism. On the one hand, it is above all the place where God puts on a face, that of a man, where the human face of God appears unveiled; on the other hand, the place where man can contemplate at the same time—reminiscence—the original image of the Face that was his before the cosmic catastrophe, and—anticipation—that of the Face that will be his in Celestial Jerusalem: one and the same Face in the glory of Pleroma.

There is no greater miracle than seeing the Invisible become visible; no better confirmation than discovering that the Face of God is also that of humanity. But the wonder of wonders is that this Face has a gaze, a tear through which Heaven surges, unfurls to meet our eyes.

The third and last aspect concerns the liturgical and sacramental role of the icon. The liturgy of the here below only reproduces the one that, uninterrupted, takes place in the other world. The icon is perhaps the visual echo of this Liturgy. Placed on the iconostasis that simultaneously separates the nave from the altar, the profane from the sacred, and regards the profane as sacred for presenting them to the Kingdom, the Holy Images are located at the confluence of the terrestrial and the celestial; and as the divine truths are reflected in the human mind by images, they reflect likewise Heaven on Earth.

The icon sanctifies the gaze of the one who looks at it, transform-ing the former into a "sense of vision." Free from any sensualism, it inaugurates the "fasting of the eyes," pacifies, illuminates. It is also a support for meditation, canalizing the mental and psychic currents. It facilitates the repetition of the Divine Name pronounced before it by helping concentration—an exercise that recalls that of the Hindu *manasapuja*. Moreover, the contemplation of the icon is this gaze of the silence that awakens within us the appearance of the archetypes and the desire to bring them together. Little by little, the divine-human Face becomes part of the firmest tissue of the human being; it gives him order, purifies him, prepares him for the vision of God. Has it not been said that "he who has not seen God in this life will not see him in a future life either?" And because "man becomes what he contemplates," said Plotinus, he who has contemplated Love will obviously become Love, first by reflection, then by imitation, and lastly by identification. Likewise, the one who has contemplated ugliness, vulgarity, violence and hatred will become ugly, vulgar, violent and hateful, and the seed of criminality will germinate in him. In the rampant "image oriented civilization" that marks the times, it is unfortunate that the actuality of the icon, mirror of holiness, is so poorly understood by our contemporaries.

This *impregnation* works toward inner transformation and is the preparation for the Face-to-face meeting at the moment of the great passage. The icon is a tool for the acceptance of death. It immerses, empowers the deep layers of the unconscious. Its memory is kept above the immediate and superficial memory of the brain; and the face it represents and buries in the depths of the human being lets him recognize the Face located on the *other side,* and to feel, in the beyond, that he is in the land of knowledge.

The supporters of the goddess of Reason, with her authorization, denounce the worship of Images. In the eighth century, the Iconoclasts were already criticizing Christians for wanting to represent God, and in the way of the pantheists, of deifying matter. Constantine V *Copronymus* (surnamed Dung) would have them tortured and dragged through the streets, sewn into sacks then thrown into the sea. One can admit the possible existence of superstitious deviations, of an idolatry. But let the debate be raised to the level of the Fathers.

The latter reply, on the one hand, that if God cannot be represented, the Word became flesh, and it is possible from that moment on to "represent the likeness of The One who showed himself"; on the other hand, the substance is not adored, but through it, the Principle is. In a definitive formula, Saint John Damascene explains, "I do not worship matter but the Creator of matter who, because of me, became matter, and with that matter saved me." A strange irony of sorts: the one nicknamed *Chrysorroas*—"Gold flowing" (because of the eloquence of his words), had to defend the icon in the Muslim state, not against the Muslims, but against iconoclastic Christians: he was lain to rest in a mosque. According to the Council of Nicaea in 787, "Anyone who worships an icon worships the person it represents." The holy Fathers have said it more than enough that "honor given to the image passes to the being embellished by imagery," and that "by looking at an icon, the spirit ascends to its prototype." By becoming flesh, God did not divinize matter, he deified it; he made it the Spirit's receptacle.

By turning to abstract art, Western religious art proves today its complete lack of understanding of the meaning of Incarnation, and that by doctrinal weakness or out of concern for demagogic adaptation it has lost intellectuality to intellectualism. Insofar as abstract art can be appreciated in Islam, the religion of divine Impersonality, it is unjustifiable in the religion where, par excellence, God gives concrete expression to the Face. As for profane art, faced with the world of icons, it only translates a fragmented world of decomposed shapes that favor the appearance of imprisoned structures instead of the essence; a world where matter, unfamiliar with assumption, disintegrates under the aspect of haunting monsters or mechanical grins, where the psyche, uprooted from all references, agonizes in the dregs of the human misadventure. . . . Nightmarish depiction of a glacial Hell into which Christ did not deign to descend. Exaltation of the Triad of inversed hypostases: titanic *Arrogance*, facing the discretion, obliteration and absence of all rhetoric from the Word; hateful *Folly*, with respect to God's "passion" for mankind; *Nothingness*, like the parodic reply to the divine kenosis, made from spareness, renunciation, and sacrifice until death.

Contrary to the dryness that is characteristic of naturalism, cubism and tachism, the art of the "saints and precious icons" soothes the eyes and rejuvenates the soul; it arouses a dream that is truer than reality, presents the plenary Truth. After having discovered the splendor and diverse levels of meanings, one can only turn once again toward this sea that brings us everything to see if other icons won't sail toward us; this sea that, from ages to ages, has brought to the shores of Mount Athos, these floating images, slowly pushed by the wind, collected by a monk, and that the traditions loaded with miracles, and piety, with flowers.

ARE THE CRAFTS AN ANACHRONISM?

Brian Keeble

In this chapter consideration is given to the question of what might be the deeper implications of the fact that, in a world in which they have only a marginal social role and almost no economic justification, the handicrafts never entirely concede defeat to the by now global industrial method of manufacture. In essence this amounts to asking whether the crafts are an anachronism or whether they have an intrinsic significance for a society that is sustained minute by minute by a highly sophisticated array of technological products that are about as far away from the world of traditional handicrafts as it is possible to get.

Yet that slow, painstaking, time-consuming method of making things by hand will not die even in the face of a system of production, distribution and consumption that by all reasonable estimates should long ago have eradicated it. Have we not, after all, solved the problem of making sufficient things for our needs? Surely our machines do that for us? And as a result are we not freed to engage with higher things? Somehow a stubborn, nagging doubt persists.

The current state of our post-industrial society would seem to suggest that the "higher" things have eluded our grasp and we have been left empty-handed. There is a widespread sense that the "leisure-society" does not provide us with those long-promised—yet so often postponed—life-sustaining satisfactions. And alongside this there is the growing realization that the material wealth of our society has been achieved at the expense of meaningfulness in the workplace.

In asking whether or not the crafts are an anachronism are we not tacitly admitting to the fact that there is something more to them than simply the methods and procedures they employ: that they are more than an outmoded way of making things? For if the whole question of *how* things should be made could be answered without reference to the question, by *whom?* and for *what?*, then we would scarcely be interested at all in any particular method of manufacture. Each improvement in efficiency would automatically make any previous method obsolete and, except for a certain antiquarian application, the crafts would certainly have disappeared in the face of two centuries of industrial enterprise and all that that implies.

The fact that the crafts have never been entirely done away with as a way of meeting certain of our needs must suggest that they involve a dimension of human experience that goes beyond the complex interplay of intuitive, imaginative and manipulative skills which go toward mastering the material substance of the craft itself. And this in turn suggests that our enquiry as to the significance of the crafts must address itself not so much to the actual method of production as to the agent whose task it is to master and deploy the method of skill in question. For a thing to have significance it must signify something. It must be a sign of something, and signs point to values. And it is the unique gift of men and women to recognize values and the necessity to act upon them.

In view of our possession of this gift it is little use our arguing that the modern world has progressed beyond a crafts-based civilization, as if the mere passage of time itself were capable of imposing upon human activity a value and a significance it would not otherwise have. For the world that surrounds contemporary urban man is in reality man's own construct, itself the result of adopting or rejecting certain values in favor of others. It cannot be argued that history makes us what we are, unalterably and inevitably, and therefore that history has decreed that the crafts have no necessary place in human affairs. For history is nothing more than the sum of human activities. Any world we make we can just as surely unmake. The fact that we currently express deep misgivings about the condition of the environment, a condition we ourselves have created, points to the fact that we are able to make an objective assessment and judgment from beyond the evolutionary process that is simply historical change as such. We are not, in other words, hapless victims of our time and place; we do have access to a set of values that transcend what would otherwise be our total confinement to historical causality. This tells us more about the nature of man than perhaps it does about the nature of any process of manufacture. And it points to the importance and the necessity of our asking the fundamental question, "What or *who* is man?"

This question, posed in one way or another, has been at the root of that now lengthy and continuing school of radical thought that has seen fit to call into question the direction and goals that industrial—and now by extension, post-industrial—society has set itself. This school of thought has, with reference to the manual trades and handicrafts, challenged the very foundations of modern society, built as it is on the almost total monopoly of industrial, mechanized production. What each of its dissenting voices has sounded is a warning against the danger of allowing the mechanical system a free rein in satisfying our human needs. These dissenters have seen, sometimes wholly, sometimes in part, that it is inherent in the very nature of such a system that it would eventually enslave men to those monetary and quantitative considerations that nourish merely the gods of economic efficiency. Such a system must inevitably lead not only to the dehumanization of man but also to widespread social manipulation of the factors that determine what a "need" is. That their fears were not ill-founded should by now be obvious. In every exhortation, in every forecast, in every appeal from our leaders as they urge us along the path of progress, the inducement is almost always exclusively that of "economic growth." And this in the face of a daily experience of life in which for great numbers of humanity "the economy" is as vengeful a god as was ever dreamed of by our ancestors. (It was recently reported that one-and-a-half per cent of the workforce is displaced annually as a direct result of technological innovation and development.)

Even to pose our initial question is, of course, to admit to our conditioning by an environment which is almost entirely the product of the machine: an environment which harbors an inherent confusion as to the intrinsic merits of art, craft and work. For industrial man the distinction between art and work is quite clear. Art is the domain of aesthetic sensibility and work is the domain of productive effort. And modern crafts inhabit an ill-defined terrain between the two, uneasily drawing from both. On the aesthetic side, the modern craftsman (seduced by the "prestige" of the fine arts) sees temptation in the fact that the accidents of individual sensibility weigh favorably in the judgment of artistic success. On the side of skill, he recognizes the necessity to demonstrate a disciplined mastery of materials as a mark of mature accomplishment. But because he is forced to operate within a society in which he has no natural patron (one who knows what *ought* to be made), the craftsman is marginalized by two dysfunctional conditions: on the one hand, the wide acceptance that "artistic freedom" has a value in isolation from moral, rational and practical criteria, and on the other hand, the almost unquestioned assumption in the market-place that the necessities of life are taken care of by a method of production that places little or no value on manual skills. All this is symptomatic of a conflict in industrial society *because* it is a conflict within industrial man himself. For the modern worker is obliged to seek a livelihood in a system where the justice that is due to his humanity is in direct conflict with his economic survival. For we have set in place a society where the artist in us is free to work for the good of his feelings provided he does not expect, in so doing, the right to earn a livelihood. At the same time the workman in us is free to work for the good that is material necessity provided he does not thereby expect the right to an inherent satisfaction from the work he must do to secure a livelihood. What has been made all but impossible by the industrial system is that men and women can attain a livelihood by doing what is both aesthetically and morally sound and economically and practically valid, by a means that allows them both intellectual and spiritual responsibility.

We can perhaps sense more vividly the degree of impoverishment imposed by such a system if we contrast it with the value accorded the handicrafts by our ancestors, whose artifacts fill our ethnographical museums where they are revered for their skill and ageless beauty, and whose concept of the handicrafts is one that grants them nothing less than a sacred function. For it was traditionally the role of the crafts that, over and above serving practical ends, they were to serve the maintenance of the subtle link that binds together beauty and being, the severance of which has had such devastating consequences for the modern world. Unlike the situation that faces the modern worker, in the traditional and sacred context of the crafts each member of society, in so far as he or she practices an art, is responsible as a moral being for the good use of the community, while at the same time being personally responsible for the intrinsic good of the thing he or she makes.

In *Ecclesiasticus* (38) it is said of the craftsman that in trusting to his hands "every one is wise in his work," by which wisdom he "will maintain the state of the world." We can hardly fail to notice the parallel between such words and those quoted by the Indian scholar Stella Kramrisch, who says that according to traditional Indian belief and practice, every creature has a function (actually a craft vocation) which is fulfilled in the universe and deviation from which "might even endanger the order of the universe." This suggests that if the crafts have become an anachronism in our time this is not due to any inherent weakness or fault in the crafts themselves, but that we have assigned them a status that is considerably beneath the full dignity of their normal function.

The juggernaut of modern industrial enterprise is based upon the moral neutrality of capitalist investment which exploits the nature of usury to exert unrelenting pressure towards a purely quantitative, economic expansion. This essentially "blind" process has created a society in which it is all but impossible to determine what qualitative criteria might apply to the concept of human needs and how those needs might best be met. In other words we are embroiled in a pattern of life that is hardly able to distinguish between what is a *real* need and what is an artificially stimulated appetite and so cannot distinguish satisfaction from superfluity. This makes it virtually impossible to determine what *must* be done (as opposed to what *can* be done) in order to unite our everyday life of making and doing with the reality that is the ultimate nature of our humanity. Indeed, such a system has an obvious vested interest in seeing that such divisions are never healed, all the better to manipulate the confusion and disharmony that inevitably manifest themselves in a demand for material consolations.

All men and women make things, and it is by skill, by the deliberate intent of the mind and its exertion towards what is other than mind—some occasion or material circumstance outside of the mind—that things get made. And since each and every one of us makes things by the exercise of skill (which is the root meaning of art) each and every one of us is in some degree an artist. But behind our doing and making there is an agent or being who remains free and objective in relation to what is produced by the action that is applied skill. How we do and make does not determine our being so much as how we do and make is the very signature of our humanity. For if, by our "fruits" we shall be "known," then work, far from being nothing more than a utilitarian process must in some sense be capable of revealing the proper nature of our humanity. In other words action follows being. The converse would be to propose that action possesses within itself its own sufficient reason. The metaphysical objection to such a proposition is clearly stated by Eckhart:

> The work has no being, nor has the time in which it occurred, since it perishes in itself. Therefore it is neither good nor holy nor blessed, but rather the man is blessed in whom the fruit of the work remains, neither as time nor as work, but as a good disposition which is eternal with the spirit as the spirit is eternal in itself, and it is the spirit itself.

So we perhaps begin to see that work is not something we must be freed from—indeed cannot be freed from unless we are freed entirely from action—but something we must engage in, in such a way and at such a level that it is revealing of our deepest nature. It must contribute to our spiritual life while serving our bodily needs.

The very opposite is the case with the industrial pattern of work which is part and parcel of a social ethos that continually holds out the promise of leisure as the reward for the time and effort put into work. But this escape to a state of freedom *from* work is not offered as something that will serve our spiritual needs. Far from it. The so-called "leisure" of our consumer society is a parody of that spiritual condition of true inactivity, the contemplative interiority of a state of being in which we must finally acknowledge that we are only truly "free" when we are released from the necessity to re-act to the demands of the external world.

The idleness that characterizes the leisure society (where no one has time to do nothing) is a condition of sloth in which the will to act to some meaningful end is, as it were, suspended in a state of restless neutrality. The medieval schoolmen understood this to be *acedia* which, as Josef Pieper explained in *Leisure as the Basis of Culture*,

> means that a man prefers to forgo the rights, or if you prefer, the claims, that belong to his nature. In a word, he does not want to be as God wants him to be, and that ultimately means that he does not wish to be what he really, fundamentally, *is*. . . . Metaphysically and theologically, the notion of *acedia* means that a man does not, in the last resort, give the consent of his will to his own being; that behind or beneath the dynamic activity of his existence, he is still not at one with himself, or, as the mediaeval writers would have said, face to face with the divine good within him.

From the Christian perspective the starting point of all discussion of work has to begin with man's expulsion from Paradise—the loss, or rather "annexing," of the spiritual domain entailed by our being brought into our bodily life. Here the "sweat" of labor is made necessary by our material needs and is suffered in the knowledge that it may form a channel or path along which the original undivided unity of being of our nature may be traced and re-made whole. In this primary sense the work of right-livelihood (it is the traditional role of the crafts to foster and preserve the sanctification of labor) is analogous to adopting the vocation of the contemplative life of prayer: the life of true inactivity. Work is prayer. Man at prayer and man at work, both turn in an inward direction away from the diverging, multiple impulses of the external world in order to effect a convergence of the soul's faculties towards a state of equilibrium that is an internal act of harmony and unity.

But whereas the "work" of contemplative prayer is a withdrawal from the world, the work of making and doing necessarily involves us with the world. It is given to very few to withdraw from the world to live a life of prayer and solitude. The mass of men and women, unable to surmount the inevitable distractions and entanglements of their bodily and social existence, need the concentration and discipline of a practical vocation in order to restore the inner balance and harmony that is their proper being.

So we may recognize that at its highest point of efficacy, inspired work, as with prayer, arrests the scattered sentient powers of the soul so that the workman becomes by degrees dead to his empirical ego as he approaches a state of perfect action. In this convergent movement of his being, initiated by the discipline of a skill (the very words "discipline" and "skill" imply of necessity a mastery over something "other" that is the opposite of *self*-indulgence), the subtle process whereby the workman comes "face to face with the divine good within him" can begin. Thus, by degrees we become detached from the contrary states that constitute the dualistic nature of our existence; life and death, spirit and matter, inner and outer, subject and object, pain and joy, so we are less the passive recipient of these contrary demands and more the instrument of the harmony and balance that transcends them. Thus conformed to the intelligible order of the Logos within, we become more the subject and vessel of the Creator and less the object of external contradictions. To use apophatic, Eckhartian terms, it is already a step towards God to see the Creation as his abundant gifts to us. It is another step nearer to want Him more than his gifts.

But, it is one thing to allow that because the mass of men and women are more or less excluded from the state of contemplative perfection, so they must be allowed the relative "freedom" of exploring their creativity, and quite another to claim that such creativity must proliferate on its own terms. For human action, let it be repeated, cannot be its own justification. For man is, primarily, called upon to understand the reason for his existence. Without such an understanding he cannot hope, beneficially, to relate his thoughts and subsequent actions to the underlying order of the reality of which he comprises only a part. Action cannot be free from the rigor and necessity of the primordial qualities of beauty and perfection if it is to take account of the "divine good within."

All traditions speak of human intelligence as having a sacred function precisely because the human *per se* is indefinable except in terms of the Divine. Suspended as he is between celestial and diabolic forces it is in turn only man's capacity to recapitulate what transcends him that grants him a legitimate dominion over the world of nature. Which is why only man can conceive of an earthly paradise and why, conversely, in denying what is above him, only man can create a hell on earth.

While it is certainly true that the crafts, in their material aspect, have their foundation in the external necessities of our existence which demands that we feed, shelter and clothe our bodies, none the less, the origin of the crafts is rooted in the cosmological idea that the very substance of the world, in virtue of its being part of the Creation, is the "body" of God—the manifest aspect of the unmanifest Divine Principle. It is the reflection of this on the human plane that permits the analogous symbolism of the craftsman as one who creates in imitation of God's act of creating the world. The sacred crafts re-enact, at the existential level of the material creation, the primordial act of cosmogenesis. That is to say, on the human plane, perfect doing and making consists in the true alignment of mind, eye and hand as a recapitulation of the Divine perfection of the world that is the true alignment of the spiritual, the psyche (of the soul) and the bodily in a movement from potentiality to act.

If the crafts were not able to effect such a true alignment then we would not find in all traditional texts passages that speak of the craftsman as upholding and maintaining the order of the universe. What is implied in all such texts is the idea that one's first and immediate duty and one's last or ultimate end must become coincident as comprising a unity. *Justice* is that which is conformable to a law, or to a rule, *order* is due place or rank and *proportion* a due share or order of a part in relation to a whole. These ideas are semantically related in signifying a relationship of harmonious unity among disparate parts, a unity that reflects the equilibrium of the universal order. Obviously there can be no right-livelihood in the things of injustice, disorder and disproportion any more than it is conceivable that men and women could consecrate to God work that is flippant, indulgent and superfluous.

Even the most cursory glance at the contents of our ethnographical museums will give abundant evidence of the symbolic aspect of the crafts. For not only in those things produced by the crafts—pottery, weaving, building, clothes, carpentry and so on—but also in the very instruments of the crafts themselves, we find a rich language of symbolism indicative of their spiritual status. For instance, Christ, as the incarnate Divine Principle, and thus "in whom all things are made," was a carpenter—one who works wood. Owing to its ubiquity as the primary substance to be worked in meeting so many practical and material needs, as well as its plasticity in accepting so many diverse forms, wood symbolically conforms to the *prima materia* of the Creation. (Swedenborg received a revelation of wood as the symbol of the celestial goodness in its lowest corporeal plane.)

St. Bonaventure points out in his treatise *The Reduction of the Arts to Theology,* that St. Augustine said the Son of God is the "art of the Father": through whom, it may be added, we are enabled to see the beginning and end of all things; that is, what is right and true. As St. Bonaventure also points out, one sense of the word "right" is that a thing's middle is not out of line with its extreme points. In the similar way a carpenter works a piece of wood, checking to see that it is *true* (from "fidelity," "trust," OE *tréo,* giving English "tree"—"as firm and straight as a tree"), by the use of a *rule* (from "regular," measuring-bar, pattern of conduct, a discipline) that tells him if the middle is aligned with its beginning and its end. His tools are no less symbolically assimilable to the Divine process or causes that shape the *materia* of the universe. Moreover, Christ, as the "beginning" and "end" of all things, was sacrificed on a wooden cross, in turn assimilable to the tree of life or world axis that holds heaven and earth together. The richness of such symbolic correspondences, which could easily be elaborated, should be sufficient to illustrate the cosmic function of the craftsman.

What we do not find is that the mass of men and women in remote ages satisfied their material needs in some unsophisticated and brutish fashion with an eye only to efficient and pragmatic solutions. On the contrary, in serving material needs the maker keeps his ocular vision on the immediate and contingent requirements of the task at hand. But at the same time he keeps the inner eye of spiritual vision on those things that relate to his final end—the fact that he is a created and creative part of that sacred reality that is the world. By so doing he produces an environment that forms the living context for the human spirit to participate in the cyclic rhythms of nature that are themselves a reflection of the cosmic rhythms of the universe. For just as the principle of nature is rhythmic organization and order, so the principle of manufacture is the ordering of matter according to an intelligible pattern. By his most common and repeated actions the craftsman integrates himself with the vast, powerful, fructifying sources of reality so that his individual existence is not projected into a meaningless expanse of time and space. For, essentially, the arts and crafts are the application of a science of rhythm, as René Guénon has pointed out; the phonetic arts being the application of the rhythm of succession deployed in time and the plastic arts being the application of the rhythm of simultaneity deployed in space. By contrast, in the industrial milieu, time is speeded up and space becomes merely indefinite extension. In so doing they erode, and eventually abolish, the meaningful relationship of the temporal with the eternal and the finite with the infinite. Time and space lose their spiritual significance as the primary ordering principles of orientation for the "place" and "direction" of human vocation and destiny.

The technological environment projects man into a progress that disrupts the cyclical and periodic rhythms of time, to replace them with the open-ended future of an indefinite development. In such an environment, space that is normally experienced as locally qualified extension—as the "container" of events—becomes the generalized field of a "freedom" paradoxically experienced as oppressive and where man is subject to the forces of inertia and compression in the physical realm and acceleration and dispersion in the psychological realm.

The sacramental and ritual character of the traditional crafts, on the other hand, actualizes the numinous context of time and space by formalizing and embodying the link between the inner contemplative domain of the soul on the one hand and the outer active domain of the body on the other. These two domains are, however, not discrete or disjunctive but complementary, dual facets of the one same reality in its transcendent and immanent, objective and subjective modes. This sacramental character places a heavier emphasis on the agent of action—the quality of the humanity of the maker—in the productive process than it does on the technical means of manufacture. This is again quite the opposite situation facing the industrial worker whose complicity is with a mechanized technique in which almost his entire work function has been systematized as a result of someone else's conception and design. This is to devitalize the work process, emptying it of precisely those external, manipulative challenges and internal, psychological satisfactions that give meaning and value to the experience of work. And what else could what we call soul-destroying work be but just such an absence or devitalization? Seen in this light we can better appreciate what is lost in the progressive model of industrial production, where the worker is always prey to the indiscriminate development of the working environment, a process that anaesthetizes his soul as the price demanded for its own survival.

With the traditional crafts the means of production are kept as close as possible to the fundamental interaction of hand and mind, with the eye as intermediary, sight being the agent of both perception and action. This economy of instrumental means allows the manipulative and visual faculties their closest collaboration with the intellect, which then acts as the motive source of the worker's skill.

The intimate link between the crafts and ritual, work and prayer, action and spirituality, has been fostered and transmitted by the guild societies in all traditional cultures. In India, for instance, the presiding god of craftsmen is Visvakarma, sum total of consciousness, knowledge and inspiration, the architect of the universe, in whom resides the Divine skill that is revealed to the craftsman through the sacred texts and oral transmission of traditional doctrines and disciplines.

In the Christian tradition, all wisdom, knowledge and ability ultimately descends through Christ, from the Father. St. Bonaventure, for instance, conceives the mechanical arts as resulting from the illumination of knowledge, which illumination (or light) is, in the final analysis, coterminous with the Divine Light that is the Logos that illumines each and every being and goodness present in the world.

From the Islamic perspective, the arts and crafts are like so many formal crystallizations in the realm of multiplicity of the Divine Unity that is the inner reality of the Koran made manifest by the Prophet and his companion 'Ali, the founder of Islamic calligraphy and patron of all the guilds.

The existence of the guilds, in both East and West, was for the purpose of nurturing and sustaining an initiatory knowledge in which art, craft, work, science, mechanics, dynamics, geometry and so on are all categories of thought and forms of wisdom—*sapientia*. This illumination of the mind corrects and perfects the intuitive knowledge of a thing's essence and how it is to be realized in some outward form and is analogous to the transmundane light of the

Divine Intellect throwing an illuminated pattern on the mirror of the human intelligence. The rays or threads of this transcendent light can be likened to translucent states of being held in hierarchic suspension from their ultimate source in the infinite perfection of the Divine Principle that is the spirit of God.[1] The purpose of the activity that is the particular craft skill is to follow the rigors of a discipline such that, in accomplishing inner and outer mastery, there is a perfect integration of bodily activity, imaginative conception and spiritual illumination—wholeness of being, in fact. This traditional practice of the trades presupposes that each thing to be made, each action to be undertaken, has itself a norm of perfection—that which enables it, through the agency of intellectual determination and manual skill, to attain its true and essential nature.[2]

From the foregoing observations it will be clear that an answer to the question "are the crafts an anachronism?" cannot be simple, for it

[1] That such a doctrine was still dependably current among his readers could be assumed by George Herbert when in the 1630s he wrote in the last stanza of his poem "Mattens,"

> Teach me thy love to know
>   That this new light, which now I see,
> May both the work and workman show:
>   Then by a sunne-beam I will climb to thee.

However, by around 1810 perhaps fewer of William Blake's readers would have recognized the allusion to the same doctrine in these famous lines:

> I give you the end of a golden string,
>   Only wind it into a ball:
> It will lead you in at Heaven's gate
>   Built in Jerusalem's wall.

[2] "The Tea Ceremony signifies that we ought to perform all the activities and manipulations of daily life according to primordial perfections, which is pure symbolism, pure consciousness of the Essential, perfect beauty and self-mastery. The intention is basically the same in the craft initiation of the West—including Islam—but the formal foundation is then the production of useful objects and not the symbolism of gestures; this being so, the stone mason intends, parallel to his work, to fashion his soul in view of union with God. And thus there is to be found in all the crafts and all the arts a spiritual model that, in the Muslim world, often refers to one of the prophets mentioned in the Koran; any professional or homemaking activity is a kind of revelation. As for the adherents of Zen, they readily seek their inspiration in 'ordinary life,' not because it is trivial, to be sure, but because—inasmuch as it is woven of symbolisms—it mysteriously implies the 'Buddha nature'" (Frithjof Schuon, *The Eye of the Heart* [Bloomington, IN: World Wisdom, 1997], pp.140-41).

depends upon what we admit is involved in their practice. If we see all work as simply the pragmatic means by which we satisfy our material needs, then of course the crafts are outmoded as a way of producing the necessities of life. But any study of the traditional conception of the crafts, and of the human self-image that is integral to them, reveals a more complex picture; one that touches upon spiritual factors that at best have been obscured or debased in the way work is understood in the modern world. However, such a study obliges us to recognize that there are social, economic, as well as spiritual conditions required for the traditional conception of human vocation to function properly; conditions hardly in providential alignment in the modern world. Indeed, it should be said that the modern world is the result of having these conditions misaligned. But that does not permit us to dismiss as speculative fancy what a study of the crafts is capable of revealing, both about the nature of the human agent of the crafts and about the spiritual milieu the crafts are capable of embodying. From the standpoint of contemporary conditions we are in the position of one who, faced with a mountain and not having the full means to ascend it, is none the less neither in a position to deny that the ascent is possible, nor to deny that the view from the summit is what it is.

The story of the Fall, of man's expulsion from the Heavenly Paradise, is the story of man's having to live "by the sweat of his brow." That much is inescapable. But does it follow that we are condemned to a life of brute exertion without redemption? Machines may have relieved us of a good deal of physical hardship but at the price, to say the least, of introducing a scale and pattern of work that makes for much soulless drudgery. And we know ourselves to have a soul as surely as we register when our soul is not given its due. As to our redemption, from the standpoint of a study of the crafts as the instrument and repository of sacred culture, the answer is unequivocal. In their natural habitat the crafts presuppose an analogical and effective relationship between labor and spiritual edification in which work has both dignity and sanctity. To work in this context is to seek purification through discipline. And because there is no freedom without discipline, so it is possible for our vocation to be exemplified in the mastery of a practical skill as the best and most natural means to dispose our salvation.[3] This makes it possible for our first duty as spiri-

---

[3] "Let every man abide in the same calling wherein he was called. Art thou called *being*

tual beings to be coincident with our responsibility as social beings. For as surely as "rights" incur responsibilities, so ultimately we can only concede our neighbors' "rights" on the basis of their spiritual freedom to realize his or her deiformity. We are surely entitled to ask whether the industrial system presents a more dignified, and in the end, a more realistic paradigm.

But if we insist that the answer to our initial question—Are the crafts an anachronism?—is yes, then what have we admitted? We have admitted to there being no possibility of an inner perfection in whatever we labor at. With that confirmed and in the name of consistency, we must go on to admit that labor is a monstrous encumbrance without value, and that learning is a mere gathering of information without meaning, the final goal of both being mechanical efficiency. In which case both had better be dealt with by machines, as indeed we see is attempted, by the "leisure industry" on the one hand and by the computer on the other. But this does not answer, so much as shelve, the question of *why* we should labor and think at all! As we have already suggested, it is precisely spiritual and qualitative values and meanings[4] that determine what *ought* to be done as opposed to what simply *can* be done.

The extensive range of mechanized contrivances we call modern industry assumes the destruction of the crafts as inimical to its survival. Such indeed is its very *raison d'être*. It is not in the interests of such a system to awaken in those it enslaves any intimation of possibilities the system itself cannot satisfy. There is an exact common measure between the fact that in the post-industrial society the body, no longer challenged as the instrument of creative work, has become a complex of organs appealed to only in as much as they are able to *feel*. How else can we explain that the blandishments of the advertising industry are directed almost exclusively towards convenience and gratification—the stimulation and indulgence of bodily sensation? A

---

servant? care not for it: but if thou mayest be made free, use *it* rather" (1 Corinthians 7:20-21).

[4] To mean something is to have in mind a cognitive intent. Hence it is to signify the actual and effective penetration of the intelligence by a cognitive value. The value of anything implies an equivalent exchange of something; here a cognitive worth that enters a given state of being by that which is adequate to it. In such an effective penetration Beauty, Goodness and Truth presuppose the possibility of our elevation from lower to higher states of being.

consumer society such as we know it could not function except in a world where the body has little to do but concern itself with its appetites—and these a mere palliative.

What alienates us from an environment made up almost entirely of the products of industrial technology is the fact that such products could not exist except by means of a system of manufacture that is first and foremost founded upon the destruction of the sacred status of human vocation. And, as an entailment of that destruction, the erosion and eventual obliteration of the natural context of that vocation—the direct, vital experience of birth, death, generation, the natural and lunar cycles, the whole panoply of the heavens and the earth, water, land, river, tree, stone and flower through which the order of the sacred is mediated to man's experience.

If we look to the beauty of the crafts and all that they have engendered, it is to seek liberation from the enslavement of our own misdoings. Nothing is more natural to man than that he should achieve a lasting standard as a bulwark against the inevitable transience of his earthly life. What is that standard to be? That is the real question posed by the crafts.

Why do the crafts continue to occupy our attention? Surely it is because we are still capable of recognizing in them a mirror image, however faint, of what it is we might yet become. We do best to honor that image by acknowledging that, in all but abandoning the crafts in favor of industrial means of production, we have lost a significant portion of what it means to be fully human. The anachronism of the crafts is achieved at the cost of our own disfigurement.

IV

Comparative
Religion

"God shows no partiality; but in every nation, anyone that fears Him and does what is right, is accepted by Him."—Acts 10:34-35

"Have we not all one father? Hath not one God created us?"—Malachi 2:10

"And other sheep I have, which are not of this fold."—John 10:16

"That which today is called the Christian religion existed among the Ancients, and has never ceased to exist from the origin of the human race, until the time when Christ Himself came, and men began to call Christian the true religion which already existed beforehand."—St. Augustine (354-430)

"And now, O philosophy, hasten to set before me not only this one man Plato, but many others also, who declare the one and only true God to be God, by his own inspiration, if so be they have laid hold of the truth."—Clement of Alexandria (c.150-c.220)

"Among all peoples, in all times, God is worshiped because it is natural to do so, though not with the same rites and methods."—Marsilio Ficino (1433-1499)

"How consoling it is for me that, all over the world, there are millions of people who, five times a day, bow down before God."—Pope Pius XII (1876-1959)

"We have been taught that Christ is the First begotten of God, and have testified that he is the Intellect (*logos*) of which every race of man partakes. Those who lived in accordance with Intellect are Christians, even though they were called godless, such as, among the Greeks, Socrates and Heraclitus and others like them. . . . Those who lived by Intellect, and those who so live now, are Christians, fearless and unperturbed."—St. Justin Martyr (c.100-c.165)

"The eternal Word or Son of God did not then first begin to be the Savior of the world when He was born in Bethlehem of Judea; but that Word which became man in the Virgin Mary did from the beginning of the world enter as a word of life, a seed of salvation, into the first father of mankind. . . . Hence it was that so many eminent spirits, partakers of a divine life, have appeared in so many parts of the heathen world; glorious names, sons of wisdom, that shone as lights hung out by God in the midst of idolatrous darkness."—William Law (1686-1761)

"O wonder, the Son of God has been from all eternity,
And his mother has only given birth to him today!"—Angelus Silesius (1624-1677)

"There is therefore one sole religion and one sole worship for all beings endowed with understanding, and this is presupposed through a variety of rites. To different countries Thou hast sent different prophets and different masters, the ones at one time, the others at another time. But it is a law of our condition as men of this earth that a long habit becomes for us second nature, that it is taken for a truth and defended as such. It is from this that great dissensions arise, when each community opposes its own faith to other faiths. And if it should be that it is impossible to remove this difference as to rites, and that this difference should even seem desirable in order to increase devotion (each religion attaching itself with more devotion to its ceremonies as if they had the more to please Thy Majesty), nevertheless . . . as Thou art unique, there is but one religion and one worship."—Nicholas of Cusa (1401-1464)

"We see Muslim and Catholic princes not only allied, when the power of a dangerous co-religionist had to be curbed, but also aiding one another generously to suppress disorders and revolts. The reader will learn, no doubt to his surprise, that in one of the battles for the Caliphate of Córdoba in 1010, Catalan forces saved the situation and on this occasion three bishops gave their lives for the 'Prince of the Believers' (*amir al-mu'minin*). Al-Mansur had in his entourage several counts who joined him with their troops, and the presence of Christian guards in the courts of Andalusia was by no means exceptional. When an enemy territory was conquered, the religious convictions of the population were respected as far as possible; let us recall only that Mansur—who was not usually over-scrupulous—took care, at the assault on Santiago, to protect the church containing the tomb of the Apostle from all profanation and that, in many other cases, Caliphs seized the opportunity to manifest their respect for the sacred things of the enemy. In similar circumstances, the Christians had a similar attitude: for centuries Islam was respected in the reconquered territories, and it was only in the 16th century that it was systematically persecuted and exterminated, at the instigation of a fanatical clergy which had grown too powerful. During the whole of the Middle Ages, on the other hand, tolerance with regard to the others' conviction and respect for the sentiments of the enemy accompanied the incessant battles between Moors and Christians, greatly diminishing the rigors and miseries of war, and conferring on the combats as chivalrous a character as possible. In spite of the linguistic abyss, respect for the adversary as well as high esteem for his virtues—and in the poetry of both sides, an understanding of his sentiments—became a common national bond. This poetry bears eloquent witness to the love or friendship which often united Muslims and Christians beyond all obstacles."—Ernst Kühnel

PATHS THAT LEAD TO THE SAME SUMMIT

Ananda K. Coomaraswamy

There is no Natural Religion. . . . As all men are alike (though infinitely various), so all Religions, as all similars, have one source.
—William Blake

There is but one salvation for all mankind, and that is the life of God
in the soul.   —William Law

The constant increase of contacts between ourselves, who for the
purposes of the present essay may be assumed to be Christians, and
other peoples who belong to the great non-Christian majority has
made it more than ever before an urgent necessity for us to understand the faiths by which they live. Such an understanding is at the
same time intrinsically to be desired, and indispensable for the solution by agreement of the economic and political problems by which
the peoples of the world are at present more divided than united. We
cannot establish human relationships with other peoples if we are
convinced of our own superiority or superior wisdom, and only want
to convert them to our way of thinking. The modern Christian, who
thinks of the world as his parish, is faced with the painful necessity of
becoming himself a citizen of the world; he is invited to participate
in a symposium and a *convivium*; not to preside—for there is Another
who presides unseen—but as one of many guests.

It is no longer only for the professed missionary that a study of
other religions than his own is required. This very essay, for example,
is based upon an address given to a large group of schoolteachers in
a series entitled "How to Teach about Other Peoples," sponsored by
the New York School Board and the East and West Association. It has,
too, been proposed that in all the schools and universities of the post-
war world stress should be laid on the teaching of the basic principles
of the great world religions as a means of promoting international
understanding and developing a concept of world citizenship.

The question next arises, "By whom can such teaching be properly given?" It will be self-evident that no one can have understood,

213

and so be qualified to teach, a religion, who is opposed to all religion; this will rule out the rationalist and scientific humanist, and ultimately all those whose conception of religion is not theological, but merely ethical. The obvious ideal would be for the great religions to be taught only by those who confess them; but this is an ideal that could only be realized, for the present, in our larger universities. It has been proposed to establish a school of this kind at Oxford.

As things are, a teaching about other than Christian faiths is mainly given in theological seminaries and missionary colleges by men who do believe that Christianity is the only true faith, who approve of foreign missions, and who wish to prepare the missionary for his work. Under these conditions, the study of comparative religion necessarily assumes a character quite different from that of other disciplines; it cannot but be biased. It is obvious that if we are to teach at all it should be our intention to communicate only truth: but where a teaching takes for granted that the subject matter to be dealt with is intrinsically of inferior significance, and the subject is taught, not *con amore*, but only to instruct the future schoolmaster in the problems that he will have to cope with, one cannot but suspect that at least a part of the truth will be suppressed, if not intentionally, at least unknowingly.

If comparative religion is to be taught as other sciences are taught, the teacher must surely have recognized that his own religion is only one of those that are to be "compared"; he may not expound any "pet theories" of his own, but is to present the truth without bias, to the extent that it lies in his power. In other words, it will be "necessary to recognize that those institutions which are based on the same premises, let us say the supernatural, must be considered together, our own amongst the rest," whereas "today, whether it is a question of imperialism, or of race prejudice, or of a comparison between Christianity and paganism, we are still preoccupied with the uniqueness . . . of our own institutions and achievements, our own civilization."[1] One cannot but ask whether the Christian whose conviction is ineradicable that his is the only true faith can conscientiously permit himself to expound another religion, knowing that he cannot do so honestly.

*

* *

[1] Ruth Benedict, *Patterns of Culture*, 1934, p. 5.

We are, then, in proposing to teach about other peoples, faced with the problem of tolerance. The word is not a pretty one; to tolerate is to put up with, endure, or suffer the existence of what are or appear to be other ways of thinking than our own; and it is neither very pleasant merely "to put up with" our neighbors and fellow guests, nor very pleasant to feel that one's own deepest institutions and beliefs are being patiently "endured." Moreover, if the Western world is actually more tolerant today than it was some centuries ago, or has been since the fall of Rome, it is largely because men are no longer sure that there is any truth of which we can be certain, and are inclined to the "democratic" belief that one man's opinion is as good as another's, especially in the fields of politics, art, and religion. Tolerance, then, is a merely negative virtue, demanding no sacrifice of spiritual pride and involving no abrogation of our sense of superiority; it can be commended only in so far as it means that we shall refrain from hating or persecuting others who differ or seem to differ from ourselves in habit or belief. Tolerance still allows us to pity those who differ from ourselves, and are consequently to be pitied!

Tolerance, carried further, implies indifference, and becomes intolerable. Our proposal is not that we should tolerate heresies, but rather come to some agreement about the truth. Our proposition is that the proper objective of an education in comparative religion should be to enable the pupil to discuss with other believers the validity of particular doctrines,[2] leaving the problem of the truth or falsity, superiority or inferiority, of whole bodies of doctrine in abeyance until we have had at least an opportunity to know in what respects they really differ from one another, and whether in essentials or in accidentals. We take it for granted, of course, that they will inevitably differ accidentally, since "nothing can be known except in the mode of the knower." One must at least have been taught to recognize equivalent symbols, e.g., rose and lotus (Rosa Mundi and Padmavati); that Soma is the "bread and water of life"; or that the Maker of all things is by no means accidentally, but necessarily a "carpenter" wher-

---

[2] To illustrate what I mean by "discussion" here, I refer the reader to my article entitled, "On Being in One's Right Mind," in the *Review of Religion*, Vol. VII, New York, 1942, pp. 32-40 [Editor's Note: This article is also published in Ananda Coomaraswamy's *What is Civilization? And Other Essays* (Ipswich: Golgonooza Press, 1989)]. Although in fact by one author, this article is in effect a collaboration of Christian, Platonist, and Hindu, expounding a doctrine held in common.

ever the material of which the world is made is *hylic*. The proposed objective has this further and immediate advantage, that it is not in conflict with even the most rigid Christian orthodoxy; it has never been denied that some truths are embodied in the pagan beliefs, and even St. Thomas Aquinas was ready and willing to find in the works of the pagan philosophers "extrinsic and probable proofs" of the truths of Christianity. He was, indeed, acquainted only with the ancients and with the Jews and some Arabians; but there is no reason why the modern Christian, if his mental equipment is adequate, should not learn to recognize or be delighted to find in, let us say, Vedantic, Sufi, Taoist, or American Indian formulations extrinsic and probable proofs of the truth as he knows it. It is more than probable, indeed, that his contacts with other believers will be of very great advantage to the Christian student in his exegesis and understanding of Christian doctrine; for though himself a believer, this is in spite of the nominalist intellectual environment in which he was born and bred, and by which he cannot but be to some degree affected; while the Oriental (to whom the miracles attributed to Christ present no problem) is still a realist, born and bred in a realistic environment, and is therefore in a position to approach Plato or St. John, Dante or Meister Eckhart more simply and directly than the Western scholar who cannot but have been affected to some extent by the doubts and difficulties that force themselves upon those whose education and environment have been for the greater part profane.

Such a procedure as we have suggested provides us immediately with a basis for a common understanding and for cooperation. What we have in view is an ultimate "reunion of the churches" in a far wider sense than that in which this expression is commonly employed: the substitution of active alliances—let us say of Christianity and Hinduism or Islam, on the basis of commonly recognized first principles, and with a view to an effective cooperation in the application of these principles to the contingent fields of art (manufacture) and prudence—for what is at present nothing better than a civil war between the members of one human family, children of one and the same God, "whom," as Philo said, "*with one accord* all Greeks and Barbarians acknowledge together."[3] It is with reference to this state-

---

[3] Philo Judaeus, *De specialibus legibus* II, 65; E. R. Goodenough, *Introduction to Philo Judaeus*, 1940, pp. 105, 108.

ment that Professor Goodenough remarks that, "So far as I can see Philo was telling the simple truth about paganism as he saw it, not as Christian propaganda has ever since misrepresented it."

It need not be concealed that such alliances will necessarily involve an abandonment of all missionary enterprises such as they are now; interdenominational conferences will take the place of those proselytizing expeditions of which the only permanent result is the secularization and destruction of existing cultures and the pulling up of individuals by their roots. *You* have already reached the point at which culture and religion, utility and meaning, have been divorced and can be considered apart, but this is not true of those peoples whom you propose to convert, whose religion and culture *are one and the same thing* and none of the functions of whose life are necessarily profane or unprincipled. If ever you should succeed in persuading the Hindus that their revealed scriptures are valid only "as literature," you will have reduced them to the level of your own college men who read the Bible, if at all, only as literature. Christianity in India, as Sister Nivedita (Patrick Geddes' distinguished pupil, and author of *The Web of Indian Life*) once remarked, "carries drunkenness in its wake"[4]—for if you teach a man that what he has thought right is wrong, he will be apt to think that what he has thought wrong is right.

We are all alike in need of repentance and conversion, a "change of mind" and a "turning round": not, however, from one *form* of belief to another, but from unbelief to belief. There can be no more vicious kind of tolerance than to approach another man, to tell him that "We are both serving the same God, you in your way and I in His!" The "compassing of sea and land to make one proselyte" can be carried on as an institution only for so long as our ignorance of other peoples' faiths persists. The subsidizing of educational or medical services accessory to the primary purpose of conversion is a form of simony and an infringement of the instruction, "Heal the sick . . . provide neither gold nor silver nor brass in your purses, nor scrip for your journey . . . [but go] forth as sheep in the midst of wolves." Wherever you go, it must be not as masters or superiors but as guests, or as we might say nowadays, "exchange professors"; you must not return to betray the confidences of your hosts by any libel. Your vocation must

---

[4] *Lambs among Wolves*, 1903. See also my "Christian Missions in India" in *Essays in National Idealism* (1st ed., 1909; or 2nd ed.).

be purged of any notion of a "civilizing mission"; for what you think of as "the white man's burden" here is a matter of "white shadows in the South Seas" there. Your "Christian" civilization is ending in disaster—and you are bold enough to offer it to others! Realize that, as Professor Plumer has said, "the surest way to betray our Chinese allies is to sell, give or lend-lease them our [American] standard of living,"[5] and that the hardest task you could undertake for the present and immediate future is to convince the Orient that the civilization of Europe is in any sense a Christian civilization, or that there really are reasonable, just, and tolerable Europeans amongst the "barbarians" of whom the Orient lives in terror.

The word "heresy" means choice, the having opinions of one's own, and thinking what we *like* to think: we can only grasp its real meaning today, when "thinking for oneself" is so highly recommended (with the proviso that the thinking must be "100 per cent"), if we realize that the modern equivalent of heresy is "treason." The one outstanding, and perhaps the only, real heresy of modern Christianity in the eyes of other believers is its claim to exclusive truth; for this is treason against Him who "never left himself without a witness," and can only be paralleled by Peter's denial of Christ; and whoever says to his pagan friends that "the light that is in you is darkness," in offending these is offending the Father of lights. In view of St. Ambrose's well-known gloss on I Corinthians 12:3, "all that is true, *by whomso-ever it has been said*, is from the Holy Ghost" (a dictum endorsed by St. Thomas Aquinas), you may be asked, "On what grounds do you propose to distinguish between your own 'revealed' religion and our 'natural' religion, for which, in fact, we also claim a supernatural origin?" You may find this question hard to answer.

The claim to an exclusive validity is by no means calculated to make for the survival of Christianity in a world prepared to prove all things. On the contrary, it may weaken enormously its prestige in relation to other traditions in which a very different attitude prevails, and which are under no necessity of engaging in any polemic. As a great German theologian has said, "human culture [*Menschheitsbildung*] is a unitary whole, and its separate cultures are the dialects of one and

---

[5] J. M. Plumer, "China's High Standard of Living," *Asia and the Americas* February, 1944.

the same language of the spirit."[6] The quarrel of Christianity with other religions seems to an Oriental as much a tactical error in the conflict of ideal with sensate motivations as it would have been for the Allies to turn against the Chinese on the battlefield. Nor will he participate in such a quarrel; much rather he will say, what I have often said to Christian friends, "Even if you are not on our side, we are on yours." The converse attitude is rarely expressed; but twice in my life I have met a Roman Catholic who could freely admit that for a Hindu to become a professing Christian was not essential to salvation. Yet, could we believe it, the Truth or Justice with which we are all alike and unconditionally concerned is like the Round Table to which "al the worlde crysten and hethen repayren" to eat of one and the same bread and drink the same wine, and at which "all are equal, the high and the low." A very learned Roman Catholic friend of mine, in correspondence, speaks of Sri Ramakrishna as "another Christ . . . Christ's own self."

*

* *

Let us now, for a moment, consider the points of view that have been expressed by the ancients and other non-Christians when they speak of religions other than their own. We have already quoted Philo. Plutarch, first with bitter irony disposing of the Greek euhemerists "who spread atheism all over the world by obliterating the Gods of our belief and turning them all alike into the names of generals, admirals and kings," and of the Greeks who could no longer distinguish Apollo (the intelligible Sun) from Helios (the sensible sun), goes on to say: "Nor do we speak of the 'different Gods' of different peoples, or of the Gods as 'Barbarian' and 'Greek,' but as common to all, though differently named by different peoples, so that for the One Reason (Logos) that orders all these things, and the One Providence that oversees them, and for the minor powers [i.e., gods, angels] that are appointed to care for all things, there have arisen among different peoples different epithets and services, according to

---

[6] Alfred Jeremias, *Altorientalische Geisteskultur*, Vorwort. "A long metaphysical chain runs throughout the world and connects all races" (Johannes Sauter, in *Archiv für Rechts- und Sozialphilosophie*, Berlin, October, 1934).

their different manners and customs."[7] Apuleius recognizes that the Egyptian Isis (our Mother Nature and Madonna, Natura Naturans, Creatrix, Deus) "is adored throughout the world in divers manners, in variable customs and by many names."[8]

The Mussulman Emperor of India, Jahangir, writing of his friend and teacher, the Hindu hermit Jadrup, says that "his Vedanta is the same as our Tasawwuf":[9] and, in fact, Northern India abounds in a type of religious literature in which it is often difficult, if not impossible, to distinguish Mussulman from Hindu factors. The indifference of religious forms is indeed, as Professor Nicholson remarks, "a cardinal Sufi doctrine." So we find Ibn al-Arabi saying:

> My heart is capable of every form: it is a pasture for gazelles and a convent for Christian monks, And idol-temple and the pilgrim's Ka'ba [Mecca], and the tables of the Torah and the book of the Koran; I follow the religion of Love, whichever way his camels take; my religion and my faith is the true religion.[10]

---

[7] Plutarch, *Isis and Osiris*, 67 (*Moralia*, 377). So William Law, in continuation of the citation above, "There is not one [salvation] for the Jew, another for the Christian, and a third for the heathen. No, God is one, human nature is one, and the way to it is one; and that is, the desire of the soul turned to God." Actually, this refers to "the baptism of desire," or "of the Spirit" (as distinguished from baptism by water, which involves an actual membership in the Christian community) and only modifies the Christian dogma *extra Ecclesiam nulla salus*. The real problem is that of the proper meaning of the words "Catholic Church"; we say that this should mean not any one religion as such, but the community, or universe of experience, of all those who love God. As William Law says also: "The chief hurt of a sect is this, that it takes itself to be necessary to the truth, whereas the truth is only then found when it is known to be of no sect but as free and universal as the goodness of God and as common to all names and nations as the air and light of this world."

Cf. F. W. Buckler: "The layman, Dissenter, schismatic or the heathen, who wittingly or unwittingly has taken up his Cross, is a child of the kingdom of God on earth and a *Khalifah* of our Lord, as the priest or bishop, who has not taken up his Cross, however unquestionable his Apostolic continuity, is not" (*The Epiphany of the Cross*, 1938). It should also be borne in mind that (as the last mentioned author has often shown) the Christian concept of the "kingdom of God" cannot be properly understood except in the light of the Oriental theory of Kingship and Divine Right.

[8] Apuleius, *Golden Ass*, XI, 5. Cf. Alfred Jeremias, *Der Kosmos von Sumer* (*Der Alte Orient*, 32, Leipzig, 1932), Ch. III, "*Die eine Madonna.*"

[9] *Tuzuk-i-Jahangiri* (Memoirs of Jahangir), in the version by Rogers and Beveridge, 1905, p. 356.

[10] R. A. Nicholson, *Mystics of Islam*, 1914, p. 105. Similarly, "If he [the follower of any particular religion] understood the saying of Junayd, 'The color of the water is the

That is to say that you and I, whose religions are distinguishable, can each of us say that "mine is the true religion," *and* to one another that "yours is the true religion"—whether or not either or both of us be truly religious depending not upon the form of our religion but upon ourselves and on grace. So, too, Shams-i-Tabriz:

If the notion of my Beloved is to be found in an idol-temple,
'Twere mortal sin to circumscribe the Ka'ba!
The Ka'ba is but a church if there His trace be lost:
My Ka'ba is whatever "church" in which His trace is found![11]

Similarly in Hinduism; the Tamil poet-saint Tayumanavar, for example, says in a hymn to Siva:

Thou didst fittingly . . . inspire as Teacher millions of religions. Thou didst in each religion, while it like the rest showed in splendid fullness of treatises, disputations, sciences, [make] each its tenet to be the truth, the final goal.[12]

The *Bhaktakalpadruma* of Pratapa Simha maintains that "every man should, as far as in him lieth, help the reading of the Scriptures, whether those of his own church or those of another."[13]

In the *Bhagavad Gita* (VII, 21) Sri Krishna proclaims: "If any lover whatsoever seeks with faith to worship any form [of God] whatever, it is I who am the founder of his faith," and (IV, 11), "However men approach Me, even do I reward them, for the path men take from every side is Mine."[14]

color of the water containing it,' he would not interfere with the beliefs of others, but would perceive God in every form and in every belief" (Ibn al-Arabi, Nicholson, *Studies in Islamic Mysticism*, 1921, p. 159). And, "Henceforth I knew that there were not many gods of human worship, but one God only, who was polyonomous and polymorphous, being figured and named according to the variety of the outward condition of things" (Sir George Birdwood, *Sva*, 1915, p.28).

[11] R. A. Nicholson, *Diwani Shams-i-Tabriz*, 1898, p. 238, cf. 221. Cf. Faridu'd Din Attar, in the *Mantiqu't Tayr*: "Since, then, there are different ways of making the journey, no two [soul-] birds will fly alike. Each finds a way of his own, on this road of mystic knowledge, one by means of the Mihrab, and another through the Idol."

[12] Sir P. Arunachalam, *Studies and Translations*, Colombo, 1937, p. 201.

[13] Translation by Sir George Grierson, *JRAS*, 1908, p. 347.

[14] Schleiermacher rightly maintains (*Reden*, V) that the multiplicity of religions is

We have the word of Christ himself that he came to call, not the just, but sinners (Matthew 9:13). What can we make out of that, but that, as St. Justin said, "God is the Word of whom the whole human race are partakers, and those who lived according to Reason are Christians even though accounted atheists. . . . Socrates and Heracleitus, and of the barbarians Abraham and many others." So, too, Meister Eckhart, greatest of the Christian mystics, speaks of Plato (whom the Moslem Jili saw in a vision, "filling the world with light") as "that great priest," and as having "found the way ere ever Christ was born." Was St. Augustine wrong when he affirmed that "the very thing that is now called the Christian religion was not wanting amongst the ancients from the beginning of the human race, until Christ came in the flesh, after which the true religion, which already existed, began to be called 'Christian'"? Had he not retracted these brave words, the bloodstained history of Christianity might have been otherwise written!

We have come to think of religion more as a set of rules of conduct than as a doctrine about God; less as a doctrine about what we should *be*, than one of what we ought to *do*; and because there is necessarily an element of contingency in every application of principles to particular cases, we have come to believe that theory differs as practice must. This confusion of necessary means with transcendent ends (as if the vision of God could be earned by works) has had unfortunate results for Christianity, both at home and abroad. The more the Church has devoted herself to "social service," the more her influence has declined; an age that regards monasticism as an almost immoral retreat is itself unarmed. It is mainly because religion has been offered to modern men in nauseatingly sentimental terms ("Be good, sweet child," etc.), and no longer as an intellectual challenge, that so many have been revolted, thinking that *that* "is all there is to" religion. Such an emphasis on ethics (and, incidentally, forgetfulness

grounded in the nature of religion itself, and necessary for its complete manifestation—"*Nur in der Totalität aller solcher möglichen Formen kann die ganze Religion wirklich gegeben werden.*" But Schleiermacher claims the highest position for Christianity—on the grounds of its freedom from exclusiveness!

Una veritas in variis signis varie resplendeat: and in the words of Marsilio Ficino, "Perhaps, indeed, this kind of variety, ordained by God himself, displays a certain admirable adornment of the universe" (*De christiana religione*, c. 4).

Cf. also Ernest Cassirer's exposition of Pico della Mirandola's "defence of the *libertas credendi*," in the *Journal of the History of Ideas*, III, 335.

that Christian doctrine has as much to do with art, i.e. manufacture, making, what and how, as it has to do with behavior) plays into the skeptic's hands; for the desirability and convenience of the social virtues is such and so evident that it is felt that if that *is* all that religion means, why bring in a God to sanction forms of conduct of which no one denies the propriety? Why indeed?[15] At the same time this excessive emphasis upon the moral, and neglect of the intellectual virtues (which last alone, in orthodox Christian teaching, are held to survive our dissolution) invite the retorts of the rationalists who maintain that religion has never been anything but a means of drugging the lower classes and keeping them quiet.

Against all that, the severe intellectual discipline that any serious study of Eastern, or even "primitive," religion and philosophy demands can serve as a useful corrective. The task of cooperation in the field of comparative religion is one that demands the highest possible qualifications; if we cannot give our best to the task, it would be safer not to undertake it. The time is fast coming when it will be as necessary for the man who is to be called "educated" to know either Arabic, Sanskrit, or Chinese as it is now for him to read Latin, Greek, or Hebrew. And this, above all, in the case of those who are to teach about other peoples' faiths; for existing translations are often in many different ways inadequate, and if we are to know whether or not it is true that all believing men have hitherto worshiped and still worship one and the same God, whether by his English, Latin, Arabic, Chinese, or Navajo names, one must have searched the scriptures of the world—never forgetting that *sine desiderio mens non intelligit*.

Nor may we undertake these activities of instruction with ulterior motives: as in all other educational activities, so here the teacher's effort must be directed to the interest and advantage of the pupil himself, not that he may do good, but that he may be good. The dictum that "charity begins at home" is by no means necessarily a cynicism: it rather takes for granted that to do good is only possible when we are good, and that if we are good we shall do good, whether by action or inaction, speech or silence. It is sound Christian doctrine that a man

---

[15] The answer can be given in the words of Christopher Dawson: "For when once morality has been deprived of its religious and metaphysical foundations, it inevitably becomes subordinated to lower ends." As he also says, the need for a restoration of the ethics of vocation has become the central problem of society—"vocation" being that station of life to which it has pleased God to call us, and not the "job" to which our own ambitions drive.

must first have known and loved himself, his inner man, before he loves his neighbor.

It is, then, the pupil who comes first in our conception of the teaching of comparative religion. He will be astounded by the effect upon his understanding of Christian doctrine that can be induced by the recognition of similar doctrines stated in another language and by means of what are to him strange or even grotesque figures of thought. In the following of the *vestigia pedis*, the soul "in hot pursuit of her quarry, Christ," he will recognize an idiom of the language of the spirit that has come down to us from the hunting cultures of the Stone Age; a cannibal philosophy in that of the Eucharist and the Soma sacrifice; and the doctrine of the "seven rays" of the intelligible Sun in that of the Seven Gifts of the Spirit and in the "seven eyes" of the Apocalyptic Lamb and of Cuchulainn. He may find himself far less inclined than he is now to recoil from Christ's harder sayings, or those of St. Paul on the "sundering of soul from spirit." If he balks at the command to hate, not merely his earthly relatives, but "yea, and his own soul also," and prefers the milder wording of the Authorized Version, where "life" replaces "soul," or if he would like to interpret in a merely ethical sense the command to "deny himself," although the word that is rendered by "deny" means "utterly reject"; if he now begins to realize that the "soul" is of the dust that returns to the dust when the spirit returns to God who gave it, and that equally for Hebrew and Arabic theologians this "soul" (*nefesh, nafs*) imports that carnal "individuality" of which the Christian mystics are thinking when they say that "the soul must put itself to death"; or that our existence (distinguishing *esse* from *essentia*, γένεσις [*genesis*] from οὐσία [*ousia*], *bhu* from *as*) is a crime; and if he correlates all these ideas with the Islamic and Indian exhortation to "die before you die" and with St. Paul's "I live, yet *not I*," then he may be less inclined to read into Christian doctrine any promise of eternal life for any "soul" that has been concreated with the body—and better equipped to show that the spiritualists' "proofs" of the survival of human personality, however valid, have no religious bearings whatever.

The mind of the democratic student to whom the very name of the concept of a "divine right" may be unintelligible is likely to be roughly awakened if he ever realizes that, as Professor Buckler often reminds us, the very notion of a *kingdom* of God on earth "depends for its revelation on the inner meaning of eastern kingship," for he may have forgotten in his righteous detestation of all dictatorships, that the classical definition of "tyranny" is that of "a king ruling in his own interests."

Nor is this a one-sided transaction; it would not be easy to exaggerate the alteration that can be brought about in the Hindu's or Buddhist's estimate of Christianity when the opportunity is given him to come into closer contact with the quality of thought that led Vincent of Beauvais to speak of Christ's "ferocity" and Dante to marvel at "the multitude of teeth with which this Love bites."

"Some contemplate one Name, and some another? Which of these is the best? All are eminent dues to the transcendent, immortal, unembodied Brahma: these Names are to be contemplated, lauded, and at last denied. For by them one rises higher and higher in these worlds; but where all comes to its end, there he attains to the Unity of the Person" (*Maitri Upanishad*). Whoever knows this text, but nothing of Western technique, will assuredly be moved by a sympathetic understanding when he learns that the Christian also follows a *via affirmativa* and a *via remotionis*! Whoever has been taught a doctrine of "liberation from the pairs of opposites" (past and future, pleasure and pain, etc., the Symplegades of "folklore") will be stirred by Nicholas of Cusa's description of the wall of Paradise wherein God dwells as "built of contradictories," and by Dante's of what lies beyond this wall as "not in space, nor hath it poles," but "where every where and every when is focused." We all need to realize, with Xenophon, that "when God is our teacher, we come to think alike."

For there are as many of these Hindus and Buddhists whose knowledge of Christianity and of the greatest Christian writers is virtually nil, as there are Christians, equally learned, whose real knowledge of any other religion but their own is virtually nil, because they have never imagined what it might be to *live* these other faiths. Just as there can be no real knowledge of a language if we have never even imaginatively participated in the activities to which the language refers, so there can be no real knowledge of any "life" that one has not in some measure lived. The greatest of modern Indian saints [Ramakrishna] actually practiced Christian and Islamic disciplines, that is, worshiped Christ and Allah, and found that all led to the same goal: he could speak from experience of the equal validity of all these "ways," and feel the same respect for each, while still preferring for himself the one to which his whole being was naturally attuned by nativity, temperament, and training. What a loss it would have been to his countrymen and to the world, and even to Christianity, if he had "become a Christian"! There are many paths that lead to the summit of one and the same mountain; their differences will be the more apparent the lower down we are, but they vanish at the peak; each will naturally take the one that starts from the point at which he finds himself; he who goes round about the mountain looking for another is not climbing. Never let us approach another believer to ask him to become "one of *us*," but approach him with respect as one who is already "one of *His*," who *is*, and from whose invariable beauty all contingent being depends!

A CHRISTIAN APPROACH TO THE
NON-CHRISTIAN RELIGIONS:
ALL TRUTH IS OF THE HOLY SPIRIT
Bernard Kelly

Omne verum, de quocumque dicatur, Sancti Spiritus est.
(All that is true, by whomsoever it is said, is from the Holy Spirit.)
—St. Jerome

In Gredt's *Elementa Philosophiae Aritotelico-Thomisticae*, "Brahmanism" is listed under Pantheism as *monismus emanationis*. Before attempting any closer approach to Indian traditional teaching it is well to give some account of the relative truth of such a judgment. Gredt's brief summary of pantheistic doctrine is "*Absolutum a se emittit et dividit partes suae substantiae.*" The absurdity of an "absolute" which is a substance susceptible of division into parts is, of course, patent. What at first arouses our incredulity is that anyone with knowledge of "Brahmanism" should impute so crass an error to an intellectual tradition which is nothing if not subtle.

Neither the 19th century nor our own possesses a philosophical language able to render metaphysical truth with precision. The attempt to find words for exact metaphysical terms has baffled the translators of St. Thomas no less than of the Upanishads. There is however a difference, for while the translators of St. Thomas may be presumed to have one traditional intellectual discipline at their finger tips, the translators of the Upanishads who needed to have two generally had neither. It has been said, with some justice, that they appear to have taken their philosophical language from the newspapers. The Indian texts are not the cause of confusion but the occasion for its display. Although it is absolutely false to equate Hindu metaphysics with pantheism, in a relative and practical sense there is a great deal of truth in the judgment that "Brahmanism" is to be shunned as pantheistic. For "Brahmanism" in that sense is the child of Western sensationalism and a mirror of our own intellectual chaos.

What is of quite vital importance is to seek a position which will not falsify evidence when we see it. This task belongs fundamentally to the kingdom of Heaven where the final answers reside. But the kingdom of Heaven is always now, and there is unhappily no escape from the labor imposed by it on the plea that a century of preparation would be needed . . . . The ability to discern truth . . . depends, not primarily on mental qualifications, but on purity of heart.

Obviously, then, there can be no question at this stage of finding an adaptable portion of Thomist teaching to accommodate some fragment of Oriental doctrine already mediated by Westernizing swamis. That is to trifle. At a certain level of incomprehension the attitude of Gredt is the only tenable one. But to keep that attitude in the face of increasing light would be a monstrous perversion of intelligence.

*

*　*

I take it that the serious interest of, for example, Hinduism is its truth. Its truth rather than its difference. Here a preliminary attitude of *crede ut intelligas* is I think necessary, and if this seems to be begging the question I can only insist that unless you do not disbelieve you can never hope to make the transition even momentarily from a Western to an Indian point of view. The differences involved are much deeper than the differences of language but they are not the primary concern of the serious interest I assume.

As a practical observation, I would say that an approach by Christians to Eastern religions which involved our being satisfied with a clarification of each according to its specific difference would condemn us from the outset to an external and superficial point of view, one which merely reflected our own world view and theological attitude. It would then be in the light of what we might take to be the *difference* of the Christian revelation that we would tend to view revealed truth as such, as well as the revelations, if we allowed them that term, on which other traditions are founded. From this point of view it is not the primordial revelation to mankind, in which, in their origins, other traditions may be deemed to share, which is the vitalizing source of light to us, but uniquely the historical canalizing of this revelation towards the fulfillment of all revelation in Christ. The differences of other traditions are from this point of view their straying from this source of light and life.

But the truth of a given tradition is the measure of its not straying from Christ.

If it is the truth of Hinduism that one is looking for, one can set no limit at the outset to what one is going to find. It will require from us an interior rather than an external approach and will set in a very different light the question of differences.

For any here who are not Christians, I should perhaps explain that the reference to the truth of other traditions to the truth of Christ does not mean that I propose to judge those other traditions by a limited truth external to them, but that I refer them to the illimitable radiance of Truth itself.

For a Christian, it seems to me that a certain theological emphasis is required by this approach based on the supernatural truth implicit in the primordial revelation to mankind, of which we have a record guaranteed to us in the first chapters of Genesis—an emphasis wholly consonant, as far as I am aware, with patristic and liturgical tradition. The consequences of this way may be very far-reaching. As I see it, the present availability to us of the light of other religions does and must revive the interest of Christian thinkers in a vast field of truth to which they may have become accustomed to give a less than central importance.

When I say that the truth of other religions requires of us an interior rather than an external approach, I mean that neither that truth nor the mind understanding it may be separated from the truth of Christ, and until we have got it and see it in that perspective, we may be only chasing a will-of-the-wisp. To seek the truth of another religion as something extrinsic is to run after strange gods and to make divisions in Truth itself.

As something intrinsic to Truth itself, the truth of Hinduism, for example, is the making explicit of depths available to us in principle in the Truth of Christ, but relatively inaccessible in the circumstances of our place and time without the stimulus and discipline of finding them in strange forms. I do not doubt for a moment that the availability of the scriptures of other peoples made so indiscriminately easy by modern publication, is for our education—not in encyclopedic knowledge, but in truth.

What is called in question by such an approach is not the uniqueness of Christ, but may well be our understanding of that uniqueness.

THE CHRISTIANS OF MOORISH SPAIN

Duncan Townson

In Muslim Spain, those who remained Christian were well treated, as they were throughout the Islamic Empire.[1] Both Jews and Christians were regarded as "People of the Book," that is, as people who had their own holy writings, the Old and the New Testaments of the Bible.[2] In Córdoba, the Christians continued to worship in the Cathedral of St. Vincent, though they were not allowed to disturb the Muslims with hymn-singing or bell-ringing.

Muslims and Christians usually got on very well together, lived much the same life, and dressed alike. Muslims took pleasure in attending Christian celebrations and were frequent visitors at monasteries on saints' days. Even warfare did not divide them. Christians in Muslim Spain were loyal to the emir and fought for their Muslim ruler against the Christian kings of the north. In peacetime Christian kings sent their sons to be taught manners at the court of Córdoba. They married their daughters to Muslim princes and these brides became Muslims too.

Arabic language and literature fascinated Spanish Christians, as did Muslim architecture and science. A Christian of Córdoba named Álvaro wrote in 854: "Innumerable are the Christians who can express themselves in Arabic and compose poetry in that language with greater art than the Arabs themselves."

A popular recreation for rich and poor alike was getting together for picnics and garden parties. People in Córdoba had a passion for them and any occasion would do. Marriages and circumcisions—all Muslim boys were circumcised—called for splendid celebrations. Then there were the Muslim and Christian feast days. At the Christian feast of the Epiphany the whole population joined in the torch-lit

---

[1] Editor's Note: "You will find that the best friends of believers [i.e. Muslims] are those who say: 'We are Christians.' This is because there are priests and monks amongst them, and because they are not proud" (Koran 5:82).

[2] Editor's Note: "Verily the Faithful [i.e. Muslims] and the Jews and the Sabians and the Christians whoso believeth in God and the Last Day and doeth deeds of piety—no fear shall come upon them neither shall they grieve" (Koran 5:69).

processions that went on all night. There were saint's day pilgrimages to Christian monasteries where the monks gave lavish hospitality. . . . The feast days were great occasions.

THE BISHOP OF TRIPOLI

Duke Alberto Denti di Pirajno

Jemberié (my servant) was much astonished when, opening the door one evening, he found himself face to face with the Bishop of Tripoli, who had come to visit me. The idea that such a high dignitary was ready to enter a newly whitewashed *fonduq* quite upset him, since he could not decide which was the greater: the honor of such a visit or the shame of being obliged to receive such an eminent person in a hut until recently used only by camel-herds. The Apostolic Vicar, however, was not bothered by such considerations.

He was a man of over fifty, thickset, obese and short-necked. He looked at people through half-closed eyes behind thick glasses, his nose raised like a hound on the scent and his fingers, on one of which he wore the episcopal ring, combing his bushy beard. After he had listened to an argument and made up his mind about it, he would join his hands as if in prayer and in a deep ponderous voice would define the situation or give his view in a few precise and unadorned phrases which admitted no further argument.

He had an excellent knowledge of Hebrew, Arabic, Persian, Turkish and Albanian. No one in the whole city, with the exception of the head of the Muntasser family, was able to converse with him in classical Arabic, which was a delight to hear. When the chief's nephews were present, they listened open-mouthed without understanding a word, and the Bishop would turn to the chief and, speaking in the local dialect, say that he was astounded to find young Moslems unable to understand their own tongue; feigning indignation, he would call attention to the fact that he, a Christian and foreigner, knew Arabic better than they, who were Arabs and Moslems. The old Muntasser was greatly diverted and rubbed his hands with glee at their discomfiture.

Islamic canonical law held no mysteries for the Bishop; his knowledge of it was such that the High Court often submitted to him the most complicated questions and asked for his opinion.

The first time he invited me to his house he refused to let me examine him, talked to me of his diabetes as though it had no connection with him, and finished by telling me the history of Muhyi 'd-Dîn

Ibn 'Arabî, a famous Arab mystic of about the year 1200, of whom I had never heard, but of whose life he knew every detail.

I had already lost the thread of this story when the *Kâdî* entered with a packet of papers under his arm. They put their heads together and began to talk rapidly in lowered voices. The papers were passed from one to the other, turned over and back, while with their forefingers they ran along the lines of the text, stressing phrases and words. Every now and again the Bishop struck the papers with the back of his hand, exclaiming that there was no doubt at all: the case was exactly that. The *Kâdî* assented and then whispered some suggestion which started the examination of the case all over again.

*

*   *

For some reason or other the Bishop took a liking to me. The incorrigible vulgarity of my speech in Arabic amused him. In a fruity voice, with his hands on his hips, he would ask me in what low haunts I had picked up such unorthodox expressions.

He had an exceptional capacity for seeing the grotesque and humorous situations, and this contrasted strangely with his grave appearance, his dignified bearing, and his solemn episcopal vestments with their amethyst-colored buttons.

The Jewish community had as its head a Rabbi who was universally respected for his integrity and the soundness of his doctrine. This worthy Talmudist was afflicted with a nose of such melancholy proportions that it overhung his mouth. He had such a permanently desolate expression that he always seemed to have just left the Wailing Wall. I asked the Bishop why the Rabbi had such an unhappy air and what could be done to console him.

"Nothing," he replied, with a grave shake of his head, "absolutely nothing. This man, who knows the Talmud as very few know it, has every reason to look like that. I wonder how many times you have pulled a long face waiting for a train that was half an hour late. Well, you can hardly expect light-heartedness and jollity from someone who has been waiting thousands of years for the Messiah."

*

*   *

It was the same Bishop who introduced me to his best friend in the town—the Arab mayor of Tripoli.

The friendship between the Bishop and the pasha was one of the most extraordinary I have ever seen. I have never met two men who were, on the surface, more directly opposed in temperament, and rarely have I come across a deeper and closer friendship. The Italian was of modest origin, the Arab the head of a princely family which had once ruled the country; the Bishop held to the simple and pure faith of St. Francis of Assisi, the prince was a fervent and practicing Moslem; the humble Christian had an encyclopedic erudition, the Moslem nobleman was unlettered.

The pasha never refused alms to a beggar, but if the beggar addressed him as *Sîdî* ("my Lord"), he would say: "Your Lord, my Lord, is Allah." He was not rich, but every day food for about forty poor people was prepared in his kitchen.

I had often asked the Bishop about his friendship with the pasha, endeavoring in my curiosity to discover on what it was based. He was always evasive in his reply; sometimes he did not reply at all, and confined himself to raising his shoulders and blowing into his beard.

The more I came to know the Arab nobleman, however, the more I discovered what they had in common—for example, their indifference to illness, their complete disregard of material considerations, their deep understanding of human suffering and misery, and their charity, which was unsmirched by egoism and knew no limits. Both of them submitted to a higher Will with the blind faith of children.

At a certain point I realized that, just as the various elements in a mosaic form a single design when pieced together, so the mental attitudes of the two friends were part of a single spiritual conception which I was at last able to recognize.

One day, as I was helping the Bishop to put his books on his library shelves, I announced that I had finally understood why he and the pasha were such close friends; I said that their friendship was a friendship between Franciscans. He continued to turn the pages of a volume he held in his hand, as though seeking a reply there. After a few moments of silence he closed the book, and said: "You express yourself badly. You ought to know that a Moslem cannot be a Franciscan friar, and I myself am too unworthy of the robe I wear to call myself a Franciscan. The pasha is a man of great heart and exemplary humility who practices the three canonical virtues in a most admirable manner. . . . I have learned much from this man; that is why we are friends."

The younger of the two friends died first. I was far away from Tripoli when it happened, and only later did I learn how the Apostolic Vicar had died serenely, surrounded by his *confrères* and nuns, gripping the hand of his old friend the pasha, who in sorrow turned to stone; while in the cathedral, the mosque, and the synagogue, men of different faiths prayed that God would postpone the appointed hour.

THE MONK AND THE CALIPH
Angus Macnab

One of the greatest of the Caliphs of the Umayyad dynasty in medieval Spain was 'Abd ar-Rahmân III, and many Christian kings sent ambassadors to his court. His patient and insightful handling of a particularly obstinate ambassador provides a case history that might profitably be studied by any budding diplomat set on attaining a higher than average competence in his profession. The date is 957, when yet another embassy was sent to 'Abd ar-Rahmân III, this time by Otto the Great, King of Germany and later Emperor. The central point of the story is really the same as that of the old puzzle: "What happens when an irresistible force meets an immovable object?" Clearly there is no answer; the only hope is to stop them from meeting, and that is what caused the Caliph to take much trouble, for although in its own sphere his power was irresistible, the will of the monk concerned was no less immovable.

The deadlock came about thus. For reasons which are not known, 'Abd ar-Rahmân had sent an embassy some years before to the "great chief of Alemanya." The letter he sent contained the usual phrases about the greatness of the Western Caliphate, but they went too far, and contained some expressions intolerable to Christian ears. As 'Abd ar-Rahmân was neither a fool nor a fanatic, it is likely that the objectionable passages were due to the blunder of a Court official, but they enraged King Otto, who detained the ambassadors for three years, while steadily refusing to enter into further relations with them.

However, something had to be done, and so Otto determined to send a counter-embassy, not so much to deal with political affairs as to retort in kind to the passages in which the Caliph's letter were deemed to be offensive to the Christian religion. The letter was composed by Otto's brother, St. Bruno the Great, Archbishop of Cologne, in the same language as that of the Caliph's letter, namely Greek, regarded as the intermediary language between Arabic and Latin. As the letter was couched in strong terms, a stout-hearted messenger was required to bear it, a man not afraid to face the potential anger of the Caliph.

A monk named John from the Benedictine Abbey of Gorze (or Görtz) in Alsace-Lorraine volunteered for the mission, fully prepared to sacrifice his life if need be (*Johannes sese offert spe martyrii*); he later became abbot of the monastery and is canonized as St. John of Gorze. With him, as companion, went a disciple named Garamannus (?Hermann), who wrote an account of the whole mission. Gorze Abbey itself provided rich gifts for the monk to take to the Caliph.

The two monks traveled on foot as far as Vienne, where they took shipping down the Rhône and thence across by sea to Barcelona. The first Moslem city they came to was Tortosa, where the governor treated them with great consideration and assisted them to make the rest of their journey to Córdoba.

On arrival there, they were lodged in a house two miles from the royal palace, and treated with regal generosity, but were not invited to present their letters of credence. Their state was in fact one of luxurious imprisonment. When they asked the reason for the delay, they were told that since the Córdoban ambassadors had been detained for three years in Germany, they would be detained for nine years in Córdoba. In fact, however, the Caliph was merely stalling for time in order to decide what to do. He had really got himself into an impossible position, for he had a very fair idea of what was in the letters, and so, unfortunately, had some of his subjects. Now, if he received the ambassadors and let them read their letters, he would be legally bound to put them to death for blasphemy against Islam and Mohammed; the law allowed of no exception. Yet to kill a guest, even if he be your worst enemy—not to speak of an ambassador—is an unspeakable crime in Moslem eyes. On the other hand, if he listened to the letters without retaliation, he would be committing a capital crime himself, for Islamic law said that anyone who tolerated blasphemy against the Prophet was just as guilty as the actual blasphemer. If this applied to all Moslems, however humble, what of the Caliph himself, the Commander of the Faithful? Thus it looked as if 'Abd ar-Rahmân would have to order either his own head, or the two ambassadors'—or possibly all three—to be cut off! Further awful consequences might include a popular upsurge against the Christians, and even a war with the German empire. When it was put about in Córdoba that the Caliph was thinking of receiving the monks, there were protestations, and an appeasing official statement had to be issued by the Palace.

After much thought, the Caliph commissioned a leading Jew, as a neutral third party, to try and persuade the monks to visit the Palace but without presenting their documents. John refused, and the two monks were left in solitude for some months more. The next visitor they had was the Mozarabic bishop of the Christians in Córdoba. As the Mozarabic bishop and the German monk could talk freely in Latin, we possess an account of the conversation, which throws an interesting light on the state of the Church under Moslem overlordship at that time. The two clerics first spoke of all manner of things, but finally the bishop revealed the real reason for his visit, namely 'Abd ar-Rahmân's desire to receive the embassy with its presents only.

"And what shall I do with the letters?" asked John. "Have I not been sent especially to deliver them? He was the first to utter blasphemies, and all we do is to refute them."

The text is not complete, but we can read a great part of the bishop's reply:

"You do not know the conditions under which we live. The Apostle forbids us to resist the powers of the world. . . . It is a great consolation to us . . . to live according to our own laws. . . . The most fervent observers of the Christian precepts are regarded most highly, whereas the Jews [who did not recognize the Messiah] are looked down on by both communities. Our situation demands from us the conduct we follow, and we do nothing contrary to our religion. In other respects we behave obediently, and that is why I think it would be better to suppress that letter, which may needlessly arouse passions against you and us."

John hesitated for a moment, but speedily rallied, and refused to give way:

"How can you use such language, you who purport to be a bishop? Are you not a confessor of the faith, and have you not been raised to the post you hold in order to defend it?. . . Yet for human considerations you depart from the truth, and far from urging the rest to proclaim it, you yourself evade your duty. Better would it have been, and more proper for a truly Christian man, to suffer all the straits of misery, rather than to accept from the enemy a nourishment prejudicial to the salvation of others."

John then criticized a number of the practices of the Mozarabic church. "How can you possibly live such a life? I have heard that you submit to what the Catholic Church regards as odious: I have been told that your people circumcise themselves despite the command of the Apostle, and abstain from certain foods, merely because their doctors forbid them."

"Custom and necessity constrain us," replied the Bishop, "otherwise we could not live among our conquerors, and besides, all that we do was already done by our forefathers, and their usage has taught us to do the same."

"Never," said John, "can I approve the doing of anything other than what is commanded, whether from love or from fear." And he added that nothing in the world would make him waver in his resolution. When this was reported to the Caliph, who was a man well skilled in working on the human heart, he let some time pass before trying to do anything else.

Six or seven weeks later, when further messengers from the Caliph had met with no better success, and it was clear that personal threats would be of no avail, it was hinted to John that his attitude might bring down a general persecution on the Christians. Garamannus relates the affair as follows:

"On the Lord's day and on certain of the principal feasts of our religion, such as Christmas, Epiphany, Easter, the Ascension, Whitsun, St. John's and some others, the Christians were allowed to repair to a church outside the city dedicated to St. Martin," and undoubtedly they must have done so in procession, for he states that they were afterwards accompanied by twelve guards, whom he calls *sagiones*, from the church back to the city. John had obtained leave to go with them, and on the way a messenger handed him a letter—remarkable for its size, for it was written on a square sheepskin—making the threats mentioned above. However, not even this made the monk deviate from his purpose.

Finally, the Mozarabic Christians themselves approached him to try to find a solution. John then suggested the only possible one, namely to send a messenger to King Otto with full information, and to ask for further instructions. The Caliph agreed, but as he could not find anyone ready to undertake such a long and hazardous journey, he published an edict offering a special boon to anyone who would volunteer to go, and all manner of rewards on his return.

In the palace secretariat was a Christian official called Recemundus (Raimundo), who was renowned for his perfect knowledge of Arabic and Latin. He was duly attracted by the possibility of preferment, but before volunteering, he applied for leave to visit the ambassador in order to find out what manner of man Otto was, and whether, if he went, he was likely to be imprisoned himself in revenge for the detention of Otto's ambassador in Córdoba. John assured him that he need have no apprehension on these points, and gave him letters of recommendation to Gorze Abbey. Raimundo returned to the palace prepared to undertake the embassy, but requested that he be presented to the bishopric of Iliberis, which was then vacant. The Mozarabic authorities agreed and Raimundo was consecrated bishop. He was provided with the necessary instructions, and set out on his journey. In ten weeks he arrived at Gorze, where he was well received. It was then August, and the Bishop of Metz kept him there during the autumn and winter, and then accompanied him to the Emperor's court at Frankfurt. Otto was probably glad enough to call the whole thing off, and agreed to all that was suggested; a new letter was composed, and Raimundo was back at Gorze by Easter, and at Córdoba by June 959, accompanied by the new ambassador, Dudo. The new letter authorized John not to present the former one, but instead to negotiate a treaty of friendship and peace, to put an end to the incursions of Arab pirates and filibusters who were causing a great deal of trouble in imperial territories, including southern France, Lombardy, and even Switzerland. These were simply bands of adventurers who had got across into Provence from Catalonia, and the Córdoba emirate had never given them any protection or encouragement.

The new ambassadors presented themselves at the palace, but 'Abd ar-Rahmân said: "No, by my life; let the former ambassadors come first; no-one shall see my face before that courageous monk who has defied my will for so long!" But even now, there were still difficulties. When the viziers arrived at the monk's house to conduct him to the palace, they found him with his hair and beard uncombed and in the penitential monastic robe. This would not do, the officials said, and the Caliph sent him a gift of ten pounds of silver to buy a court dress. John returned thanks, but gave the money to the poor. "I do not scorn the gift of kings," he said, "but I cannot wear any other dress than the habit of my order." When the Caliph heard this, he exclaimed: "Let him come anyhow he likes, even clad in a sack; I shall not receive him the less well for that!"

So at last the interview took place. The monks were led to the palace with immense splendor through streets lined with troops in gala uniform, and preceded along the road by dancing dervishes. "It was the summer solstice," writes Garamannus, "and from the city to the palace these Moors never ceased to raise a fearful dust." He was of course unaware of the true nature of the sacred dance of the dervishes (the Persian word *darvish* being the equivalent of the Arabic

word *faqîr*, meaning "poor man," in the same sense as the "holy poverty" of the Franciscans), and of the high honor being rendered thus by
the representatives of one religion to those of another.

The chief dignitaries of the Caliphate came out to meet the
Christian ambassador, then led him through dazzling saloons into
the presence of the Caliph, who now, almost at the end of his reign
of half a century, appeared very seldom in public, and "like a god"
(*quasi numen quoddam*) hid himself from the eyes of his subjects. Amid
surroundings of untold riches, the Caliph sat cross-legged upon a
couch; he gave John the palm of his hand to kiss, an honor which
Moslem princes reserved only for the greatest of lords. As a Christian,
the monk was given an armchair to sit in (Moslems generally sitting
on the carpeted floor), and after a prolonged silence 'Abd ar-Rahmân
began to speak of the reasons which had obliged him to delay this
interview for so long. John replied, and a conversation ensued, in
which the Caliph proved so courteous and amiable that he won John's
heart despite the natural prejudice with which the monk had approached him. The presents were offered and accepted, and the monk
asked leave to return to his own country; but 'Abd ar-Rahmân would
not permit him to do so until he had seen John several times more
and got to know him better.

In the growing acquaintanceship John developed a deep affection
for the Caliph, and he returned from the palace to his sumptuous
lodging convinced that the Arabs "did not deserve the name of barbarians that they were constantly given in Europe." At subsequent
interviews, now on more familiar terms, they discussed questions of
state. The Caliph inquired minutely concerning the power, wealth,
and military affairs of Otto; he debated many points with John, who
would not allow that anyone was Otto's superior in arms and horses.
In this, 'Abd ar-Rahmân praised his staunchness, but criticized Otto's
conduct in leaving unpunished the rebellion of his son and son-in-law,
who had not hesitated to call in the Hungarians to ravage the empire
they sought to usurp.

As to the rest, and the agreements, if any, that were concluded
between the two empires, we are not told, for the chronicle of
Garamannus ends at this point; but one thing is certain: before the
"immovable object," St. John of Gorze, returned home, he had conceived as great a respect and admiration for 'Abd ar-Rahmân, as 'Abd
ar-Rahmân, the "irresistible force," already had for him.

During the last two years of his life, 'Abd ar-Rahmân almost entirely delegated the administration of his realm to his son Al-Hakam. He appointed no chief minister since the death of Mundhir ibn Sa'îd, the "unknown young man" who was at the Byzantine ambassadors' reception in 949. He seldom left his retreat in the Orange-blossom palace, where he solaced himself with the company of his women, children, and poets. The Arab chronicle mentions some of the women in whose conversation he delighted: Muzna, who sang her own verses, and acted as his secretary; 'Â'isha, a Córdoban maiden whom Ibn Hayyân calls the most chaste, beautiful, and learned woman of her age; Safîya, also a beautiful and learned poetess; and finally the slave-woman Noiratedia, whose ready wit and amusing sallies delighted him. He also conversed daily with his old friend Sulaimân ibn 'Abd al-Ghâfir, a nobleman who had been a great soldier, and now lived a retired life of asceticism. Knowing his charitable spirit, the Caliph had chosen him as an agent for good works, and through him conveyed assistance privately to a large number of families.

Shortly before his death, the chronicler Al-Makkârî relates, he wrote the following confession, which was found among his papers: "I have reigned fifty years, and my realm has always either been at peace or victorious. Beloved by my subjects, feared by my enemies, respected by my allies the greatest princes on earth, I had all I could desire: honors and wealth, pleasures and power. No earthly good was wanting to me; yet on scrupulously reckoning up the days on which I have tasted felicity without bitterness, I have found only fourteen in my long life." In this state of mind, says Al-Makkârî, 'Izrâ'îl, the Angel of Death, translated him from his alcázar at Madînat az-Zahrâ ("the Orange-blossom palace") to the eternal mansions of the beyond on the night of Wednesday 2nd *Ramadân* 350 A.H. (15th November 961 A.D.) at the age of seventy-two. Two days later his body was borne to Córdoba amid vast crowds who lamented: "Dead is our father, gone is his sword, the sword of Islam: the succor of the weak and needy, and the terror of the proud."

V

The Universality
of the
Christian Mystics

"Men go abroad to wonder at the height of mountains, at the huge waves of the sea, at the long courses of the rivers, at the vast compass of the ocean, at the circular motion of the stars—yet they pass by themselves without wondering."—St. Augustine (354-430)

"That you may be able to know God, first know yourself."—Cyprian of Carthage (d.258)

"Whosoever will come after me, let him deny himself."—Mark 8:34

"All scripture cries aloud for freedom from self."—Meister Eckhart (1260-1327)

"Blessed are the pure in heart for they shall see God."—Matthew 5:8

"There is but one salvation for all mankind, and that is the life of God in the soul."—William Law (1686-1761)

"God became man so that we might become God."—St. Irenaeus (c.120-c.202)

"With Christ I am crucified; nevertheless I live, yet not I, but Christ in me."—Galatians 2:20

"The Father is begetting his Son unceasingly."—Meister Eckhart (1260-1327)

"The Virgin I must be and bring God forth from me,
Should ever I be granted divine felicity."—Angelus Silesius (1624-1677)

"Thou hast made us for thyself, O Lord, and our hearts are restless until they rest in Thee."—St. Augustine (354-430)

"God is a Spirit: and they that worship Him must worship Him in spirit and in truth."—John 4:24

"Dost thou tell me that he who has not the sacraments of God cannot be saved? I tell thee that he who has the virtue of the sacraments of God cannot perish. Which is better, the sacrament or the virtue of the sacrament—water or faith? If thou wouldst speak truly, answer 'faith.'"—Hugh of Saint-Victor (c.1096-1141)

"What is man's chief end? Man's chief end is to glorify God and enjoy Him forever."—Westminster Catechism

"The kingdom of God is within you."—Luke 17:21

Preghiera Semplice	Simple Prayer
Oh! Signore, fa' di me un istrumento della tua pace:	O Lord, make me an instrument of Thy peace:
Dove è odio, fa' ch'io porti l'Amore;	Where there is hatred, let me bring love;
Dove è offesa, ch'io porti il Perdono;	Where there is injury, let me bring pardon;
Dove è discordia, ch'io porti l'Unione;	Where there is discord, let me bring union;
Dove è dubbio, ch'io porti la Fede;	Where there is doubt, let me bring faith;
Dove è errore, ch'io porti la Verità;	Where there is error, let me bring truth;
Dove è disperazione, ch'io porti la Speranza;	Where there is despair, let me bring hope;
Dove è tristezza, ch'io porti la Gioia;	Where there is sadness, let me bring joy;
Dove sono le tenebre, ch'io porti la Luce.	Where there is darkness, let me bring light.
Oh! Maestro, fa' che io non cerchi tanto:	O Divine Master, grant that I may not so much seek
Ad essere consolato, quanto a consolare;	To be consoled as to console;
Ad essere compreso, quanto a comprendere;	To be understood as to understand;
Ad essere amato, quanto ad amare.	To be loved as to love.
Poichè, si è:	For it is
Dando, che si receve;	In giving that we receive;
Perdonando, che si è perdonati;	In pardoning that we are pardoned;
Morendo, che si risuscita a Vita Eterna.	In dying that we rise to eternal life.

—St. Francis of Assisi (1182-1226)

SAINT BERNARD
René Guénon

Amongst the great figures of the Middle Ages, there are few whose study is more effective than that of Saint Bernard for the purpose of dissipating certain prejudices dear to the modern mind. What indeed could be more disconcerting for the modern mind than to see a pure contemplative—one who always wished to be and to remain as such—called upon to play a dominant role in conducting the affairs of Church and State, and often succeeding where all the prudence of professional diplomats and politicians had failed? What could be more surprising and even more paradoxical, according to the ordinary way of judging things, than a mystic who has nothing but contempt for what he called "the quibblings of Plato and the niceties of Aristotle," but who nonetheless triumphed over the most subtle dialecticians of his day? All of Saint Bernard's life seems destined to show, by means of a brilliant example, that, in order to solve problems of an intellectual, and even of a practical order, there exist means quite other than those which we have become accustomed to considering as the only effective ones, no doubt because they are the only ones within reach of purely human discretion, this "discretion" being something that is not even a shadow of true wisdom. Thus the life of Saint Bernard could be seen as a refutation in advance of the errors of rationalism and pragmatism, errors considered to be opposed to each other, but in fact interdependent; at the same time, for those who examine his life impartially, it confounds and upturns all the preconceived ideas of "scientific" historians, who believe—with Renan—that "the negation of the supernatural constitutes the very essence of critical thinking"—a thesis with which we readily agree, but for the reason that we see in this incompatibility the exact opposite of what the moderns do, namely, a condemnation, not of the supernatural, but of "critical thinking." What lesson, indeed, could be more profitable for our era than this?

*

* *

247

Bernard was born in 1070 in Fontaines-lès-Dijon; his parents belonged to the upper ranks of Burgundy's nobility, and, if we mention this fact, it is because it seems that some features of Bernard's life and doctrine, which we will discuss in the following pages, can be attributed to this origin. We do not simply wish to imply that this accounts for the sometimes bellicose ardor of his zeal, or the violence that he often brought to bear on the polemics in which he was engaged—something that was entirely superficial, for goodness and mildness were unquestionably the basis of his character. What we allude to above all is his relationship with the institution and ideal of chivalry, something that must be given serious consideration if we are to understand the events and the spirit of the Middle Ages.

At about the age of twenty, Bernard decided to withdraw from the world; and he quickly succeeded in getting all his brothers, some of his other relatives, and several of his friends, to accept his views. In his early apostleship, and in spite of his youth, his force of persuasion was such that, according to his biographer, "he became the terror of mothers and wives; friends were afraid to see him approach their friends." Here, already, there was something extraordinary, and it would surely be inadequate to attribute it simply to the force of his "genius," in the profane sense of this word. Would it not be more true to see here the action of divine grace which, in a sense, penetrated the whole person of the apostle and which, by bountifully radiating outwards, was communicated through him as through a channel, if we may use a simile which he himself later used to describe the Holy Virgin, and which can also be applied, with certain limits, to all saints?

It was thus that Bernard, accompanied by thirty young men, in 1112 entered the monastery of Cîteaux, which he had chosen because of the rigor with which the Rule was observed there—a rigor that contrasted with the laxness that had introduced itself into all the other branches of the Benedictine Order. Three years later, his superiors, in spite of his inexperience and uncertain health, did not hesitate to entrust him with the leadership of twelve monks who were going to found a new abbey, called Clairvaux, which he governed until his death, always resisting the honors and privileges offered to him in the course of his career. The renown of Clairvaux soon spread wide and far, and the abbey's quick growth was truly prodigious: when its founder died, it was said to have housed about seven hundred monks, and to have given birth to more than sixty new monasteries.

*

* *

The care that Bernard brought to the administration of Clairvaux, personally overseeing, as he did, everything down to the most minute details of everyday life; the part that he took in the direction of the Cistercian Order, as head of one of its foremost abbeys; the skill and the success of his interventions aimed at smoothing over the difficulties that frequently arose with rival orders—all those things suffice to prove that what one calls "common sense" was indeed strong in him, and moreover was accompanied by a very high degree of spirituality. There was more than enough there to absorb all the energy of an ordinary man; yet Bernard soon saw a whole new field of activity open up before him, completely in spite of himself, for he feared nothing so much as being forced to leave his cloister to become involved in the affairs of the outside world, from which he had intended to isolate himself forever by abandoning himself completely to asceticism and contemplation, with nothing to distract him from what, in his eyes, and in the words of the Evangelist, was "the one thing needful." In this hope, he was greatly disappointed; but all those "distractions"—in the etymological sense of the word, those things which he could not screen out and which he would complain about with some bitterness—in no way prevented him from attaining the heights of mystical life. This is indeed remarkable; and what is no less so is that, in spite of his humility and all the efforts he made to live in seclusion, his collaboration was requested for all sorts of important affairs, and, since he had no regard for the world, everyone, including high civil and ecclesiastical dignitaries, always spontaneously bowed before his compelling spiritual authority; and whether this be due to his own saintliness or to the age in which he lived, is hard to tell. There is indeed a contrast between our own time and one when a simple monk, uniquely through the radiation of his eminent virtues, could become in a sense the center of Europe and of Christianity, the unchallenged judge of all conflicts, both political and religious, where public interest was at stake, the judge of the most highly reputed masters of philosophy and theology, the restorer of the unity of the Church, the mediator between the Papacy and the Empire, and finally one who was to see armies numbering several hundred thousands of men come into being because of his preaching.

*

* *

Bernard had begun early on to denounce the luxurious living of most of the members of the secular clergy and even of the monks in some abbeys; his reproofs had provoked resounding conversions, including that of Suger, the illustrious Abbot of Saint-Denis, who, though he did not officially hold the title of prime minister to the King of France, nevertheless fulfilled all the functions.

It was this conversion that brought the Abbot of Clairvaux's name to the attention of the French Royal Court, where, it seems, he was regarded with a respect mixed with fear, for one saw in him the indomitable foe of all abuses and injustices; and very soon, in fact, he did intervene in conflicts that had broken out between Louis le Gros and various bishops, and he protested loudly against any infringements of civil authority against the rights of the Church. In actual fact, it was still only a question of purely local affairs, of interest only to this or that monastery or diocese; but in 1130, considerably graver events occurred, which put in peril the whole Church, which became divided by the schism of the anti-pope, Anaclete II, and it was this that caused Bernard's renown to spread throughout all Christendom.

We need not retrace here all the details of the history of that schism: the cardinals, split into two rival factions, had elected in succession Innocent II and Anaclete II; the first of the two, who was forced to flee from Rome, never despaired of the rightness of his cause and appealed to the universal Church. It was France that responded first; at a council convened by the King at Étampes, Bernard appeared (in the words of his biographer) "like a true envoy of God" among the united lords and bishops; all followed his advice on the question before them and recognized the validity of the election of Innocent II. The latter was on French soil at the time, and it was to the Abbey of Cluny that Suger came to inform him of the council's decision; he traveled through all the main dioceses and was welcomed everywhere with enthusiasm; this momentum created support for Innocent throughout almost all of Christendom. The Abbot of Clairvaux made his way to the King of England and quickly overcame his hesitations; perhaps he also had a part in gaining the recognition of Innocent II by King Lothaire and the German clergy. He then went to Aquitaine to combat the influence of Bishop Gérard d'Angoulême, a partisan of Anaclete II; but it was only during a second visit to that region, in 1135, that he succeeded in destroying the schism by effecting the conversion of the Count of Poitiers. Between the visits, he had to go to Italy, summoned by Innocent II, who had returned there with the aid of Lothaire, but who had been impeded by unforeseen difficulties due to hostility between Pisa and Genoa; Innocent had to find a compromise between the two rival cities to make them accept it; it was Bernard who was in charge of this difficult mission, and he performed it with marvelous success. Innocent was able to return to Rome, but Anaclete remained ensconced in St. Peter's, from which it was impossible to extract him; Lothaire, crowned emperor, at the basilica of St. John Lateran, withdrew shortly with his army; after his departure, the anti-pope again took the offensive, and the legitimate pontiff had to flee and take refuge in Pisa.

The Abbot of Clairvaux, who had returned to his cloister, was dismayed by the news; shortly afterwards he heard news of the efforts of Roger, King of Sicily, to win all of Italy to the cause of Anaclete, thereby ensuring his own supremacy at the same time. Bernard immediately wrote to the inhabitants of Pisa and Genoa to encourage them to remain faithful to Innocent; but this faithfulness constituted only a feeble prop, and to conquer Rome, it was Germany alone from whom effective aid could be expected. Unfortunately, the Empire was always prey to division, and Lothaire could not return to Italy before he was assured peace in his own country. Bernard left for Germany and worked for the reconciliation of the Hohenstaufens with the Emperor; there again, his efforts were crowned with success; there he witnessed the consecration of the happy outcome the Diet of Bamberg, after which he made his way to the council that Innocent II had convened in Pisa. On this occasion, he had to address the misgivings of Louis le Gros, who opposed the departure of the bishops from his kingdom; Louis' prohibition was lifted, and the principal members of the French clergy were able to respond to the appeal of the head of the Church. Bernard was the soul of the council; between the meetings, as historians of the day describe it, his door was besieged by those who had some serious matter to resolve, as if this humble monk were endowed with the power to decide at will all ecclesiastical questions. He was then delegated to Milan to bring back that city to the side of Innocent II and Lothaire; there he was acclaimed by the clergy and the faithful, who in a spontaneous show of enthusiasm, wanted to make him their archbishop, an honor from which he freed himself only with great difficulty. He wished only to return to his monastery and did in fact go back there, but not for long.

At the beginning of 1136, Bernard once more had to abandon his solitude, in compliance with the Pope's wishes, to come to Italy to join the German army, commanded by Duke Henry of Bavaria, son-in-law of the Emperor. A misunderstanding had arisen between Henry and Innocent II; Henry, little concerned with the rights of the Church, chose consistently to align himself only with the interests of the State. But the Abbot of Clairvaux was strongly in favor of re-establishing harmony between the two powers and reconciling their rival claims, especially in certain questions of investiture, in which he seems to have regularly played the role of moderator. Meanwhile Lothaire, who had himself taken command of the army, subdued all of southern Italy; but he made the mistake of rejecting the peace proposal of the King of Sicily, who quickly took his revenge, putting everything to fire and sword. At that Bernard did not hesitate to appear at Roger's camp, but Roger was ill-disposed towards his words of peace; Bernard then predicted his defeat, which in fact happened; then retracing his steps, Bernard followed Roger to Salerno and made every effort to turn him away from the schism into which ambition had drawn him. Roger consented to listen to the partisans of both Innocent and Anaclete, but, while pretending to conduct the inquiry impartially, he was only trying to gain time and refused to make a decision; at least the debate had the happy result of bringing about the conversion of one of the principal authors of the schism, Cardinal Peter of Pisa, whom Bernard won to the side of Innocent II. This conversion dealt a severe blow to the cause of the anti-pope; Bernard knew how to profit from this, and even in Rome, through his ardent and convincing words, he managed in a few days to win over most of the dissidents from Anaclete's side. This happened around Christmas 1137; a month later, Anaclete suddenly died. Some of the cardinals most involved in the schism elected a new anti-pope who took the name Victor IV, but their resistance did not last for long, and, on the eighth day of Pentecost, they all made their submission; the next week, the Abbot of Clairvaux again headed home to his monastery.

This brief account should suffice to give an idea of what might be called Saint Bernard's political activity, which however did not stop there: from 1140 to 1144, he was to protest about the mischievous interference of King Louis le Jeune in the episcopal elections; then he had to intervene in a major conflict between the same king and Count Thibaut of Champagne; nevertheless he was fastidious in becoming involved in such matters. In brief, one could say that Saint Bernard's conduct was always determined by the same intentions: to defend what was right, to combat injustice, and, perhaps most of all, to maintain unity in the Christian world. It was this constant preoccupation with unity which animated his struggle against schism; this also caused him to undertake, in 1145, a journey to Languedoc to bring back to the Church the neo-Manichean heretics who were starting to spread in this region. It seems that he unfailingly kept in mind the Gospel words: "That all may be one, even as my Father and I are one."

*

* *

However, the Abbot of Clairvaux did not have to struggle only in the world of politics, but also in the intellectual realm, where his triumphs were no less astonishing, since they were marked by the condemnation of two eminent adversaries: Abelard and Gilbert de la Porrée. The former, through his writings and teachings, had acquired for himself the reputation of being one of the most skillful dialecticians; he even made excessive use of dialectic, for instead of seeing in it only what it really is—a simple means for reaching an understanding of the truth—he regarded it almost as an end in itself, which tended to lead to an over-reliance on words. It seems also that, either in his method, or in the very basis of his ideas, he was drawn to a pursuit of novelty all too similar to that of some modern philosophers; but, in an age in which individualism was something almost unheard of, this fault ran no risk of being taken for a quality, as happens today. Some people were soon upset by these innovations, which offered nothing more than confusion between the realms of reason and faith; it was not that Abelard could rightly be called a rationalist, as has sometimes been suggested, for there were no rationalists prior to Descartes; but he did not know how to distinguish between what pertained to reason and what was higher than it; between profane philosophy and sacred wisdom; between purely human knowledge and transcendent knowledge; it was here that lay the root of all his errors. Did he not go as far as to maintain that philosophers and dialecticians enjoyed a habitual inspiration comparable to the supernatural inspiration of prophets? One can easily understand why Saint Bernard, when his attention was drawn to such theories, rose up against them forcefully and even with passion, and that he bitterly reproached their author for having taught that faith was no more than simple belief. The controversy between these two very different men, which had begun in private conversations, soon caused a great stir in schools and monasteries. Abelard, confident of his skill in manipulating reasoning, demanded that the Archbishop of Sens call a council before which he might justify himself publicly, for he thought he could easily lead the discussion in such a way to confuse his adversary. Things turned out quite differently: the Abbot of Clairvaux, in fact, saw the council as only a tribunal before which the suspect theologian was appearing as the accused; in a preparatory meeting, he produced Abelard's writings and indicated their most reckless propositions, which he proved were heterodox; the next day, the author having been introduced, Bernard enunciated these propositions and summoned Abelard to either renounce them or justify them. Abelard, instantly foreseeing a condemnation, did not await the judgment of the council but declared immediately that he would appeal the decision to the court of Rome; the trial, nonetheless, followed its course, and when the condemnation was pronounced, Bernard wrote such powerfully eloquent letters to Innocent II and the cardinals that six weeks later, the sentence was confirmed in Rome. Abelard had no other course than to surrender; he took refuge in Cluny, the abbey of Peter the Venerable, who arranged an interview for him with the Abbot of Clairvaux and succeeded in reconciling them.

The Council of Sens took place in 1140; in 1147, at the Council of Reims, Bernard obtained in similar manner the condemnation of the errors of Gilbert de la Porrée, Bishop of Poitiers, regarding the mystery of the Trinity; these errors arose from the fact that their author applied to God the concrete distinction of essence and being, which is applicable only to created beings. However Gilbert made a retraction without much difficulty; so he was simply forbidden to read or transcribe his writings until they had been corrected; his authority, apart from the specific points which were involved, was not affected, and his teaching remained in good repute in the schools throughout the Middle Ages.

*

* *

Two years before this last affair, the Abbot of Clairvaux had had the joy of seeing one of his fellow Cistercian monks, Bernard of Pisa, rise to the pontifical throne; the new pope took the name of Eugene

III and Bernard always maintained the most warm-hearted relations with him. It was this new pope who, towards the start of his reign, charged Bernard to preach the Second Crusade. Until then, the Holy Land had held—at least so it seems—only a minor place in Saint Bernard's preoccupations; however, it would be wrong to think that it was completely alien to his concerns, and the proof of this is a fact which is not usually given the attention it deserves: namely, the part Bernard played in the founding of the Order of the Temple, the first of the military orders, by date and by importance, which was to serve as a model for all the others. It was in 1128, about ten years after its foundation, that the order received its Rule at the Council of Troyes, and it was Bernard who, as secretary of the council, was charged with drawing up this Rule, or at least delineating its chief features, for it seems that it was only some time later that he was called upon to complete it, and he finished the final wording of it only in 1131. He then commented on this Rule in *De laude novae militiae* ("In Praise of the New Militia"), in which he set forth, in terms of magnificent eloquence, the mission and the ideal of Christian chivalry, which he called the "militia of God." These connections between the Abbot of Clairvaux and the Order of the Temple, which modern historians regard as merely a rather secondary episode in his life, assuredly had a completely different importance in the eyes of men of the Middle Ages; and we have shown elsewhere that these connections undoubtedly constitute the reason that Dante chose Saint Bernard as his guide in the highest circles of Paradise.

*
* *

In 1145, Louis VII formulated a plan to go to the aid of the Latin principalities in the Orient, which were being menaced by the Emir of Aleppo; but the opposition of his advisers had constrained him by postponing the plan's execution, and the definitive decision had been left to a plenary assembly which was to take place in Vézelay at Easter the following year. Eugene III, detained in Italy by a revolution provoked in Rome by Arnaud of Brescia, charged the Abbot of Clairvaux to take his place at this assembly; Bernard, after having read aloud the papal bull which invited France to the Crusade, delivered a speech which was, to judge by the impact it produced, the most important speech of his life; everyone in the audience knelt to receive the cross from his hands. Encouraged by this success, Bernard traversed the cities and provinces, preaching the Crusade everywhere with indefatigable zeal; when he could not travel in person, he sent out letters no less eloquent than his speeches. Then he went to Germany, where his preaching had the same result as in France; the Emperor Conrad, after resisting for a while, changed his mind under Bernard's influence and joined in the Crusade. Toward the middle of the year 1147, the French and German armies set off on this expedition, which, despite its formidable appearance, was to end in disaster. The causes of this failure were many; the main ones seem to be the treason of the Greeks and the lack of cooperation between the various leaders of the Crusade; but some critics, quite unjustly, sought to lay responsibility for the failure on the Abbot of Clairvaux. He had to write a veritable apology for his conduct, an apology which was, at the same time, a justification of the defeat as an act of God, showing that the unhappy outcome was not attributable only to the faults of Christians, and that therefore "the promises of God remain intact, for they do not contradict the rights of justice"; this apology is contained in the book *De Consideratione* ("On Contemplation"), addressed to Eugene III, a book which is like Saint Bernard's testament, and which contains especially his views on the rights of the papacy. Moreover, not everyone was discouraged, and Suger, the eminent prime minister of Louis VII, quickly conceived a plan for a new Crusade, of which the Abbot of Clairvaux himself would be the leader; but Suger's death halted the execution of this plan. Saint Bernard himself died shortly afterwards, in 1153, and his last letters testify that he was preoccupied until the end with the deliverance of the Holy Land.

Since the immediate purpose of the Crusade had not been attained, could one therefore say that such an expedition had been entirely useless, and that the efforts of Saint Bernard had been squandered to no avail? We do not think so, despite what may be said by historians who are concerned only with external appearances; for these great movements of the Middle Ages had—for various profound reasons, only one of which we will note here—a character which was both political and religious. The reason to which we refer was the wish to maintain within Christendom a living awareness of its unity. Christendom was identical with Western civilization, which was thus founded on an essentially traditional basis, as is every normal civilization, and which reached its peak in the 13th century; the loss of this traditional character could not but follow a split in the unity of Christendom.

This split, which was later accomplished in the religious realm by the Reformation, was achieved in the political realm by the emergence of nationalities following the destruction of the feudal regime; and, with this last point in mind, it could be said that the person who dealt the first blow to the grand edifice of medieval Christianity was Philip le Bel, who, through a coincidence that was by no means accidental, destroyed the Order of the Temple, thereby directly attacking the most profound of Saint Bernard's works.

*

* *

In the course of his journeys, Saint Bernard frequently reinforced his preaching by miraculous healings, which, for the crowds, were visible signs of his mission; these facts have been reported by eye-witnesses, but Bernard himself was unwilling to speak of them. Perhaps he imposed this restriction on himself because of his great modesty; but he undoubtedly attributed only a secondary importance to these miracles, considering them simply a concession accorded by divine mercy to the weakness of the faith of the majority of the populace, in keeping with the words of Christ: "Blessed are they that have not seen and yet have believed!" This attitude was in accord with the disdain that Bernard generally showed towards all outward and material means, such as the pomp of ceremonies and the ornamentation of churches; some have nevertheless reproached him, with some seeming justification, for having only contempt for religious art. Those who made this criticism however overlooked a necessary distinction, which Bernard himself established between what he called church architecture and monastic architecture: it was only the latter that should observe the austerity that he advocated; it was only to the religious orders and to those who followed the road of perfection that he forbade the "cult of idols," that is to say, of forms, which, he proclaimed, were on the contrary useful as a means of education for the simple and the imperfect. If he protested against the abuses of representations devoid of meaning and having only purely ornamental value, he did not wish, as has been falsely maintained, to forbid symbolism in architectural art, since he himself frequently made use of symbolism in his sermons.

*

* *

Saint Bernard's doctrine is essentially mystical: by this we mean that he envisages divine things especially from the point of view of love, something which it would be wrong to interpret in a merely affective or emotive sense, as do modern psychologists. Like many great mystics, he was particularly drawn to the Song of Solomon, which he commented on in many sermons, sermons which were part of a long series that continued throughout almost all of his career; this commentary, which was never completed, describes all the degrees of the love of God, up to the supreme peace which the soul reaches in ecstasy. The ecstatic state, as he understood it, and certainly experienced it, is a sort of death with regard to the things of this world; along with sensory images, all natural feeling disappears; everything is pure and spiritual within the soul itself, as in its love. This mysticism reflected itself naturally in the dogmatic treatises which Saint Bernard wrote; the title of one of the principal ones, *De diligendo Deo* ("On Loving God"), clearly indicates the place that love held in his thought, but it would be wrong to believe that this was to the detriment of true intellectuality. If the Abbot of Clairvaux always sought to remain apart from the vain subtleties of the academics, it was because he had no need of the laborious artifices of dialectic; he resolved at a single blow the most arduous questions because his thinking did not proceed by means of a long series of discursive operations; what philosophers strove to reach by a circuitous route and by proceeding tentatively, he arrived at immediately, through intellectual intuition, a faculty without which no real metaphysics is possible, and without which one can only grasp a shadow of the truth.

*

*　　*

Finally, we must draw attention to a pre-eminent characteristic of Saint Bernard, namely, the central place which the cult of the Holy Virgin played in his life and in his writings. This produced a great flowering of legends, which may be the reason why Bernard has remained so popular. He loved to give the Holy Virgin the title of Our Lady, a usage which subsequently became generalized, doubtless due in large part to his influence; it is as if he were, as has been said, a true "knight of Mary," and truly regarded her as his "lady," in the chivalric sense of the word. If one links this fact regarding the role played by love in his teaching, and also played, in more or less symbolic forms, in the ideas of the chivalric Orders, one understands easily why we took care to mention his noble family background. Having become a monk, Bernard always remained a knight, as did all those of his class; at the same time, one could say that he was in some way predestined to play (as he did in so many instances) the role of intermediary, conciliator, and arbiter between religious power and political power, since he combined in his person the nature of each. He was both monk and knight: these two characteristics were those of the members of the "militia of God," of the Order of the Temple; they were also, first and foremost, those of the author of their Rule, the great saint who was called the last of the Fathers of the Church, and whom some would regard, not without reason, as the prototype of Galahad, that perfect knight without blemish, the victorious hero of the quest for the Holy Grail.

CHARACTERISTICS OF VOLUNTARISTIC MYSTICISM

Frithjof Schuon

Voluntaristic mysticism is a path of love which—in contrast with Hindu *bhakti*—is characterized by the fact that no intellectual element intervenes in an active fashion in its method; thus the qualifications it demands are almost exclusively moral: at most it demands a general predisposition which, together with moral factors and on contact with grace, becomes a "vocation". It is true that this mysticism thrives on dogmatic symbols and theological concepts, but not on intellections: it is entirely centered on love—on the will with its emotive concomitances—and not on gnosis. In a certain sense, passional mysticism is "negative", since its method—apart from sacramental graces—consists above all in the negation of the natural appetites, whence the cult of suffering, and the importance of trials and consolations; the activity is purely moral and ascetic, as the following opinion of Saint John of the Cross shows well: "By its nature, this [our mind] is limited to natural science; but God has nevertheless endowed it with an obediential power in regard to the supernatural, so that it can obey whenever it pleases Our Lord to make it act supernaturally. Strictly speaking, no knowledge is accessible to the mind except by natural means; therefore all knowledge must pass through the senses" (*The Ascent of Mount Carmel*, I, 2). This is the negation of the intellect, the reduction of the intelligence to reason alone. In such a perspective, there is no place for the intellective man; there is no path for him. The consequence is that he is condemned to occupy himself with philosophy; given his need for logic and the nature of his aspiration, he cannot follow the path of love—the only one offered to him—except on the margin; his particular vocation falls so to speak into the void.

A particularly striking characteristic of voluntaristic mysticism is sentimental humility, which appears as an end in itself and which excludes all help from the intelligence. Humility as such is certainly everywhere a condition of spirituality; but it is only in "passional" mysticism that it is situated on the plane of sentimentality, which proves that the human groups to whom it is addressed have a fundamental tendency to the sort of obsession with the "ego" that is individualism; this obsession or this "pride" has an influence on the intelligence, whence the propensity to Promethean thought, to rationalism, to philosophical adventures, to the divinization of passional art, to ego-centricity in all its forms. In human groups whose mentality is not centered on the individual and on the individual point of view, asceticism could not put the emphasis on a systematic and blind humiliation that is contrary to the nature of things and also to the intelligence. If we divide men into two groups, contemplatives and those whose natural vocation lies in action, we could say that the first are much less obsessed with the ego than the second, and even that the passional element in them has something quasi-impersonal about it, in the sense that their passion is much more passion as such than that of a particular ego; it hardly encroaches on their intelligence, especially since the latter determines passion and not conversely. What perhaps most distinguishes the born metaphysician from the ordinary man is that in the former, passion stops where intelligence begins, whereas in the latter, the intelligence does not by itself oppose the passional element, of which, all too readily, it even becomes the vehicle. Moreover, it is important to know that anti-intellectual mysticism is not an exclusively Christian phenomenon; it is also to be found in the two other monotheistic religions and even, incidentally, in Hindu bhaktism.

*
* *

Sentimental humility seeks out pride because it has need of it, and is fundamentally fearful of any perspective that transcends the moral alternative on which it lives, and this explains the sacrifice of the intelligence in the name of virtue. Saint Theresa of Avila, whose intelligence was keen, had no difficulty in recognizing the dangers of this position, but she did not bring any decisive remedy for it, given the empirical character of her own point of view. She did not wish us to remain "sunk in the consideration of our own misery", and she believed that "never will the stream of our works come out clean and pure from the mire of fear, weakness, cowardice, and a thousand troublesome thoughts, such as these: are not people looking at me? In taking this road, am I not going to be led astray? Is it not presumption to dare undertake this good work? Is it not pride, is it not worse still, that a creature like me should occupy herself with a matter as lofty as prayer? Will people not have too good an opinion of me if I abandon the common and ordinary way? Must one not avoid all excess, even in virtue? Sinner that I am, will the wish to raise myself not simply expose myself to the risk of falling from higher up? Perhaps I shall stop short on the way; perhaps I shall be for some good souls a cause of scandal? Finally, being what I am, is it right for me to aspire to anything at all? O my daughters, what a lot of souls there must be to whom the demon brings great losses by thoughts of this kind! They take for humility what I have just said, and many other similar things. . . . This is why I say, my daughters, that, if we wish to learn true humility we must fix our eyes on Jesus Christ, the sovereign good of our souls, and on his saints" (*The Interior Castle*, I, 2). Now, if scruples like these—which are actually pieces of foolishness—are current coin, it is because the very conception of humility has become superficial; only individualistic sentimentalism can give rise to finicalness of this sort on the spiritual plane, and the true remedy would be to purify the idea of humility by bringing it back to its profound meaning, which implies above all a sound knowledge of the nature of things. If humility is subject to so many contortions of the mind, and if the demon has at his disposal so many doors to slip through and take on the appearance of virtue, the reason obviously lies in the sentimental and individualistic corruption of humility itself; in a word, the whole chaos of these entirely artificial difficulties and these almost inextricable psychological subtleties, is due to the abolition—which in its fashion also smacks of pride—of the intelligence. Man no longer "knows" that, metaphysically, he is nothing; he must therefore always be reminding himself, with much effort and sighing, that he is base, unworthy, and ungrateful; something that he has difficulty believing in his heart of hearts. It is not sufficiently realized that the devil is not merely in official "evil", but also, although indirectly, in the insipid exaggeration with which one surrounds the "good", as if to make it suffocating and improbable; whence a pendulum-like play between an "evil" considered as being absolute and endowed with arbitrary aspects, and a "good" detached from truth and compromised by the unintelligence of the sentimentalism which accompanies it. Be that as it may, this play of the pendulum between an "evil" made positive and a "good" made improbable and almost inaccessible, cannot be displeasing to the demon, for he has every interest in contributing to a quasi-insoluble alternative which burdens the mind, and to an exaggeration which, basically, does wrong to God.[1]

In the same order of ideas, to search after sins denotes a rather outward perspective for, if man is a sinner, it is not in this superficial and quantitative way that he can free himself from his nature. The sound attitude, on this plane, comes down to this: to do what is prescribed, to abstain from what is forbidden, to strive towards the three fundamental virtues from which all others derive, namely humility, charity, and veracity; on this basis, our mind can concentrate on God, who will Himself undertake to transform our purely symbolical virtue into an effective and supernatural virtue; for good can come only from Him. Every other attitude is contradictory and unsound; the exaggeration of sin is not possible without individualism; to everywhere and always look for sin is to cultivate it, whereas the aim of spirituality is to transcend the human, not to magnify it. "Be ye therefore perfect, even as your Father which is in heaven is perfect", said Christ; now the perfection of God is a blessed one, which means that the perfection of man must also have an aspect of serenity and peace, which the contemplation of truth confers. It is true that man is free will; but freedom comes from the intelligence, and it is the latter that characterizes man in the first place.

*

* *

Saint John's doctrine is that of emptiness or obscurity according to faith, hope, and charity: emptiness of understanding, memory, and will. This conception of hope and charity is universal, but not that of

---

[1] An example of a healthy attitude is the following meditation of Saint Ignatius of Loyola, in which instead of abasing himself in an unintelligible sentiment of gratitude—or culpability—he relies, with intelligence, on the nature of things: ". . . I will consider God present in all creatures. He is in the elements, giving them being; in plants, giving them vegetation; in animals, giving them feeling; in men, giving them intelligence; He is in myself in these different manners, giving me at one and the same time being, life, feeling, and intelligence. He has done more: He has made of me his temple; and, to this end, He has created me in the likeness and image of his Divine Majesty. . . . I will consider God acting and working for me in all created objects, since He is in fact in the heavens, in the elements, in plants, in fruits, in animals, etc. as an agent, giving to them and conserving for them being, vegetation, feeling, etc. . . . Then, considering seriously my own self, I will ask myself: what do reason and justice oblige me on my part to offer and to give to His Divine Majesty, and that is, all the things that are mine, and myself with them. . . ." (*Spiritual Exercises*).

faith: for here emptiness should be, not the negation of pure intelligence, but the negation of the mental element and of formal thought; in other words, instead of comprehension being extinguished before dogma, it is the mental element that has to be extinguished, not before dogma, but before pure intellection, before direct and supra-formal intellective vision. This is obvious, for if love is emptiness of the will, and hope emptiness of the memory, then faith must logically be emptiness of a faculty situated on the same level, namely the mind or reason; faith cannot be emptiness of a faculty incomparably more eminent—because transcending the individual—than will and memory, and above all, it cannot sacrifice the greater for the less, otherwise one could also demand the "emptiness of virtue" by emptying virtue of its contents.

When Saint John of the Cross says that "the soul is not united to God, here below, either through understanding, or through enjoying, or through imagining", one should be entitled, in the case of the first of these three faculties, to read: "through thinking"; and when it is said that "Faith despoils understanding and by its night prevents it from comprehending", one would like to read: "it prevents it from reasoning". One cannot put pure intelligence—which is "something of God"—on the same plane as the strictly individual faculties.

If Saint Paul says that "Faith is the substance of the things which one hopes, a conviction about those things which one does not see", this does not of itself mean—though it may do so inclusively and accidentally—what the Spanish Doctor means: "Although the reason adheres absolutely to these things with firmness, they do not disclose themselves to the intelligence, for if they did so, Faith would no longer exist." The most perfect theoretical knowledge cannot abolish existential ignorance; the proof of this is that it does not suffice to have this knowledge in order to behave as if one saw God; on the other hand, metaphysical knowledge is the unquestionable key for the realization of Truth; intellection, by itself, already has the power to purify the heart, so that many of the more or less hazardous complications of individualistic asceticism become superfluous. The difference between faith as belief and faith as gnosis consists in this: that the obscurity of faith, in the ordinary believer, is in the intelligence, whereas in the metaphysician it is in the will, in the participation of his being: the seat of faith is then the heart, not the mind, and the obscurity comes from our state of individuation, not from a congenital unintelligence. The faith of the sage—or of the "gnostic"—has two veils: the body and the ego; they veil, not the intellect, but ontological consciousness. Wisdom, however, comprises degrees.

It would be entirely illogical and disproportionate to ask oneself how the limitations of mystical individualism can accord with sanctity and the most obvious signs of divine grace, ecstasies, levitations, and other such phenomena, for religious genius and heroicalness of virtues furnish a sufficient explanation both for the miracle of sanctity and for the miracles of the saints. The scope of the intelligence is an entirely different question: it is only too clear that one cannot say, from a Catholic point view any more than from any other traditional point of view, that heroicalness of virtues and miracles suffice to prove the universal value of a doctrine, otherwise Catholicism for example would have to accept, not only Palamitic theology on account of such saints as Seraphim of Sarov, but even the Asiatic doctrines on account of the unquestionable sanctity of certain of their representatives; one cannot therefore adduce, as a criterion of value or of intellectual perfection of the Johannine and Theresian doctrines, the sanctity of their authors, although this sanctity is a guarantee of intrinsic orthodoxy, and even more than that.

This is to say that all spiritual paths tend towards Union; it is therefore normal that sanctity as such may comprise "states" and "stations" that surpass the possible narrowness of its point of departure or of its initial form; if the aim is Union,[2] this has to be able to manifest itself on the way. In this regard let us again quote Saint Theresa of Avila: "What distinguishes this abode is, as I have said, the almost continual absence of dryness; in it the soul is free from the inward troubles which it experiences from time to time in all other abodes and it nearly always enjoys the purest calm. Far from fearing that the demon can counterfeit so sublime a grace, it remains perfectly assured that God is the author of it; firstly, as has been said, because the senses and the faculties have no part in it, and also because Our Lord, in revealing himself to the soul, has put it with him in a place, which, to my mind, the demon would not dare to enter, and to which moreover the sovereign Master forbids him access. . . . There, our Lord favors the soul and enlightens it amidst a peace so profound and of such great silence that it reminds me of the construction of the temple of Solomon, where no sound had to be heard."

---

[2] It is true that Union comprises modes and degrees, but here it is a question of "Union as such" and not of "such and such a Union".

SAGES AND SAINTS OF OUR EPOCH IN THE LIGHT OF THE PERENNIAL PHILOSOPHY

Mateus Soares de Azevedo

Our aim here is to survey some of the most important and influential spiritual guides of our time in the light of the teachings of the Perennial Philosophy. In this endeavor we will make reference to illustrious representatives of the various great religions, and through the "universalism" of the Perennial Philosophy, their essential messages will be brought together inwardly. Each of the mystics to be presented here brings the particular "color" of his or her own religion of origin, while the Perennial Philosophy endows each of their messages with an underlying unity through its access to the "uncolored Light." For this wisdom means both essentiality and universality; it is simultaneously center and radiation, and it therefore does not pertain specifically to the Occident or to the Orient, but rather comprehends them both and transcends them.

In our own epoch, among the masters that expounded and experienced this wisdom most profoundly are the influential figures of Frithjof Schuon (1907-1998) and Shri Ramana Maharshi(1879-1950); the first having as his primary—but not exclusive—ray of action the West as a whole and the second a considerable part of the East, namely India. Both were "universalists," which is to say they believed in—and in the case of Schuon, explicitly taught—the idea of the "transcendent unity of religions"; both expounded the purest (and also the most intrinsically orthodox) form of perennial gnosis, but each in his own way; and both attracted admirers from all the major religions. Schuon was in fact a sage in the double capacity of a pure metaphysician—in the philosophical current of Shankara, Plato, and Eckhart—and of an "extra-confessional," sapiential spiritual guide, with a profound love for all authentic religions, but without attachment to their more "formalistic" and "nationalistic" aspects. Schuon was a teacher of the pure Truth, of the Truth beyond form.[1] There are, of course, distinctions to be made in the scope, completeness, and universality of the

---

[1] In the world of Christianity, Schuon can be viewed as belonging to the lineage of the "gnostics" (the term is not here used in a sectarian or heretical sense), such as

metaphysical doctrines which Schuon and the Maharshi expounded, and in the methods of spiritual realization which they advocated, and we shall consider these questions in what follows.

In selecting the German "philosopher" (in the original sense of "lover of wisdom") and the Hindu sage as the main objects of this study, we do not forget the immense importance—especially in the domain of traditional metaphysics, religious symbolism, and the critique of the modernist deviation in all its aspects—of the remarkable French metaphysician and esoterist René Guénon (1886-1951). Guénon was, in a sense, the founder of the traditionalist or perennialist school, a "school" in which Schuon's works are the most complete and final flowering. If Guénon is unquestionably the originator of this unique phenomenon—an unprecedented influx of intellectual and spiritual light in an epoch almost completely impervious to true intellectuality and spirituality—Schuon is its conclusion and fulfillment. The French esoterist was the seed, and the German metaphysician the flower and the fruit. Guénon was the pioneer and Schuon the consummation; Guénon was like a river whereas Schuon was like an ocean, so profound and diversified was the metaphysical doctrine which he expounded, the spiritual counsel which he imparted, and the poems and paintings which he produced.

*

* *

In beginning our journey of bringing to light the spiritual luminaries of our day, we think especially, in what concerns Western Christianity, of two spiritual descendants of the great St. Francis of Assisi, both of them Italian capuchins: Sister Consolata Betrone (1903-1946) and Padre Pio da Pietrelcina (1887-1968).

Soror Consolata Betrone was in a sense a successor to the 19th century St. Theresa of Lisieux.[2] She was a pious and devoted soul whom Christ directly taught regarding the way of ejaculatory prayer and

---

St. John the Evangelist, St. Clement of Alexandria, Meister Eckhart, and Angelus Silesius. In the world of Islam, he can be said to belong especially to the line of Ibn 'Arabi, Rumi and the Shaikh al-Alawi.

[2] St. Theresa of Lisieux was loved by Schuon because of her complete trust in God, her profound humility, her spiritual "common sense," and her way of offering up everything, pleasures and pains, to God.

the perpetual invocation of the Holy Name, a way which is viewed by the Perennial Philosophy as the quintessence itself of all spirituality. The message of Sister Consolata is very significant for contemporary Christians; for Schuon, it is in fact a central message in that she links the way of spiritual childlikeness and trust in God of Saint Theresa of Lisieux with the invocation of the Holy Name.

The stigmatist[3] Padre Pio taught and practiced the invocation of the Holy Name, and was the spiritual director of thousands of Catholics. It was in this sense that Schuon could write in a letter to an Italian correspondent of the 1950s, signor Guido di Giorgio, that Padre Pio was "une protection, sinon bien plus" ("a protection, if not much more than that") for the Christian world.

It is natural that a pope should also have a place in this survey. We refer to Pius XII (r. 1939-1958), who is included here by virtue of his excellence, but also in view of the cowardly calumniation he has received from the enemies of tradition (for he was the last traditional pontiff of the Catholic Church), whose main weapon is the false allegation that he was indifferent to the fate of European Jewry during World War II.[4] The truth is that, in contradistinction to many of the secular leaders of the period, who did almost nothing to help the Jews, Pius XII clearly acted in their defense during the war.[5] When vicious, racist anti-Semitism was rampant, it was he who boldly declared: "We are all Semites!" Here he had in mind the Abrahamic monotheistic tradition that is common to Jews, Christians, and Moslems. The Pope also referred to the fact that if by mere racial or ethnic criteria the Europeans are not Semites, they in a certain sense became so spiritually by their adherence to a religion of Semitic origin, namely Christianity. In this respect it is important to recall that, in 1942, many thousands of Jews were being sheltered in convents, monasteries, and

[3] Padre Pio is the only stigmatized priest in the history of the Catholic Church (St. Francis bore the stigmata of Christ, but he was not a priest). It may be of interest to note that Padre Pio was from the same generation as Guénon, and had a marked facial resemblance to Schuon.

[4] One must assume that the reason he has recently been attacked is precisely because he was the last papal representative of the traditional Roman Catholic Church, being therefore a privileged target for the enemies of tradition.

[5] As was the case with the populist leaders Getúlio Vargas in Brazil and Juan Domingo Perón in Argentina, and even to a certain extent Franklin D. Roosevelt in the United States, who until 1942 refused the pleas of Pius XII to accept more Jewish refugees from Europe.

schools under the auspices of the Supreme Pontiff. The Vatican City itself harbored many of them, and Castelgandolfo, the summer residence of the popes, sheltered more than 15,000 Jews. In 1944, Pius XII put the papal seal on the entrance to the main Roman synagogue before the city was invaded by Nazi troops, in order to protect its sacred contents. And, in 1946, no less than the chief rabbi of Rome, Israel Zolli, embraced Catholicism, with all his family, saying that one of the reasons for this spectacular change of religion was precisely Pius XII's defense of his people during the war. Moreover, the rabbi took as his Christian name "Eugenio," which was the baptismal name of Pius XII. Here, then, is more than enough evidence to show that the accusations leveled against him do not have any concrete basis in fact, and are ideologically and politically motivated; by attacking Pius XII, one attacks the traditional Church, which has been destroyed by Vatican II and its sequelae.

Let us say a little more on this topic. Already two years before becoming Pope in 1937—when he was the Vatican's Secretary of State—Pius XII collaborated with the then Pope Pius XI[6] in the drafting of his famous encyclical *Mit brennender Sorge*, which strongly condemned the Nazi racist ideology. And when some critics allege that the encyclical was not strong enough, one should remember that until well towards the end of the war, not even Jewish organizations knew fully that the Nazi persecutions had in view the complete extermination of the Jewish people. Moreover, in the case of Pius XII, he was sometimes obliged to moderate his tone or maintain a prudent silence, when the opposite might have dangerously and cruelly aggravated the situation.[7]

---

[6] Achille Ratti, pope Pius XI (Roman pontiff from 1922 to 1939), may perhaps deserve a place in this synopsis. Beyond his work of clarifying Christian social doctrines with his vigorous condemnations of Fascism (1931), Communism (1937), and Nazism (1937), he was also a man of vision in pronouncing the following bold "universalistic" words to his *Nuncio* to Libya: "Do not think you are going to a country of heathens. Muslims attain to salvation. The ways of God are infinite."

[7] Some readers may be interested to know that Pius XII once granted a private audience to Titus Burckhardt in Castelgandolfo, during which they talked about the sacred art of the Middle Ages. The Pope must surely have appreciated the conversation and presence of an eminent representative of the Guénon-Schuon current of spirituality—just as Burckhardt appreciated the Pope's—for the pontiff's final words to Burckhardt were: "I bless you, your colleagues, your family, and your friends." Surely a wonderful and blessed link between traditional Catholicism and the exponents of the *philosophia perennis*!

Interestingly enough, the main source of these attacks (disguised of course) are the modernists and revolutionaries who have taken control of the Vatican since the time of John XXIII, Paul VI, and the Vatican II council. It was then that they established, so to speak, a "new religion," a religion of Man and "this world," in total opposition to the old and perennial religion of God and eternal life.[8] In spite of the fact that some call him a "conservative," it is indisputable that this control by the "revolutionaries" is currently maintained by John Paul II.[9]

Pius XII, so orthodox and traditional in doctrinal, ritual, and moral matters, and so profoundly compassionate and humble as a human being, had a particular gift for the teaching and transmitting of an ample corpus of doctrinal guidance on a vast number of themes. He was also deeply conscious of the dignity, not only of his function as Supreme Pontiff, but also of man as such, as God's representative on earth. This can be seen in those pictures that allow us to witness his dignified gestures (one might even use the Hindu term *mudrâs!*)— especially as he gave his papal blessing to the faithful—which are unsurpassed by those of even the greatest of the Hindu or Buddhist masters![10]

*

* *

Let us turn now to the world of Islam. Perhaps the greatest figure of modern times is the Algerian Sheikh Ahmed al-Alawi (1869-1934). He is highly relevant to the Perennial Philosophy in that he was a master of gnosis and an exponent of the spiritual method of invocation or God-remembrance. He was also profoundly interested in other religions, especially Christianity. At a certain moment, the Sheikh al-Alawi is said to have had more than 200,000 disciples throughout the

---

[8] In the words of Cardinal Suenens, Vatican II was the "French Revolution in the Church." According to the well-known theologian, and later cardinal, Yves Congar, it was like "the October 1917 revolution." See Rama P. Coomaraswamy, *The Destruction of the Christian Tradition* (Pates Manor, Bedfont: Perennial Books, 1981) for an informed traditional view of Vatican II.

[9] John Paul II's sympathetic view of Vatican II can easily be seen in his choice of name—a combination of the papal names John XXIII and Paul VI, both of whom orchestrated and presided over the revolutionary council.

[10] The gesture of folding the hands when praying is a typical Christian "*mudrâ.*"

Islamic world, which caused his spiritual order (or "brotherhood") to be influential even in cultural and political matters. What a contrast to contemporary pseudo-Islamic leaders, such as Khomeini and Gaddafi (both of them false mystics), and Saddam Hussein and Hafiz Assad who, despite being anti-Moslem secularists, have shamelessly exploited religion for their own personal and political ends! Schuon had a personal knowledge of the Sheikh al-Alawi, and has written beautifully of him:

> The idea which is the secret essence of each religious form, making each what it is by the action of its inward presence, is too subtle and too deep to be personified with equal intensity by all those who breathe its atmosphere. So much the greater good fortune is it to come into contact with a true spiritual representative of one of those forms, to come into contact with someone who represents in himself, and not merely because he happens to belong to a particular civilization, the idea which for hundreds of years has been the very life-blood of that civilization.
>
> To meet such a one is like coming face to face, in mid-20th century, with a medieval saint or a Semitic patriarch, and this was the impression made on me by the Sheikh Al-Hajj Ahmad Bin-'Aliwa, one of the greatest masters of Sufism. . . . In his brown *jellaba* and white turban, with his silver-gray beard and long hands which seemed, when he moved them, to be weighed down by the flow of his *baraka* (spiritual radiance), he exhaled something of the pure archaic ambience of the Prophet Abraham. . . . His eyes, which were like two sepulchral lamps, seemed to pierce through all the objects, seeing in the outer shell merely one and the same nothingness, beyond which they saw always one and the same reality—the Infinite. Their look was very direct, almost hard in its enigmatic unwavering-ness, and yet full of charity. . . . The cadence of the singing, the dances and the ritual incantations seemed to continue vibrating in him perpetually; his head would sometimes rock rhythmically to and fro, while his soul was plunged in the unfathomable mysteries of the Divine Name, hidden in the *dhikr*, the Remembrance. . . . He was surrounded at one and the same time, with all the veneration that is due to saints, to leaders, to the old, and to the dying.[11]

---

[11] Frithjof Schuon, *Rahimahu 'Llah*, in *Cahiers du Sud* (Paris), 1935. Quoted in Martin Lings, *A Sufi Saint of the Twentieth Century* (Cambridge, UK: Islamic Texts Society, 1993), pp. 116-117.

*
* *

Moving now further East, we find in India a great precursor of Shri Ramana Maharshi—and also of the perennialists—in Shri Ramakrishna (1836-1886), known as the *Paramahamsa* ("the supreme swan"), the highest honorific designation for a mystic in the Hindu tradition. Ramakrishna was a forerunner of the idea of the universality of revelation, as was later expounded by the proponents of the Perennial Philosophy. To mention one particular instance of his uniqueness and importance: at different periods in his life he willingly practiced two non-Hindu religions, namely Christianity and Islam, in a profound and sincere manner, fully recognizing their spiritual validity; and thus did he manifest, by direct personal participation, the metaphysical concept of the "transcendent unity of religions"—a thesis later developed by Schuon in an influential book bearing this title. As William Stoddart says in his book *Outline of Hinduism*,[12] Ramakrishna was the first spiritual authority in modern times to explicitly teach this idea. He was also a practitioner of the spiritual method of the invocation of the Divine Name, a technique traditionally considered as the best-suited for the end of the *Kali Yuga*, or Iron Age, which, the Hindu cosmological doctrines teach, we now inhabit. Ramakrishna had a saying that Schuon would later expound in manifold forms, namely that "God and His Name are one."

One cannot leave India without mentioning two important figures: the great *bhakta* ("devotee," "divine lover") Swami Ramdas (1884-1963) and the 68th Jagadguru ("universal teacher" in Sanskrit) of Kanchipuram (1894-1994). Like the "Russian pilgrim" in the 19th century, Swami Ramdas traveled as a wandering monk through the whole of the Indian subcontinent, ceaselessly invoking the Sacred Name, in which he had an unshakable trust as a privileged means of attaining to God. Moreover, during his only visit to the West, he had occasion to meet Schuon who made a deep impression on him. After the meeting, Ramdas wrote of the Swiss sage: "The tall and stately figure [of Schuon] stood out in great prominence above us all—a very prince among saints."[13] Concerning the Jagadguru of Kanchipuram, it can be said that he was an authentic and traditional descendant

---

[12] *Outline of Hinduism* (Washington, DC: The Foundation for Traditional Studies, 1993), p. 90.

[13] See Swami Ramdas, *World is God* (Kerala: Anandashram), p. 107.

of the greatest exponent of the sapiential way (*jnana*) in India, Shri Shankaracharya (788-820). A teacher of *jnana* for 90 years—he assumed his function as early as 1907 (the same year Schuon was born)—Schuon dedicated his important book on Hinduism, *Language of the Self*,[14] to the venerable Jagadguru—proof of the high esteem in which he was held. Besides being an official representative of *Advaita Vedanta*, he was a universalist well-versed in Christianity, Islam, and even in the old religion of the Indians of North America, being an admirer of the Sioux visionary Black Elk.

*
* *

Finally, in the primordial world of the shamanist tradition of the American Indians, one must mention the extraordinary figure of the holy man from the Oglala Sioux, the medicine-man Black Elk (Hekaka Sapa [1862-1950]). A man of deep contemplation, he received many visions from the spiritual world, and explained to new generations of Indians the meaning of their religion and the utility of its ancient rites.[15] In a series of penetrating essays, especially in *The Feathered Sun: Plains Indians in Art and Philosophy*,[16] Schuon showed his understanding and love for the Red Indian spiritual patrimony and demonstrated its universality and convergence with the other great religions, proving thereby its intrinsic truth and orthodoxy. Interestingly enough, Black Elk ended his long life not only revered as a kind of prophetic figure by the American Indians, but also as a holy man by the Christian missionaries, who taught him the love of Jesus Christ, a love which in a sense he incorporated in his native religion of the Sun Dance and Sacred Pipe.

*
* *

[14] Published by Ganesh Books in 1959; a more recent edition was published by World Wisdom Books in 1999.

[15] See especially *Black Elk Speaks*, as told through John G. Neihardt (Lincoln and London: University of Nebraska Press, 1961) and Joseph Epes Brown, *The Sacred Pipe* (Norman & London: University of Oklahoma Press, 1989).

[16] Published by World Wisdom Books, 1990.

As much earlier precursors of the Perennial Philosophy, one could mention two great figures: Muhyi'd-Din ibn 'Arabi in Islam (1165-1240) and Cardinal Nicholas of Cusa in Western Christianity (1401-1464). Ibn 'Arabi is particularly renowned for the declaration he made in one of his poems:

> My heart has opened unto every form; it is a pasture for gazelles, a cloister for Christian monks, a temple for idols, the Kaaba of the pilgrim, the tables of the Torah, and the book of the Koran. I practice the religion of love; in whatsoever directions its caravans advance, the religion of love shall be my religion and my faith.

Surely an inspired confession both of "universality" and of the love of God by the greatest of the Moslem "gnostics"!

For his part, Cardinal Nicholas of Cusa wrote, amongst other things, a commentary on the Koran, as well as an imaginary dialogue between followers of different religions, entitled *De Pace Fidei* ("On Peace between the Faithful"), in which he advocated an understanding between the different faiths of the world.

*
* *

We now focus our attention again on Schuon and the Maharshi, each the very epitome of spirituality in our time. In this connection, one must consider Guénon and Schuon as belonging to one and the same spirit—having, nevertheless, different functions and styles—of traditional metaphysics, intrinsic and universal orthodoxy, and a radical and devastating critique of modern art, culture, and science, which they castigate as materialistic, relativistic, individualistic, and harmful to man and his environment. As mentioned above, Guénon and Schuon are the two *chefs d'école* of the traditionalist or perennialist school of thought, and the difference mentioned refers to the fact that the French esoterist was like the embodiment of intellectual or metaphysical doctrine, whereas Schuon was a master of both intellectuality and spirituality. Guénon never wished to have disciples. As Schuon himself has aptly written: "The work [of Guénon] is 'theoretical' since it does not directly envisage spiritual realization, and even refrains from assuming the role of a practical teaching. . . . The role of René Guénon was to state principles rather than to show how to apply them. . . ." He states further: "Guénon was like the personification, not of spirituality as such, but uniquely of metaphysical certainty. . . ."[17]

We can now return to Shri Ramana Maharshi. In reality, he was not a spiritual master in the strict sense, for the reason that he was a *fard* (a "solitary"), a term which we borrow from Sufism. This means that he was one of those saints who did not have a spiritual master to teach him the Way, but gained his exceptional condition purely by grace, by direct divine illumination.[18] Not having been the disciple of a master, he was not himself a master of disciples. He thus did not teach a spiritual method properly so called. His permanent and constantly reiterated preoccupation was the self-inquiry, "Who am I?," in which he pointed to the Self, the Divine Being as our authentic center.[19] In his case the divine was, as it were, in his powerful spiritual presence. The Maharshi's "spiritual way," if one may put it thus, consisted in his own presence; through his *darshan* he blessed all those who sought his *baraka* (another applicable Sufi term); he was a born contemplative and a born gnostic, the most extraordinary spiritual phenomenon that India produced in the 20th century.

This sage, who lived on and around the sacred mountain of Arunachala, near Tiruvannamalai in South India, conferred his blessings through contemplative silence, not only to the followers of the *Sanatana Dharma* (Hinduism), who came to him from all over India, but also to Europeans and Americans, Catholics, Protestants, Jews, Buddhists, and Moslems—even to persons without a religious affiliation. This aspect of the Maharshi's activity could be considered problematical: since he did not explicitly require from his visitors a traditional affiliation (the purpose of which is to guarantee a structure or framework for the spiritual path), his non-Hindu followers for the most part remained without ritual and doctrinal support, and therefore did not prepare themselves to attain something solid and permanent in the spiritual way.

---

[17] Both quotations are from Schuon's appreciation: "René Guénon: L'Oeuvre" in *Études Traditionnelles*, Paris, juillet-novembre, 1951. (An English translation was published in *Sophia*, vol. 1, No. 2, Winter 1995, pp. 5-11, entitled "René Guénon: Definitions".)

[18] Apart from this last aspect, Guénon can also be considered as one of the "solitaries" (*afrad*).

[19] This fundamental aspect of the Maharshi's message converges perfectly with Schuon's teaching, being in fact its finality.

Most probably Schuon had this in mind when he included the following in his long cycle of poems:

Ein Weiser sagte: fragt euch — wer bin Ich?
Dies ist kein Weg. Der Weise meinte sich,
Beschrieb sein Geisteswesen, gottgeschenkt;
Es ist nicht euer, weil ihr Gleiches denkt.

Man kann nicht ohne Gott die Welt verbrennen —
"An seiner Frucht wird man den Geist erkennen."

A sage said: ask yourselves — who am I?
But this is not a spiritual way. The sage referred to himself,
He described his spiritual state, granted by God;
This state is not yours, just because you think the same.

One cannot overcome the world without God —
"Ye shall know the Spirit by its fruits."

Be that as it may, Schuon has more to say about this Indian saint, and we conclude our section on the great Shri Ramana Maharshi with the following profound words of Schuon:

In Shri Ramana Maharshi one meets again ancient and eternal India. . . . The spiritual function which can be described as "action of presence" found in the Maharshi its most rigorous expression. Shri Ramana was as it were the incarnation, in these latter days and in the face of the modern activist fever, of what is primordial and incorruptible in India. He manifested the nobility of contemplative "non-action" in the face of an ethic of utilitarian agitation. . . . The great question "Who am I?" appears, with him, as a concrete expression of a reality that is "lived," if one may so put it, and this authenticity gives to each word of the sage a flavor of inimitable freshness—the flavor of Truth when it is embodied in the most direct way. The whole of the Vedanta is contained in the Maharshi's question "Who am I?" The answer is the Inexpressible.[20]

As regards Frithjof Schuon himself, the spiritual method he taught was far from ignoring the question of traditional affiliation,

---

[20] Frithjof Schuon, *Spiritual Perspectives and Human Facts* (Pates Manor, Bedfont: Perennial Books, 1987), p. 127.

since, for him, the *sine qua non* for receiving spiritual guidance was the commitment to practice with sincerity and discernment an orthodox religion. In his circle of admirers and followers were Moslems, Christians (Catholics, Orthodox, and traditional Protestants), Jews, Buddhists, and members of the religion of the Sun Dance and the Sacred Pipe.

Those to whom destiny gave the opportunity of meeting the remarkable man that is Frithjof Schuon[21] invariably left the encounter as if walking above the clouds, even though, more often than not, they required weeks or months of reflection and meditation in order to digest everything that he had imparted. Implacable discernment, infinite nobility, sincere courtesy, unfailing good sense: these are some of the recurrent expressions that have been used to describe him following such encounters. Every question put to him, be it regarding philosophy, religion, mysticism, esthetics, the modern world, and even one's personal life—even the most simple—was received with interest and answered with brilliance. Of course he did not gladly suffer presumptuous or pedantic people, nor stupid questions. It was as if Schuon's extraordinary discrimination was a magical sword—like that of Sir Galahad, the invincible warrior of the Round Table—which, in the most efficient and painless way, cut the Gordian knot of our illusions. One would arrive at his house as a poor orphan and leave as if walking on air. A profound gratitude was the main sentiment of all those whom Schuon's love and intelligence marked, and it is with this sentiment that I now end this rough and very incomplete appraisal of this contemporary sage.

With the death of Frithjof Schuon, the 20th century was deprived, in its twilight, of its most penetrating and inspired intelligence; of a philosopher, poet, and painter whose lucidity confronted our time, obsessed as it is with banal novelties, with the permanent truth and beauty of the Perennial Philosophy. Through his writings, he taught us, his readers, how to think with objectivity, how to see the causes of things in their remote effects, and how to foresee the remote effects of present causes. Schuon the man has gone, it is true, but his books, poems, and paintings remain. His message, paradoxically, seems to become more and more relevant with the passage of time, as if to confirm its oneness, precisely, with the Perennial Philosophy which

---

[21] His remarkable nature is partly evident in the words he wrote about the sages of the different traditions, words which in part have been reproduced in this article.

he so staunchly embodied. His message is thus at the disposition of all those—be they from the East or from the West—who genuinely seek the profound reason of things, who seriously wish to plumb the "why" of the world and of men, and who deeply desire true certainty and serenity, which alone are the bases of that peace of spirit that is so lacking in the agitated and anxious contemporary world.

VI

The Modern
Deviation

"This know also, that in the last days perilous times shall come. For men shall love nothing but money and self; they will be arrogant, boasters, proud, blasphemers, disobedient to parents, unthankful, unholy, without natural affection . . . lovers of pleasure more than lovers of God; men who preserve the outward form of religion, but are a standing denial of its reality . . . ever learning, and never able to come to a knowledge of the truth."—II Timothy 3:1-7

"Now the Spirit speaks expressly, that in the latter times some shall depart from the faith, giving heed to subversive doctrines. . . ."—I Timothy 4:1

"For this people's mind has become gross, and their ears are dull of hearing, and their eyes they have closed."—Matthew 13:15

"Thus saith the Lord: 'Stand ye in the ways, and see, and ask for the old paths, where is the good way, and walk therein, and ye shall find rest for your souls.' But they said: 'We will not walk therein.'"—Jeremiah 6:16

"The fool hath said in his heart, 'There is no God.'"—Psalm 14:1

"Thus, because they have not seen fit to acknowledge God, he has given them up to their own depraved reason. This leads them to break all rules of conduct. They are filled with every kind of injustice, mischief, rapacity, and malice; they are one mass of envy, murder, rivalry, treachery, and malevolence; whisperers and scandal-mongers, hateful of God, insolent, arrogant, and boastful; they invent new kinds of mischief. . . ."—Romans 1:28-31

". . . In religion,
What damned error, but some sober brow
Will bless it and approve it with a text,
Hiding the grossness with fair ornament."—Shakespeare (1564-1616)

"Never does one triumph over error by sacrificing any right whatsoever of the truth."—St. Irenaeus (c.120-c.202)

"The view is false which holds that it is indifferent, with regard to the truth of faith, whether one has a wrong opinion about creation, as long as one has a right opinion about God; for an error concerning creation engenders a false knowledge regarding God."—St. Thomas Aquinas (1224-1274)

"The rejection of heretics makes the tenets of Thy Church and sound doctrine to stand out more clearly. 'For there must also be heresies, that the approved may be made manifest among the weak (I Corinthians 11:19).'"—St. Augustine (354-430)

"For the time will come when they will not endure sound doctrine; but after their own lusts shall they heap to themselves teachers, having itching ears; and they shall turn their ears from the truth, and shall be turned unto fables."—II Timothy 4:2-4

"Riches and piety will diminish daily, until the world will be completely corrupted. In those days it will be wealth that confers distinction, passion will be the sole reason for union between the sexes, lies will be the only method for success in business, and women will be the objects merely of sensual gratification. The earth will be valued only for its mineral treasures, dishonesty will be the universal means of subsistence, a simple ablution will be regarded as sufficient purification. . . .

"The observance of laws and institutions will no longer be in force in the Dark Age, and the ceremonies prescribed by the *Vedas* will be neglected. Women will obey only their whims and will be infatuated with pleasure. . . . Men of all kinds will presumptuously regard themselves as the equals of *brahmins* [priests]. . . . The *vaishyas* [the middle class of craftsmen, farmers, and merchants] will abandon agriculture and commerce and will earn their living by servitude or by the exercise of mechanical professions. . . . The path of the *Vedas* having been abandoned, and man having been led astray from orthodoxy, iniquity will prevail and the length of human life will diminish in consequence. . . . Then men will cease worshiping Vishnu, the Lord of sacrifice, Creator and Lord of all things, and they will say: 'Of what authority are the *Vedas*? Who are the Gods and the *brahmins*? What use is purification with water?' The dominant caste will be that of *shudras* [servants, laborers]. . . . Men, deprived of reason and subject to every infirmity of body and mind, will daily commit sins: everything which is impure, vicious, and calculated to afflict the human race will make its appearance in the Dark Age."—*Vishnu Purana* (3rd century)

"At the horrible time of the end, men will be malevolent, false, evil, and obtuse, and they will imagine that they have reached perfection, when it will be nothing of the sort."—*Saddharma-Pundarika* (c.200)

THE ABOLITION OF MAN
C. S. Lewis

It came burning hot into my mind, whatever he said and however he
flattered, when he got me home to his house, he would sell me for a
slave.—John Bunyan

"Man's conquest of Nature" is an expression often used to describe
the progress of applied science. "Man has Nature whacked," said
someone to a friend of mine. In their context the words had a certain
tragic beauty, for the speaker was dying of tuberculosis. "No matter,"
he said, "I know I'm one of the casualties. Of course there are casualties on the winning as well as on the losing side. But that doesn't alter
the fact that it is winning." I have chosen this story as my point of
departure in order to make it clear that I do not wish to disparage all
that is really beneficial in the process described as "Man's conquest,"
much less all the real devotion and self-sacrifice that has gone to make
it possible. But having done so I must proceed to analyze this conception more closely. In what sense is Man the possessor of increasing
power over Nature?

Let us consider three typical examples: the airplane, the wireless,
and the contraceptive. In a civilized community, in peace-time, anyone who can pay for them may use these things. But it cannot strictly
be said that when he does so he is exercising his own proper or individual power over Nature. If I pay you to carry me, I am not therefore
myself a strong man. Any or all of the three things I have mentioned
can be withheld from some men by other men—by those who sell,
or those who own the sources of production, or those who make the
goods. What we call Man's power is, in reality, a power possessed by
some men which they may, or may not, allow other men to profit by.
Again, as regards the powers manifested in the airplane or the wireless,
Man is as much the patient or subject as the possessor, since he is the
target both for bombs and for propaganda. And as regards contracep-
tives, there is a paradoxical, negative sense in which all possible future
generations are the patients or subjects of a power wielded by those
already alive. By contraception simply, they are denied existence; by

contraception used as a means of selective breeding, they are, without their concurring voice, made to be what one generation, for its own reasons, may choose to prefer. From this point of view, what we call Man's power over Nature turns out to be a power exercised by some men over other men with Nature as its instrument.

It is, of course, a commonplace to complain that men have hitherto used badly, and against their fellows, the powers that science has given them. But that is not the point I am trying to make. I am not speaking of particular corruptions and abuses which an increase of moral virtue would cure: I am considering what the thing called "Man's power over Nature" must always and essentially be. No doubt, the picture could be modified by public ownership of raw materials and factories and public control of scientific research. But unless we have a world state this will still mean the power of one nation over others. And even within the world state or the nation it will mean (in principle) the power of majorities over minorities, and (in the concrete) of a government over the people. And all long-term exercises of power, especially in breeding, must mean the power of earlier generations over later ones.

The latter point is not always sufficiently emphasized, because those who write on social matters have not yet learned to imitate the physicists by always including Time among the dimensions. In order to understand fully what Man's power over Nature, and therefore the power of some men over other men, really means, we must picture the race extended in time from the date of its emergence to that of its extinction. Each generation exercises power over its successors: and each, in so far as it modifies the environment bequeathed to it and rebels against tradition, resists and limits the power of its predecessors. This modifies the picture which is sometimes painted of a progressive emancipation from tradition and a progressive control of natural processes resulting in a continual increase of human power. In reality, if any one age really attains, by eugenics and scientific education, the power to make its descendants what it pleases, all men who live after it are the patients of that power. They are weaker, not stronger: for though we may have put wonderful machines in their hands we have pre-ordained how they are to use them. And if, as is almost certain, the age which had thus attained maximum power over posterity were also the age most emancipated from tradition, it would be engaged in reducing the power of its predecessors almost as drastically as that of its successors. And we must also remember that, quite apart from this, the later a generation comes—the nearer it lives to that date at which the species becomes extinct—the less power it will have in the forward direction, because its subjects will be so few. There is therefore no question of a power vested in the race as a whole steadily growing as long as the race survives. The last men, far from being the heirs of power, will be of all men most subject to the dead hand of the great planners and conditioners and will themselves exercise least power upon the future.

The real picture is that of one dominant age—let us suppose the hundredth century A.D.—which resists all previous ages most successfully and dominates all subsequent ages most irresistibly, and thus is the real master of the human species. But then within this master generation (itself an infinitesimal minority of the species) the power will be exercised by a minority smaller still. Man's conquest of Nature, if the dreams of some scientific planners are realized, means the rule of a few hundreds of men over billions upon billions of men. There neither is nor can be any simple increase of power on Man's side. Each new power won *by* man is a power *over* man as well. Each advance leaves him weaker as well as stronger. In every victory, besides being the general who triumphs, he is also the prisoner who follows the triumphal car.

I am not yet considering whether the total result of such ambivalent victories is a good thing or a bad. I am only making clear what Man's conquest of Nature really means and especially that final stage in the conquest, which, perhaps, is not far off. The final stage is come when Man by eugenics, by pre-natal conditioning, and by an education and propaganda based on a perfect applied psychology, has obtained full control over himself. *Human* nature will be the last part of Nature to surrender to Man. The battle will then be won. We shall have "taken the thread of life out of the hand of Clotho"[1] and be henceforth free to make our species whatever we wish it to be. The battle will indeed be won. But who, precisely, will have won it?

For the power of Man to make himself what he pleases means, as we have seen, the power of some men to make other men what *they* please. In all ages, nurture and instruction have, in some sense, attempted to exercise this power. But the situation to which we must

---

[1] Editor's Note: In classical mythology Clotho is the Fate that spins the thread of life.

look forward will be novel in two respects. In the first place, the power will be enormously increased. Hitherto the plans of educationalists have achieved very little of what they attempted and indeed, when we read them we may well thank the beneficent obstinacy of real mothers, real nurses, and (above all) real children for preserving the human race in such sanity as it still possesses. But the man-molders of the new age will be armed with the powers of an omnicompetent state and an irresistible scientific technique: we shall get at last a race of conditioners who really can cut out all posterity in what shape they please.

The second difference is even more important. In the older systems both the kind of man the teachers wished to produce and their motives for producing him were prescribed by the *Tao*—a norm to which the teachers themselves were subject and from which they claimed no liberty to depart. They did not cut men to some pattern they had chosen. They handed on what they had received: they initiated the young neophyte into the mystery of humanity which overarched him and them alike. It was but old birds teaching young birds to fly. This will be changed. Values are now mere natural phenomena. Judgments of value are to be produced in the pupil as part of the conditioning. Whatever *Tao* there is will be the product, not the motive, of education. The conditioners have been emancipated from all that. It is one more part of Nature which they have conquered. The ultimate springs of human action are no longer, for them, something given. They have surrendered—like electricity: it is the function of the Conditioners to control, not to obey them. They know how to *produce* conscience and decide what kind of conscience they will produce. They themselves are outside, above.

The Conditioners, then, are to choose what kind of artificial *Tao* they will, for their own good reasons, produce in the Human race. They are the motivators, the creators of motives. But how are they going to be motivated themselves? For a time, perhaps, by survivals, within their own minds, of the old "natural" *Tao*. Thus at first they may look upon themselves as servants and guardians of humanity and conceive that they have a "duty" to do it "good." But it is only by confusion that they can remain in this state. They recognize the concept of duty as the result of certain processes which they can now control. Their victory has consisted precisely in emerging from the state in which they were acted upon by those processes to the state in which they use them as tools. One of the things they now have to decide is whether they will, or will not, so condition the rest of us that we can go on having the old idea of duty and the old reactions to it. How can duty help them to decide that? Duty itself is up for trial: it cannot also be the judge. And "good" fares no better. They know quite well how to produce a dozen different conceptions of good in us. The question is which, if any, they should produce. No conception of good can help them to decide. It is absurd to fix on one of the things they are comparing and make it the standard of comparison.

To some it will appear that I am inventing a factitious difficulty for my Conditioners. Other, more simple-minded, critics may ask, "Why should you suppose they will be such bad men?" But I am not supposing them to be bad men. They are, rather, not men (in the old sense) at all. They are, if you like, men who have sacrificed their own share in traditional humanity in order to devote themselves to the task of deciding what "Humanity" shall henceforth mean. "Good" and "bad," applied to them, are words without content: for it is from them that the content of these words is henceforward to be derived. Nor is their difficulty factitious. We might suppose that it was possible to say, "After all, most of us want more or less the same things—food and drink and sexual intercourse, amusement, art, science, and the longest possible life for individuals and for the species. Let them simply say, 'This is what we happen to like,' and go on to condition men in the way most likely to produce it. Where's the trouble?" But this will not answer. In the first place, it is false that we all really like the same things. But even if we did, what motive is to impel the Conditioners to scorn delights and live laborious days in order that we, and posterity, may have what we like? Their duty? But that is only the *Tao*, which they may decide to impose on us, but which cannot be valid for them. If they accept it, then they are no longer the makers of conscience but still its subjects, and their final conquest over Nature has not really happened. The preservation of the species? But why should the species be preserved? One of the questions before them is whether this feeling for posterity (they know well how it is produced) shall be continued or not. However far they go back, or down, they can find no ground to stand on. Every motive they try to act on becomes at once a *petitio*. Stepping outside the *Tao*, they have stepped in the void. Nor are their subjects necessarily unhappy men. They are not men at all: they are artifacts. Man's final conquest has proved to be the abolition of Man.

We have been trying, like Lear, to have it both ways: to lay down our human prerogative and yet at the same time to retain it. It is impossible. Either we are rational spirit obliged for ever to obey the absolute values of the *Tao*, or else we are mere nature to be kneaded and cut into new shapes for the pleasures of masters who must, by hypothesis, have no motive but their own "natural" impulses. Only the *Tao* provides a common human law of action which can over-arch rulers and ruled alike. A dogmatic belief in objective value is necessary to the very idea of a rule which is not tyranny or an obedience which is not slavery.

I am not here thinking solely, perhaps not even chiefly, of those who are our public enemies at the moment. The process which, if not checked, will abolish Man goes on apace among Communists and Democrats no less than among Fascists. The methods may (at first) differ in brutality. But many a mild-eyed scientist in pince-nez, many a popular dramatist, many an amateur philosopher in our midst, means in the long run just the same as the Nazi rulers. Traditional values are to be "debunked" and mankind to be cut out into some fresh shape at the will of some few lucky people in one lucky generation which has learned how to do it. The belief that we can invent "ideologies" at pleasure, and the consequent treatment of mankind as mere ὕλη, specimens, preparations, begins to affect our very language. Once we killed bad men: now we liquidate unsocial elements. Virtue has become *integration* and diligence *dynamism*, and boys likely to be worthy of a commission are "potential officer material." Most wonderful of all, the virtues of thrift and temperance, and even of ordinary intelligence, are *sales-resistance*.

The true significance of what is going on has been concealed by the use of the abstraction Man. Not that the word Man is necessarily a pure abstraction. In the *Tao* itself, as long as we remain within it, we find the concrete reality in which to participate is to be truly human: the real common will and common reason of humanity, alive, and growing like a tree, and branching out, as the situation varies, into ever new beauties and dignities of application. While we speak from within the *Tao* we can speak of Man having power over himself in a sense truly analogous to an individual's self-control. But the moment we step outside and regard the *Tao* as a mere subjective product, this possibility has disappeared. What is now common to all men is a mere abstract universal, an H. C. F., and Man's conquest of himself means simply the rule of the Conditioners over the conditioned human material, the world of post-humanity which, some knowingly and some unknowingly, nearly all men in all nations are at present laboring to produce.

Nothing I can say will prevent some people from describing this lecture as an attack on science. I deny the charge, of course: and real Natural Philosophers (there are some now alive) will perceive that in defending value I defend *inter alia* the value of knowledge, which must die like every other when its roots in the *Tao* are cut. But I can go further than that. I even suggest that from Science herself the cure might come.

I have described as a "magician's bargain" that process whereby man surrenders object after object, and finally himself, to Nature in return for power. And I meant what I said. The fact that the scientist has succeeded where the magician failed has put such a wide contrast between them in popular thought that the real story of the birth of Science is misunderstood. You will even find people who write about the sixteenth century as if Magic were a medieval survival and Science the new thing that came in to sweep it away. Those who have studied the period know better. There was very little magic in the Middle Ages: the sixteenth and seventeenth centuries are the high noon of magic. The serious magical endeavor and the serious scientific endeavor are twins: one was sickly and died, the other strong and throve. But they were twins. They were born of the same impulse. I allow that some (certainly not all) of the early scientists were actuated by a pure love of knowledge. But if we consider the temper of that age as a whole we can discern the impulse of which I speak.

There is something which unites magic and applied science while separating both from the wisdom of earlier ages. For the wise men of old the cardinal problem had been how to conform the soul to reality, and the solution had been knowledge, self-discipline, and virtue. For magic and applied science alike the problem is how to subdue reality to the wishes of men: the solution is a technique; and both, in the practice of this technique, are ready to do things hitherto regarded as disgusting and impious—such as digging up and mutilating the dead.

Perhaps I am asking impossibilities. Perhaps, in the nature of things, analytical understanding must always be a basilisk which kills what it sees and only sees by killing. But if the scientists themselves cannot arrest this process before it reaches the common Reason and kills that too, then someone else must arrest it. What I most fear is the reply that I am "only one more" obscurantist, that this barrier, like all previous barriers set up against the advance of science, can be safely passed. Such a reply springs from the fatal serialism of the modern imagination—the image of infinite unilinear progression which so haunts our minds. Because we have to use numbers so much we tend to think of every process as if it must be like the numeral series, where every step, to all eternity, is the same kind of step as the one before. I implore you to remember the Irishman and his two stoves. There are progressions in which the last step is *sui generis*—incommensurable with the others—and in which to go the whole way is to undo all the labor of your previous journey. To reduce the *Tao* to a mere natural product is a step of that kind. Up to that point, the kind of explanation which explains things away may give us something, though at a heavy cost. But you cannot go on "explaining away" for ever: you will find that you have explained explanation itself away. You cannot go on "seeing through" things for ever. The whole point of seeing through something is to see something through it. It is good that the window should be transparent, because the street or garden beyond it is opaque. How if you saw through the garden too? It is no use trying to "see through" first principles. If you see through everything, then everything is transparent. But a wholly transparent world is an invisible world. To "see through" all things is the same as not to see.

THE END OF A TRADITION
Rama P. Coomaraswamy

It is often stated that "traditional man"—by which we mean men whose lives are rooted in the great religious traditions that have their source and origin in a Divine Revelation—has no "historical sense." With this one can agree, provided one understands by a "historical sense" the attitude that modern and so-called "enlightened" man has assumed towards all that has gone before him in the sphere of time. In point of fact however, traditional man has a profound and much more accurate historical sense than his modern counterpart. He does not see the modern world as the result of "evolutionary" and "progressive" achievement brought about by "historical processes" and "dynamic forces" that will inevitably lead to higher and higher states of "civilization," and ultimately to the "perfection of mankind." Rather, he sees the present situation as the outcome of regressive and degenerative patterns of behavior arising from the sequential abandonment of those principles and truths divinely revealed by God in some remote age for the guidance of mankind. In his view, the crisis in which the world finds itself is due to the replacement of traditional values and truths with "humanistic" principles, and the precepts of "Faith, Hope, and Charity" with the pseudo-ideals of "Liberty, Equality, and Fraternity" which in the practical order mean: a liberty from the restrictions God has placed on mankind; an equality of the profane with the sacred; and the brotherhood of all men in their opposition to traditional values. For him, it is not religion, but these distortions of reality along with the superstitions of "progress" and "evolution" that are the "opiates of the people," giving man a false "faith" in humanity, and holding out to him the false "hope" of an earthly millennium in which society will be so organized as to remove from mankind the very need to be good. Within such a worldview "charity" is profaned to the level of "helping mankind" along its pilgrim road to this false utopia.

Insofar as such ideas permeate the world in which we find ourselves, traditional man recognizes that we have arrived at what has been called the "latter days," the *Kali Yuga* or "dark age" when those faithful to tradition are but a "remnant," and a persecuted remnant

291

at that; an Iron Age in which all the lesser possibilities inherent in creation will have their brief but all too deadly opportunity to come to fruition. And thus it is that the Christian Scriptures describe the nature of the *civitas mundi* built in opposition to the *civitas Dei* by a society that at best ignores, and at worst openly wars upon the sacred.

> This know also, that in the last days perilous times shall come. For men shall be lovers of their own selves, covetous, boasters, disobedient to parents, unthankful, unholy, without natural affections, trucebreakers, false accusers, proud, blasphemers, incontinent, fierce, despisers of those that are good, traitors, heady, high-minded, lovers of pleasures more than lovers of God; having a form of godliness, but denying the power thereof: . . . ever learning, and never able to come to the knowledge of the truth. (2 Timothy 3:1-5; 7)

> Now the Spirit speaketh expressly, that in the latter times some shall depart from the faith, giving heed to seducing spirits and doctrines of devils; speaking lies in hypocrisy; having their conscience seared with a hot iron. (1 Timothy 4:1-2)

Hippolytus, one of the early church fathers, in his discourse, "On the End of the World," describes the last days in these words:

> The temples of God will be like houses, and there will be overturnings of the churches everywhere. The Scriptures will be despised and everywhere they will sing the songs of the adversary. Fornications, and adulteries, and perjuries will fill the land; sorceries, and incantations, and divinations will follow after these with all force and zeal. And, on the whole, from among those who profess to be Christians will rise up then false prophets, false apostles, imposters, mischief-makers, evil-doers, liars against each other, adulterers, fornicators, robbers, grasping, perjurers, mendacious, hating each other. The shepherds will be like wolves; the priests will embrace falsehood; the monks will lust after things of the world; the rich will assume hardness of heart; the rulers will not help the poor; the powerful will cast off all pity; the judges will remove justice from the just, and blinded with bribes, they will call in unrighteousness.

From the Catholic point of view, if one can be allowed to simplify the situation somewhat, it can be said that when God created the Angels, and man "in His own image," He endowed them with both an "Intellect" and "Free-will." In doing so, He not only provided them with a means of "knowing, loving, and serving" Him, He also endowed them with the possibility of refusing obedience and of rebelling against Him. Thus it was that Lucifer, the Angel of Light, refused to serve and fell from heaven with a host of his fellows. So also man, tempted by the serpent in the Garden of Eden, chose to disobey, and, as a result, he was cast forth from his paradisic state, and carries with him for all time that "stain" of rebellion which the Church characterizes as "original sin." Such was required by Divine Justice.

Fortunately, His Mercy is greater than His Justice, and so God provided man with a means of returning to that condition which God always envisioned as being "natural" to him. We have little detailed knowledge of the "paths" provided to early man for regeneration, but paths there certainly were. Thus it was that Abel, born of Adam shortly after his "fall," made sacrifice, "and the Lord had respect to Abel and his offerings" (Genesis 4:4). He further established moral codes of behavior and said to Cain, "if thou do well, shall thou not be accepted?" Throughout the Old Dispensation, or the tradition as established before the historical coming of Christ, we have a series of repeated manifestations of God's intent to save His Creation, followed by a series of "falling aways" as mankind rejected grace and turned away from his true and proper end. St Clement speaks of the Spirit of Christ "who has changed his forms and his names from the beginning of the world and so reappeared again and again in the world" (Homilies, III.20). That is to say, God repeatedly renewed His Covenant with man, calling man back to the rightful dignity of his vocation; and time and again man broke this Covenant and followed in the paths of his own "lusts." All this is summarized in the historical aspects of the Old Testament, the prophets of which are venerated by the Catholic Church as Saints, even as their utterances are venerated as being inspired by the Holy Spirit. This all culminated with the coming of Christ who established the New Covenant which was to last till "the end of time."

Inevitably then, Christians look back with fervor and veneration to the times when the Divine touched the earth, whether by means of the great Prophets or, as in the present dispensation, through Christ and the Apostles as they actually walked upon the earth. What greater time to be alive than when one might have sat at His feet and listened to His words, or at least to those of the men who were His immediate followers? And if Catholics listen to the traditional Church today, it is because she preserves as a precious "deposit" what He and the Apostles taught and did—those doctrines and those rites provided for their regeneration and their salvation even down to the present time.

Now every efficacious Divine intervention has to allow for man's "freedom" to oppose it, for grace can only build on a nature that accepts its saving intervention. The Spirit can blow when and where it will, but man is always at liberty to refuse it entrance into his own heart. Thus it was that from the moment Christ manifested Himself on earth, forces rallied to oppose and even to destroy Him. If the Magi came to pay Him reverence, Herod slaughtered the Holy Innocents. If the Apostles rallied round Him, Judas betrayed Him. If the true Jews followed Him, the "perfidious" Jews (perfidious to their own tradition) crucified Him. The battle lines were established between those who sought to be *alteri Christi*—other Christs—and those who were to be "anti-Christs." It is a battle as old as Adam, but still played out in our own times, and above all, in our own hearts. If the majority of mankind are indifferent to this *Jihâd*, it must be remembered that, in the Divine economy, as Christ said, "those who are not with Me are against Me," and He warned that the "lukewarm" would be "vomited forth."

Now Satan has always attempted to confuse the issues, and above all, to convince mankind that there is no battle to be fought at all. Throughout history he has used a variety of different ploys with varying degrees of success. It would seem that in modern times he has been successful to an extraordinary degree; such is not only permitted by God, but even predicted in the sacred writings of all the traditions. "The final coming of Christ will be immediately preceded by a very awful and unparalleled outbreak of evil, called by St Paul an Apostasy. . . . This will be when revolutions prevail and the present framework of society breaks to pieces. . . ."[1] Thus it is that modern man is a collectivity deprived of any true roots and alienated both from his neighbor and himself. But if throughout history this process of alienation has always gone on, God has provided in his love an antidote: TRADITION. To quote a passage from the *Chandogya Upanishad* (VII.26.2), "from taking hold of the traditional teachings there is release from all the knots [of the heart]." A true historical perspec-

---

[1] Taken from Cardinal Newman's description of the latter days.

tive therefore requires that we see in tradition the preservation of the Divine Revelation, and in a departure from this precious deposit the source of all the aberrations that prevail in our times.

Etymologically, "tradition" simply means "that which is transmitted" or "handed on." According to the *Catholic Encyclopedia* (1908), "traditional truth was confided to the Church as a deposit which it would guard and carefully transmit as it had received it without adding to it or taking anything away. . . ." It should of course be abundantly clear that the Christian Revelation was complete with the death of the last Apostle. There is no such thing as "ongoing revelation" or of revelation constantly adapting itself to the changing exigencies of time and circumstance. Thus it is a *de fide* (must be believed) proposition that:

> The Revelation made to the Apostles by Christ and by the Holy Spirit whom he sent to teach them all truth was final, definitive. To that body of revealed truth nothing has been, or ever will be added.
>
> The meaning of the sacred dogmas must always be retained which Holy Mother Church has once taught, nor may it ever be departed from under the guise of or in the name of deeper insight. . . . If anyone shall say that, because of scientific progress, it may be possible at some time to interpret the Church's dogmas in a different sense from that which the Church understood and understands, let him be Anathema! . . . The doctrine of the faith which God has revealed has not been proposed to human intelligence to be perfected by them as if it were a philosophical system, but as a divine deposit entrusted to the Spouse of Christ to be faithfully guarded and infallibly interpreted.

Now what the traditional Catholic Church teaches, its "Magisterium," is precisely this Tradition. Neither the Pope, nor the hierarchy, nor an ecumenical council, can depart from it legitimately. Hence it is important to understand the meaning of the term.

If this Tradition is defined from the point of view of its subject matter as dogmas (truths) and disciplines (rites etc.), from the point of view of origins it can be said to derive not only from Revelation itself but also from ecclesiastical traditions which are precepts and customs long observed in the Church and which, even if they might be revelatory, can only be traced back to post-Apostolic times. Thus, for example, in the Canons of the traditional Mass apart from the words of consecration we can by no means be sure which parts are of

Apostolic origin and which parts derive from ecclesiastical traditions although it would be reasonable to assume that the post-Apostolic authors to whom innovations were Anathema, codified many "customs, precepts, disciplines, and practices" that were truly Apostolic in origin, and hence the Church has always venerated them as being part and parcel of the revealed Tradition, such an attitude being incorporated in the Canons of various Ecumenical Councils which "insisted that the unwritten traditions shall have sway," and that "if anyone disregards any ecclesiastical tradition, written or unwritten, let him be anathema."[2] It will thus be seen that Tradition (with a capital T) as a source of Revelation refers to immutable things which cannot be rejected or changed.

Inevitably, a further extension of the concept of "tradition" is to be found in the various "organs" that are used to transmit the "customs, precepts, institutions, disciplines, and practices" of the Church to our generation. Among these "organs" are the dogmatic definitions of the Roman Pontiffs, of Ecumenical Councils, Professions of the Faith and theological censures. Equally important are such things as the universal customs or practices associated with dogma and, above all, the traditional liturgical forms.

The Magisterium which is defined as the "teaching function of the Church," as a whole as well as in its constituent parts, is as the *Catholic Encyclopedia* states, "the official organ of tradition." The faith is totally dependent upon tradition and cannot under any guise depart from it. "Tradition is thus the faith that the Church teaches, for she has received it from the Apostles, and it is the norm of truth." And how could it be otherwise, for as Cardinal St Bellarmine has said, one of the characteristics of tradition is that it is "perpetual—for it was instituted that it might be continuously used till the consummation of the world...."

There is of course a still broader sense in which the word "tradition" can be legitimately used—this broader sense is, as the *Catholic Encyclopedia* states,

---

[2] The first of these quotations is taken from the Councils of Gangra (Canon XXI) and of Carthage (Canon III), and the second, from the 7th Ecumenical Council. Converts to the Catholic Church are required to promise that they "admit and embrace most firmly the apostolic and ecclesiastical traditions and all other conditions and prescriptions of the Church." Saints have repeatedly stressed the importance of accepting all the "traditions" that fall under this heading.

not always clear, but we endeavor to explain it to ourselves in the following manner: we are all conscious of an assemblage of ideas or opinions living in our minds . . . a common sentiment . . . a common spirit. . . . The existence of tradition in the Church must be regarded as living in the spirit and the heart, thence translating itself into acts and expressing itself into words and writings. . . . This sentiment of the Church is peculiar in this that it is itself under the influence of grace. The thought of the Church is essentially a traditional thought.

And why is this so? It is because those who are deeply steeped in their faith, whose patterns of life conform to the established and formal "traditions," find that their every act and thought is correspondingly influenced. Generosity, gentleness, courtesy, dignity and a whole host of similar qualities that reflect the divine virtues become a normal part of living—qualities that are conspicuously absent from the modern world which is in its essence anti-traditional.

Finally, it should be clear that the sacred Scriptures—constituting what we call the Bible—are themselves a part of tradition. As Cardinal Manning has pointed out:

> We neither derive our religion from the Scriptures, nor does it depend upon them. Our faith was in the world before the New Testament was written.

This is not to say that the Scriptures do not hold an important place within tradition, but rather that it is tradition that guarantees to us their validity, and that to understand them correctly one must have recourse to the writings of the Church Fathers and the Saints. As Tanqueray, a most authoritative theological source, puts it clearly,

> [Tradition] is more extensive than Scripture, and embraces truths which are not at all contained in Scripture or are contained there only obscurely; also Tradition is more essential to the Church than is sacred Scripture, for revealed truth at first was handed down orally by the Apostles, it was always proclaimed orally, always and everywhere. . . .

Indeed, it is thought that parts of the New Testament were written as long as six decades after the death of Christ, and the definitive corpus of the Bible was not established until the fourth century.

Those familiar with the Christian Scriptures are aware that, even in the days of St Paul, there were those who departed from Tradition and taught doctrines other than those revealed by Christ and the Apostles. Such were described by him as "clouds without water" and "clouds tossed in whirlwinds, to whom the mist of darkness is reserved." They were "seducers," "anti-Christs," and "dissolvers of Christ" who brought in "sects of perdition." These were to be shunned by the faithful who were instructed to "stand fast, and hold the traditions which they had learned, whether by word or by our epistle. . . ." Such an attitude has always been preserved throughout the history of the Church which has ever shown herself intolerant of error, though always tolerant of the repentant sinner. And always, Western man has had the Church as an ever-living witness to that tradition established by Christ—indeed, the history of Western civilization can be described as the waxing and waning of this very "force," and of mankind's willingness to accept or reject its teachings and practices. Prior to the Renaissance, despite its many defects and problems, the Western world was in effect a Catholic world, a world in which the dominant political, social, and economic structures were Christian in principle and practice. With the revival of what is termed the "new learning," which was in fact a return to the pagan and pre-Christian values of the Graeco-Roman world, the Christian Tradition was progressively eroded.

Nevertheless, it is perhaps erroneous to place the break with the Renaissance as such. Prior to this historical phenomenon, there had been a decline in spiritual values which tended to give the Church an increasingly "exoteric" character, and which further obscured the always tenuous relationship between the "sacerdotium" and the "regnum": between the spiritual authority and the temporal power, between Church and State. An increasingly worldly quality manifested itself in both orders by which one was greatly weakened and the other virtually destroyed. Economic forces came increasingly to control the civil order, till, as R. H. Tawney says, men persuaded themselves that "greed was enterprise, and avarice economy." Religion was tolerated only in so far as it did not interfere with economic development, while on the political level, royalty was either forced to cooperate with the rising moneyed classes, or else were simply deposed in favor of the so-called "democratic governments," that is to say, governments more easily manipulated by the new power structure. As proof of this new orientation one can point to the destruction of societal structures based on hierarchy such as caste or function, and its replacement with a new aristocracy based exclusively on money and power. Usury, condemned by all orthodox traditions, becomes accepted, and indeed, extolled in what is called "the art of making money."

On the theological level, under the slogan "Reformation," Calvin and Luther attacked the Church and refused to accept any aspect of the Christian tradition which was not based on Scripture alone. And if the Reformation theologians refused to acknowledge Revelation as an ultimate source of truth, the philosophers of the age in turn restricted the function of the Intellect to one of its faculties only—that of Reason. Thus we have the birth of what has been called the "Age of Reason," as if what had preceded it had been an age of un-reason, and as if *manas* could exist in the absence of *bodhi*.

Underlying this altered outlook on life in the spiritual, political, and philosophical spheres was the principle that it was man himself—man *qua* man—that was central to all creation, and hence that he alone, not immutable and supernatural tradition, was to be the judge of what was just, true, and beautiful. And if man was to replace God as a source of truth, it rapidly followed that the world replaced heaven as the goal of his activities. Reason, no longer guided by Revelation, became the mistress of the emotions, of feelings, and what is worse, of the "unconscious" so beloved of contemporary psychiatrists. Religion became a private affair, a matter of personal feelings; one was entitled to them, but one was supposed to keep them to oneself. They had no role to play in the public forum and everyone's private judgment was as good as his neighbors. Western man, disenfranchised from tradition, was given a host of slogans to assuage his hunger. First, "Liberty, Equality, and Brotherhood" and then the ideas of "dynamic progress" and the "evolution" of man into some higher state of existence. Those who refused to accept this new and "modern" worldview were now described as "backward"—the term historically being first applied to the Catholics who during the reign of Queen Elizabeth I refused to conform to the new religion of the Anglican Church.

In order to establish the new economic basis of society, it was necessary to disinherit the landed classes and to rob the Church of its wealth—a wealth held in trust for the poor from whom it was originally derived. Just as in India no real modernization could occur without the destruction of the caste system, so also in Europe it was necessary to first destroy the social and economic structure of Christendom. The idea of progress was created in order to provide those who were the victims of "dynamic processes" with a sop to assuage their pain.

The laboring classes, the expropriated serfs with no craft skills, were told that it was only a matter of time before all their problems would be solved, before the "new world" would be created in which all men would be "free"—that is, with no limits apart from those they imposed upon themselves. And because this new philosophy could in no way explain the vast differences between human beings with regard to their abilities, nor in any way justify the economic disparities that resulted, the newly created "proletariat" were also promised that poverty would be abolished.

Throughout the period of breakdown that followed the Renaissance, the Church remained a bulwark and a witness to certain truths, and as such became the enemy of a false "progress" predicated on the "evolution" and "advancement" of man's intellectual abilities from the "primitiveness" of his dependence upon Church and tradition. It was not that she opposed the discoveries of science and the material betterment of man, but that she constantly demanded that the universal principles of justice and truth had to prevail—justice and truth that is, as understood from a traditional point of view. It was inevitable that she would as such come into conflict with the State, which in reality meant, with the economic powers that controlled the State. This conflict was resolved in many ways, but primarily by what is described as the complete separation of Church and State.

There have always been those within the Church who felt that her rigidity (is not one meant to be rigid about the truth, and were not the martyrs who died for the faith guilty of this "sin"?) was the principal reason why modern man refused to listen to her, those who felt that she should adapt herself to the modern world and somehow be brought up to date. After all, they argued, how could contemporary man ever accept a belief in "mystical rites," in rosaries, in exorcism, in miracles, and how could truths that were valid for primitive man, still be valid for a generation that had intellectually advanced so far along the path of "progress"? It was not that such people wanted the Church to use airplanes and telephones; they wanted her to adopt modern ways of thinking, to accept their belief in "progress," in "evolution," in "dynamic processes," and "historical determinism," and in essence to achieve an *aggiornamento* with all that had resulted from the apostasy of the present age. When she refused to do this, some departed from her bosom, while others remained within her to corrupt the faithful from within. Over and above this, education was removed from her control and became, in the practical order, the means to success in the modern world. Through the process of secular education her ablest members were frequently seduced into being proponents of this "modernism" as it came to be called. Even during the 20th Ecumenical Council—Vatican I—held towards the end of the last century, powerful forces gathered in an attempt to make this new outlook part of the official teaching of the Church, and those who are familiar with the Church documents of that era know how promptly and vigorously this intrusion and violation of the truth were rejected.[3] But time was on the side of the innovators, and by the time Vatican II was convened, many of these individuals had insinuated themselves into high positions in the Church hierarchy. This factor coupled with superb organization allowed for the second Vatican Council to be captured by those who were at heart not Catholic at all.[4]

With Pope Paul VI the Church underwent a series of the most drastic changes—almost no aspect of its traditions being left unre-versed—and a host of modern ideas incorporated within the official body of her teachings. To quote from documents directly:

> The human race has passed from a rather static concept of reality to a more dynamic evolutionary one. . . . It is a fact bearing on the very person of man that he can come to an authentic and full human-ity only through culture, that is, through the cultivation of natural goods and values. . . . The progress of the human person and the advance of society itself hinge on each other. . . . The goal of all social institutions is and must be the human person. . . .

Indeed, the faithful are instructed to:

> Blend modern science and its theories and the understanding of the most recent discoveries with Christian morality and doctrine. Thus their religious practice and morality can keep pace with their scien-tific knowledge and with an ever advancing technology. . . .

---

[3] See the Encyclical letters of Pope St Pius X, *Pascendi Dominici Gregis* and *Lamentabili Sane* (1907).

[4] Those who are interested in how this was done are referred to Father Ralph Wiltgen's *The Rhine Flows into the Tiber*, Augustine Publishing Company, Devon, England, 1978, a book which carries the official Nihil Obstat and Imprimatur declar-ing it free of doctrinal or moral error.

One could give a myriad examples. Private judgment in religious matters is approved; common worship with those who deny the teachings of the Church is encouraged; the Pope surrenders his authority and allows it to be shared with the College of Bishops in a "democratization of the Church." Moreover, everything is so vaguely worded as to allow a multitude of contradictory interpretations. But all this would not in itself have effectively changed the Church without the alteration and adulteration of her Apostolic rites, and especially the Holy Mass preserved throughout history by the Catholic tradition. This, the most central and most sacred rite in Christendom was altered, only those parts being retained that would give the new service some appearance of being similar.[5]

Thus it is that the Christian tradition has been all but destroyed from within.[6] That such would happen before the "end of the world" had always been predicted, both by the saints and by certain passages in Scripture. But for those who have eyes to see, and ears to hear, the unfolding of this process is laid out before their very noses.[7] As Paul VI himself admitted, the "smoke of Satan" has been billowing through the halls of the Vatican. It is this that explains the abandonment of the priesthood by thousands of those committed to the consecrated life, the emptying out of the religious orders, and the falling away of millions of the faithful.

Many are under the mistaken idea that a Pope has the authority to change the faith, to alter the rites, and to depart from tradition. Such of course is not the case, for as Vatican I says in a *de fide* (must be believed) statement:

> The Holy Spirit is not promised to the successors of Peter so that, through His revelation, they might bring new doctrines to light, but that, with His help, they might keep inviolate and faithfully expound the revelation handed down through the Apostles, the deposit of faith. . . .

[5] See Michael Davies' *Pope Paul's Mass*, Augustine Publishing Company, Devon, England, 1980.

[6] See my *The Destruction of the Christian Tradition*, Perennial Books, Bedfont, Middlesex, England, 1981.

[7] For a complete documentation of these facts see Michael Davies' *Pope John's Council*, Augustine Publishing Company, Devon, England, 1977.

Most Catholics do not realize that the Pope can be a heretic, and should he in his public statements prior to election give evidence for this, his election is invalid as are all his acts. This is why, if a Pope should take steps to destroy the Church, the faithful are instructed by Cardinal St Bellarmine to actually "hinder the execution of his will."

Some may well ask what has become of the promise of Christ that the Gates of Hell would not prevail against His Church, and that it would last till the end of time. The promise is fulfilled in the fact that there are significant segments of the traditional Church still viable in the modern world—a remnant faithful to tradition to use the words of Scripture. These groups are of course reviled by the New Church and openly accused of schism for their refusal to abandon the faith that their fathers believed and practiced. Such are the times in which we live, for truly, the *Kali Yuga* is upon us. The New Church has not only abandoned tradition, it has gone as far as to introduce with all the weight of its usurped authority, a "counter-tradition" that can only be seen as a vehicle for hastening the completion of the present cycle of time. It has forgotten the warning of Christ:

> Woe unto the world because of offences; for it must needs be that offences come; but woe to that man by whom the offence cometh. (Matthew 18:7)

THE DRAGON THAT SWALLOWED ST. GEORGE

Whitall N. Perry

Whosoever implores my aid shall receive it.—St. George

In a remarkable study, *The Myth of the Eternal Return*,[1] Mircea Eliade traces the shift in humanity's orientation across the centuries from a cyclical or atemporal perspective to one that is linear or historical.

Archaic and traditional man both East and West lived out a rhythmic perpetuity of recurring events that referred always to an archetypal Source—mythical prototypes "repeated because they were consecrated in the beginning ('in those days,' *in illo tempore, ab origine*) by gods, ancestors, or heroes." As Ananda Coomaraswamy says in his *Hinduism and Buddhism*, "'In the beginning' (*agre*), or rather 'at the summit,' means 'in the first cause': just as in our still told myths, 'once upon a time' does not mean 'once' alone but 'once for all.'" And Eliade's use of the word Myth (from the root MU, "Mystery") must be understood the way Coomaraswamy defines it, as "the penultimate truth, of which all experience is the temporal reflection." Likewise, in speaking of archetypes, it is Platonic Ideas or Essences that are intended.

Contemporary or secular man by contrast lives in a linear flow of history conceived as commencing one single time at some undetermined point in the past and progressing towards an indeterminate temporal future.

The first perspective could be considered "spatially" as vertical and static, the second "temporally" as horizontal and dynamic.

It is "the idea of Center and the idea of Origin" that dominates all early and traditional cultures, writes Frithjof Schuon in his *Light on the Ancient Worlds*. Spatially,

> every value is related back in one way or another to a sacred Center, to the place where Heaven has touched the earth; in every human

---

[1] Princeton University Press, 1971.

world there is a place where God has manifested Himself to spread His grace therein. Similarly for the Origin, the quasi-timeless moment when Heaven was near and when terrestrial things were still half-celestial; but the Origin is also, in the case of civilizations having a historical founder, the time when God spoke, thereby renewing the primordial alliance for the branch of humanity concerned. To conform to tradition is to keep faith with the Origin, and for that very reason it is also to be situated at the Center; it is to dwell in the primordial Purity and in the universal Norm. Everything in the behavior of ancient and traditional peoples can be explained, directly or indirectly, by reference to these two ideas, which are like landmarks in the measureless and perilous world of forms and of change.

It is a "mythological subjectivity" of this kind that makes understandable . . . the fact that each ancient civilization can be said to live on a remembrance of the lost Paradise, and that it believes itself—in so far as it is the vehicle of an immemorial tradition or of a Revelation that restores the "lost word"—to be the most direct branch of the "age of the Gods".

And Eliade cautions against confusing this exemplary Paradise—the paradigm of Reality—with some fictional "lost paradise of animality": primeval man had a "thirst for the 'ontic,'" for the real, and "everything that we know about the mythical memories of 'paradise' confronts us, on the contrary, with the image of an ideal humanity enjoying a beatitude and spiritual plenitude forever unrealizable in the present state of 'fallen man.'" If, then, archaic man rejected history in the degree possible, which for him was equatable with "the measureless and perilous world of forms and of change," that is, with accident, incongruity, misfortune, sin, suffering, and punishment—and confined himself "to an indefinite repetition of archetypes, . . . this behavior corresponds to a desperate effort not to lose contact with *being*." The only qualification to be made here is that the expression "desperate" should be changed to some other word such as "intense" or "cognizant," since the very rhythm itself of the "eternal return" is characterized by a serenity that in its nature excludes any suggestion of *angst*.

The purpose of this paper will be to examine the pattern of the eternal return (*anakuklêsis*) in relation to a particular archetypal entity—in the present case, St. George; and then to see, both how it happens that, and what the consequences are when, "myth" declines into desuetude.

Mythology

The St. George chronicle comprises two poles: that of martyrdom, and that of Solar Hero or Dragon-Slayer. Starting with the first pole, such were the ordeals endured by this celebrated Christian knight that if St. Stephen can be called the proto-martyr, then certainly next to Christ St. George can be considered the prototype of martyr, or "Great Martyr," as he is known to the Greeks. The earliest acts in the Bollandist archives on this subject are in Greek and belong to the sixth century; there are also some eighth century Latin acts considered to be translations of a work antedating the Greek ones just mentioned and attributed to Pasikrâs, the servant of the hero. Erudite research, it hardly needs adding, now takes all this literature for apocryphal. Pope Gelasius (494) says that George is of those "whose names are justly reverenced among men, but whose acts are known only to God." The thirteenth century account of Jacobus de Voragine (1230?-?1298) will mainly suffice our purposes—particularly as his *Golden Legend* did most to familiarize Western tradition with the dragon.

George, then, was a native of Cappadocia who served in the Roman army in Palestine with the rank of tribune during the reign of Diocletian and Maximian. When he witnessed the persecutions the Christians were suffering under the proconsul Dacian (in the Greek acts it is Diocletian, and in the Latin, the Emperor of the Persians), he changed his soldier's garb for the robes of a Christian and denounced Dacian's gods in public as mere demons. This daring earned him dismemberment by iron hooks, while stretched across a rack with torches setting fire to his body and salt poured over his exposed entrails, but he was healed the following night through a vision of the Lord. The next day a magician poisoned his wine, but by making the sign of the cross over it George both saved himself and converted the magician, who for his failure was beheaded. The saint was then thrust upon a wheel bristling with double-edged swords, but the wheel snapped at the first movement. After this Dacian plunged him into a cauldron of molten lead; George made the sign of the cross and experienced pure refreshment.

"Look here, my dear George," said Dacian, forcing a smile, "see with what indulgence our gods treat you: be persuaded of their good intentions. Sacrifice unto them, and behold what honors you shall reap!"

"Is this the brunt of your purpose? With pleasure, then," replied St. George. "I only fail to understand why you did not invite me civilly in the first place instead of resorting to all these torments." Dacian, overjoyed, ordered with flourish of trumpets the whole city to assemble at the great temple for George's conversion. Here the saint fell on his knees and prayed that the temple with all its idols be straightway destroyed, whereupon fire flashed down from heaven and consumed everything, while the earth in turn yawned open, swallowing up the priests. George then proposed further "sacrifice to idols" in another temple, telling the infuriated proconsul, "If your gods cannot help themselves, how can they be of help to you?"

At this point Dacian's wife (who in the Greek and Latin acts is the Empress Alexandra) converted to Christianity, for which deed he had her suspended by the hair and beaten with staves. The effusion of blood in these circumstances, St. George reassured her, answered for baptism, and she rendered up her soul. On the following day, Dacian ordered St. George to be dragged through the town and then beheaded. The martyr had a prayer granted that *whosoever implored his aid would have his petition answered*, after which he was decapitated. A bolt of lightning forthwith struck down Dacian and his ministers.

Since the Christian persecutions under Diocletian began in the year 303, St. George's death is associated with this date. The scene of his martyrdom is variously given as Diospolis (Lydda) in Palestine, or Nicomedia in Asia Minor. His name is from the Greek *georgos*, "a tiller of the earth," and his feast is 23 April (when the sun has entered Taurus). Apart from his extensive cult in the East, he has been chosen as patron in the West by England, Portugal, Aragon, Valencia, Barcelona, Malta, and Genoa; he is likewise the patron of prisoners, soldiers, and shepherds. The martyr's banner consists of a red cross on a white background.

*

* *

It is clear from the foregoing passages that we have to do with events of a cosmic magnitude. Veneration for St. George enjoyed a popularity in the Middle Ages only surpassed perhaps by that for the Blessed Virgin, countless churches and religious and military orders being dedicated to him; and although he miraculously intervened to aid the Crusaders in their capture of Jerusalem (which had to be preserved as a sanctuary for all Monotheism), he was nevertheless revered by the Saracens as the "White-horsed Knight." Nay, they went even further, claiming according to the Arab historian Mas'ûdî that Jirjîs—as Muslims call the saint—was sent by God during the Prophet's reign to the king of Mosul with the command that he embrace the new faith. The king proved intractable and had Jirjîs slain. God, however, revived him and again sent him to the king, resulting in the same slaying and resurrection as before. When the martyr performed this mission a third time, his persecutor ordered him burned, with his ashes scattered on the Tigris. But God once more miraculously restored the saint to life, this time destroying the king and all his subjects. The Swiss traveler Johann Ludwig Burckhardt noted that "the Turks pay great veneration to St. George."

Now this Jirjîs is identified by Muslims with Elias and al-Khidr (lit. "The Green One"), a mysterious personage or prophet, who like Melchizedek ("King of Righteousness") seems to have "neither beginning of days, nor end of life" (Hebrews 7:3). S. Baring-Gould, for one, has researched the St. George annals from the viewpoint of comparative mythology, and he cites from an *Essay on the Age and Antiquity of the Book of Nabathaean Agriculture*, by Ernest Renan.[2] The book in question is an ancient Nabathaean text by Kûthâmî the Babylonian, which was translated into Arabic around the year 900 by the Chaldaean Muslim, Ibn Wahshîya al-Kasdani. Kûthâmî tells of a divinity named Yanbûshâdh over whose death the gods lamented, "just as all the angels and *sekâ'in* lamented over Tammûzî." This latter event took place at Babylon in the temple of the Sun, whose great golden image was suspended "between heaven and earth," surrounded by images of all the planets. The Babylonian author related how he would weep along with the people when present in the temple during the feast of Tammuz, which was in the month (July) named after the divinity, but that he wept with far greater fervor when it came to the turn of Yanbûshâdh. "The reason is this, that the time of Yanbûshâdh is nearer to our own than the time of Tammuz, and his story is, therefore, more certain and worthy of belief."

Al-Kasdani, the translator, intervenes at this point, saying that in his efforts to ascertain the identity of Tammuz, he came upon full details of the legend in another Nabathaean book: "How he summoned a king to worship the seven (planets) and the twelve (signs), and how the king put him to death several times in a cruel manner, Tammuz coming to life again after each time, until at last he died;

[2] London, 1862.

and behold! it was identical with the legend of St. George that is current among the Christians." Apparently al-Kasdani was unaware of the Islamic Jirjîs, who is given moreover the surname Bâqiyâ[3] ("Surviving") because of his being raised from the dead.

This Tammuz—in the oldest texts (c. 3200 B.C.) *Dumu-zi*, "the son who rises, goes forth (from the nether world)"—was a Sumerian, Babylonian, and Assyrian divinity associated with annual vegetation cycles, and a cosmogonic paradigm of suffering, death, and resurrection. He was humiliated, flogged, imprisoned, drowned in the Euphrates and mourned by the Great Goddess, his sister-mother-lover Innini or Ishtar, by whom he was yearly accompanied into Aralû (the lower regions) and as often revived. Ezekiel (8:14) tells how the women of Jerusalem used to weep at the north gate of the temple for Tammuz, whom St. Jerome in the Vulgate renders as Adonis (*plangentes Adonidem*). J. G. Frazer writes[4] that "some of the old Canaanite kings of Jerusalem appear to have played the part of Adonis in their lifetime, if we may judge from their names, Adoni-bezek and Adoni-zedek,[5] which are divine rather than human titles. Adonizedek means 'lord of righteousness,' and is therefore equivalent to Melchizedek, that is, 'king of righteousness'. . . . Thus if the old priestly kings of Jerusalem regularly played the part of Adonis, we need not wonder that in later times the women of Jerusalem used to weep for Tammuz, that is, for Adonis."

Indeed, the Phoenician Adonis which entered into Greek mythology reveals essentially the same story. It is the identical myth, according to Lucian[6] and others, that carries back to Osiris, the Egyptian god of Judgment, Resurrection, and Immortality: of divine descent in a human body, he was a benevolent king treacherously murdered and dismembered, whereupon his sister-consort Isis and her sister Nephthys uttered a lament until out of pity Ra sent down from heaven

---

[3] Hughes, *Dictionary of Islam*; this form of the word is not given in Arabic dictionaries; it might be a Coptic variant of *bâqî*. In Syria near the Lebanese border is a Greek Orthodox monastery named Mâr Georgos where a three-day festival is annually held for St. George, and which is attended by numbers of both Christian and Muslim faithful, the latter sometimes invoking Jirjîs by the name al-Khidr and sometimes the name Abu 'l-'Abbâs.

[4] *Adonis Attis Osiris*, London, 1909.

[5] Judges 1:4-7; Joshua 10:1 sqq.

[6] *De dea Syria*, n. 7.

Anubis, who with the aid of Horus, Thoth, and the two stricken goddesses managed to piece together the broken body and restore Osiris to life.

"Under the names of Osiris, Tammuz, Adonis, and Attis [the Phrygian counterpart of Adonis]," writes Frazer, "the peoples of Egypt and Western Asia represented the yearly decay and revival of life, especially of vegetable life, which they personified as a god who annually died and rose again from the dead." But Eliade justly observes that "agriculture is only one of the planes upon which the symbolism of periodic regeneration applies. . . . What is primordial and essential is the idea of regeneration, that is, of repetition of the Creation." We have nonetheless noted that the name George etymologically derives from agriculture, and that the saint's feast comes when the sun has entered Taurus, the season of the earth's greatest fecundity.

"As a plant or tree," says Coomaraswamy, "Soma must have been green," a fact he equates with Khwâjâ Khidr ("the Green One"), under whose feet at every step the earth grows green.[7] And this in turn irresistibly conjures up the image of the uncouth warrior-stranger all green, and dressed in green, astride a green horse—in the Arthurian romance of Celtic descent, *Sir Gawain and the Green Knight.* It is the "custom" at Arthur's court on New Year's Day not to serve the banquet until some prodigy has been performed or recounted.

George Lyman Kittredge in a brilliant study on Gawain[8] assembled a large body of parallels, including ones drawn from North American Indian mythology, about heroes "who play fast and loose with their heads"; but it took Coomaraswamy in his "Sir Gawain and the Green Knight: Indra and Numaci,"[9] to demonstrate through Vedic sources the cosmological principle at stake: we are witnessing the drama of World Creation where the Primordial One, the Supreme Person (*Purusha*) has voluntarily to be dismembered through a Sacrifice *in divinis* so that a predestined portion of Infinity's fathomless bounty may be released for manifestation by this beheading, this diremption of Heaven and Earth. "The decapitation is a disenchantment

---

[7] Cf. *Ars Islamica*, I (1934), 174, 175 [Editor's Note: This same article also appears in Ananda K. Coomaraswamy, *What is Civilization? And Other Essays* (Ipswich: Golgonooza Press, 1989)].

[8] *Gawain and the Green Knight*, 1916.

[9] *Speculum*, Cambridge, Mass., January 1944.

of the victim," writes Coomaraswamy, "a liberation of the Sun from the darkness by which he had been obscured and eclipsed. But the Sacrificial death is also a making many from one, in which sense the dismemberment is a consummation desired by the victim himself; and that is the release of all the imprisoned principles, 'All this' (universe) that was contained in 'That One' by whom all beings and all things are breathed out or poured forth at his 'death' and whom . . . 'they could not overcome so long as he was one' (*Taittiriya Aranyaka* V. 1. 3)." Here, says Coomaraswamy, is the key to why "Arthur and his knights—Gods and men—may not *eat* until the champion feat has been performed." "It should be clearly understood," he adds, "and from a Christian point of view will be perfectly intelligible, that the Sacrifice is always a willing victim and the passion self-imposed [the reader may recall that this is invariably the case with George the martyr], at the same time that he is the innocent victim of a passion unjustly imposed upon him; these are only two different ways of regarding one and the same 'event.'"

Moreover, the dismembered deity has in its turn to be reconstructed by a corresponding expiatory Sacrifice here below, in this head-for-a-head requital: the many has now to "offer its neck" in the interests of restoring Unity once again. "There is thus an incessant multiplication of the inexhaustible One and unification of the indefinitely Many."[10] "It cannot be too clearly realized," continues Coomaraswamy in his Gawain article, "that we are dealing with a recurring cycle of events; in this connection it is not at all insignificant that in so many cases the story begins and ends with the 'Year.'" Although mythology is what presently concerns us, it must be stressed that the microcosmic implications in all this are paramount. Still quoting the same author: "It is . . . well known that the express purpose of the Sacrifice, as a rite enacted and to be comprehended, is to build up again, at one and the same time the sacrificer's and the deity's Self, 'whole and complete,'" and that "whoever, like Gawain, searches for the Master Surgeon, to pay his debt, and submits to *this* Headman's axe, will find himself, not without a head, but with another head on his shoulders; just as Gawain, having lain down to die, assuredly stood up again a new man."

These accumulated references, while in no way exhaustive, supply all the evidence needed to identify St. George as the embodiment

[10] Coomaraswamy, *Hinduism and Buddhism*, New York, 1943.

in Christian terms of the Universal Principle of cyclical Cosmogonic Regeneration; and homage for his person is based on the fact that Man as Heaven's Vicegerant on earth (Koran *passim*), thanks to his total intelligence and volitional liberty, is obliged on pain of forfeiting this birthright to participate actively in the "ecological" maintenance of creation in its entirety—Noumenal, animic, and phenomenal. Not that every Christian who venerates the saint is asked to understand his motives in this light, but these explanations are given to show wherein the spiritual efficacy of the worship lies.

If the reader seems to find here an indiscriminate overlapping of myths, this is because with these central solar themes we are at the very heart of the eternal return. The fact remains that all these heroes, gods, and demigods are distinct and separate entities: "Many are his forms and many his existences," says an Egyptian Hymn to Osiris,[11] who is no more Adonis than the latter is Tammuz, it only being at the timeless and omnipresent point of the eternal return that their identities converge.

*

* *

The Church today considers St. George an atavistic carrier of pagan rubbish, and there have not lacked those Christian apologists[12] who wonder in print how such an undisguised heathen could ever have found his way into the Roman Martyrology. But the question can be reversed, to ask how it is conceivable that so universal an archetypal reality could fail to enter the Christian sphere. In any case, enter it did, with the modifications entailed by the nature of the times and peoples and religion to which it was addressed. Gone is the stress on nuptial rites and fecundity, although the feminine counterparts remain, metamorphosed befitting a now chivalric context. Thus we see associated with the saint the Empress Alexandra, sharing in his martyrdom, while the other lady will prove to be the princess in the dragon story, whose chaste girdle serves George as the artifice indis-

---

[11] Margaret A. Murray, *Egyptian Religious Poetry*, London, 1949. The affinity alluded to is what the Hindus call *bhedâbheda* ("distinction without difference") or as Eckhart says, "fused but not confused." St. George and his predecessors all belong to the same spiritual family.

[12] Calvin, Gibbon, and a host of lesser luminaries.

pensable for charming the monster into docility. This theme even turns up in the Green Knight, whose lady's green silken girdle, worn at her conniving by Gawain—who as will be shown is none other than the fearsome knight's alter-ego—saves him from her husband's death-blow. The second lady in this Arthurian romance is Morgan le Fay, on whose magical powers, acquired from Merlin, the whole tale hinges.

Incidentally, the heathenish wailings for Tammuz will seem less outlandish if one remembers the central role the Passion plays in the Latin Rite. And certainly the analogies between Osiris and Christ have not been overlooked by scholars in comparative religion: both figures are celebrated for a Passion and a Resurrection, Osiris as Judge and King of the Dead corresponds to Christ the Pantocrator, and without undue speculation the two Gospel Marys might in some way be identified with Isis and Nephthys; at least it is well established that the cult of Isis passed across into that of the Blessed Virgin, as attested by the number of Marian shrines in the Middle Ages erected on temple sites formerly dedicated to pagan deities.

But why now this apparent divagation concerning Christ? The reason is that St. George was lauded in mediaeval times as though a prolongation of the Savior, and as the Virgin's right arm, or what in Buddhist terms would be called a Christian Bodhisattva: his *whosoever implores my aid shall receive it* is a direct echo of the Gospel's "whatsoever ye shall ask in my name, that will I do" (John 14:13). His is likewise the theme of martyrdom and revival; he too has the cross for emblem; they both are celebrated at Eastertide, when the Year is reborn; and just as St. Michael is the celestial champion of the Redeemer, and of her who shall crush the serpent's head, so is St. George the terrestrial counterpart, and in this Messianic context the patron of those soldiers who battle for the Heavenly Jerusalem, since "this generation [the final Year of our cosmic cycle] shall not pass, till all these things be fulfilled" (Matthew 24:34).

The same context also brings in the dragon, whose history did not just appear as a pious afterthought belatedly tacked onto the *Golden Legend,* and in fact it can be traced as far back as the sixth century. Voragine himself refers to variants in the story recounted by "other authors"; therefore apart from oral traditions there must have been written documents known at his time. The monster's credibility was doomed to expire with the close of the Middle Ages, for early in the sixteenth century Pope Clement VII boldly managed to dispatch the beast through the facile expedient of cutting out his mention upon reformation of the Missals and Breviaries. This now left the Roman Church (for the Orthodox is not partner to the act) with one problem in place of two, and it would only be a matter of time before George himself disappeared—so closely are his and the dragon's destinies intertwined. But first let us recall the version given by the Italian Dominican chronicler.

The young Cappadocian knight on his travels chanced to pass near a pagan city in Libya called Silene, bordering which lay a vast swamp infested by an insatiable dragon that repeatedly put to flight an armed host intending its destruction. In his forays against the city his pestilential breath even killed those just within the walls. To fend off the monster the citizens finally offered him two sheep a day, but the supply soon ran short, so that they had no expedient save to furnish each time along with a sheep one of their children, a boy or a girl, drawn by lots. The town was practically emptied of youths when it fell the turn of the king's only daughter to be sacrificed. The grief-stricken monarch proposed his gold and silver and half his realm in her stead—anything that could spare the maiden this horrible fate, all of which merely served to heighten the anger of his bereaved subjects, who reminded him that he it was who had issued the edict, consequently his duty now lay in abiding by it, at the risk of being put to the torch, along with his palace. Thereupon, summoning the princess, he adorned her in royal robes, lamenting the fate that was to banish evermore his dreams for her of a princely marriage.

The princess (who in old ballads is named Sabra) then fell at her father's feet to receive his benediction, after which she departed for the swamp. At this moment St. George appeared, who asked the cause of her weeping. "Good youth," she replied, "quickly mount your horse and fly, lest you perish with me!" "Have no fear of that, my child," he answered, "but tell me why are you in tears, before this crowd standing on the walls?" Finding her entreaties for his departure of no avail, she recounted the whole dismal story. Even while she spoke, the monster raised his scaly head above the marshes. All trembling, the virgin cried, "Fly, fly, sir knight!"

By way of response, George mounted his steed, and, recommending himself to God with the sign of the cross, brandished his lance and charged the dragon, now advancing upon him. With a single stroke the beast was transfixed and overthrown. George then bade the princess pass her girdle round the neck of the monster, who rose and followed her like a little dog on a leash.

When they reached the town, the people fled in terror; but St. George summoned them back, explaining that he had been sent by the Lord to deliver them of their affliction, and inviting them to join the Christian faith. On that day the king and all his people were baptized. Then the saint drew his sword and killed the dragon, whose carcass was carted away by four pairs of oxen. The king had an immense church constructed in honor of the Blessed Virgin and St. George, and from it issued a fountain whose waters cured all wasting diseases. After distributing to the poor the largesse he had received from the king, George instructed the monarch on the rules of religion, embraced him, and departed.

Some authors recount that George killed the dragon outright; while other stories tell of the princess shut up in a castle whose subjects are perishing for lack of water, the only source, at the base of a hill, being guarded by the "laidly worm," from which George duly delivers them.

*

* *

Of greater importance is the motif's universality. Perseus and Andromeda have already been mentioned. "Similar stories were prevalent in Greece. In the isle of Salamis, Cenchrius, a son of Poseidon, relieved the inhabitants from the scourge of a similar monster, who devastated the island. At Thespia, a dragon ravaged the country round the city; Zeus ordered the inhabitants to give the monster their children by lot. One year it fell on Cleostratus. Menestratus determined to save him, he armed himself with a suit covered with hooks, and was devoured by the dragon, which perished in killing him."[13]

The Aryan prototype for all this is in the Vedic encounter of Indra with the great serpent Ahi—alternatively known as Vritra, "Drought," or Namuci, "Holdfast"—who has confiscated the waters, which are only to be released when Indra dismembers the Titan with his thunderbolt. The corresponding Persian myth concerns the overthrowing of Ahriman by Mithra; there is also the Iranian hero Thraetona who slew Dahak, a three-headed dragon. For European counterparts, we have the Teutonic myth of Siegfried, who overcomes a mighty dragon and despoils him of the Rheingold belonging to the river nymphs,

[13] Baring-Gould, *op. cit.*

and which finds its Scandinavian parallel in the story of Sigurd. The Anglo-Saxon Beowulf is likewise a dragon-slayer.

Further instances outside the Aryan sphere could be gathered from the shamanistic and animistic traditions of North America and Africa; but we shall limit ourselves to one Asiatic parallel because of its pertinence here, namely, an episode recounted in that inimitable Chinese blend of wit-with-wisdom, Wu Ch'êng-ên's sixteenth-century spiritual allegory, *Monkey (Hsi Yu Ki)*, based on the travels to India of the renowned Chinese Buddhist pilgrim and scholar, Hsüan Tsang (600?-664 A.D.).

Tripitaka—as the Buddhist saint is by-named in the tale for the scriptures he is seeking—with Monkey (the Great Ego) and two other uncouth traveling companions, all pledging his protection in return for their salvation, has reached a place bordering on a great body of water presided over by a monster deity who, in exchange for bringing the local inhabitants rain in due season and fertility, demands the yearly sacrifice of a boy or girl. This time he is after Tripitaka; and it is only through Monkey's final recourse to the Bodhisattva in the Southern Ocean, the goddess Kuan-yin (Avalokitesvara), the "Regarder of the Cries of the World" (*Whosoever implores my aid shall receive it*), that the monster king is dispatched—and this by the divinity's expedient of tying to her sash (here we have again the girdle talisman) a bamboo basket in which the fiend is retrieved from the waters, and who now turns out to be nothing but a golden fish. "It is a goldfish that I reared in my lotus pond," she explains. "Every day it used to put its head out and listen to the scriptures, thus acquiring great magical powers." But one day a flood came, washing it out to sea, whence began all the mischief. The citizens gather in gratitude to do obeisance to the Bodhisattva while a skilled painter makes her portrait; "and this was the beginning of the form of Kuan-yin known as 'Kuan-yin with the Fish-basket.'"[14]

History

Our task is now to determine in the measure possible where mythology contemporizes with history. There are two historical moments in the life of every person on earth which are inexorably real and yet totally outside the reach of empirical consciousness: the moment

---

[14] *Monkey*, Arthur Waley's translation, New York, 1943, p. 253 ff.

of birth, and the moment of death. These two decisive events occur moreover exactly once, over the entire lifespan of the individual, and scarcely enter into his reflections at all—everything else considered.

The transition of timelessness into time. Ancient man, it was indicated, existed in a spatial, atemporal world, not that he lacked the notion of time—one has only to regard his astronomy—but it was less *time* as we know it than movement and rhythm, a set of recurring events perpetually related back to a static Center, the way in Hindu music that the mode or *râga* while developing never ceases weaving around the basic tonic. Schuon writes that "traditions having a prehistoric origin are, symbolically speaking, made for 'space' and not for 'time'; that is to say, they saw the light in a primordial epoch when time was still but a rhythm in a spatial and static beatitude, and when space or simultaneity still predominated over the experience of duration and change. The historical traditions on the other hand must take the experience of 'time' into account and must foresee instability and decadence, since they were born in periods when time had become like a fast-flowing river and ever more devouring, and when the spiritual outlook had to be centered on the end of the world."[15]

Eliade regards Messianism as constituting a major shift into the historical perspective, where *in illo tempore* is now projected from the Center out to the Future, thus necessitating faith in a promised Good which is yet to come. Still, even here history is rejected in the sense of something positive, and is only tolerated as the "world in travail" while awaiting its consummation in the apocatastasis, that final Event which shall definitively deliver it from time. It must of course be stressed, in keeping with what Schuon says above, that there was nothing arbitrary in this transition to a historical or Messianic view taken by the later religions, that the adaptation was cosmologically forced on them with time more and more devouring space in a world cycle now rushing towards its expiration. Even Hinduism and its emphasis on the "eternal law" or *sanâtana dharma*—the same as the eternal return—has its place for the *Kalki avatâra*, the Solar Hero who awaits the moment when the Dragon *Mâyâ* in the form of time (*kâla*) is about to swallow space (simultaneity, "staticity," Eternal Present, Supreme Center), to strike his decisive blow that will reverse all inverted values, and usher in a new cycle (Age, Year).

[15] *Light on the Ancient Worlds*, p. 14. As an example of how the present with traditional peoples predominated over time, the Mayans would graphically represent through a single composite image the birth, lifespan, and death of an individual.

This Event, as Eliade shows, is prefigured in the New Year cere-monies and rites that have prevailed in varying forms the world over, typically characterized on the one hand by the abolition of past time, the abolition of order, a flouting of normal values in favor of general permissiveness—by Saturnalian orgies, universal confusion, the extinction of the sacred fire, and chaos, namely, the "descent into hell"; and on the other hand, by confession of sins, expulsion of the scapegoat, the rekindling of the sacred fire, the return of the dead, regeneration, initiation, and consecration of the new harvest. Sometimes a combat is enacted between a divinity and the primordial dragon (the serpent often symbolizing preformal chaos). Also, the twelve days of midwinter were held in Vedic times to foretoken the twelve months of the coming year (*Rg Veda* IV. 33. 7), a belief likewise maintained in Europe concerning the twelve days between Christmas and Epiphany.

But with Christianity the Year becomes unique, macrocosmic, and historically "once for all" (Hebrews 10:10) of "this generation," although microcosmically recurrence or periodicity is still retained, as in the liturgical calendar. Whereas formerly the high priest carried out the sacrifice following "the patterns of things in the heavens" and entered "into the holy place each year with blood of others," Christ now "by his own blood . . . entered in once into the holy place," for it was not meet "that he should offer himself often. . . . For then must he often have suffered since the foundation of the world: but now once in the end of the world hath he appeared to put away sin by the sacrifice of himself" (Hebrews 9).

Christianity's conflict with the various paganisms it encountered can thus in part at least be explained as a rivalry between the classic spatial or periodic perspective and the newly revealed temporal or historical one, which—independently of other considerations—being more "timely" was precisely bound to prevail. Yet the bane of historic-ity is secularization, and man being what he is, it suffices but a subtle shift in focus for "the measureless and perilous world of forms and of change," hitherto regarded as something negative to be rejected, now to be seen as something positive to be espoused. The outer world becomes reality, matter assumes an increased importance, and man experiences a Renaissance marked by humanism with its concept of indefinite progress and human or worldly perfectibility. This entails in consequence a loss of contact with higher states of being, mythology is relegated to a realm equatable with the incredible, while sacred history itself in turn becomes "myth."

Islam, the last of the historical religions, actually seizes hold of time itself as a sword with which to destroy all time: the *Shahâdah* or Witness "*Lâ ilâha illa 'Llâh*—There is no divinity if not the Divinity" destroys through a transformation that refers and ultimately renders everything back to its Origin; the Event or Final Day or Judgment is not only ceaselessly proclaimed as immanent, Islam itself is in a way already that Event or Judgment. The past and the future are more geometric than temporal; Allah "is the First and the Last, and the Outward and the Inward";[16] there is purely the desertic fatality of the omnipresent Now, and this Now belongs to God. For the Muslim believer, the world is thus in part illusion and in part theophany, but at all events never more than a veil (*hijâb*) covering Reality.

It goes without saying that the Christian believer (wherever he still exists) is likewise no secularist: he is the first to "let the dead bury their dead" and is more predisposed than not to turn his back on the world itself as the personification of evil. He is a man who only endures history while awaiting the glory of the Kingdom to come.

*

* *

For the needs of this study, history is envisaged in a dual role: micro-cosmic and macrocosmic—inward and outward. Inward: we all have inside the brief time allotted—at the risk of ruin—to kill the dragon that holds our soul in captivity. This is the history that is transacting incessantly within us. Outward: inevitably, in the nature of things there have been monster-idols that historically more than once have held a human collectivity in thralldom, until dispatched or slain by a solar hero.

Likewise, just as it is incumbent on all men to seek redemption—and there are those who have experienced spiritual rebirth even in this lifetime—so can it be acknowledged on trustworthy religious testi-

---

[16] Koran LVII. 3. Cf. Schuon, *Forme et Substance dans les Religions*, Paris, 1975 the chapter "La croix 'temps-espace' dans l'onomatologie koranique" [Editor's Note: See Frithjof Schuon, *Form and Substance in the Religions* (Bloomington, IN: World Wisdom, 2002), the chapter "The Cross of Space and Time in Koranic Onomatology"]

mony that Christ and certain saints of earlier ages have exceptionally raised the dead back to life. Again, as man is intended to be a creature capable of walking on the waters, in the sense of dominating his psychic substance, so indeed must there have been holy men capable upon spiritual occasion of outwardly walking on water, especially given that miracles themselves are none other than inward truths dramatized in outward events. The same with alchemy as an initiatic technique: just as the "artist" strives to transform base substances into "gold," so are there cases on record of alchemists achieving literal transmutations.

Myth is easier to "trace" than exceptional historical events, because the former is perennial, while the latter are "effaced" in the passage of time, with the added difficulty that a historical event which is sacred in character is already partially lifted out of the stream of time—as will be shown in the last section of this article.

In bafflement people face the stark "fact" of Stonehenge, the masonry at Cuzco, the monuments of Easter Island, the Nazca line drawings discernible only at high altitude, or the great menhir of Locmariaquer—possibilities the world today would scoff at, had the evidence not yet vanished. For how to account for a menhir (now lying broken in four pieces) that was originally over twenty-three meters high and weighing three hundred tons, which would have required three thousand men to raise after being transported from a distant quarry on a well-made road (of which no trace exists at Locmariaquer)? One often finds menhirs, moreover, as it were casually set in the earth without apparent regard for engineering or the specifics of gravity, the broad end up and the pointed end down—as though suspended from heaven.

Our modern world as such would have been totally inconceivable—not to say incomprehensible—to the men of these former cultures, yet we blandly assume that anything out of the ordinary reported of their times which cannot be authenticated in a monument, museum, shard, or scientific archive, quite simply never existed. If St. George was a historical personage, then where is a bone to prove it? And the same goes for dragons.

And yet if we are to allow for the hypothesis that the peoples of these former periods might have been something more than mere evolutionary monsters groping towards the daylight, we ought at least in the interests of objectivity to credit their traditions with a modicum of good faith. To do the contrary is all the more illogical when our science itself is continually running up against possibilities which yesterday would scarcely have crossed the imagination.

The fabulous creatures of antiquity can be envisaged in three categories: those which have a purely mythological symbolism, such as the sphinx and the winged lion; those which additionally are materializations of beings from the subtle domain, such as perchance the mermaid or the unicorn; and those which existed physically according to fossil evidence or the accounts of early naturalists and compilations in bestiaries, such as the dinotherium, and possibly the sea serpent, the behemoth, and basilisk. The dragon appears to belong to all three categories, although its historical verification is what most interests us for the moment.

In the great zoological work of Conrad von Gesner, *Historia animalium* (Zurich, 1551-58), dragons figure as part of the fauna known to science. By Solinus' account (3rd century A.D.), the Egyptians kept a species tame in their houses as good geniuses, an observation which brings to mind the thirty-two thousand pottery figurines discovered in the region of Acambaro, some hundred and sixty kilometers northwest of Mexico City, in 1945 by Waldemar Julsrud, and among which is a statuette dating around 2,500 B.C. of a young girl nude playing with a creature about her size, that looks for all the world like a dinosaur? Without attempting to claim a foothold for dinosaurs in the Quaternary period, we can nonetheless propose that there could be a closer parentage between dragons and prehistoric monsters than is known to modern science. In the Pentateuch (Numbers 21:6) we read that "the Lord sent fiery serpents among the people, and they bit the people; and much people of Israel died." And Deuteronomy (8:15) speaks about "that great and terrible wilderness, wherein were fiery serpents, and scorpions, and drought."

Whatever the beast St. George encountered, it was clearly more than just a physical monster, otherwise the king's army in Voragine's account would speedily have dispatched it, nor would the citizens in the Eastern version have been provoked into idolatry. No, it had to be a being incarnating a tenacious diabolical force of an intensity such that only an intervention from heaven could dissolve, and this at an age when the cosmos was less "solidified" than now—and thus more accessible to the interpenetration of powers both from above and below.

*

* *

Concerning the "historicity" of St. George, which was first really put in doubt by Calvin,[17] it is at the outset inconceivable that with countless thousands of known Christian martyrs to choose from, the early Church would have singled out for the greatest veneration of all some "unknown soldier": the ancient Church authorities may have been "primitive" by our lights, but they were not imbeciles; and the verbal dueling excelled in by the likes of the Dyophysites, Monophysites, Aphthartodocetaes, Phthartolatraes, Agnoetaes, and Aktistetaes does not betoken a mentality that would let a spurious saint of such magnitude slip through the net were there the slightest doubt of his authenticity.

The Transactions of the Royal Society of Literature[18] refer to a Greek inscription from an ancient church converted out of a heathen temple in Ezra, Syria, dated 346, wherein St. George is named as a holy martyr. Constantine (r. 306-337) dedicated a great church to the saint over his tomb near Lydda, and later according to one tradition the Emperor had the martyr's bones translated to a church in Constantinople that was originally a temple of Juno. A church dating from the fourth century was built to him at Thessalonica, and more inscriptions are found in ruined churches in Egypt and Mesopotamia. Clovis erected the monastery at Baralle in honor of St. George c. 512. Ramula, the ancient Arimathaea, also bore the name of Georgia. It was around the year 1348 that King Edward III made him patron of England.

St. Ambrose (340?-397) within a century of George's day was extolling his virtues in referring to the destruction of Dacian's temple: "George, the faithful soldier of Christ, at a time when Christianity was hidden, alone dared courageously to proclaim his faith in the Son of God. . . . And not only did he never let himself be seduced by temporal power, but, making game of his persecutor, he annihilated the temple with all its idols." Ambrose also signals out the torment of the Empress Alexandra as proof "that martyrdom in the absence of

---

[17] "*Nil eos Christo reliquum facere qui pro nihilo ducunt ejus intercessionem, nisi accedant Georgius aut Hippolitus, aut similes larvae.*"

[18] Second Series, vol. vii. pt. i.

baptism, makes it possible to possess the kingdom of heaven." Now to convince this learned Church Doctor that he was the victim of a pious hoax would be tantamount to convincing the present-day Sioux that Crazy Horse (killed in 1877) was nothing but a legend.

The sanctity of St. George is likewise attested and conveyed through a vast iconographical tradition ascending the centuries to the earliest times, and it suffices to say that the dulia accorded to icons is under a rigid ecclesiastical control which would far from tolerate the heroes of fairy tales being admitted into the company of the saints. "In the charismatic economy of every intrinsically orthodox religion there is in fact a protective power which keeps a watchful eye on the integrity of the various elements of worship, even if they are no more than secondary, and this power results from the presence of the Holy Spirit, and is thus not unconnected with the mystery of infallibility. . . . When it comes to ancient cults, historically dubious, but deep-rooted and hence efficacious, the Holy Spirit, or what Muslims would call the *barakah*, must be 'given a free hand'. . . ; one must have a feeling for the concrete meaning of sacred phenomena, and trust in the para-cletic and charismatic power which animates the body of religion."[19]

These considerations have to do with what theology has always recognized as *the rights of immemorial custom.*

*
*   *

One April day in 1961, the late Richard Cardinal Cushing, then Roman Catholic archbishop of Boston, was being chauffeured in his black limousine some seventeen miles southwest of the city through the greening Massachusetts landscape, on route to dedicate the first Catholic church in the little town of Dover—red brick St. Philomena's, which the three-year-old parish had just completed, when suddenly his attention froze on an item in the newspaper he was scanning: the Vatican's Sacred Congregation of Rites had stricken St. Philomena, "the virgin martyr," from the register of saints. Already the cardinal had distributed eight hundred statuettes of St. Philomena to Dover's Catholics, and the stained-glass window to her was in place. Solemnly

---

[19] Schuon, "On Relics," *Studies in Comparative Religion*, Summer 1975 [Editor's Note: This same article appears in Frithjof Schuon, *Esoterism as Principle and as Way* (Pates Manor, Bedfont: Perennial Books, 1981)].

before the startled congregation, Cardinal Cushing dedicated their new edifice as the "Church of the Most Precious Blood." "It was a difficult job," he said afterwards. "It was like telling the Irish there was no St. Patrick."

Little could he suspect that the Church would presently be telling the Irish—or at any rate the non-Irish—just that. But there was nothing to be done. Archaeology was triumphing over credulity, and the faithful could take it or leave it. What after all was Philomena for exact science but the fractured skull of an adolescent girl and a clot of something suggesting blood in a glass phial, discovered on 24 May 1802 in the catacomb of St. Priscilla on Rome's Via Saleria Nova, with fragments of Latin on tiles jumbled over the grave: *Lumena paxte cum fi*, which religious zeal made to read *Pax tecum Filumena?*

However, symbols adjacent to the tomb—two anchors, three arrows, a palm, and a flower or torch—were, including the rest, enough to convince the "credulous" that they had to do with a bona fide martyr; and in 1805 Pope Pius VII allowed a priest, Don Francis di Lucia, to have the bones enshrined in the church of Mugnano del Cardinale near Naples, which inaugurated a flood of miracles. With a Neapolitan nun, Sister Mary Louisa of Jesus, receiving a series of revelations on the saint's life and martyrdom that formed the substance of a biography compiled by Don Francis, Philomena's identity was complete, and in 1837 Pope Gregory XVI authorized her public veneration with 11 August as feast day, for which Pope Pius IX approved a Mass and office in 1855. The churches dedicated to her number in the hundreds upwards. Perhaps the saint's most celebrated triumph was the devotion she showered on St. John Vianney (1786-1859), France's famed Cure d'Ars: "my dear little saint," and "agent in heaven," as he called her.

Given this emotionally charged "cult," the complete success of Philomena's desanctification proved a signal victory for Rome and the spirit of Vatican II, and soon a taste for blood far stronger than that desiccated crumb in a phial was reaching from the Eternal City to Brussels, where the venerable Bollandists labored overtime at the Collège de St. Michel on their *Analecta Bollandiana* and *Acta Sanctorum* carving the Martyrology down to proposed scientific proportion. Hagiology would never be the same again. They hacked away at the Fourteen Holy Helpers until the Vatican decided that this company was to be disbanded if not entirely liquidated, thus removing Sts. Catherine of Alexandria (whose "legend," according to Donald

Attwater's updated version[20] of Alban Butler's eighteenth-century *Lives of the Saints,* is one of the "most preposterous of its kind," there being no "positive evidence that she ever existed outside the mind of some Greek writer who first composed what he intended to be simply an edifying romance"), Barbara (no more than a "spurious legend" for Attwater, and "pious romance"), Christopher, and George (here Attwater, being English, demurs, professing that the endeavors to eliminate him "are more remarkable for their ingenuity than for their cogency"; and in fact the Church has had to let George remain in England, contenting itself with demoting him there to a "second-rank" saint—which is a way of "damning with faint praise").

The wonder is that St. Margaret survived, she whom Attwater dismisses as "a fictitious romance," and among whose unpardonable ordeals was that of being swallowed by a dragon—her emblem to boot. Other saints, of course, not in the aforementioned holy company (which received an enormous veneration, originating in Germanic countries from the time of their intercession during the Black Death of the fourteenth century, and later spreading out to Italy and America) have been given the ax, such as Cecilia ("a fabrication" in Attwater's book), and of all people, Louis of France, who although lauded by Attwater as the epitome of integrity, was demoted to second rank—for being too regal, perchance. Then how did St. Ursula, the subject of "false relics" and "forged epitaphs" . . . "preposterously elaborated through the mistakes of imaginative visionaries" (Attwater), escape—if indeed she has? And why for the rest, may we ask, is the Vatican out to out-martyr the martyrdoms of the ancient pagan Rome—even if it is child's work to massacre what are now held to be no more than names?

Eliade again furnishes the clue: in the "primitive" ontological conception, "an object or an act becomes real only insofar as it imitates or repeats an archetype. Thus, reality is acquired solely through repetition or participation; everything which lacks an exemplary model is 'meaningless,' i.e., it lacks reality. . . . [Hence] the man of a traditional culture sees himself as real only to the extent that he ceases to be himself (for a modern observer) and is satisfied with imitating and repeating the gestures of another. In other words, he sees himself as real, i.e., as 'truly himself,' only, and precisely, insofar as he ceases

---

[20] *The Penguin Dictionary of Saints.*

to be so. Hence it could be said that this 'primitive' ontology has a Platonic structure."

The second aspect of archaic ontology according to Eliade is "the abolition of time through the imitation of archetypes and the repetition of paradigmatic gestures. . . . All sacrifices are performed at the same mythical instant of the beginning. . . . There is an implicit abolition of profane time, of duration, of 'history'; and he who reproduces the exemplary gesture thus finds himself transported into the mythical epoch in which its revelation took place."

The conclusion is inescapable: a church dedicated to temporizing must of necessity "demythologize"; it is impossible to plunge into the mainstream of history, with all that secularization implies, while pretending that "my kingdom is not of this world"; accordingly it is the "non-historical" saints—that clutter of "dead" hagiographical lumber—which have to go; those fabulous martyrs of the first Christian centuries whose lives are cloaked in the miraculous. These are the great apotropaic and intercessionary saints, the Bodhisattvas of Christianity; they are, citing Schuon, "like the appearance of stars on earth; they reascend after their death to the firmament, to their eternal home; they are almost pure symbols, spiritual signs only provisionally detached from the celestial iconostasis in which they have been enshrined since the creation of the world."[21]

As with St. George, St. Christopher emerges from an interfusion of archetypal entities, he being "successor" to Anubis, Hermes, Atlas, and Herakles; St. Ursula for her part can be traced back to the Swabian goddess Ursel or Hörsel, whose emblem was a ship, and whom Tacitus in his *Germania* (ix) relates to Isis: "A part of the Suevi sacrifice to Isis."[22] If Ursula has been left unmolested by the authorities, it may be that her cult in recent years has had nothing matching the amplitude of that for Christopher, Philomena, and others; besides, those powers committed to the task of "social involvement" are concerned with a work of dismemberment rather than extermination, which would be too transparent and thus self-defeating—almost like trying to eliminate the Blessed Virgin herself, a possibility which if not wholly excluded, has nonetheless yet to see its time.

---

[21] *Light on the Ancient Worlds*, p. 34.

[22] Baring-Gould, *op. cit.* This hagiographer adduces Ursula's pagan antecedents as "painful" proof of her spuriousness; whereas we take exactly the opposite view, namely, that her filiation in the eternal return attests to her authenticity.

In "burying" St. George and thereby pretending he who offers perpetual intercession does not even exist, the "official" Church is announcing a truth: namely, that it has become secularized and cut off from the sacred, from its whole *raison d'être*. In its worldly zeal to make—rather than transcend—history, the tables are thus turned, for it now has inescapably taken over the role of "Holdfast," keeping back the Waters of Life. Says Coomaraswamy: "A church or society—the Hindu would make no distinction—that does not provide a way of escape from its own regimen, and will not let its people go, is defeating its own ultimate purpose."[23]

The Confluence of the Sacred and the Secular

Myth connotes Mystery: there is a discontinuity and inviolable barrier between each plane of existence as well as in the reversal of values between the sacred and the profane that leaves the former inaccessible to the reaches of purely human calculation and endeavor. This "Cloud of Unknowing" is called in Islam a *barzakh*, separating the higher from the lower, this life from the next; it is the veil (*hijâb*) in Sufic symbolism: "Seventy Thousand Veils separate Allah, the One Reality, from the world of matter and of sense";[24] and but for these "veils," the intensity of the Supernal Sun would consume the whole world in an instant, being why they are only withdrawn at the end of time. Their "weaving" and manipulation so to speak are wrought through *Mâyâ*.

On the other hand, were there no communication whatsoever between different levels of reality, "myth" would forever remain *in potentia*, and "history" would never be transformed by the divine act of Creation from chaos into cosmos.[25] There has accordingly to be some manner of interpenetration, and this is represented symbolically by the double spiral, of which the *yin-yang* is an Eastern variant; or again, by what traditional geometry understands when speaking about "the squaring of the circle," an example of which is offered in Islamic architecture, where the round dome ("heaven") of a mosque is harmoniously blended into the cubic base ("earth") through means of an intermediary octagonal structure. It is to the same liaison that

[23] *Hinduism and Buddhism*, p. 29.

[24] This teaching, cited in Reynold A. Nicholson's *The Mystics of Islam*, London, 1963, p. 15, is based on a saying (*hadîth*) of Muhammad.

[25] Eliade, p. 10.

the "strait gate" in the Gospels refers, and of which the neck in the hourglass affords a symbol.

The passage from time to Eternity is somehow unseizable, like the instant between wakefulness and sleep, life and death; for it involves an inversion of values, a *metanoia* ("intellectual metamorphosis" in Coomaraswamy's rendering). "The road leading to the center," writes Eliade, "is a 'difficult road' (*dûrohana*), and this is verified at every level of reality. . . . The road is arduous, fraught with perils, because it is, in fact, a rite of the passage from the profane to the sacred, from the ephemeral and illusory to reality and eternity, from death to life, from man to the divinity. Attaining the center is equivalent to a consecration, an initiation; yesterday's profane and illusory existence gives place to a new, to a life that is real, enduring, and effective." By the same token, death for archaic man is nothing other than a return to *illud tempus*, since he identifies with the gods (archetypes) and not simply with a higher animal existence (history).

In demonstrating that the eternal archetypes alone are truly real, however, Eliade does not develop the corollary just mentioned that without manifestation (history) they remain for us on our level only *in potentia*, which is to say that if the solar hero and the dragon belong purely to the domain of mythological archetypes, this condemns St. George to a wingless duplication of St. Michael, given that the latter perfectly executes on the supernal plane (Rev. 12:7) all the functions attributed to George in his historical role "down here." Yet even were this the case, which it is not, the fact holds that the veneration offered to a non-historical entity would still carry across to the everlasting archetype, which ultimately belongs to that sphere out of which inter-cession operates. "In defining myth," writes Schuon, "one should not lay undue stress on this supposed lack of historical basis, for the func-tion of myth is such that once it has been properly understood the question of historicity ceases to have any practical importance. What guarantees the spiritual function of a sacred story is its symbolism, on the one hand, and its traditional character, on the other."[26] Not to mention its proven salvatory efficacy over the centuries.

The Japanese, who manifest a contemplative "plasticity" more pronounced than that shown by most Westerners, have no difficulty

---

[26] *Logic and Transcendence*, New York, 1975, the chapter "Dharmâkara's Vow." Considerations pertinent to this article are also to be found in the chapter, "Some Observations on the Symbolism of the Hourglass."

accepting the historical existence of the Bodhisattva Dharmâkara, whose cult as the Buddha Amitâbha receives enormous veneration in the different schools of Amidaism—and this without the aid of archaeology or relics, Dharmâkara belonging to a world system antedating ours by ten *Kalpas* (meaning, figuratively, some forty-three billion, two hundred million solar years). There is only the Buddha Shâkya-Muni's word for it, whose own existence has been cast in doubt by certain European orientalists. Now Dharmâkara's Vow not to enter Nirvana except on condition that the invocation of his name be the means for saving myriad souls, finds a resonance in St. George's *Whosoever implores my aid shall receive it*; and the fact that Amitâbha belongs to a category of Buddhas classed as *anupapadaka* "without parentage" relates with what was noted earlier concerning al-Khidr and Melchizedek.

Saying that the essential in mythology is its spiritual symbolism and not its historical substantiation is somewhat the same as proclaiming that *Âtman* alone is real and the world illusory: while this is perfectly true metaphysically, for us on a less exalted plane the world does indeed exist, since we are caught willy-nilly in the teeth of history, or the world of forms, time and space.

Certainly the inward truth takes precedence over its outward expression; but to infer from this that the outward is "merely" symbolical and qua *event* never happened nor need happen, is to "Protestantize" everything and by consequence cut oneself off from very real and *substantial* means of grace. Muhammad said the inner Holy War is greater than the outer; he did not deny the outer, either in his words or actions—to say the least. Were the Logos "purely of the next world," there would be no reason for Jesus and the founders of other religions to manifest in history. Yet for this matter, what is known of the Nazarene in profane documents, apart from incidental references by Josephus, Tacitus, and Suetonius? As for Gautama Buddha, we possess no independently verifiable historical records whatever to authenticate his existence.

The overwhelming evidence of the Incarnation launched the early Church; the dilemma tearing it apart in the Arian and Christological controversies was not a scrupling about *whether* Christ existed—*quod absit*—but about *how* he existed: an excruciating examination of theological conscience bent on reconciling the hypostatic union of incorruptible Essence with limitative form—this confluence between the Sacred and the temporal, the Infinite and finite, Myth and history, Archetype and image—an interpenetration in Nicaean terminology neither Monophysitic (one nature) nor Monothelitic (one will) nor Homoiousian (the Son essentially like the Father), but rather Homoousian (identical) or "consubstantial," that is, "one person with two natures and wills." In brief, the mystery surrounding the manner of God's confrontation with the world is only resolvable, as Schuon's writings demonstrate, through recourse to the doctrine of *Mâyâ*, a concept missing in Christian theology. No major religion, however, is lacking any of the necessary truths expressed in one form or another, and a fascinating Christian parallel to *Mâyâ* is found in Jacob Boehme's *Sex Puncta Mystica* (V. 1. f.), where as Coomaraswamy says, one has only to substitute "*Mâyâ*" for the author's "Magic" to obtain the Hindu doctrine. Given the considerations on *Mâyâ* brought up in this article, it is worth citing a few extracts from Boehme:

> Magic [*Mâyâ*] is the mother of eternity, of the being of all beings; for it creates itself, and is understood in desire.

> It is in itself nothing but a will, and this will is the great mystery of all wonders and secrets, but brings itself by the imagination of the desireful hunger into being.

> It is the formative power in the eternal wisdom . . . a mother in all three worlds, and makes each thing after the model of that thing's will . . . and lends itself to good or to evil. . . .

> It is without understanding, and yet comprehends all; for it is the comprehension of all things. . . .

> In sum: Magic [*Mâyâ*] is the activity in the Will-spirit.

*
* *

Witnessing the dance-dramas in Bali when the island's traditions were still shielded under a perceptive Dutch rule, this author felt a peculiar incertitude as to whether the dancers were simply enacting sacred history, or whether instead some archetypal cosmic event itself was about to burst through the fragile structure of the dance—so interpenetrated was ritual with Reality. And these dancers did in their trances pass for the time being into that archetypal world which their dance commemorates.[27]

Obviously, a major "historical" cosmological event cannot take place but exceptionally. It was shown that the New Year ceremonies celebrate the "end of the world" and the beginning of a new one annually; the historical occurrence happens only once in aeons; but like death which strikes exactly once in a lifetime, the point is: it *does* happen. And these primary moments—whether macro- or microcosmic—are fundamentally ungraspable and unimpartible, being situated on the margin of history and time, "as a thief in the night."

Yet this very margin (veil or *barzakh*) borders on the eternal return, for as René Guénon has demonstrated,[28] where time (or history) stops, there is no more succession; everything is accordingly in perfect simultaneity, that is, integrally and undividedly present in an Eternal Now, which will be more or less partial or total depending on the level of reality envisaged. From this Center the archetypal saints, gods, and mythological heroes allied to any particular world-sector radiate outward like multiple sparkles from a same family of gems to various historical "moments"—thus accounting for the ostensible overlapping of spiritual entities, so baffling to proponents of the historical or scientific approach.

The dichotomy between the sacred and the profane—something scarcely existent *in illo tempore* when gods and men still intermingled—makes it, moreover, so that the left hand can never really know the works of the right, even if it would; for citing Hermes: "That which is mortal cannot draw near to that which is immortal, nor that which is for a time [history] to that which is everlasting, nor that which is corruptible to that which is incorruptible."[29] "The things of God," according to St. Paul, "knoweth no man, but the Spirit of God" (1 Cor. 2:11).

Holy personages pass largely unperceived by the world, being mainly known by the traces they leave, and their reverberations on religion. But history fails to capture the aggregate of factual detail or

---

[27] True theater is precisely spellbinding through its power momentarily to convert (in differing degrees) accident into essence.

[28] *The Reign of Quantity*, London, 1953, the chapter "Time Changed into Space."

[29] *Hermetica*, Fragments, no. 7; tr. Walter Scott, Oxford, 1924-36.

outward "accident," and their portraits best cohere in sacred myth.[30] A striking exception is the life of Muhammad, which has been scrupulously recorded to the last detail, and this because of Islam's insistence on the Unicity of God: Muhammad had to be "fixed" into history to preclude his being divinized. The Islamic miracle is accordingly not in the Prophet's personage but rather in his religion's global expansion over a few years' time. With the generality of saints, by contrast, their traces when subjected to the searingly erudite scrutiny of such as the Bollandists,[31] melt away like snow in the midday sun.

*

* *

Does this then mean that nothing sacred is finally knowable through other than blind faith? Admitting a certain latitude for hyperbole, embroidering, exaggeration, and credulity—phenomena most frequently associated with popular cults of local saints and folk divinities whether apocryphal or not, there still indelibly remains the perpetual veneration of holy figures central throughout Christendom the same as with all religions, and, *vox populi, vox Dei.* The Church has every reason to regard with the utmost caution claims for isolated apparitions, miracles, visions, or sanctity, and this out of vital concern for safeguarding the priceless spiritual graces accompanying genuine dulia; but what to think when the very sacrament of veneration is endangered through undermining some of its most hallowed pillars? As though, for example, the Psalms were to be deleted from the Bible on grounds of spurious authorship, it being in any case for Christians the Gospels that matter.

Naiveté enters in where competence leaves off; this is a frailty of human nature, or what Schuon calls "the human incapacity to exert the intelligence on all planes at once." Modern man as an instance is extremely sophisticated in the domain of scientific technology, and

---

[30] Even a Hermetic figure like William Shakespeare eludes the biographer's grasp, since the essential dimension of his function transcends the domain accessible to the historian and literary critic.

[31] Their *Acta* was expressly censured in 1695 by the Spanish Inquisition as heretical when the Bollandists cast doubt on the Carmelites' claim of descent through the Essenes, the Blessed Virgin, and the apostles from the Prophet Elias, whose statue in St. Peter's bears the inscription: *Universus Ordo Carmelitarum Fundatori Suo S Eliae* ("The Entire Order of Carmel to its Founder, St. Elias").

quasi-totally ignorant on the spiritual plane. But he naively projects this unintelligent sector in his perceptive apparatus onto ancient—and even medieval—man, himself naive if one wishes by our standards of analytical enquiry, and presumes that the latter's preoccupation with religion was largely an affair of superstition.

We live on the frontier of two immensities, one inward and one outward; ideally we should be at home in both since true man is the mediator between Heaven and Earth, the measure of all things, and abridgement of the Universe. Now in practice, ancient man directed his energies primarily towards the inner things, whereas modern man due to his centrifugal orientation applies his best energies to the outer world, striving in the degree possible to live by bread alone. He reaches for the stars, which the setting of his inner Sun have made him think are all there is.

The deduction to be drawn from these considerations is that if we find ourselves without competence regarding the spiritual domain, then the "sophisticated" response is to refrain from plunging in where angels fear to tread, and further, to believe with something more than blind faith that in the nature of things, our ancient forebears as human beings could hardly be stupid concerning that realm where they elected to concentrate their highest intellectual powers. A spiritual intelligence confronted with St. Margaret's dragon or St. Ursula's eleven thousand virgin martyrs will defer judgment on the literal and historical plane while searching out the allegorical, tropological, and anagogical factors, wherein with the reverberations of their sanctity, lie the essential graces which these saints have to transmit.

If now it be asked, does not the Church's competence have specifically to do with the things of the spirit? The answer is, those Christians concerned with the spiritual life are jealous for their saints and martyrs; conversely, if those principalities and powers managing ecclesiastical affairs today are not jealous for their saints and martyrs, then their concern is not for the spiritual life.

The following passage, from the work of S. Baring-Gould already cited, was written more than a century ago:

> In the time of Antichrist, the Church will be divided: one portion will hold to the world-power, the other will seek out the old paths, and cling to the only true Guide. The high places will be filled with unbelievers in the Incarnation, and the Church will be in a condition of the utmost spiritual degradation, but enjoying the highest

State patronage. The religion in favor will be one of morality, but not of dogma; and the Man of Sin will be able to promulgate his doctrine, according to St. Anselm, through his great eloquence and wisdom, his vast learning and mightiness in the Holy Scriptures, which he will wrest to the overthrowing of dogma. He will be liberal in bribes, for he will be of unbounded wealth; and at the last, he will tear the moral veil from his countenance. . . .

It need only be added that since morality is but an appendage of dogma, a church already exercised in destroying liturgy will certainly be capable at the opportune moment of destroying morality also—a maneuver moreover even now visibly in progress, and this quite independently of speculations about when that final day shall fall.[32] Meanwhile, the thinly-disguised Powers manipulating change are simply executing the *mot d'ordre* of their cabal: "The reform must be carried out in the name of obedience."

*
* *

No dragon of course ever has, or will—or could in the end—swallow St. George; but if the menace were not there, the story would carry no suspense.

What has been swallowed is the archaeological "proof" of the non-existence of the hero—the apocryphal Mother Goose that modern

---

[32] In fairness to Baring-Gould, it should be noted that the material he was documenting went counter to his credence: "How the Abomination of Desolation can be considered as set up in a Church where every sanctuary is adorned with all that can draw the heart to the Crucified, and raise the thoughts to the imposing ritual of heaven, is a puzzle to me. . . . Rome does not fight against the Daily Sacrifice, and endeavor to abolish it. . . . Rome does not deny the power of the godliness of which she makes show, but insists on that power with no broken accents. . . . However, this is not a question into which we care to enter, our province is myth not theology." In other words, how could he possibly be expected to have foreseen Vatican II, which, be it said, expunged St. Michael along with St. George by eliminating the following Prayer after Mass :

St. Michael, the archangel, defend us in battle, be our protection against the malice and snares of the devil. We humbly beseech God to command him, and do thou, O Prince of the heavenly host, by the divine power thrust into hell Satan and the other evil spirits who roam through the world seeking the ruin of souls. Amen.

science has fed to ecclesiastical savants. Taking a clue from Diocletian, the antiliturgical and neopagan Church today has seen fit to cast St. George, martyr, into the abyss of oblivion; the Bollandists, however, should not prematurely jubilate, as betwixt the twain, it is George the indestructible.

Whosoever implores my aid shall receive it. In history's deepening twilight he still awaits—lance poised, with the hand of God always above, the supplication of his devotees crying out like Sabra for its master stroke.

CHRISTENDOM AND CONSERVATISM

Titus Burckhardt

Leaving aside any political overtones which the word may have, the conservative is someone who seeks to conserve. In order to say whether he is right or wrong, it should be enough to consider what it is he wishes to conserve. If the social forms he stands for—for it is always a case of social forms—are in conformity with man's highest goal and correspond to man's deepest needs, why shouldn't they be as good as, or better than, anything novel that the passage of time may bring forth? To think in this way would be normal. But the man of today no longer thinks normally. Even when he does not automatically despise the past and look to technical progress for humanity's every good, he usually has a prejudice against any conservative attitude, because, consciously or unconsciously, he is influenced by the materialistic thesis that all "conserving" is inimical to constantly changing life and so leads to stagnation.

The state of need in which today every community finds itself that has not kept up with technical progress, seems to confirm this thesis; but it is overlooked that this is not so much an explanation as a stimulus for even further development. That all must change is a modern dogma that seeks to make man subject to itself; and it is eagerly proclaimed, even by people who consider themselves to be believing Christians, that man himself is in the grip of change; that not only such feeling and thinking as may be influenced by our surroundings are subject to change, but also man's very being. Man is said to be in the course of developing mentally and spiritually into a superman, and consequently 20th century man is looked on as being a different creature from the man of earlier times. In all of this one overlooks the truth, proclaimed by every religion, that man is man, and not merely an animal, because he has within him a spiritual center which is not subject to the flux of things. Without this center, which is the source of man's capacity to make judgments—and so may be called the spiritual organ vehicling the sense of truth—we could not even recognize change in the surrounding world, for, as Aristotle said, those who declare everything, including truth, to be in a state of flux, contradict themselves: for, if everything is in flux, on what basis can they formulate a valid statement?

Is it necessary to say that the spiritual center of man is more than the psyche, subject as this is to instincts and impressions, and also more than rational thought? There is something in man that links him to the Eternal, and this is to be found precisely at the point where "the Light which lighteth every man that cometh into the world" (John 1:9) touches the level of the psycho-physical faculties.

If this immutable kernel in man cannot be directly grasped—anymore than can the dimensionless center of a circle—the approaches to it can nevertheless be known: they are like the radii which run towards the center of a circle. These approaches constitute the permanent element in every spiritual tradition and, as guidelines both for action and for those social forms that are directed towards the center, they constitute the real basis of every truly conservative attitude. For the wish to conserve certain social forms only has meaning—and the forms themselves can only last—if they depend on the timeless center of the human condition.

In a culture which, from its very foundations (thanks to its sacred origin), is directed towards the spiritual center and thereby towards the eternal, the question of the value or otherwise of the conservative attitude does not arise; the very word for it is lacking. In a Christian society one is Christian, more or less consciously and deliberately, in an Islamic society one is Moslem, in a Buddhist society Buddhist, and so on; otherwise one does not belong to the respective community and is not a part of it, but stands outside it or is secretly inimical to it.

Such a culture lives from a spiritual strength that puts its stamp on all forms from the highest downwards, and in doing this it is truly creative; at the same time it has need of conservational forces, without which the forms would soon disappear. It suffices that such a society be more or less integral and homogeneous for faith, loyalty to tradition, and a conserving or conservative attitude to mirror one another like concentric circles.

The conservative attitude only becomes problematical when the order of society, as in the modern West, is no longer determined by the eternal; the question then arises, in any given case, which fragments or echoes of the erstwhile all-inclusive order are worth preserving. In each condition of society (one condition now following the other in ever more rapid succession) the original prototypes are reflected in some way or other. Even if the earlier structure is destroyed, individual elements of it are still effective; a new equilibrium—however dislocated and uncertain—is established after every break with the past. Certain central values are irretrievably lost; others, more peripheral to the original plan, come to the fore. In order that these may not also be lost, it may be better to preserve the existing equilibrium than to risk all in an uncertain attempt to renew the whole.

As soon as this choice presents itself, the word "conservative" makes its appearance—in Europe it first received currency at the time of the Napoleonic wars—and the term remains saddled with the dilemma inherent in the choice itself. Every conservative is immediately suspected of seeking only to preserve his social privileges, however small these may be. And in this process, the question as to whether the object to be preserved is worth preserving goes by default. But why shouldn't the personal advantage of this or that group coincide with what is right? And why shouldn't particular social structures and duties be conducive to a certain intelligence?

That man seldom develops intelligence when the corresponding outward stimuli are lacking, is proved by the thinking of the average man of today: only very few—generally only those who in their youth experienced a fragment of the "old order," or who chanced to visit a still traditional Oriental culture—can imagine how much happiness and inward peace a social order that is stratified according to natural vocations and spiritual functions can bring, not only to the ruling, but also to the laboring classes.

In no human society, however just it may be as a whole, are things perfect for every individual; but there is a sure proof as to whether an existing order does or does not offer happiness to the majority: this proof inheres in all those things which are made, not for some physical purpose, but with joy and devotion. A culture in which the arts are the exclusive preserve of a specially educated class—so that there is no longer any popular art or any universally understood artistic language—fails completely in this respect. The outward reward of a profession is the profit which its practice may secure; but its inner reward is that it should remind man of what, by nature and from God, he is, and in this respect it is not always the most successful occupations that are the happiest. To till the earth, to pray for rain, to create something meaningful from raw material, to compensate the lack of some with the surplus of others, to rule, while being ready to sacrifice one's life for the ruled, to teach for the sake of truth—these, amongst others, are the inwardly privileged occupations. It may be asked whether, as a result of "progress," they have been increased or diminished.

Many today will say that man has been brought to his proper measure, when, as a worker, he stands in front of a machine. But the true measure of man is that he should pray and bless, struggle and rule, build and create, sow and reap, serve and obey—all these things pertain to man.

When certain urban elements today demand that the priest should divest himself of the signs of his office and live as far as possible like other men, this merely proves that these groups no longer know what man fundamentally is; to perceive man in the priest means to recognize that priestly dignity corresponds infinitely more to original human nature than does the role of the "ordinary" man. Every theocentric culture knows a more or less explicit hierarchy of social classes or "castes." This does not mean that it regards man as a mere part which finds its fulfillment only in the people as a whole; on the contrary, it means that human nature as such is far too rich for everyone at every moment to be able to realize all its various aspects. The perfect man is not the sum total, but the kernel or essence of all the various functions. If hierarchically structured societies were able to maintain themselves for millennia, this was not because of the passivity of men or the might of the rulers, but because such a social order corresponded to human nature.

There is a widespread error to the effect that the naturally conservative class is the bourgeoisie, which originally was identified with the culture of the cities, in which all the revolutions of the last five hundred years originated. Admittedly the bourgeoisie, especially in the aftermath of the French revolution, has played a conservative role, and has occasionally assumed some aristocratic ideals—not however without exploiting them and gradually falsifying them. There have always been, amongst the bourgeoisie, conservatives on the basis of intelligence, but from the start they have been in the minority.

The peasant is generally conservative; he is so, as it were, from experience, for he knows—but how many still know it?—that the life of nature depends on the constant self-renewal of an equilibrium of innumerable mutually interconnected forces, and that one cannot alter any element of this equilibrium without dragging the whole along with it. Alter the course of a stream, and the flora of a whole area will be changed; eliminate an animal species, and another will be given immediate and overwhelming increase. The peasant does not believe that it will ever be possible to produce rain or shine at will.

It would be wrong to conclude from this that the conservative viewpoint is above all linked with sedentarism and man's attachment to the soil, since it has been demonstrated that no human collectivity is more conservative than the nomads. In all his constant wandering, the nomad is intent on preserving his heritage of language and custom; he consciously resists the erosion of time, for to be conservative means not to be passive.

This is a fundamentally aristocratic characteristic; in this the nomad resembles the noble, or, more exactly, the nobility of warrior-caste origin necessarily has much in common with the nomad. At the same time, however, the experience of a nobility that has not been spoiled by court and city life, but is still close to the land, resembles that of the peasant, with the difference that it comprises much wider territorial and human relationships. When the nobility, by heredity and education, is aware of the essential oneness of the powers of nature and the powers of the soul, it possesses a superiority that can hardly be acquired in any other way; and whoever is aware of a genuine superiority has the right to insist upon it, just as the master of any art has the right to prefer his own judgment to that of the unskilled.

It must be understood that the ascendancy of the aristocracy depends on both a natural and an ethical condition: the natural condition is that, within the same tribe or family, one can, in general terms, depend on the transmission by inheritance of certain qualities and capabilities; the ethical condition is expressed in the saying *noblesse oblige*: the higher the social rank—and its corresponding privilege— the greater the responsibility and the burden of duties; the lower the rank, the smaller the power and the fewer the duties, right down to the ethically unconcerned existence of passive people. If things are not always perfect, this is not principally because of the natural condition of heredity, for this is sufficient to guarantee indefinitely the homogeneous nature of a "caste"; what is much more uncertain is the accomplishment of the ethical law that demands a just combination of freedom and duty. There is no social system that excludes the misuse of power; and if there were, it would not be human, since man can only be man if he simultaneously fulfills a natural and a spiritual law. The misuse of hereditary power therefore proves nothing against the law of nobility. On the contrary, the example alone of those few people, who, when deprived of hereditary privilege, did not therefore renounce their inherited responsibility, proves the ethical calling of the aristocracy.

When, in many countries, the aristocracy fell because of its own autocracy, this was not so much because it was autocratic towards the lower orders, but rather because it was autocratic towards the higher law of religion, which alone provided the aristocracy with its ethical basis, and moderated by mercy the right of the strong.

Since the fall, not merely of the hierarchic nature of society, but of almost all traditional forms, the consciously conservative man stands as it were in a vacuum. He stands alone in a world which, in its all opaque enslavement, boasts of being free, and, in all its crushing uniformity, boasts of being rich. It is screamed in his ears that humanity is continually developing upwards, that human nature, after developing for so and so many millions of years, has now undergone a decisive mutation, which will lead to its final victory over matter. The consciously conservative man stands alone amongst manifest drunks, is alone awake amongst sleep-walkers who take their dreams for reality. From understanding and experience he knows that man, with all his passion for novelty, has remained fundamentally the same, for good or ill; the fundamental questions in human life have always remained the same; the answers to them have always been known, and, to the extent that they can be expressed in words, have been handed down from one generation to the next. The consciously conservative man is concerned with this inheritance.

Since nearly all traditional forms in life are now destroyed, it is seldom vouchsafed to him to engage in a wholly useful and meaningful activity. But every loss spells gain: the disappearance of forms calls for a trial and a discernment; and the confusion in the surrounding world is a summons to turn, by-passing all accidents, to the essential.

ACKNOWLEDGMENTS

We would like to thank the following authors, editors, and publishers for their consent to publish the articles in this anthology.

1. "The Question of Evangelicalism": Frithjof Schuon, *Christianity/Islam: Essays in Esoteric Ecumenicism,* translated by Gustavo Polit. World Wisdom Books, 1984, pp. 15-53. New translation for this volume by Mark Perry in collaboration with Jean-Pierre Lafouge, Deborah Casey, and James S. Cutsinger.
2. "The Veil of the Temple: A Study of Christian Initiation": Marco Pallis. In *The Sword of Gnosis,* edited by Jacob Needleman. Penguin Books, 1974, pp. 81-103.
3. "Mysticism": William Stoddart, *Sacred Web,* vol. 2, 1998, pp. 65-77.
4. "The Power of the Name: The Jesus Prayer in Orthodox Spirituality" (abridged): Bishop Kallistos Ware, *The Power of the Name: The Jesus Prayer in Orthodox Spirituality.* SLG Press, 1986.
5. "The Rosary as Spiritual Way" (abridged): Jean Hani, *Sophia,* vol. 8, no. 1, Summer 2002, pp. 55-78, translated by G. John Champoux.
6. "The Virgin": James S. Cutsinger, *Sophia,* vol. 6, no. 2, Winter 2000, pp. 115-194.
7. "The Royal Door": Titus Burckhardt, *Chartres and the Birth of the Cathedral,* translated by William Stoddart. World Wisdom Books/ Golgonooza Press, 1996, pp. 65-73.
8. "Shakespeare in the Light of Sacred Art": Martin Lings, *The Sacred Art of Shakespeare.* Inner Traditions, 1998, pp. 3-13.
9. "Theology of the Icon": Jean Biès, *Returning to the Essential: Selected Writings of Jean Biès,* translated by Deborah Weiss-Dutilh. World Wisdom, 2004, pp. 109-112.
10. "Are the Crafts an Anachronism?": Brian Keeble, *Art: For Whom and For What?* Golgonooza Press, 1998, pp. 136-151.
11. "Paths that Lead to the Same Summit": Ananda K. Coomaraswamy, *The Bugbear of Literacy.* Perennial Books, 1979, pp. 50-67.
12. "A Christian Approach to the Non-Christian Religions: All Truth is of the Holy Spirit" (abridged): Bernard Kelly. In *Religion of the Heart: Essays Presented to Frithjof Schuon on His 80th Birthday,* edited by Seyyed Hossein Nasr and William Stoddart. The Foundation for Traditional Studies, 1991, pp. 155-176; and a lecture to the Aquinas Society of Cambridge, 1955.
13. "The Christians of Moorish Spain" (abridged): Duncan Townson, *Muslim Spain.* Cambridge University Press, 1973, pp. 18, 25.

14. "The Bishop of Tripoli" (abridged): Duke Alberto Denti di Pirajno, *A Cure of Serpents*. Pan Books, London, 1957, pp. 151-160.
15. "The Monk and the Caliph": Angus Macnab, *Spain Under the Crescent Moon*. Fons Vitae, 1999, pp. 62-70.
16. "Saint Bernard": René Guénon, *Sophia*, vol. 4, no. 1, pp. 21-38, translated by Rob Baker (with amendments by William Stoddart for this edition).
17. "Characteristics of Voluntaristic Mysticism": Frithjof Schuon, *The Transfiguration of Man*. World Wisdom Books, 1995, pp. 79-86.
18. "Sages and Saints of Our Epoch in the Light of the Perennial Philosophy": Mateus Soares de Azevedo, *Sacred Web*, vol. 10, 2003, pp. 185-195 (enlarged and revised for this edition).
19. "The Abolition of Man" (extract): C. S. Lewis, *The Abolition of Man*. C. S. Lewis Pte. Ltd., 1978, pp. 34-48.
20. "The End of a Tradition": Rama P. Coomaraswamy. In *The Unanimous Tradition*, edited by Ranjit Fernando. Sri Lanka Institute of Traditional Studies, 1991, pp. 185-192.
21. "The Dragon that Swallowed St. George" (abridged): Whitall N. Perry, *Challenges to a Secular Society*. The Foundation for Traditional Studies, 1995, pp. 112-152.
22. "Christendom and Conservatism": Titus Burckhardt, *The Essential Titus Burckhardt: Reflections on Sacred Art, Faiths, and Civilizations*, translated and edited by William Stoddart. World Wisdom, 2002, pp. 181-186.

NOTES ON CONTRIBUTORS

(In order of appearance)

FRITHJOF SCHUON was born in Basle, Switzerland in 1907, and was the twentieth century's pre-eminent spokesman for the "traditionalist" or "perennialist" school of comparative religious thought. Until his later years Schuon traveled widely, from India and the Middle East to America, experiencing traditional cultures and establishing lifelong friendships with Hindu, Buddhist, Christian, Muslim, and American Indian spiritual leaders. A philosopher in the tradition of Plato, Shankara, and Eckhart, Schuon was a gifted artist and poet as well as the author of over twenty books on religion, metaphysics, sacred art, and the spiritual path. Of his first book, *The Transcendent Unity of Religions*, T. S. Eliot wrote, "I have met with no more impressive work in the comparative study of Oriental and Occidental religion," and world-renowned religion scholar Huston Smith has said of Schuon that "the man is a . . . wonder; intellectually apropos religion, equally in depth and breadth, the paragon of our time." Schuon's books have been translated into over a dozen languages and are respected by academic and religious authorities alike. More than a scholar and writer, Schuon was a spiritual guide for seekers from a wide variety of religions and backgrounds throughout the world. He died in 1998. World Wisdom is presently engaged in the publication of the Essential Writings of Frithjof Schuon, the first title of which is called *The Fullness of God: Frithjof Schuon on Christianity*, edited by James S. Cutsinger.

MARCO PALLIS was born of Greek parents in Liverpool, England in 1895, and received his education at the universities of Harrow and Liverpool. He was widely respected as a teacher and writer of religious and metaphysical works, and was also a gifted musician and composer, as well as a mountaineer, traveler, and translator of perennialist works. For many years he corresponded with the eminent perennialist writers Ananda K. Coomaraswamy, René Guénon, and Frithjof Schuon. His writings include the best-selling *Peaks and Lamas*, an engaging account of his mountain experiences in Tibet before its invasion by Chinese Communist troops, and *The Way and the Mountain*, a collection of articles on Tibetan Buddhist themes informed by a universalist perspective. He also wrote many articles for the British journal *Studies in Comparative Religion*, the most important of which formed the basis of his work *A Buddhist Spectrum: Contributions to Buddhist-Christian Dialogue*, recently published by World Wisdom. Marco Pallis died in 1990.

Notes on Contributors

BISHOP KALLISTOS WARE was born in Bath, Somerset in 1934 and was educated at Westminster School and Magdelan College, Oxford, where he obtained a double First in Classics and Theology. He was received into the Orthodox Church in 1958, ordained as a priest in 1966, and in the same year took monastic vows at the Monastery of St. John the Theologian on the island of Patmos. In 1982 he was consecrated Bishop of Diokleia and appointed assistant Bishop in the Orthodox Archdiocese of Thyateira and Great Britain. He also has charge of the Greek Orthodox parish in Oxford. From 1966 to 2001 he led a distinguished career as Spalding Lecturer in Eastern Orthodox Studies at the University of Oxford. He is the author of best-selling works on Orthodoxy such as *The Orthodox Church, The Orthodox Way*, and *The Power of the Name: The Jesus Prayer in Orthodox Spirituality*, and is one of the translators of the influential compendium of Hesychast mystical writings called *The Philokalia* (four volumes completed; a fifth and final volume in progress). Volumes one and two (of a projected six) of his Collected Works have recently been published and are entitled *The Inner Kingdom* and *In the Image of the Trinity*.

JEAN HANI is Professor Emeritus at the University of Amiens in France, where he has specialized in the study of Greek literature, philosophy, and Christian theology. He has written several books on Christian esoterism and traditional symbolism, including, *Le Symbolisme du temple Chrétien, Mythes, rites, et symboles: Les chemins de l'invisible, La Vierge noire et le mystère marial*, and *La Divine liturgie*.

JAMES S. CUTSINGER is Professor of Theology and Religious Thought at the University of South Carolina and also serves as secretary to the Foundation for Traditional Studies. A widely recognized writer on the Perennial Philosophy and the traditionalist school, Professor Cutsinger is an Orthodox Christian and an authority on the theology and spirituality of the Christian East. Works edited by him include, *Reclaiming the Great Tradition: Evangelicals, Catholics, and Orthodox in Dialogue, Not of This World: A Treasury of Christian Mysticism, Paths to the Heart: Sufism and the Christian East, The Fullness of God: Frithjof Schuon on Christianity* and *Prayer Fashions Man: Frithjof Schuon on the Spiritual Life*. The recipient of numerous teaching awards, he was honored in 1999 as a Michael J. Mungo University Teacher of the Year. He is currently editing the Essential Writings of Frithjof Schuon series for World Wisdom.

TITUS BURCKHARDT, a German Swiss, was born in Florence in 1908 and died in Lausanne in 1984. An eminent member of the perennialist school, he is perhaps best known to the general public as an art historian. Already a generation ago, he won much acclaim for producing and publishing the first successful full-scale facsimiles of the Book of Kells, a copy of which he presented to Pope Pius XII at his summer residence at Castelgandolfo. In more recent years he acted as a specialist advisor to UNESCO, with particular reference to the preservation of the unique architectural heritage of Fez, which was then in danger. Besides his studies in Islamic art, mysticism, and culture, such as *Introduction to Sufi Doctrine, Fez: City of Islam*, and *Moorish Culture in Spain*, his best known works are: *Sacred Art in East and West, Siena: City of the Virgin, Chartres and the Birth of the Cathedral*, and *Alchemy: Science of the Cosmos, Science of the Soul*. Two notable compendiums of his works have also been published: *Mirror of the Intellect: Essays on Traditional Science and Sacred Art* and *The Essential Titus Burckhardt: Reflections on Sacred Art, Faiths, and Civilizations*, both edited by William Stoddart.

MARTIN LINGS was born in Burnage, Lancashire, in 1909. After a classical education he read English at Oxford where he was a pupil and later a close friend of C. S. Lewis. In 1935 he went to Lithuania where he lectured on Anglo-Saxon and Middle English at the University of Kaunas. After four years he went to Egypt and was given a lectureship in English Literature at Cairo University where he lectured mainly on Shakespeare. In 1952 he returned to England and took a degree in Arabic at London University. He later joined the staff of the British Museum where he was Keeper of Oriental Manuscripts. He is the author of *The Sacred Art of Shakespeare* (with a Foreword by HRH the Prince of Wales), *Ancient Beliefs and Modern Superstitions, The Eleventh Hour: The Spiritual Crisis of the Modern World in the Light of Tradition and Prophecy*, and *Symbol and Archetype: A Study of the Meaning of Existence*. Among his works on Islamic mysticism are: *The Book of Certainty, A Sufi Saint of the Twentieth Century: Shaykh Ahmad al-'Alawi*, and *What is Sufism?* His biography of the Prophet, entitled *Muhammad: His Life Based on the Earliest Sources*, has been internationally acclaimed as a masterpiece.

JEAN BIÈS was born in Bordeaux, France, in 1933. He studied Classics at the University of Algiers and later at the Sorbonne. Thereafter he worked as a teacher of French at the High School in Nay and as a Professor of Greek Literature at the University of Pau. The discovery of René Guénon's writings in 1951 was to become a determining influence on his life by revealing to him the existence of initiatory teachings. In 1973, he defended his doctoral dissertation in which he studied the relationship between French literature and Hindu thinking (*Littérature française et Pensée Hindoue*). This work was awarded the Prix d'Asie by the Académie des Sciences d'Outremer. Jean Biès' works, written in his native French, consist of presentations of traditional teachings, travel and personal accounts, testimonies, and collections of poetry—some 10,000 pages of published and unpublished texts. He retired in 1993 in order to devote his time entirely to his works. In 1997, he was named Chevalier of the French Legion of Honor. A compendium of his writings, entitled *Returning to the Essential: Selected Writings of Jean Biès* was recently published by World Wisdom.

BRIAN KEEBLE has long been devoted to the promulgation of the traditional arts and crafts in Britain. He is the founder of Golgonooza Press and co-founder of the Temenos Academy. Sponsored by the Prince's Foundation of HRH the Prince of Wales, the Temenos Academy is a teaching organiza-tion dedicated to the central idea that inspired the earlier *Temenos Review* (a journal devoted to the arts of the Imagination). Scholars and teachers, committed to what is now generally known as the Perennial Philosophy, are invited to lecture and hold study groups and to teach the ever-growing num-ber of devoted friends and students. He recently edited *Every Man an Artist: Readings in the Traditional Philosophy of Art* for World Wisdom, while his other works include *Art: For Whom and For What?* and *Conversing with Paradise.*

ANANDA K. COOMARASWAMY was born in 1877, of Anglo-Ceylonese parents. After completing studies in Geology he soon became interested in the arts and crafts of his native Ceylon and India. In 1917 he relocated to the USA where he became Keeper of Indian and Islamic Art at the Boston Museum of Fine Arts, establishing a large collection of Oriental artifacts and presenting lectures on their symbolic and metaphysical meaning. An encounter with the seminal writings of perennialist author René Guénon served to confirm and strengthen his view on the perspective of the Perennial Philosophy, or "transcendent unity of religions"—the view that all authentic Heaven-sent religions are paths that lead to the same summit. From this period onwards Dr. Coomaraswamy began to compose his mature—and undoubtedly most profound—works, adeptly expounding the Perennial Philosophy by draw-ing on his unparalleled knowledge of the arts, crafts, mythologies, cultures, folklores, symbolisms, and religions of the Orient and the Occident. In 1947 his plans to retire to India and take on *sannyasa* (renunciation of the world) were cut short by his sudden and untimely death. A representative collection of his extensive writings, entitled *The Essential Ananda K. Coomaraswamy,* was recently edited by his son Rama P. Coomaraswamy for World Wisdom.

BERNARD KELLY was a Catholic neo-scholastic and traditionalist especially con-cerned with the recalling of contemporary Christian thought to Thomism, and with the provision of a traditional and scholastic critique of the modern world. He also endeavored to prepare the ground for a sound Christian approach to the Eastern religions and in this regard corresponded regu-larly with perennialist author Ananda K. Coomaraswamy. He was a frequent contributor to Catholic journals such as *Blackfriars, The Life of the Spirit,* and *Dominican Studies.* Bernard Kelly died in 1958.

DUNCAN TOWNSON is a professional historian and the author of *The New Penguin Dictionary of Modern History, 1789-1945, A Dictionary of Contemporary History: 1945 to the Present*, and *Muslim Spain*.

DUKE ALBERTO DENTI DI PIRAJNO was a physician, scholar, and Governor of Tripoli who worked in Italy's former North African colonies. His experiences are recounted in his books *A Cure for Serpents* and *Ippolita*. He died in 1968.

ANGUS MACNAB was born in London of New Zealand-Scots parents. He received a classical education at the ancient "Public School" of Rugby and at Christ Church College, Oxford. He was a gifted translator of Latin and Greek poetry but as a profession he chose teaching. His interest in Spain began in 1936, and after the Second World War, in which he served as a volunteer ambulance driver, he learned Spanish and decided to make Spain his home. In 1938, under the influence of G. K. Chesterton and Hilaire Belloc, he embraced neo-scholasticism and traditional Catholicism. In conjunction with his classical roots and later oriental studies, traditional neo-scholasticism provided him with a fine philosophical tool for a subtle examination of the two traditional cultures of medieval Spain: Islam and Christianity. The fruits of his investigation were his engaging books *Spain Under the Crescent Moon* and *Toledo: Sacred and Profane*.

RENÉ GUÉNON was born in Blois, France in 1886 and was to become the forerunner-cum-originator of the "traditionalist" or "perennialist" school of thought. Frithjof Schuon said of him that he had "the central function of restoring the great principles of traditional metaphysics to Western awareness," and he added that Guénon "gave proof of a universality of understanding that for centuries had no parallel in the Western world." Guenon's powerful indictment of the modern world is to be found in his works of civilizational criticism, *Crisis of the Modern World* and *The Reign of Quantity and the Signs of the Times*, wherein he criticizes the prevailing ideologies of materialism, occultism, evolutionism, progressivism, individualism, and relativism. His major expositions of traditional symbolism are contained in *The Symbolism of the Cross* and *Fundamental Symbols: The Universal Language of Sacred Science*, while his exposition of pure metaphysics is most notably presented in *The Multiple States of the Being* and *Man and His Becoming According to the Vedanta*. René Guénon died in Cairo in 1951. The publisher Sophia Perennis is presently engaged in the English publication of the Collected Works of René Guénon.

C. S. LEWIS was born in Ireland in 1898. He gained a triple First at Oxford and was a Fellow and Tutor at Magdalen College, Oxford from 1925 to 1954. In 1954 he became Professor of Mediaeval and Renaissance English Literature at Cambridge. He was an outstanding and popular lecturer and had a lasting influence on his pupils. C. S. Lewis was for many years an atheist, and described his conversion in his autobiography, *Surprised by Joy*: "In the Trinity Term of 1929 I gave in, and admitted that God was God. . . . [I was] perhaps the most dejected and reluctant convert in all England." It was this experience that helped him to understand not only apathy but active unwillingness to accept religion, and, as a Christian writer, gifted with an exceptionally brilliant and logical mind and a lucid, lively style, he was without peer. Among his most popular works are *The Screwtape Letters*, *Mere Christianity*, *The Problem of Pain*, and *Letters to Malcolm: Chiefly on Prayer*. He is also the author of several children's stories. He died at his home in Oxford in 1963.

RAMA P. COOMARASWAMY was born in New York in 1929, the son of Ananda and Doña Louisa Coomaraswamy. He received his early education in Canada, India, and England, before undertaking undergraduate studies at Harvard University, and medical studies at New York University, where he graduated in 1959. Parallel with his distinguished medical career, Dr. Coomaraswamy has retained a deep interest in theological matters and was professor of Ecclesiastical History at St. Thomas Aquinas Seminary in Ridgefield, Connecticut for a period of five years. He is one of the most forceful exponents of traditional Christian teachings—he converted to Catholicism at age 22—and is the author of over fifty articles, as well as *The Destruction of the Christian Tradition*, *The Problems with the New Mass*, and *The Invocation of the Name of Jesus: As Practiced in the Western Church*. Dr. Coomaraswamy is also co-editor of *The Selected Letters of Ananda Coomaraswamy* and editor of *The Essential Ananda K. Coomaraswamy*.

WHITALL N. PERRY has ties with authorities in Hindu, Buddhist, Islamic, Roman Catholic, Orthodox, and Native American circles. In addition to his monumental *A Treasury of Traditional Wisdom*, he has contributed articles on metaphysics, cosmology, and modern counterfeits of spirituality to various journals, several of which were collected together to form his book *Challenges to a Secular Society*. More recently he has published a traditional cosmological critique of Darwinist evolution entitled, *The Widening Breach*. He has been called "the most authoritative traditionalist of American background," and "a latter-day transcendentalist in the tradition of Emerson and Thoreau." Travels in his youth through Europe, the Near, Middle, and Far East sparked an interest in Platonism and Vedanta, which brought him under the personal influence of Ananda K. Coomaraswamy. He spent five years in Egypt in close contact with René Guénon, after whose death he moved to Switzerland with his family where he became a close associate of Frithjof Schuon. When Schuon moved to the United States in 1980, Perry and his family relocated to America to remain in contact with him.

BIOGRAPHICAL NOTES

MATEUS SOARES DE AZEVEDO is a writer and journalist from Minas Gerais, central Brazil. He studied Journalism at the Catholic University and modern languages at the University of the State of São Paulo, and for many years worked as a journalist in the International Affairs section of major newspapers. He also holds a Master's degree in the History of Religions from the University of São Paulo, with a thesis on the relevance of the Perennial Philosophy for contemporary thought.

He is the author of four books and dozens of articles and essays dealing with the importance of traditional religion and spirituality in the contemporary world, some of them translated into English and Spanish. More recently, he has contributed articles to *Dossier H: Frithjof Schuon,* and the North American perennialist journals *Sophia* and *Sacred Web.* He has also translated and introduced books by C. S. Lewis, Frithjof Schuon, Martin Lings, and Rama P. Coomaraswamy into Portuguese. His latest book is entitled *Iniciación al Islam y al Sufismo.*

WILLIAM STODDART was born in Carstairs, Scotland, lived most of his life in London, England, and now lives in Windsor, Ontario. He studied modern languages, and later medicine, at the universities of Glasgow, Edinburgh, and Dublin. He was a close associate of both Frithjof Schuon and Titus Burckhardt during the lives of these leading perennialists and translated several of their works into English. His books include *Outline of Hinduism, Outline of Buddhism,* and *Sufism: The Mystical Doctrines and Methods of Islam.* For many years Dr. Stoddart was assistant editor of the British journal *Studies in Comparative Religion.* Pursuing his interests in comparative religion, he has traveled widely in Europe (including a visit to Mount Athos), North Africa, India, Ceylon, and Japan. He recently edited *The Essential Titus Burckhardt: Reflections on Sacred Art, Faiths, and Civilizations* for World Wisdom.

INDEX

Abraham, 83, 107, 129, 222, 271

Adam, 10, 33, 41, 51, 99, 115-116, 128, 136, 143, 152, 178, 185, 189, 293-294

Adam-Eve, 98

Advaita Vedanta, 145, 273

Alawî, Ahmad al-, 107, 145-146

Albertus Magnus, 61

Alchemy, 99, 114, 145, 320

Allah, 16, 94, 128-129, 132, 142, 225, 234, 319, 327

Ambrose, 218, 322

American Indian, 161, 310

Amida, 16, 24-25, 45-46, 94

Amitabha, 17, 45-46, 329

Angelic Salutation, 100, 115, 124-125

Angels, 29, 90, 111, 124, 129, 131-132, 167, 170-172, 219, 292, 308, 333

Angelus Silesius, 35, 61, 211, 245, 267

Annunciation, 105-106, 117, 124, 129, 137, 169, 177

Anselm, Saint, 3, 111, 334

Apocalypse, 123, 145, 172

Apostles, 31, 35, 84, 90, 111, 114, 139, 168, 172, 292-298, 302, 332

Archetype, 5-7, 18, 90, 98-99, 106, 116, 165, 187, 325, 328, 330

Aristotle, 15, 173, 247, 336

Art, 8, 12, 17, 46, 65, 75, 80-81, 85, 96, 112, 117, 124, 128-129, 134, 146, 159-161, 163, 168-169, 171-174, 176-179, 181, 183-188, 192, 195-197, 201, 203, 205, 212, 215-216, 223, 230, 257, 261, 269, 273-274, 287, 299

Ascension, 36, 105-106, 167, 171-172, 239

Asceticism, 22, 242, 249, 261, 264

Assumption, 105-106, 192, 195

Athos, Mount, 49, 55, 80, 90, 192

Âtmâ, 59, 145, 150, 155

Augustine, Saint, 10, 19-20, 62, 73, 103, 201, 211, 222, 245, 281, 301-302

Avalokitesvara, 43, 316

Avatâra, 64, 138, 143-145, 149, 162, 317

Ave Maria, 64, 100, 124, 158

Baptism, 51-53, 77, 112, 220, 307, 323

Beauty, 31, 63, 68, 77, 99, 109, 118-120, 125, 143, 146, 149-150, 157, 160, 165-166, 175, 190, 196, 200, 204, 206-207, 226, 277, 283

Being-Consciousness-Bliss, 61-62

Being-Wisdom-Life, 62

Bellarmine, Cardinal Saint, 296, 303

Bernadette of Lourdes, Saint, 126, 165

Bernard, Saint, 12, 28, 117, 119, 121, 143, 161, 170, 176, 247-259

Bernardino of Siena, Saint, 66, 165

Beyond-Being, 60-61, 63-64, 147-148

Bhagavad Gita, 103, 221

Bible, 10, 14, 16, 110, 113, 118, 121-122, 128, 140, 176, 217, 230, 297, 332

Biblical, 35, 84, 89, 96, 115, 119, 144

Bishop of Tripoli, 232-233, 235

Black Elk, 273

Boehme, Jacob, 32, 34, 330

Boethius, 173, 175

Brother Lawrence, 80

For a glossary of all key foreign words used in books published by World Wisdom, including metaphysical terms in English, consult:

www.DictionaryofSpiritualTerms.com.

This on-line Dictionary of Spiritual Terms provides extensive definitions, examples and related terms in other languages.

Titles in The Perennial Philosophy Series by World Wisdom